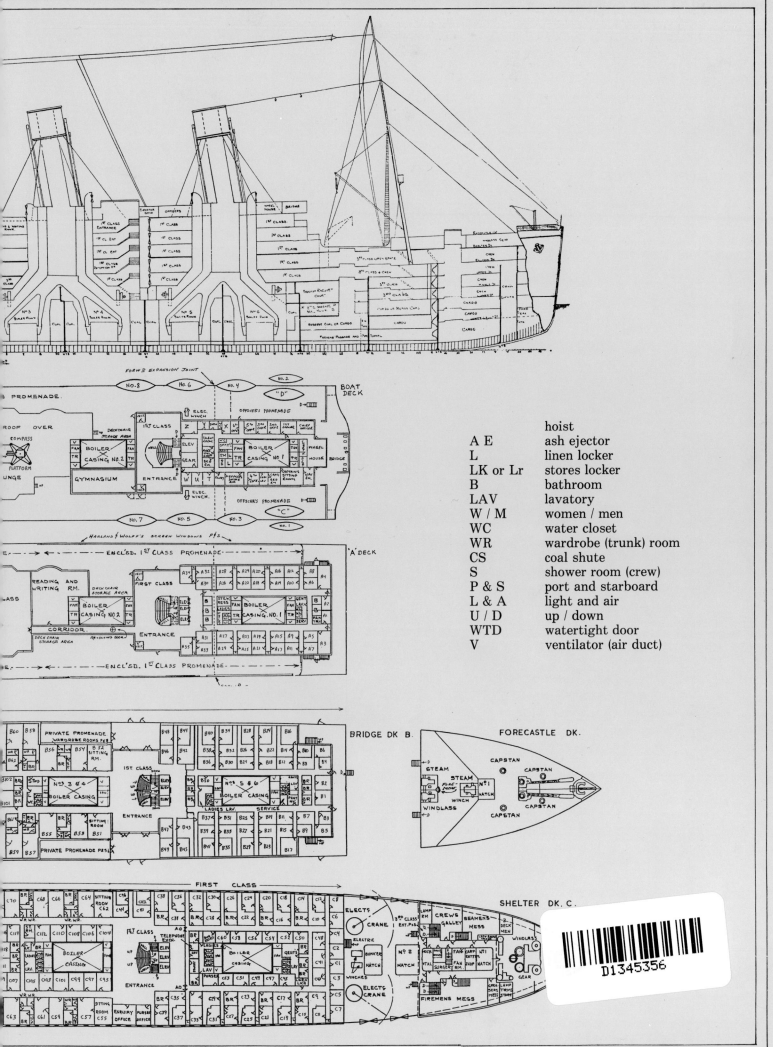

TITANIC
TRIUMPH AND TRAGEDY
A Chronicle in Words and Pictures

TITANIC
TRIUMPH AND TRAGEDY

JOHN P. EATON AND CHARLES A. HAAS
Foreword by John Maxtone-Graham

Patrick Stephens, Wellingborough

First published in 1986

British Library Cataloguing in Publication Data

Eaton, John P.
  Titanic: Triumph and Tragedy.
  1. Titanic (*Ship*)
  I. Title   II. Haas, Charles A.
  363.1′23′091631   G530.T6

  ISBN 0-85059-775-7

*Patrick Stephens Limited is part of the
Thorsons Publishing Group*

Printed and bound in Great Britain
by Butler & Tanner, Frome, Somerset.

For our dear friends Elizabeth and Arnold Watson, and for the brave men and women who are the Spirit of *Titanic*.

CONTENTS

ACKNOWLEDGEMENTS

The preparation of this book has involved dozens of individuals and institutions on both sides of the Atlantic. Their assistance is most gratefully acknowledged.

Our heartfelt thanks and appreciation are expressed to our great friends and invaluable assistants, Michael A. Findlay and Michael V. Ralph, whose many contributions and hours of work literally made this book possible.

We express our deep gratitude to these fine people, who also demonstrated in words and deeds the true meanings of scholarship, friendship and sharing:

R. Douglas and Virginia Anderson; Stella Archer, Administrator, National Maritime Museum of Ireland, Dun Laoghaire; Philip Atkins, National Railway Museum, York, England; Terrence Atkins, Lloyd's of London; Martin Bayerle and Gerard Spring, Maritime Analysts Group, Inc; Frank O. Braynard; Joel Buckwald, Administrator, National Archives — New York Branch; Barrie Rogers Davis; Robert DiSogra; Arthur and Maria Dodge; Thomas Decker; Don Dunn; Shelley Dziedzic; Cmdr Norman C. Edwards and Lt (jg) Neil B. Thayer, United States Coast Guard; Mr and Mrs George A. Fenwick; Bob Forrest; Richard Hill and Catherine Marquard, New York Public Library; Richard Horline; David F. Hutchings; Walter Lord; Russ Lownds; Donald Lynch; Walter Macauley, *Belfast Telegraph*; Ken Marschall; John Maxtone-Graham; Russell Matthews; Lisa V. Mayne; Michael McCaughan, Curator, Ulster Folk and Transport Museum, Holywood; Elliott B. Nixon and Wade S. Hooker, Jr, Burlingham, Underwood & Lord; Linda Nixon; Wilton J. Oldham; Nigel Overton, Southampton Maritime Museum; Diane R. Prignoli; Eugene A. Shenesky, Jr; Alan Silverman, Voice of America, Washington, DC; J. Welton Smith; Phillip Chadwick Foster Smith; Bertie Traynor and May Gilliland, Harland and Wolff Ltd; Deborah Trefts, United States Senate; Mr and Mrs Edward D. Walker and family.

We also thank the staffs of the following institutions, who always made two *Titanic* researchers feel most welcome: Atlantic Mutual Insurance Company, New York; Belfast Central Library; British Newspaper Library, Colindale; Dartmouth Heritage Museum, Dartmouth, NS; Guildhall Library, London; Halifax (Nova Scotia) Regional Library; Library of Congress; Linenhall Library, Belfast; Liverpool Central Library; National Archives, Washington, DC; Mariners' Museum, Newport News, Va; Maritime Museum of the Atlantic, Halifax, NS; National Maritime Museum, Greenwich, England; National Museum of American History, Smithsonian Institution, Washington, DC; Nova Scotia Museum, Halifax; Philadelphia Free Public Library; Public Archives of Nova Scotia, Halifax; Public Record Office, Kew; Public Record Office of Northern Ireland, Belfast; Scottish Record Office, Edinburgh; Ulster Museum, Belfast. Crown copyright material in the Public Record Office is reproduced by permission of the Controller of Her Majesty's Stationery Office.

Grateful acknowledgement is made for the copyright photographs from the Father Francis M. Browne, SJ collection, housed at the Provincialate, Dublin, and made available by courtesy of the Provincial of the Irish Province of the Society of Jesus.

Our deep thanks to our respective employers, St Luke's-Roosevelt Hospital Center and the Randolph Township (New Jersey) Board of Education for their understanding, their support, the use of their facilities and their patience.

Our gratitude and love to four truly special people — Frank P. Aks, Ruth Becker Blanchard, Marshall B. Drew and Eva M. Hart.

Our special love to Beatrice V. Haas, who provided the never-ceasing support, the encouragement and the thoughtful care that only a mother can.

FOREWORD

On the 75th anniversary of her simultaneous maiden voyage and destruction, *Titanic* is on every tongue; hence, the timing of this photographic pantechnicon by John Eaton and Charles Haas is exquisitely appropriate.

It is a rich and rewarding collection. The authors have included sufficient illustrations within these covers to satisfy the most ardent *Titanic* buff. Some are familiar, some show *Olympic* interiors to suggest probable duplication on her successor and several are new. I am especially pleased that Ken Marschall's superlative work is represented, as well. The combined impact is stunning. Included in the text are haunting details about *Titanic*'s trials in Belfast Lough on 2 April 1912: 'While the ship travelled at 20½ knots on a straight course, the helm was ordered hard over'. (*Titanic* executed a full circle, 'heeling slightly'.) 'During the turn the ship's forward movement was about 2,100 feet.' Subsequently, when Captain Smith ordered *Titanic*'s engine-room telegraphs swung from Full Ahead to Full Astern, it was ascertained that from that instant until the vessel stopped, half-a-mile's inexorable momentum had continued, co-incidentally the estimated distance between sighting the iceberg and impact. No-one on the new ship's bridge that bright spring day off Belfast could have guessed that identical 'crash' manoeuvres would have to be implemented in mid-ocean only a fortnight later. The juxtaposition of these routine trial rituals with the vessel's ensuing fate is the stuff of high drama.

Trials completed, *Titanic* steamed to Southampton for a week in port before entering service just after Easter, on 10 April 1912. There followed four uneventful days of a spring crossing, radioed ice warnings, ominous bone-chilling cold on Sunday evening, 14 April, an almost imperceptible collision near midnight and an ensuing horror of foundering and drowning. The *Titanic* saga moves with the implacable progression of Greek tragedy and the authors have seen to it that we are privy to every gripping detail.

Parallels with a tragedy of our own time are easily drawn. The after-effects of the explosion of the shuttle/orbiter *Challenger* in January of 1986 recall the post-April mood of 1912. In both cases overwhelming technological advances were taken for granted: space and sea could be conquered with impunity, encouraging complacency no less in the engineers responsible than we who watched and marvelled. NASA launched rockets into orbit as blithely as Edwardian shipwrights launched seemingly impervious hulls into dangerous Atlantic service: *Challenger* ascended heavenward as presumptuously as *Titanic* departed Southampton. Unexpected, disastrous nightmares consumed them both. The ordinary became, in two horrendous instances, the extraordinary. Both ordeals left us with the sobering reality that no human enterprise is immune from sudden failure; that NASA's orbiter should have failed as catastrophically as White Star's steamer points up the folly of relying on presumedly foolproof technology.

Whence *Titanic*'s inexhaustible preoccupation? Some must derive from the fatal interruption of that maiden voyage. RMS *Titanic* departed on schedule from three harbours, Southampton, Cherbourg and Queenstown, each to have been a regular trans-atlantic call. But she did not reach her western terminus and the welcoming scenario at New York's Pier 59 was not played out. That she never completed her voyage, that she vanished beyond our ken, that a brand-new vessel and hundreds of lives were lost initiated a compelling *Titanic* angst from which, perhaps, we have never fully recovered.

The *Titanic*'s legendary notoriety has intensified since the sunken ship was discovered and photographed on the ocean floor in late 1985. Against all expectations, she rests upright, save for her damaged stern section, remarkably well-preserved. In death as in life, *Titanic* astonishes.

John Maxtone-Graham
New York City, March 1986

AUTHORS' INTRODUCTION

She was not the world's fastest ship. Nor was she the first of a new class. She was not the 'largest liner ever built', nor the most costly. The documentation of her conception, design and construction has not withstood the passage of time well. Two world wars, indifference, corporate rivalries, accident, neglect and even late 20th century political activity have conspired to deprive historians of much that might be known about her.

It is through the appalling tragedy that befell her during her one voyage that the world best knows of her today. Perhaps history's most famous ship, she is remembered through memorials and motion pictures; through songs (more than 300 at the last count) and scraps of yellowing newspapers; through reminiscences of her survivors and recurring anniversary observances. And, fortunately, she is remembered through pictures. For during the brief span of her existence, the new hobby and profession of photography ensured a record of her beauty, her people and their loss.

It is our hope, through the illustrations that follow, to record the splendour of this ship; to examine new information about her; to reflect upon the heroism and human drama during her final hours; and to recall the important lessons she has taught mariners and the public alike. In doing so, it is not within the scope of our work to reiterate the detailed descriptions of *Titanic*'s story available in splendid books by other authors. Readers who seek these are referred to the excellent accounts by Walter Lord, Geoffrey Marcus, Wyn Craig Wade *et al*.

We have had the assistance of many people and institutions — their names are listed elsewhere — in our fascinating task. To them, and to the late Elizabeth and Arnold Watson, who encouraged and supported our work as a researching team, our deepest thanks.

Finally an *apologia*: while cameras did preserve some of *Titanic*'s features, they have provided a very incomplete record. In several instances — all clearly indicated — we have used photographs of the virtually identical *Olympic* to tell the story, in the belief that a picture quite representative of *Titanic*, though not actually *of* her, is preferable to no photograph at all. In other cases, the capabilities of 1912 photography have provided pictures which, while historically significant, are less than ideal in quality.

The year 1987 marks the 75th anniversary of this great vessel's loss, and the second anniversary of her re-discovery on the North Atlantic's floor. Through her name and those of her gallant passengers and crew, and through what she has taught mankind, *Titanic* is her own memorial.

John P. Eaton
New York,
New York

Charles A. Haas
Randolph,
New Jersey

February, 1986

PROLOGUE

Interwoven in the fabric of history are tales of coincidence and premonition. One of the best known and, at the same time, most remarkable of these is the novel *Futility*, published in 1898, by the American author Morgan Robertson. Fourteen years before the *Titanic* disaster — indeed, nine years before the vessel's conception — the 36-year-old writer concocted a story whose early pages vividly describe the April crossing of an immense liner and its subsequent loss through collision with an iceberg.

Dimensions, equipment and even top speed of the two vessels are strikingly similar. The names of the ships complete the aura of incredibility: the fictional 1898 ship was named *Titan*; the liner of 1912, *Titanic*.

	Titan	*Titanic*
Flag of registry	British	British
Time of sailing	April	10 April 1912
Displacement	70,000 tons	66,000 tons
Length	800 feet	882.5 feet
Number of propellers	3	3
Top speed	24-25 knots	24-25 knots
Capacity	c 3000	c 3000
Number of passengers		(Total aboard)
aboard	2,000	2,230
Number of lifeboats	24	20
Capacity of lifeboats	500	1,178
Number of watertight		
bulkheads	19	15
Engines	triple	triple expansion and turbine
Side of ship striking iceberg spur	starboard	starboard

Born in September 1861, and the product of an early life at sea, Morgan Robertson wrote fourteen novels about sailors and the sea. Somewhat of a psychic, he claimed to be inspired by what he called his 'astral writing partner'. During his later years, his inspiration deserted him and he could write no more.

He never profited from the similarity of his work to the actual event. Even though the novel was serialized regionally throughout the United States public interest appears to have been centred on the enormity of the disaster itself. With the calamity's horror described in almost hourly bulletins, there was small need for a fictionalized version.

Morgan Robertson died in 1915, never having gained full recognition for the depiction of his glimpse into the future, of the dream which came so tragically true.

Another writer with more than a passing interest in clairvoyance and psychic research was the British journalist William Thomas Stead. As assistant- and then editor of the *Pall Mall Gazette*, his crusading efforts for causes, both popular and unpopular, and his innovative approach to reporting public affairs, brought a contemporary sense to the presentation of news.

While editor of the *Pall Mall Gazette*, Stead wrote for the issue of 22 March 1886 an article, 'How the Mail Steamer Went Down in Mid Atlantic, by a Survivor'. The unnamed steamer sinks after colliding with another vessel and many aboard are lost because there are too few lifeboats. Stead concluded his article with the notation, 'This is exactly what *might* take place and *will* take place if the liners are sent to sea short of boats. — Ed'.

After leaving the *Gazette*, Stead was founder in 1890 and editor of the influential monthly periodical, *Review of Reviews*. Its 1892 Special Christmas Number contained a 123-page story entitled 'From the Old World to the New'. In it, Stead depicted a visit to the Chicago World's Fair of 1893. During the fictional Atlantic voyage — which is in early May aboard the White Star liner *Majestic* — a clairvoyant passenger has a vision of survivors from the wreck of the vessel *Ann and Jane*, which foundered after striking an iceberg. The survivors are rescued and *Majestic* steers south to avoid the ice-field that sank the other craft.

In April 1912 W. T. Stead was himself on the way from the Old World to the New — from England to New York where, at President William Howard

Morgan Robertson
(Empire State Notables)

William T. Stead
(Illustrated London News)

Celia Thaxter
(Authors' collection)

Taft's personal request, he was to address a great peace conference on 21 April at Carnegie Hall. The vessel on which he crossed. . .*Titanic*.

It is highly doubtful that the irony of his own prophecies was entirely lost to Mr Stead.

Celia Laighton was born in 1836. At the age of five, she moved to the Isles of Shoals, off Portsmouth, New Hampshire, where her father was keeper of the White Island lighthouse. Her girlhood was spent in marine surroundings. Later, when she began to write verse, her work, which is mostly lyrical, dealt with aspects of the sea.

Married at an early age to Levi Thaxter, a serious student of Robert Browning's poetry, the young girl matured in a home which was the summer residence of several Harvard University faculty members.

A volume of her work published in 1874 contained a poem, 'A Tryst', which was strangely predictive of an event which would not occur for 38 years. There are no specific biographic details concerning her source for this poem. But it is quite probable that Celia Thaxter listened to and absorbed the telling and retelling by the islands' fishermen of the story of a ship lost in a long-forgotten encounter with an iceberg '. . .out of the desolation of the North'.

'A Tryst'

From out of the desolation of the North
An iceberg took its way,
From its detaining comrades breaking forth,
And travelling night and day. . .

To the warm airs that stir in the sweet South,
A good ship spread her sails;
Stately she passed beyond the harbor's mouth,
Chased by the favoring gales;

And on her ample decks a happy crowd
Bade the fair land good-by;
Clear shone the day, with not a single cloud
In all the peaceful sky.

Brave men, sweet women, little children bright,
For all these she made room,
And with her freight of beauty and delight
She went to meet her doom.

Storms buffeted the iceberg, spray was swept
Across its loftiest height;
Guided alike by storm and calm, it kept
Its fatal path aright. . .

Dawn kissed it with her tender rose tints, Eve
Bathed it in violet,
The wistful color o'er it seemed to grieve
With a divine regret. . .

Like some imperial creature, moving slow,
Meanwhile, with matchless grace,
The stately ship, unconscious of her foe,
Drew near the trysting place.

For still the prosperous breezes followed her,
And half the voyage was o'er;
In many a breast glad thoughts began to stir
Of lands that lay before. . .

Was not the weltering waste of water wide
Enough for both to sail?
What drew the two together o'er the tide,
Fair ship and iceberg pale?. . .

O helmsman, turn thy wheel! Will no surmise
Cleave through the midnight drear?
No warning of the horrible surprise
Reach thine unconscious ear?

She rushed upon her ruin. Not a flash
Broke up the waiting dark;
Dully through wind and sea one awful crash
Sounded, with none to mark.

Scarcely her crew had time to clutch despair
So swift the work was done:
Ere their pale lips could frame a speechless prayer,
They perished, every one!

Celia Thaxter, *Poems of Celia Thaxter*,
Boston, reprinted 1896.

Having spent almost all her life on Appledore, one of the Isles of Shoals, Celia Thaxter died in August 1894, never to realize how closely her poetry depicted an event of such tragic proportion.

Robertson. Stead. Thaxter. A strange trio, not likely to be found in company with one another. Yet, they are forever joined through their own tales of wind and ice and improbable incident.

Prediction and premonition? Who can say? The improbable incident occurred in 1912.

Chapter One

PART ONE:
THE OWNERS

The story of *Titanic* begins in 1867. At the end of that year the 31-year-old Thomas Henry Ismay purchased for the sum of £1,000 the name, house flag and goodwill of the White Star Line, a bankrupt company whose sailing fleet had been in the Australian trade. Ismay intended to enter the highly competitive North Atlantic passenger business. He was encouraged in his endeavour by Gustav Schwabe, a Liverpool financier and uncle of Gustav Wolff, junior partner in the Belfast ship-building firm of Harland and Wolff. Mr Schwabe assured Ismay of financial backing if the new company would order its ships from his nephew's yard.

Together with George Hamilton Fletcher, a close friend, Ismay arranged to have Harland and Wolff design three vessels of slightly less than 4,000 tons each. During contract negotiations, a fourth vessel was added, as were two more of slightly larger size. The final agreement was made on 30 July 1869, and on 6 September the Oceanic Steam Navigation Company Ltd was registered with a capital of £400,000.

Harland and Wolff did not disappoint the new company's owners. Their first ship, *Oceanic*, was launched at Belfast on 27 August 1870 as yard number 73, and incorporated many innovative features for North Atlantic liners. The ratio of length to beam was ten-to-one, instead of the usual eight-to-one; first class cabins and the dining saloon were amidships instead of aft; and instead of separate deck houses there was a single structure surrounded by open railings, an arrangement which provided generous deck space. Individual cabins were larger than those on any other liner, and there were electric bells for summoning stewards, as well as running water in each cabin. While the engines were not novel in design, their arrangement was: four-cylinder compound engines were provided, so that each pair of cylinders formed a complete engine in case of accident.

Oceanic's maiden voyage was scheduled for 2 March 1871, but was delayed until 16 March due to engine problems. The voyage, once begun, was extremely successful and she was greeted at New York as 'the new leviathan'. Indeed, the *Oceanic*, a triumph of shipbuilding for her time, rightly has been called 'the mother of modern liners'.

Together with her sisters, *Atlantic, Baltic, Republic, Celtic* and *Adriatic*, the vessel formed the basis for a relationship between the builders and the owners which was to endure as long as the red, swallow-tailed pennant with its white star dominated the North Atlantic and Australian services. From the pioneering *Oceanic* and her five sisters emerged an impressive succession of tenders, freighters and liners, each bearing the unmistakable stamp of the builders' integrity, and each operated with the efficiency of the owners' expertise.

As the scope of the company widened, so did the prestige of its management. In 1870 Ismay invited his old friend William Imrie to join his firm and afterwards the White Star Line was managed by the firm of Ismay, Imrie and Company. The line soon became pre-eminent on the Australian run, and while several experimental routes — Central and South America, a trans-Pacific run, and one to the Orient — were never successfully established, the company's North Atlantic services soon became the standard against which all other passenger services were measured.

Thomas Ismay's eldest son, Bruce, was admitted to partnership in the firm on 1 January 1891 and, exactly one year later, Thomas Ismay retired. Bruce Ismay, with his younger brother James, who had also joined the firm, were thus in control when the decision was made that future vessels of the company would excel in comfort and excellence of design, rather than in speed.

To this end, Harland and Wolff designed and constructed for White Star the great *Oceanic* (II) of 1899, without doubt the culmination of 19th century shipbuilding art and science. The vessel caused great attention when launched, and even

greater acclamation on her 6 September 1899 maiden voyage from Liverpool to New York.

Control of the White Star Line passed from the hands of its British stockholders in 1902, following its purchase for £10,000,000 by the International Mercantile Marine Company, a vast shipping combine created by American financier J. Pierpont Morgan. Based on the smaller International Navigation Company of New Jersey (which was formed in 1893 from the American, Red Star and Inman Lines), the firm changed its name in 1902, raised its capital from $15,000,000 to $120,000,000 and began through share purchases to acquire control of the Atlantic Transport, Leyland and Dominion Lines. Although the White Star purchase offer was at first opposed by the Ismay family, the terms were accepted by a majority of the shareholders, and the first payment of £3,000,000 was made on 31 December 1902. The takeover saw the retirement of three of the company's partners — William Imrie, James Ismay, and W. S. Graves — but Bruce Ismay and Harold Sanderson remained. They were soon joined by William J. Pirrie, managing director and controlling chairman of Harland and Wolff who, it was said, had been instrumental in arranging White Star's purchase by the Morgan interests.

International Mercantile Marine's incumbent president, Clement Griscom, was ill; with J. P. Morgan's full support, Bruce Ismay was offered the job. He accepted in February 1904, and at the age of 41 became president and managing director of IMM, with unlimited control.

The White Star Line's position within the IMM was somewhat complex: White Star was owned by the Oceanic Steam Navigation Co, whose directors were J. Bruce Ismay, Harold A. Sanderson and Pirrie. Ismay was chairman and managing director. All Oceanic Steam Navigation shares, except six shares individually held, were owned by the International Navigation Company, which in turn was controlled by the Fidelity Trust Company, of Philadelphia, Pennsylvania (USA), a holding company.

All the International Navigation Company's stock was actually owned by the International Mercantile Marine Company, whose president was Ismay, and among whose officers were five 'voting trustees', Pirrie, Charles Steele, Ismay, P. A. B. Widener and Morgan. In 1912 the IMM corporation was capitalized at more than £37,000,000 and owned 120 ships with an aggregate gross tonnage of 1,067,425, with six additional vessels being built.

Earlier, in 1907, during dinner at Downshire, Pirrie's Belgrave Square mansion in London, Ismay had discussed construction of two huge ships (a third was subsequently added) as White Star's response to the size, luxury and speed of liners constructed by the company's rivals on the North Atlantic, the Hamburg-American Line, the North German Lloyd and the Cunard Line.

German express liners of the early 20th century — *Kronprinz Wilhelm, Kaiser Friedrich der Grosse, Kronprinzessin Cecilie* and *Prinz Friedrich Wilhelm* — were notable for their elaborate furnishing as well as their speed (and, it might be added, their vibration).

Cunard's *Lusitania* and *Mauretania* (both launched in 1906) set an equivalent standard for British passenger ships and were powered by then-innovative turbine engines.

White Star Line ships had followed the comfort-rather-than-speed policy. *Oceanic* (1899) and the latest additions to their Atlantic fleet, the 'Big Four' — *Celtic* (1901), *Cedric* (1903), *Baltic* (1904) and *Adriatic* (1907) — successively held records for size rather than rapid crossings. But in 1909 technology existed for combining the utmost luxury and stability with engines whose strength and reliability would assure consistent arrival on time.

The time for the '*Olympic* class' of liners was at hand.

Thomas H. Ismay **far left** and William Imrie **left** founded the White Star shipping dynasty. (Photos from *White Star* by Roy Anderson.)

The turbine steamships *Lusitania* **middle** and *Mauretania* **bottom** led Cunard's bid for North Atlantic supremacy. (Authors' collection.)

Above right When *Laurentic*'s machinery outperformed the conventional machinery of her sister *Megantic*, White Star chose combination turbine-reciprocating engines for the *Olympic* class. (Authors' collection.)

In 1902, American financier J. P. Morgan **right** formed the International Mercantile Marine shipping trust. He selected Joseph Bruce Ismay **far right** head of the Oceanic Steam Navigation Company Ltd to serve as its chief officer. (Authors' collection.)

On both sides of the Atlantic, preparations were begun to accommodate the new *Olympic* class of liners. **Top** In Southampton, cranes continued construction of White Star's deepwater dock, while in New York **above** the new Chelsea piers were well under way. (*Railway Magazine*, June 1911; Staten Island Ferry Maritime Museum/Ted Costa.)

PART TWO:

THE BUILDERS

At first the River Lagan had wound in gentle curves through Belfast, Ireland, on its leisurely way to where it entered Belfast Lough. But during the years 1841 to 1846 the Belfast Harbour Commissioners ordered the river's straightening, and the new straight cut became known as the Victoria Channel. Material excavated from the site was deposited on the cut's eastern side and formed an island whose bank diverted the Lagan into its new course.

The seventeen-acre plot was first known as 'Dargan's Island', after William Dargan, the contractor who carried out the work. In 1849 it was renamed 'Queen's Island' in honour of Queen Victoria, who visited that year to open the new channel.

Until 1851, all Belfast shipbuilding had been concentrated along the River Lagan's banks, but in that year the small firm of Thompson and Kirwan moved its wooden shipbuilding yard to Queen's Island, and in 1853 the iron shipbuilding yard of Robert Hickson and Company was laid out.

In December 1854, 23-year-old Edward James Harland came to Robert Hickson's yard in response to a printed advertisement. He had served his apprenticeship with Robert Stephenson & Co, and worked briefly at J. & G. Thompson's Glasgow marine engine works and Thomas Toward's Tyne yard. He was hired as Hickson's general manager.

Scarcely four years later, on 21 September 1858, Harland purchased the shipyard from Hickson for £5,000, with financial assistance from G. C. Schwabe of Liverpool. Schwabe's nephew, Gustav Wilhelm Wolff, had been Harland's private assistant for several months prior to the purchase, and he continued in this capacity until 11 April 1861 when he was taken on as partner.

The agreement contained a clause specifying that the partnership should be carried on as heretofore under the style of 'Edward James Harland' until Wolff should desire to have his name added, when the style of the partnership would be changed to 'Harland and Wolff'. It was Wolff's desire that this change take place on 1 January 1862. The firm has continued under this name ever since.

Harland's first achievement as the yard's owner and manager was the *Venetian*, for use in the Bibby Line's Liverpool-Mediterranean service. The vessel had actually been contracted to Hickson, but was completed after the yard's sale to Harland. *Venetian* — 'yard number 1' — was a single-screw, four-masted iron barque, of 290 feet overall length and 1,508 gross tons. Since the yard lacked engine works, the otherwise-completed ship had to be towed to Greenock for engine installation by MacNab and Company.

It was not until the April 1862 launch of *Arabian*, also for Bibby, that any product bore the imprimatur of 'Harland and Wolff', but many vessels for numerous shipping companies rapidly followed until the momentous yard number 73, launched on 27 August 1870. The vessel bore the name *Oceanic* — that of her proud owners, Oceanic Steam Navigation Company, operated by the White Star Line.

White Star, with which the shipbuilding firm was to become so inexorably linked, would, over the years, own 75 Harland and Wolff vessels, each constructed, with the sole exception of 1927's *Laurentic*, on a cost-plus basis, with no formal contract or fixed price, merely a 'letter of agreement'.

In 1867 the Belfast Harbour Commissioners constructed the new Hamilton Graving Dock, and in doing so connected Queen's Island with the mainland. In 1880 Harland and Wolff built its own Belfast engine works on a piece of rented land, which the Commission had reclaimed from tidal flats. In 1885 this plant constructed Harland and Wolff's first triple-expansion engine to a design which was to prove so successful in many of their subsequent ships.

William James Pirrie, who was to exercise vast influence on the firm, had been hired at the age of

fifteen as an apprentice draughtsman in 1862. He soon worked his way up to become head designer and in 1874 was admitted to partnership in the firm. He became managing director following Sir Edward Harland's death in 1895, and upon the 1906 retirement of Gustav Wolff became controlling chairman. It was under his direction that Harland and Wolff entered the 20th century.

Pirrie planned and executed the 1906-8 yard modernization, during which greatly enlarged slips, numbers two and three, were constructed in an area formerly occupied by three slips. A huge gantry designed by the shipyard and constructed by Sir William Arrol and Company Ltd, Glasgow, was erected over the two new slipways. It covered an area of 840 by 240 feet, and its height to the top of the overhead crane was 214 feet.

The work-force grew in proportion to the yard's activity. The 150 employees of 1862 increased to almost 15,000 workers in 1912. Working conditions at the 'Island' in force during the 1910-16 period, which saw completion of *Olympic, Titanic* and *Britannic**, are described by a company employee:

'Working Hours: Start at ten minutes to eight, finish at 5.30 pm. Ten minutes break at 10.00 am and a half hour lunch break. Saturday was part of the working week the

---

*Laid down as *Gigantic*, yard number 433's name was quickly changed following the *Titanic* disaster.

hours being 7.50 am to 12.30 pm.

'It was a nine-hour day, forty-nine hour working week. Working these hours a tradesman might earn £2 a week and if he worked all night Friday and all day Saturday he could boost his earnings up to £5. There were no special amenities or modern facilities such as canteens or showers.

'Holidays: Two days at Christmas, two days at Easter and one week in the summer (July). These were not paid holidays and working men's wives used to save one shilling a week from their husbands' wages to help cover these "holiday periods". The same applied at a launch in the shipyard. Those who were not required that day were told the previous day not to report for work. Therefore, when we read "The shipyard held holiday for the launch", what it really meant was that some married men's families had to endure a certain amount of hardship (the loss of a day's pay), people being so poor and money and work being so scarce.'

It may be further noted that smoking was not permitted at any place in the yard. Wages were the prevailing rate for the period. And a strict seniority system existed, so a regular worker could be certain of year-round employment.

The slips now completed, the space under the giant gantry stood empty, waiting. But not for long. The keel for yard number 400, *Olympic*, was laid down on 16 December 1908, to be followed on 31 March 1909 by the keel for yard number 401: *Titanic*.

Edward J. Harland **far left** and Gustav Wilhelm Wolff **left** formed and operated the shipyard that built virtually all White Star's ships. (Harland and Wolff Ltd.)

Downshire House, Belgrave Square, London, the home of Lord William James Pirrie, was the site where, in 1907, over after-dinner coffee, Bruce Ismay discussed with Lord Pirrie the construction of three immense new liners. (Authors' collection.)

Right Lord Pirrie guided the Harland and Wolff firm into the 20th century with his technical knowledge and his financial skills. (*Shipbuilder*.)

Far right Alexander M. Carlisle, general manager at Harland and Wolff, headed construction of the *Olympic*-class vessels. (Private collection.)

The owners' specifications for *Titanic* were translated into hundreds of blueprints and working drawings in Harland and Wolff's Queens Island draughting office. (Harland and Wolff Ltd.)

Chapter Two

CONSTRUCTION AND LAUNCH

A party of distinguished guests arrived at Harland and Wolff on 29 July 1908. They had come from the White Star Line's main office to examine the shipbuilder's concept plan for the huge new ships which had recently been discussed between Lord Pirrie and J. Bruce Ismay. The party, which included among others Ismay and Harold Sanderson, examined the scale drawing prepared by Harland and Wolff draughtsmen under the direct supervision of Pirrie, assisted by his nephew, draughting department manager Thomas Andrews. The plan bore the legend

400 Plan — 29 July 1908 (Proposed General Arrangement)

S S No 400

850 × 92 × 64′ 6″

Design 'D'

In the builders' concept, the power plant consisted of two reciprocating engines and a low-pressure steam turbine. Over the great first class dining saloon was a glass dome in the manner of the Cunard liners *Mauretania* and *Lusitania*, then enjoying great popularity. The representation of the second class dining room's design included the long rows of tables still so much a part of sea travel. There was — wonder of wonders! — a passenger lift in the second class accommodation, while on F deck a gymnasium was flanked by a Turkish bath and a large plunge bath.

The owners carefully examined the 'Proposed General Arrangement'. There were questions and answers, proposals of modification, and note taking. There were nodded heads and handshakes. The owners accepted in principle what the builders had prepared for them.

Two days later, on 31 July, the contract letter was signed. The document, described later as 'a sheet of quarto paper making a formal agreement to do it, and that is all', was the understanding between the Oceanic Steam Navigation Company and Harland

and Wolff, for the construction of *Olympic* and *Titanic*, with a third sister to follow. The liners were to be built on the usual 'cost-plus' basis, with the owners specifying the particulars and amenities they desired and the builders supplying these without regard to specific contractual costs.

Lord Pirrie directly controlled the vessels' practical design, while the details — decoration, equipment and general arrangement for construction — initially were under general manager Alexander M. Carlisle's supervision. As the plans were developed, they were submitted to White Star's directors for consideration. Perhaps a shipyard manager would accompany the plans to White Star's Liverpool office; perhaps he might be asked to come over for subsequent discussion. Occasionally the White Star directors would confer directly with Pirrie at his London home. Ultimate decisions were J. Bruce Ismay's responsibility.

Perhaps the most unusual element of the great liners was their propelling machinery. The first major vessels equipped with turbine engines — the triple-screw Allan liners *Victorian* and *Virginian* of 1904 and the quadruple-screw Cunard ships *Lusitania* and *Mauretania* of 1907 — had demonstrated the turbine's superiority in speed and economy. White Star then tested its own refinement. In 1909 the company completed two liners, *Megantic* and *Laurentic*, for its Canadian service. The vessels were identical except for the engines: *Megantic* was fitted with conventional reciprocating engines while *Laurentic* had a combination of reciprocating and turbine engines. Outstanding economy was obtained with the *Laurentic*'s performance, and the owners decided to adopt the combination engines for the much larger vessels then being designed.

Work on *Olympic* had progressed fewer than fifteen weeks when *Titanic*'s keel was laid on 31 March 1909. The speed with which both ships were built represented no sacrifice to the highest quality standards. In design and construction the hulls

exceeded any regulation then in effect. Compartmentalization conformed to the British Board of Trade's current requirements. Rivets were driven by hydraulic equipment, ensuring greater plating quality than conventional methods. The quality of work was described by one company designer as 'only a question of setting a standard and working to that standard by taking pains and spending money'. And spend they did. *Titanic*, fully equipped, cost about £1,500,000, or about $7,500,000.

Motivation of administrative and supervisory personnel at Harland and Wolff merged with the skills of workers, labourers and craftsmen to form the immense hulls. The huge gantries, with their nascent giants below, were objects of wonder along the River Lagan. And in the spring of 1911, when *Olympic* was being prepared for her maiden voyage and *Titanic* was ready for launching, the prestigious *Shipbuilder* magazine devoted an entire special issue* to these newest and largest wonders of the shipping world.

At the time of her launch, *Titanic* was the largest man-made object yet moved. Preparations for the event included lubricating the 772-foot-long sliding way with 22 tons of tallow and soap, providing a one-inch-thick coating which would bear the three-tons-per-square-inch pressure of the hull's weight. To check the vessel's momentum once it entered the water, three heavy anchors were placed in the river bed on each side of the ship; each was connected with a seven-inch steel wire hawser to eyeplates riveted to the shell plating. Two parallel piles of cable drags, each weighing over eighty tons, were likewise connected with eight-inch steel wire hawsers. They were arranged so that that anchors and drags would act simultaneously in bringing the ship to a standstill once it cleared the end of the slip.

The launching, on 31 May 1911, was witnessed by more than 100,000 people, stationed both in the shipyard itself and at other vantage points on both river banks. On the County Antrim side, the Harbour Commissioners enclosed a portion of the Albert Quay and charged a small admission fee, the proceeds going to several Belfast hospitals. Sightseers without tickets swarmed at every vantage point, from the roofs of coal sheds to the masts and yards of harbour shipping. The ferry boat *Slieve Bernagh*, diverted from her customary run to Bangor, Co Down, was advertized '. . . to leave the Queen's Bridge jetty at 11.15 am and will proceed on a cruise down the Lough, returning in time to permit the passengers witnessing from the deck of the steamer the launch of the SS *Titanic*. Tickets for the cruise at 2/0 each'.

Earlier that morning special guests and members of the press were ferried across the Irish Sea from Fleetwood, Lancashire, to Belfast aboard the specially chartered steamer *Duke of Argyll*, arriving at Donegall Quay at 7.30 am. They joined the thousands who were pressing down Queen's Road to Harland and Wolff's gates, where entry was strictly by ticket only. Three stands had been erected within the yard: for the launch party, distinguished guests and the press.

The day was clear and bright, the warm May weather tempered somewhat by a southerly breeze which rippled the river's surface and caused the flags on top of the gantry to stand straight out: the British Union Jack at one side, the American Stars and Stripes at the other; and at the centre, the White Star pennant, below which signal flags spelled out the word 'Success'. Shortly before noon Lord Pirrie and his wife (both celebrating birthdays on this special day) received a group of important visitors in the shipyard office and soon thereafter the party left for the special stand set aside for their use. The group included, among others, John Pierpont Morgan, J. Bruce Ismay, E. C. Grenfell, Sanderson, Charles F. Torrey, Mr Graves, Mr Curry, Mr Hale and Mr Concannon.

Leaving the party on the stand, Pirrie made a final inspection of preparation before giving the launch signal. During the morning a small army of workmen had added final touches to pre-launch work. Now the forest of shores under the bilges had dwindled to a few stray clusters, and these were being knocked away one by one with the aid of heavy rams and rolled out past the rope barriers that guarded the ship on either side. In the gloom under the hull one vaguely could see moving figures and catch the clink of iron as wedges were driven into the ways. Finally the vessel was being held on the ways solely by hydraulic triggers. They required only the opening of a valve for release, which would allow the huge bulk to glide gracefully into the water.

As Pirrie descended the gangway and consulted briefly with Charles A. Payne, who had charge of the launching apparatus, the hoisting of a red flag on *Titanic*'s stern gave notice that the launch would soon take place. At the same moment a red rocket was fired as a warning to all shipping in the river to Stand Away! Pirrie and Payne anxiously examined the brass face of a dial which showed pressure continuing to build on the launch trigger mechanism. Knots of men still swung their sledges in the darkness under the bilges. Most of the gangs had scrambled clear of this and now lined the inside of the barriers, glancing apprehensively at their lagging comrades.

Pirrie gave a brief command and all the foremen's

*Subsequently facsimile reprinted by Patrick Stephens as *Ocean Liners of the Past: Olympic and Titanic*.

21

whistles blew shrilly. There was a cry taken up all along the lines of men, 'Stand clear!', and on this word a swarm of men came darting out of the holes in the launchways while the crew of painters, with one eye on the launching gear, dabbed hastily at the marks left by the last of the shores. Again the warning cry rang out, on this occasion with an emphatic 'Hurry on!' added to it. A few stopped to pick up their tools and foremen shouted with a hint of anxiety, 'Never mind the hammers,' and 'Hurry! Come as you are!' Speedily the foremen mustered and counted their squads.

One worker, James Dobbins, aged 43, had to be dragged out. He had been using a large cross-cut saw to separate a wood support from one of the shores, and upon release of the support the shore had collapsed and pinned his leg underneath. He was hurriedly extricated by his fellow workers and pulled to safety from under the hull. His presence was reported to a nearby foreman, who included the unconscious worker in his head count.*

Soon the words 'All right' were passed along the lines.

All was ready. A suspenseful, almost palpable silence hung on the air. At thirteen minutes past twelve o'clock Pirrie gave a signal to Payne, who spoke the final order. A second red rocket roared into the air. A couple of foremen tugged at the handle of the releasing valve, a jet of dirty black water foamed out of the escape pipe, and the large triggers canted over. On the stand bearing the launch party there was no ceremony, no bottle of champagne smashed across the heavy, though graceful, metal bows. Only a general gasp and a chorus of 'There she goes!' as, under the bows, one could see on the ways a patch of white, slimy grease spreading and spreading while a surge of workers

swept forward cheering wildly. The people on the stands and throughout the yard took up the cheering, echoed by the vast crowds across the river.

As at the launch of *Olympic* there was no screech of riven timber or rumble of tumbling shores. Amid the hooting of sirens from the river steamers the gigantic vessel moved smoothly and gracefully down the ways and into the water. Sixty-two seconds from the time she began to move, the whole bulk was afloat in the Lagan. She had not moved her whole length after entering the water before the anchors and drags brought her to a standstill. So beautifully was the whole launching conducted that the motion of the water caused by her entrance was scarcely more than that caused by the passing of a small paddle steamer. The vessel rode gracefully at her anchors, her buoyancy causing her to rock gently back and forth. The crowds, after viewing her for some time, streamed back into the city.

After workers detached the metal hawsers from the riverbed anchors and drags, tugs from Liverpool's Alexandra Towing Company — *Alexandra, Hornby, Herculaneum* and *Wallasey* — assisted by Harland and Wolff's own yard tug, *Hercules*, towed the vessel to her berth.

After the launch Lord Pirrie entertained guests, including Morgan and Ismay, to a luncheon at Queen's Island. In Belfast's Grand Central Hotel, J. W. Kempter presided at a luncheon given for a large number of visitors and yard officials. The press had its own luncheon, presided over by White Star's J. Shelley, at the Grand Central Hotel.

As the shadows of a warm spring evening crept slowly up the Lough and gradually engulfed Belfast, they also met the splendid new hull of *Titanic*, riding high at her berth, gently rocking on the tidal flow. Tomorrow the work would begin anew, work on fitting and forming and shaping a great vessel. But for now, tonight, the vessel was alone, after the splendour and clangour of her launch. Alone. Waiting . . .

---

*Mr Dobbins was removed by ambulance to the Royal Victoria Hospital where, following an operation, he died the next day from contusions and shock.

Beneath the great Arrol gantry, the double bottom of *Olympic* (left) takes shape, while in the adjacent slip number three, the keel of *Titanic* has been laid. The year is 1909. (Ulster Museum.)

As shell plating of *Olympic* reaches her upper stages, the ribs of *Titanic* (left) are in place, in this view looking aft toward the River Lagan. (Bob Forrest Collection.)

By 1910, construction of *Titanic* had reached C deck. (Harland and Wolff Ltd.)

Left *Titanic*'s plating nears completion as work on *Olympic* (right) progresses. (Harland and Wolff Ltd.)

As the nearly-complete *Titanic* looms in the background, the shipyard workers engaged in her construction, their work for the day completed, head for home. The bow of *Nomadic*, built for use as a tender at Cherbourg, is on the left. (Harland and Wolff Ltd.)

To maintain ships of the *Olympic* class, Harland and Wolff engaged in a major construction programme at the shipyard. The Thompson Graving Dock (foreground) lies empty, awaiting the launch of *Titanic* (seen in the background, left). (Authors' collection.)

Above The ship's giant anchor — one of three carried — arrives at the shipyard for installation. (*Olympic*; Harland and Wolff Ltd.)

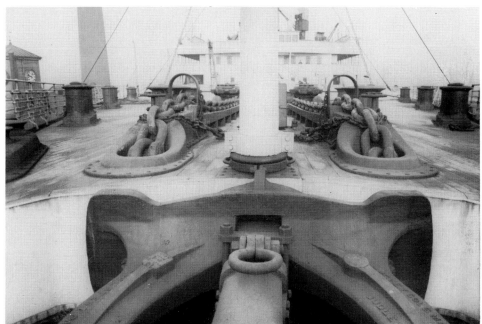

Right The bower anchor, installed on the fo'c's'le deck, has been attached to 175 fathoms of chain. (*Olympic*; Harland and Wolff Ltd.)

The shipyard lies deserted and quiet on a Sunday not long before *Titanic*'s launch. Her immense bulk fills the gantry. (Harland and Wolff Ltd.)

Above left Harland and Wolff's monstrous floating crane moves in with a portion of the drag chains intended to check *Titanic's* movement after launching. (Ulster Museum.)

Above Beneath the wooden bow cradles, the hydraulic cylinder powering the launching triggers is in place. (Harland and Wolff Ltd.)

Middle left Spectators approach the yard where, beneath her gantry, the new vessel awaits launch. Flags above the gantry signal the impending event. (*Cork Examiner*.)

Left The rare sight of a woman in the shipyard denotes the approach of *Titanic's* launching hour. (Harland and Wolff Ltd.)

Right The hydraulic system is tested on the morning of the launch. (Harland and Wolff Ltd.)

Below Crowds press forward, filling the side of the slipway near the stern as launch time approaches. (THS/Peter Phillips Collection.)

Above right The bow draws away from the launching platform. (Private collection.)

Right Red launch flag fluttering, *Titanic*'s stern enters the waters of Belfast Harbour. (Harland and Wolff Ltd.)

Left *Titanic* floats in the River Lagan, having cleared the slipway's bed of tallow and soap. (*Shipping World*.)

Left Well-wishers crane for a better look at the new liner off the end of the slipway. (THS/Peter Phillips collection.)

Left Momentum spent, *Titanic* awaits towing from mid-channel ... (Harland and Wolff Ltd.)

Above right ... as shipyard workers grapple to retrieve drag chains. (*Cork Examiner*.)

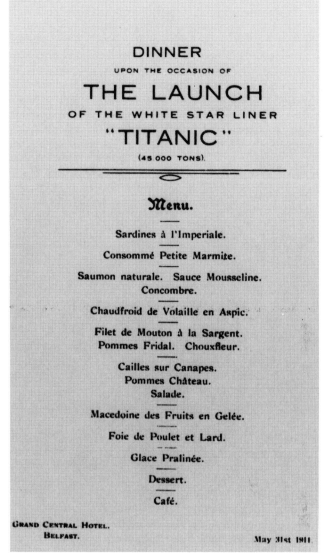

DINNER

UPON THE OCCASION OF

THE LAUNCH

OF THE WHITE STAR LINER

"TITANIC"

(45.000 TONS).

Menu.

Sardines à l'Imperiale.

Consommé Petite Marmite.

Saumon naturale. Sauce Mousseline.
Concombre.

Chaudfroid de Volaille en Aspic.

Filet de Mouton à la Sargent.
Pommes Fridal. Chouxfleur.

Cailles sur Canapes.
Pommes Château.
Salade.

Macedoine des Fruits en Gelée.

Foie de Poulet et Lard.

Glace Pralinée.

Dessert.

Café.

GRAND CENTRAL HOTEL.
BELFAST.

May 31st 1911.

Above right Launch activities completed, members of the press and invited dignitaries repair to Belfast's Grand Central Hotel for dinner. (Barrie Rogers Davis collection.)

Right The tow line tightens as the newly launched vessel is moved away from the end of the slipway. (Ulster Museum.)

Chapter Three

FITTING OUT

Titanic's hull, riding high at the fitting out basin, was a mere empty shell, awaiting the designer's skill to bring its cavernous interior to life. The attention and care lavished upon it during construction and launching now was brought to bear on her outfitting. The 'builders' specification book', an agreement between builders and owners, laid down detailed instructions regarding installation and adjustment of thousands of items and dozens of systems which would transform the hull into a vibrant entity.

Titanic's specification book was based largely on the design of *Olympic*, and contained modifications from lessons learned during the earlier ship's construction and fitting out. A document of more than 300 pages, it contained elaborate instructions by which White Star, in concert with Harland and Wolff, planned to make *Titanic* the biggest, best and most secure vessel afloat, while imbuing her with a unique character.

Even a casual perusal of the specification book shows the attention to detail which set *Titanic* apart. While many installations were themselves typical of the period, it was the sheer magnitude of quantity and highest quality which established *Titanic* as unique.

Specifications for the 'accommodation list', furnishings, decoration and details of fittings filled 120 pages. More than a page was devoted to the description of the suite rooms on B deck.

'The suite on the P[ort] side to consist of two bedrooms and a sitting room, with lavatory accommodation and wardrobe rooms arranged between the bedrooms; the sitting room being at the fore end of the suite next [to the] 1st class entrance. The after bedroom to be decorated by H & W, the walls being oak panelled and the furniture of oak in the French style; this room to contain two cot beds one 6′9″ × 2′9″, and one 6′6″ × 4′3″; a settee with an oval table in front; a two-basin washstand; a 3′0″ dressing table with chair; and an electric heater; the floor to be laid with blue carpet. The forward bedroom to have two brass cot beds of the same size as above, the other articles of furniture being as enumerated for the after bedroom, but

the decoration of the room and style of furniture to be to approval by A. Heaton & Co. The sitting room by A. H. & Co to have round table in the centre of the room, with two armchairs and two ordinary chairs, a sideboard, a cabinet, a corner writing table with chair, two other lounge chairs, a fireplace and an octagonal coffee stool; the panelling, decoration and style of furniture to be to approval. The lavatory accommodation to consist of a bathroom and WC; the bathroom containing bath with shower, an open washbasin, a hinged grating seat and an electric heater. The floor of the bathroom, WC and communicating corridor between the bathrooms to be laid with lino tiles. A wardrobe room for each bedroom to be arranged with hat and coat hooks and suitable chest of drawers.

'The suite on the S[tarboard] side to consist of two sets of rooms each comprising bedroom, wardrobe room, bathroom and WC. Each set to be separately entered from the fore and aft passageway through a vestibule and private athwartship corridor. Between the two sets of rooms a Saloon and Verandah to be arranged each separately communicating with the bedroom of either set of rooms. The Saloon to have a small Pantry at the fore end, and a servant's bedroom to be arranged adjacent to the forward set of rooms, with an entrance from the main fore and aft passageway. Each bedroom to have two cot beds, one 4′6″ and one 2′6″ wide; a settee with small round table in front; an arm chair, writing table and chair; a combined dressing table and washstand, with chair; an electric heater. The Saloon to have round table in the centre constructed so as to extend for the accommodation of four persons; four chairs to be supplied for the dining table; a sofa bed; four arm chairs; a corner writing table and chairs; a small square table and chair; a sideboard and fireplace. Bathrooms to contain bath and shower, wash basin and hinged seat.

'The verandah to have three settees with small square tables in front, two round backed chairs, two arm chairs, and two small round tables.

'The servants' rooms to be finished in dark mahogany and fitted with bed having Pullman over, sofa, wardrobe, folding lavatory, electric heater and a red carpet.'

The verandahs were new to North Atlantic liners, one on the port side and one starboard, forward of thirty 'parlour suite' cabins.

The decoration of these magnificent suites was specified:

30

'12 Rooms to have furniture in oak marked 'A' design.
14 Rooms to have furniture in oak with brass beds, marked 'B' design (Two of these rooms to have oak sparred cot beds).
6 rooms to be 'Adams' style, in white.
4 rooms to be 'Louis XVI' style, in oak.
2 rooms to be 'Louis XV' style in grey.
2 rooms to be 'Empire' style in white.
2 rooms, one P & S at fore end of this accommodation to be in mahogany.'

Descriptions and specifications for sofas, wardrobes, writing tables (five varieties) and chairs (more than thirty varieties) each occupied separate pages, while the fifty varieties of tables (for passenger cabins and dining accommodation) were described on almost two full pages.

Among the fifteen separate sections in the specification book were 'General Design and Description' (thirteen pages); 'Castings, Decks, Lockers, Doors and Bulwarks' (22 pages); 'Ventilation and Heating' (31 pages); 'Sidelights, Windows, & c' (six pages); 'Plumber Work, Etc (sixteen pages); and 'Cementing and Painting' (ten pages).

Some extracts from the more than 270 pages of specifications:

'... The sheer line to be cut in and to receive two coats of yellow [paint]. The name and Port of Registry to be cut in and to receive two coats of yellow, the letters being 18" for the name on the bow and 12" for the name and Port of Registry on the stern.

[For the first and second class galley:] '... Four steam jacketed stockpots of 80 gallons capacity made of best pan cast metal with flanges, machine faced and jointed with countersunk bolts and nuts; polished iron circular top with polished mouldings; planished copper hinged cover tinned inside and fitted with polished brass hinges and brass mounted handle; back balanced weight ...

...'BELLS. 1 — 23" dia Brass ship's bell for F'csle on Foremast.
1 — 17" dia Brass ship's bell for look-out cage on Foremast.
1 — 9½" dia Brass ship's bell for Captain's bridge.

... 'Post Office on Deck G to have warm air delivered through louvre in overhead trunks connecting with system supplied from No 69 fan on "D" deck to have also a 14" × 6" roof ventilator leading up to 20" cowl ventilator on 'C' deck.

... '12 mops with handles; 12 Squeegees with handles; 36 mounted Holystones & handles; 48 Paint cans; 48 Paint brushes, assorted; 12 sash tools; 72 Coir Brooms, 24 with handles; 1 Cwt white cotton waste; 1 solder pot ...

'The vessel to have two pole masts constructed entirely of steel, suitably stiffened with angles and raked 2" per foot. The foremast to be stepped on the Saloon Deck and the Main Mast on the Shelter Deck. A look-out cage to be fitted on the foremast at a suitable height; to be of steel

plating well stayed to the mast. An iron ladder to be fitted inside the mast to give access to the cage ...'

Once the specifications received the owners' approval, there could be no change without the owners' consent. Each modification was therefore discussed, first among the several departments at Harland and Wolff, then in a general meeting of the managing directors (department heads), usually with Pirrie present. Changes were listed and indicated in red on overlays to the vessel's plan sheets. Finally, the modifications were submitted to the owners or their representatives, sometimes by Thomas Andrews or Edward Wilding (head draughtsman and assistant chief of design), or, when the changes were major, by Pirrie himself.

Finally, one day — it may have been in July 1911 — the owners asked the builders when it might be reasonable to expect *Titanic's* completion. There were so many arrangements to be attended to — arrangements for coal, for ordering food for the voyage, for operation of the New York pier, for crew hiring — that Ismay and his directors wished to begin preparations. When could White Star's publicity department begin issuing public statments regarding the maiden voyage?

And, quite likely, Pirrie considered work still to be completed, emergencies which could arise at the yard, and his managing directors' estimates. He leaned forward to consult a calendar on the conference table.

Then he spoke a date. And the hint of a smile played on Ismay's face as he jotted it down:
'March 20 1912.'

Publicity and public relations announcements were little used in 1911, particularly by as conservative a company as the White Star Line. But the company was especially proud of *Olympic* and *Titanic*. Already there had been postcards showing *Olympic*, and noting that *Titanic* was 'now building'. A similar statement was appearing on company stationery of the period. Now, with Pirrie's estimate, it was possible for White Star to announce the long-awaited date of the maiden voyage. But, perhaps fortunately for the company, the 20 March date was not made public immediately, and an event soon occurred which made White Star's directors glad they had not rushed to make it so.

Three months after her highly-publicized maiden voyage, *Olympic* — already very popular with the travelling public — was involved in an accident which badly damaged her hull and changed the course of *Titanic's* destiny. Outward-bound from Southampton on 20 September 1911, *Olympic* collided with the British Royal Navy cruiser *Hawke*. The latter was proceeding up the Solent on her way to her home base at Portsmouth. *Olympic* was moving slowly down the Solent, approaching a shoal

named the Bramble, where a reverse S-turn was required. *Hawke* came up on *Olympic*'s starboard quarter, appeared to ease down, and then turned to port as though to pass under the liner's stern. But she struck the liner on the starboard side abreast the main mast, thrusting nearly eight feet into the *Olympic*'s hull and raking a forty-foot gash below her waterline.

The *Hawke*, after nearly capsizing, pulled away and proceeded slowly on to Portsmouth. *Olympic*, her voyage now cancelled, was unable to return to Southampton until the turn of the tide, and anchored for the night off the Isle of Wight while passengers were offloaded by a tender. *Olympic* returned to Southampton and was temporarily patched for her return to her Belfast builders, who had the only drydock large enough to accommodate her. She sailed from Southampton on the morning of 5 October, and moving at a cautious ten knots, arrived at Belfast on 6 October. Among the repairs made was replacement of her damaged starboard propeller crankshaft with a shaft planned for installation aboard *Titanic*.

Once again, owners conferred with builders, and made a difficult decision. The White Star Line's official announcement of *Titanic*'s maiden voyage date appeared in the 11 October 1911 edition of the London *Times*: 'April 10, 1912'.

Here, indeed, was a change of plan, necessitated by the unexpected diversion of yard workers and materials for the repair and hoped-for rapid return to service of the revenue-producing 'pride of the line'. The projected date of 20 March became the official date of 10 April, the first in a series of unpredictable events which were to culminate so tragically.

While *Olympic* was under repair in the new graving dock, *Titanic* lay alongside the Alexandra Wharf. With *Olympic*'s departure in late November, *Titanic* was returned to the graving dock and her own fitting out resumed.

Now it was January 1912, and the builders raced to meet the owners' deadline for *Titanic*'s entry into service, without compromising quality of workmanship. During January the sixteen wooden lifeboats, constructed at the Queen's Island boatyard, were installed under the Welin davits. (Not the 32 boats requested by the original designer, Alexander Carlisle, who no longer was employed at Harland and Wolff. Indeed, Carlisle had submitted a plan which described a complement of 64 lifeboats. However, during the period between 9 March and 16 March 1910 the decision had been reached by owners and builders to install sixteen instead of 32 boats.)

The Board of Trade regulations concerning lifeboat capacity were based on cubic footage and had been formulated with the Merchant Shipping Act of 1894. The largest vessel considered by this Act was one of '10,000 tons', a figure exceeded many times by vessels constructed during the intervening years. For *Titanic*, these now outdated regulations required a capacity of 9,625 cubic feet, which offered seating accommodation for approximately 960 passengers. *Titanic*'s sixteen boats under davits totalled 9,752 cubic feet, which was augmented by an additional 1,506 cubic feet with the installation of four Englehardt 'collapsible' boats constructed in Glasgow by McAllister & Son, boat builders, of Dumbarton. Their inclusion had been approved by White Star as part of 'Plan 6', on 5 May 1911.

Titanic's twenty lifeboats had a total capacity of 11,327.9 cubic feet, thus exceeding the Board of Trade's requirements by more than six per cent. And yet, prior to departure, *Titanic* would be certified by Board of Trade ship surveyors to be functionally capable of carrying a total of 3,547 passengers and crew.*

During January, the wireless call letters 'MUC' were assigned to *Titanic*. Wireless was a comparatively new development in communication. Following its successful use in the 1909 rescue of passengers and crew of the White Star liner *Republic* after its collision with the Italian liner *Florida*, wireless had become virtually a necessity. By 1912 nearly all North Atlantic passenger-carrying vessels were so equipped. By far the majority used the Marconi wireless system. And the Marconi apparatus aboard *Titanic* was the most powerful on any merchant vessel.

It was powered by a five kilowatt motor-generator, fed at 100 volts dc from the ship's lighting circuit; an independent oil engine generator was installed on the top deck, and a battery of accumulators also was provided as a standby.

The equipment's guaranteed working range was 250 miles under any atmospheric condition, but actually communication could be maintained up to about 400 miles, while at night the range for both receiving and transmitting was often up to 2,000 miles. Some time after January 1912, *Titanic*'s call letters were changed to 'MGY', letters previously assigned to the American vessel *Yale*.

A report on the progress of *Titanic*'s fitting out appeared in the 14 February 1912 columns of the *New York Maritime Register* and not only reflects the status of near completion, but also describes some of the countless activities necessary for a huge liner's completion:

'... The signs of progress on the vessel are plainly

*It was later calculated that 63 boats would have been needed to accommodate *Titanic*'s certified capacity — a figure curiously close to the 64 boats offered by Alexander Carlisle in one of his early proposals.

visible. The masts and all four funnels are now erected, the machinery on board, and the iron work of the superstructure well advanced. The inside work is also proceeding apace. In addition to the joiners' and carpenters' work, such as framing, panelling, etc, and laying of decks, the fitters and plumbers are proceeding throughout the ship with the fitting of baths, plumbing, pipes, scuppers, etc, etc. The first and second class elevators are fitted. The floors are well advanced and an interesting feature is the cementing and tiling of the swimming pond, which is progressing rapidly, as [is] also the elaborate decorative work in the magnificent saloon, smokeroom, restaurant and other public apartments . . .'

Titanic was successfully drydocked on Saturday, 3 February 1912 in the Belfast Harbour Commissioners' new graving dock. A little over an hour was required to move the mammoth vessel from the fitting out jetty into the dock. Pirrie, who witnessed the procedure, later expressed the builder's satisfaction regarding progress towards the liner's completion.

The two sister ships were together for a brief and final time when *Olympic* arrived at Belfast on 1 March for refitting of her port propeller, having lost a blade on 24 February during an eastbound crossing. When she departed on 6 March *Titanic* was again drydocked to provide the space needed for *Olympic's* outward turn into the River Lagan.

It is likely that the delay caused by the assignment of yard workers to again repair *Olympic* may have influenced yet another aspect of *Titanic's* maiden voyage. There is some evidence to suggest that a Liverpool stopover may have been planned for her voyage from Belfast to Southampton. *Olympic* had made a similar, brief visit to Liverpool in June 1911, and the owners may have wished to salute the city, the Line's home port, with an appearance of their newest and largest ship. But it appears that the loss of time caused by *Olympic's* second return to Belfast cut still further the number of days remaining before the officially announced 10 April sailing date for *Titanic*.

A last-minute change in *Titanic's* design also may have been a factor. Passengers aboard *Olympic* had complained that as they walked along the A deck promenade they were splashed with spray from the bow. Owners and builders agreed on a modification for *Titanic* that would permit first class passengers to promenade in dry, if somewhat isolated, grandeur. At a very late stage of construction, during the last three weeks of March, the open windows on the forward end of A deck were torn out and replaced by new sliding glass windows. The modification gave *Titanic* a distinctly different appearance from that of *Olympic*. It is seldom in the history of great liners that such a major modification was made at so late a stage in construction.

Now, indeed, time was running out for the

builders. Painters vied with carpet layers for working space. Tile layers in bathrooms and working spaces had to work around electricians who were installing wall and ceiling lights. Furniture lay in organized piles awaiting placement once floors were polished.

The interior decorators, A. Heaton & Co, placed finishing touches on the period suite rooms on B deck. Representatives of Henry Wilson & Co Ltd, of Liverpool, saw to it that their fine kitchen equipment was not damaged by careless installers. Master mechanics from R. Waygood & Co Ltd tested and re-tested the passenger elevators and the goods lifts in the victualling department. Harland and Wolff's own interior decorating department fretted over a late shipment of fabrics from H. P. Mutters and Zoon, The Hague, Netherlands. ('Their blankets and quilts arrived last week, before we really needed them. And now we have to wait to finish the settee for the restaurant reception room. Really!')

One of the glories of the entire ship, the great 21-light candelabra for the main staircase, arrived from Perry & Co, of Bond Street, London. Earlier, the brass cot beds for the de luxe cabins and the metallic berths and mattresses for the first, second and third class cabins and crew's quarters had arrived from Hoskins & Sewell Ltd, of Birmingham, and were being placed and installed. The elaborate hardware, the ormolu door fittings and electrical wall sconces arrived from N. Burt & Co Ltd, of London, and were being installed throughout the ship.

Orders had been placed for eating utensils from the Goldsmiths and Silversmiths Company Ltd, of Regent Street, London. The chinaware for the à la carte restaurant had been ordered from Royal Crown Derby, while Stonier & Co, of Liverpool, was busy delivering chinaware for the ship's other dining areas. Books and magazines for the libraries would be delivered at Southampton from *The Times* of London's own book club.

For sailing and navigating staff, items of a more practical nature were arriving daily and being stored in their appropriate departments: charts and sailing direction from Messrs Phillips, Son and Nephew; lifebelts (3,560 of them) from Fosbery, London; the navigation lamps from Messrs Wm Harvie, Glasgow; the ship's compasses, from Kelvin, Bottomley & Baird; four Milner's safes . . .

As the *Titanic's* inventory grew so, too, did her mention in record books. Signal letters, used to identify vessels on official lists of tonnage, also served as an international code of recognition. Expressed as a hoist of four flags, they were used in pre-wireless days to identify vessels at a distance. On 25 March 1912, Henry Malan, Registrar General of the General Register and Record Office of

Shipping and Seamen, signed the order allotting *Titanic* her signal letters: 'HVMP'.

The liner's crew now began to assemble at Belfast. During her building, many from the engineering department had visited the yard to observe construction of the systems with which they subsequently were to work. Now, during March, they arrived at the yard to stay with the vessel, some actually living aboard.

The coal strike then in progress in England forced many ships out of service because of lack of fuel. Among these was *Oceanic*, from which several of *Titanic*'s officers were drawn. First Officer Charles Lightoller arrived on 20 March.

The junior officers — Pitman, Boxhall, Lowe and Moody — received telegrams from the White Star Line marine superintendent to report to the company's Liverpool office at 9 am on 26 March to pick up their tickets for Belfast. Departing from Liverpool at 10 o'clock that night, they arrived at Belfast and joined *Titanic* at about 12 noon on 27 March, reporting on board to Chief Officer William Murdoch.

Francis Carruthers had been employed by the Board of Trade for sixteen years as engineer and ship surveyor at Belfast. He described his duties as, '. . . the admeasurement of vessels for tonnage and surveying the hull, machinery and equipment of vessels during construction for passenger certificate; inspecting the hull during construction, checking the scantlings and arrangements against the submitted designs, seeing that the workmanship is of good standard and that the bulkheads and

bulkhead doors are in the positions and the height specified by the regulations . . .'

During *Titanic*'s construction, Carruthers stated, he had visited the vessel close to 2,000 times. He had probed and measured, set up tests, asked countless questions, submitted numerous reports. Now, as March drew to a close, his work with *Titanic* also was approaching an end. Accompanied by Lightoller, he completed his inspection of the watertight bulkheads and doors. On 25 March, with Lightoller issuing the actual commands, the great 15½-ton forward anchor was lowered and raised, and all sixteen boats under davits were swung out, lowered and hoisted again into position. 'All the gear', in Mr Carruthers' words, 'proved satisfactory'.

By 31 March, though work was still being completed on the furbishing of passenger cabins and public rooms, everything else was in readiness. *Titanic*, her paint sparkling in the pale, early spring light of Belfast, her fuel aboard, her mechanical systems in order, stood ready for sea trials and, if these were successful, for handing over to her owners.

The evolution of her design, the integrity of her construction, the seaworthiness of her hull and practicability of her accommodation were to be put to their final test. The ultimate proof of her owners' dreams and her builders' skill was to be seen. The contents of the specification book, no longer merely page after page of closely-spaced writing, had merged to form the ship . . . the *Titanic*.

Left Soon after launching, *Titanic* is guided by the yard tug *Hercules* to the outfitting basin. (Pennwick Publishing Inc.)

The 29 boilers for *Titanic* were fabricated in Harland and Wolff's own shops ... (Private collection.)

... as were the giant reciprocating engines. (Harland and Wolff Ltd.)

Above A few of the 15,000 Harland and Wolff workers pose before *Titanic*'s hull. (*Belfast Telegraph*.)

While installation of the ship's machinery continues, shipyard interior designers prepare sketches of *Titanic*'s staterooms and public rooms for three classes of passenger . . .

Left Special first class stateroom C64. (Authors' collection).

Below left Second class stateroom. (Ulster Folk and Transport Museum.)

Below The à la carte restaurant. (Authors' collection.)

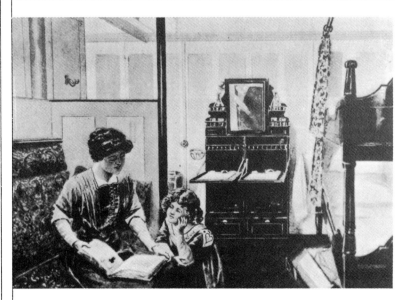

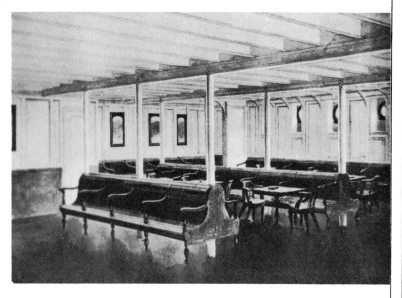

Above left Second class dining room. (Authors' collection.)

Above Third class general room. (Authors' collection.)

WHITE STAR LINE.

"OLYMPIC," (Triple-Screw) 45,000 Tons.
AND
"TITANIC," (Triple-Screw) 45,000 Tons,
Launched May 31st 1911.
THE LARGEST STEAMERS IN THE WORLD.

Left and below . . . as White Star's publicity department announces the new liners' debut in many ways, including a special postcard. (Authors' collection.)

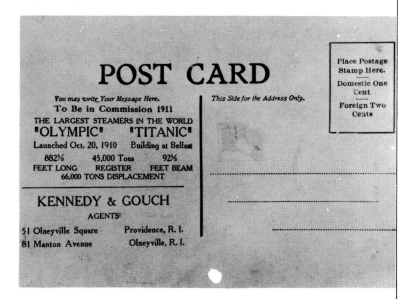

POST CARD

Place Postage Stamp Here.
Domestic One Cent
Foreign Two Cents

You may write Your Message Here.
To Be in Commission 1911
THE LARGEST STEAMERS IN THE WORLD
"OLYMPIC"   "TITANIC"
Launched Oct. 20, 1910   Building at Belfast
882½   45,000 Tons   92½
FEET LONG   REGISTER   FEET BEAM
66,000 TONS DISPLACEMENT

This Side for the Address Only.

KENNEDY & GOUCH
AGENTS
51 Olneyville Square   Providence, R. I.
81 Manton Avenue   Olneyville, R. I.

H1622
RW

LOOKING FRD.

Inset far left In mid September 1911, a tentative date for *Titanic*'s first voyage is released. Sailing schedules printed in passenger lists of other White Star liners carry the 20 March 1912 date. (Authors' collection.)

Left Within a fortnight of the schedule's publication, however, an unforseen event changes the Company's plans: *Olympic* is forced to return to her builders for repairs following her 20 September collision with HMS *Hawke*. The damage is extensive. (Harland and Wolff Ltd.)

Right The scope of the repairs necessitates diversion of workers from the completion of *Titanic*. After conferring with the builder, White Star reluctantly reschedules the maiden voyage date to 10 April. (Harland and Wolff Ltd.)

Below Upon completion of *Olympic*'s repairs, facilities again become available for continuing *Titanic*'s outfitting. She enters Thompson Graving Dock in February 1912. (1912 newsreel.)

Below right *Titanic* is safely placed in the drydock, and preparations are made to drain out the water. (*Irish Times*.)

Left With land bridge and shoring in place, *Titanic* awaits completion of outfitting. (*Cork Examiner*.)

Below left Workmen install the 16-foot-diameter manganese bronze centre propeller. (*Olympic*: Ulster Museum.)

Right Finishing touches include installation of *Titanic*'s lifeboats. Designed by Harland and Wolff's chief draughtsman Roderick Chisholm ... (*Belfast Telegraph*.)

Above far right ... and mounted in davits designed by Axel Welin... (*Shipbuilder*.)

Right ... the boats originally were planned to be 32 in number. But the expected change in British Board of Trade lifeboat regulations does not materialize, and the 32 boats are replaced by the legally required sixteen. Four additional boats — Englehardt collapsibles — are provided by the owners, in excess of requirements. A copy of the original design was later produced as evidence in an American court. (National Archives.)

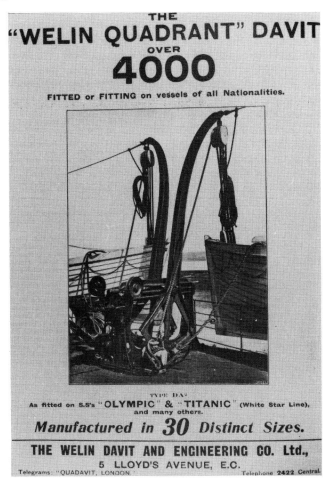

THE "WELIN QUADRANT" DAVIT

OVER
4000
FITTED or FITTING on vessels of all Nationalities.

TYPE DA²

As fitted on S.S's "OLYMPIC" & "TITANIC" (White Star Line), and many others.

Manufactured in 30 Distinct Sizes.

THE WELIN DAVIT AND ENGINEERING CO. Ltd.,
5 LLOYD'S AVENUE, E.C.

Telegrams: "QUADAVIT, LONDON."   Telephone 2422 Central.

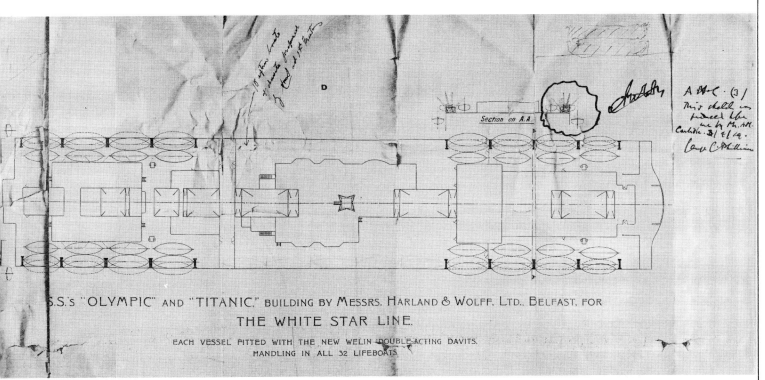

S.S.'s "OLYMPIC" AND "TITANIC," BUILDING BY MESSRS. HARLAND & WOLFF. LTD., BELFAST, FOR

THE WHITE STAR LINE.

EACH VESSEL FITTED WITH THE NEW WELIN DOUBLE-ACTING DAVITS. HANDLING IN ALL 32 LIFEBOATS

The New White Star Liner,
R.M.S. "TITANIC"
is the largest vessel
in the world.

It is not only in size but also in the luxury of her appointments that the "Titanic" takes first place among the big steamers of the world. By the provision of VINOLIA OTTO TOILET SOAP for her first-class passengers the "Titanic" also leads as offering a higher

standard of Toilet Luxury and comfort at sea.

VINOLIA OTTO TOILET SOAP

is perfect for sensitive skins and delicate complexions. Its rich, cleansing lather soothes and softens, and for regular Toilet use there is no soap more delightful.

VINOLIA COMPANY LTD.,   LONDON AND PARIS.

Top On 6 October 1911 to allow *Olympic* access to the Thompson Graving Dock, *Titanic* has been backed out and is about to be re-moored at the shipyard jetty. (Harland and Wolff Ltd.)

Above The two sisters are together again on 6 March 1912, as *Olympic* returns to Belfast for replacement of a damaged propeller. (Harland and Wolff Ltd.)

Left As the maiden voyage date approaches, the new liner is featured in a contemporary advertisement for scented soap. (Authors' collection.)

Right One of the final details prior to departure for sea trials is the insuring of the vessel. Coverage is divided among many companies on both sides of the Atlantic. (Atlantic Mutual Insurance Company.)

42

Insurance *is wanted by* OCEANIC STEAM NAVIGATION COMPANY LIMITED *for account of*

Whom it may concern.

loss, if any, payable to OCEANIC STEAM NAVIGATION
COMPANY, LIMITED.

For $ $100,000. *on* STR. TITANIC

Valued at $5,000,000.

Per

and to be insured at and from

the 30 day of March 1912 at 7 P.M.

until

the 30 day of March 1913 at 7 P.M.

This policy is subject to total loss or constructive total loss of the
vessel only, and to cover General Average and salvage charges if both
charges combined amount to $750,000., which amount is deductible.

Premium at the rate of 2-1/10% per annum, predicated on the rate of
7½¢ for each trip, and in the event of the vessel being detained in
port for any cause, the premium returned for such detention to be
based on the number of trips. But in the event of the total loss of
the Steamer during the period covered by this policy, the full annual
premium of 2 1/10% to be paid by the Assured.

To include the trip from Belfast to Southampton Sailing on
on after March 30th 1912 at 7 PM and the risk of trials on
said trip if any.

Binding

President.

Oceanic Steam Navigation Co. Applicant.

W. Johnson Higgins

} New York, March 27th 1912

43

Chapter Four

TRIALS

Titanic's sea trials were scheduled for Monday, 1 April. On 29 March 79 firemen, stokers, greasers and support crew had signed on. Escort tugs from the Alexandra Towing Company, several of which had assisted during the *Titanic*'s launch, were sent over from Liverpool. Ship's officers and representatives of the builder, owner and the Board of Trade were aboard. Galleys for crew, observers and officers were stocked and staffed.

The trials were to commence at 10 am, and at 9 am the tugs were alongside, ready to put tow lines aboard. But a brisk north-west wind swept across the region, roiling the Lough's waters and stirring the narrow confines of the River Lagan and Victoria Channel in brisk swells of white-capped waves. It was impossible to navigate *Titanic*'s huge bulk through the channel without endangering her hull. Agents of the builders and owners reluctantly decided to postpone trials until the next day.

The delay meant additional costs, fewer days at Southampton to load supplies, furnishings and food stocks. But to the engineers and officers, it meant an extra day for investigating and learning the intricacies of the new vessel and her equipment, and gaining familiarity with the seemingly endless corridors, the countless rooms and staircases of the immense liner.

The 2nd of April dawned clear and fair. The now-calm waters of Abercorn Basin, where *Titanic* had lain during her outfitting, reflected the hull's black, the white-painted superstructure and the thin gold sheer line at the hull's upper edge — all traditional White Star features, proudly carried by their newest and greatest vessel.

Even as the sun rose, the great ship already hummed with the activity of work crews. Thin wisps of smoke issuing from the second and third funnels showed the furnaces were being fired and that steam was up; smoke was also a tell-tale sign of activity in the galleys, where the first full meal to be served aboard was being prepared for men who were to take the liner out on her trial trip.

One member of the 'black gang' failed to return aboard, leaving 78 in the engine room. There were 41 officers and senior crewmen — engineers, chief stewards, cooks and storekeepers. Harold A. Sanderson, a member of the IMM's board as well as the Oceanic Steam Navigation Co Ltd, was aboard to represent the owner. Bruce Ismay was unable to attend. Thomas Andrews headed the builders' delegation, accompanied by Edward Wilding, a Harland and Wolff marine architect. Lord Pirrie had very much wished to attend the trials, but illness kept him away.

Carruthers, the Board of Trade surveyor, came aboard to observe the trials' particulars. Messrs C. J. Smith, of Southampton, placed several members of their firm aboard to adjust the ship's compasses once the vessel entered open water.

Jack Phillips and Harold Bride crouched over their wireless apparatus. The equipment had just been received from the Marconi factory, and was not yet fully in phase, though it was operable. There were adjustments to be made, wires to be connected, generators to be tested. It was a very busy day for them.

Shortly before 6 am, the tugs came up the River Lagan. They were to assist *Titanic* on the first step of her trials, escorting her away from the fitting out basin, through the Victoria Channel and into the Belfast Lough. To *Hercules*, Harland and Wolff's own yard tug, went the honour of having the first line aboard.

The hawsers which secured *Titanic* to the shore were dropped away; the massive hulk gently drifted free of the jetty. Lines were quickly attached to the tugs *Huskisson* and *Herculaneum* at the stern (port and starboard, respectively). They steadied the great ship and guided her towards the river channel while *Hornby* strained on the starboard bow line. Finally, *Herald* began to pull on the forward line, which extended directly ahead through *Titanic*'s centre anchor hawsepipe.

Away from the basin, in mid-river *Titanic* stood

poised for forward movement. Steadied and propelled by the straining tugs she moved slowly, majestically down Victoria Channel towards the wider reaches of Belfast Lough. Great gouts of oily black smoke poured from her funnels as stokers built up steam necessary for the engine trials ahead. She rode high in the water, for she had yet to bunker a full supply of coal, take aboard food, cargo, kitchen and dining room tableware and glassware.

Hundreds of spectators crowded the river banks and the low, rock-strewn edges of Victoria Channel. They murmured, then shouted their admiration as the new ship glided quietly by.

Down the channel and into the Lough, one, two, three miles and more, still steadied and propelled entirely by tugs, her engines remaining in check, *Titanic* reached a point almost two miles off the Irish town of Carrickfergus. The tugs cast off and wheeled around to return to Belfast. As the smoke from their funnels receded in the distance, *Titanic* stood for the first time alone in open water. A brief command, and the blue-and-white burgee, the signal letter 'A', was run up: 'I am undergoing speed trials'. A moment of suspenseful silence was followed by a jangle of bells in the engine room as orders from the bridge were received to set the engines in motion. Boiler steam was fed slowly, carefully into the two monstrous reciprocating engines and the centre turbine. A faint, almost imperceptible shudder radiated through the ship's frame as the immense steel and bronze propellers revolved for the first time, then again and again.

Titanic lived!

The rhythmic pulsation of the giant cylinders' vertical movement being transformed to horizontal rotation beat faster and faster. Thick crankshafts plunged, leapt up, plunged again as the triple expansion engines received full steam. The huge turbine, taking its power from spent steam emerging from the reciprocating engines, added little more than a hum while it transmitted 16,000 shaft horsepower to the centre propeller.

The vessel's sharp bow cut the waters of Belfast Lough. A plume of white spray arced outward, almost quietly at first; then, as the speed rose to almost twenty knots, hissed and foamed, leaving an ever-widening wedge of frothy spume behind the stern as the vessel moved faster, faster.

At an order from the bridge, engines were stopped but not put astern. Having attained high speed for the first time, the huge liner drifted slowly to a full stop. At the request of the owners' representatives, the vessel was restarted, stopped and again started. As before, high speed was attained, but this time, while travelling at about eighteen knots, the centre turbine was cut out, and various manoeuvres were conducted: port and starboard turns using only the rudder; slowing down and speeding up; turning,

with first the port and then the starboard propeller assisting. Once again, the ship was allowed to drift to a complete stop. Notes were taken, observations compared. Representatives consulted with officers and with one another. Mr Carruthers moved quickly here and there, taking measurements, recording observations and evaluations for the Board of Trade.

In their cabin behind the officers' quarters, the Marconi operators continued to test their circuits. Frequently they transmitted test messages to wireless stations at Liverpool and Malin Head. Then, their messages acknowledged and their frequencies confirmed, the men returned to fine-tuning the apparatus, assuring its function.

Lunch was now ready, but there was one more test to be conducted. While the ship travelled at 20½ knots on a straight course, the helm was ordered hard over. Heeling slightly, *Titanic* turned a full circle whose diameter was measured at about 3,850 feet, or a bit less than 4½ lengths of the vessel. During the turn, the ship's forward movement was about 2,100 feet. While lunch was being served in the main dining saloon the vessel was put at dead slow, and such observers, representatives and officers as could be spared sat down for their meal, still conversing, comparing, exchanging data.

Following lunch, the major stopping test was conducted. A buoy was dropped in the waters of the Lough and, after turning, *Titanic* was put at full speed and, when precisely alongside the buoy, put at full astern. Officers Moody and Murdoch, sextants ready, carefully observed the buoy's position and the vessel's approach. They relayed their observations to Edward Wilding, who signalled Captain Smith. At the captain's command, the telegraph handle was quickly put to 'full astern'. The entire vessel shuddered as the stress of full speed astern was imposed on her hull. At a twenty-knot speed, *Titanic* took a bit less than half a mile — about 850 yards — to come to a complete stop.

At about 2 pm the running test took place. In open water, out in the Irish Sea, *Titanic* turned southward and travelled a straight course for about two hours. She averaged eighteen knots, although as the liner passed Copeland Island she maintained almost 21 knots for a brief period.

Two hours down, about forty miles. A turn. Then two hours back, to the mouth of the Lough. As the ship steamed down the fifteen-mile length of the Lough, the descending sun glared in the observers' eyes. A few more turns were made and, for a brief while, the vessel was put on a serpentine course — first port, then starboard, then port again and back to starboard — to test her handling.

There was still a slight glow from the now-departed sun in the western sky as *Titanic* approached Belfast from the east, at about 7 pm. As

she glided to a halt, Mr Carruthers requested one final test: both port and starboard anchors were dropped. Satisfied that the trials had met Board of Trade standards, Carruthers signed and dated a passenger certificate, 'good for one year from today, 2.4.12'. Yard workers and members of the Harland and Wolff staffs who were not to go on to Southampton were lightered ashore. Some last-minute kitchen equipment came aboard, as did some fresh food and several special chairs for the first class reception room.

Casually, almost as an afterthought, the papers were signed, indicating acceptance by the owner (represented by Sanderson) of the builders' product as signed by Andrews. Thus was *Titanic* handed over.

A few minutes after 8 pm the anchors were winched up and secured. Deck hands worked quickly and efficiently, as a time limit created a sense of urgency. The vessel had to depart from Belfast in time to arrive in Southampton by the midnight tide, less than thirty hours away.

Titanic performed a tight turning circle as one propeller played foward against the reverse of the other. A bright yellow glow of lights along the decks and in the dining room served as cheerful contrast to the darkness in the wheelhouse forward. Once again, this time finally, *Titanic* left her birthplace. The great ship's masthead lights and red-and-green navigating lamps appeared to blink as distance made them indistinct.

The subtle pulsation of the mighty engines lingered in the air, grew fainter, then vanished. Only the distant hull — somehow darker than the blackness of the soft, Irish spring night — could be seen.

Titanic had set out to meet her destiny.

She passed out into the Irish Sea, moving southward through the night toward St George's channel. There was little sleep aboard the vessel. 'On-and-off' shifts were, of course, in effect for crew, officers and runners. But there was the excitement of the first night out and, after brief naps, many of the men were awake. There was practically no rest for the builders' representatives as measurements and tests continued: further electrical trials, tests of the sanitary arrangements, and a trying of everything in the ship under actual sea conditions. As Edward Wilding later said, '. . . And there were a good many things to try'.

While running south through the night and early morning, the vessel sustained a speed of eighteen knots. There were brief spurts above twenty knots,

but as all the boilers were not lighted no attempt was made to sustain this speed. All were satisfied.

The weather was fine until about 2 am, when fog settled around the vessel. At 4 am there was still considerable fog, but by 6 am it had largely dispersed.

The wireless was in almost constant use. Messages flowed to Mr Ismay at the Liverpool home office describing trial results, the ship's speed and her ease of handling. Communication with other wireless-equipped vessels was established as Phillips and Bride continued testing their own equipment and, perhaps boastfully demonstrated its power. *Titanic*'s special transmitter had a 400-mile daytime range; this more than trebled at night. But freak atmospheric conditions enabled *Titanic*, as she rounded Land's End, to establish communication with Teneriffe, more than 2,000 miles away, and with Port Said, more than 3,000 miles distant.

By 10.30 am on 3 April *Titanic* was reported by wireless to be 150 miles east of Fastnet. In fine though somewhat hazy weather with light swells she rounded Cornwall and passed into the English Channel. Through lengthening afternoon shadows she passed Prawle Point, St Catherine's Point . . . Darkness descended as she moved towards the Isle of Wight and into Spithead, past the Nab Light Vessel. More slowly she entered Southampton Water, the buoys' red and green marker lights spreading a colourful path before her. The pilot came aboard. The huge liner almost inched forward, her bulk looming through the night sky, outlined in dark silhouette against Gosport's distant shores to starboard and Ryde to port. Her arrival coincided with high water at Southampton.

At last the liner approached the White Star Dock, where she was met by five tugs: *Ajax*, *Hector*, *Vulcan*, *Neptune* and *Hercules*, all of the Red Funnel Line. Arc lights on the dock illuminated the area, pointing the way to the quayside.

Gently assisted by the tugs, *Titanic* was turned around ninety degrees in the newly dredged turning circle in the River Test Channel. At the anticipated time of departure, noon on 10 April, it would be low water, and there would be little room for manoeuvring. The shrill keening of the tugs' manoeuvring whistles pierced the darkness as the tiny vessels warped the huge liner stern-first into her mooring.

After a voyage of about 570 miles, *Titanic* was successfully docked and tied up shortly after midnight at Berth 44.

The first page of 'An Agreement and Account of Voyages and Crew' for *Titanic*'s voyage from Belfast to Southampton, including trials, contains a clause, 'Five shillings per day to be paid for detention in Belfast Lough commencing from midnight, Monday, 1st April, 1912'. The crew collects the bonus when the trials are delayed. (Public Record Office of Northern Ireland.)

Titanic is prepared for sea trials at 10am on 1 April. (Private collection.)

Above Tugs stand ready to assist *Titanic* into Belfast Lough. But before the tests can start, high winds, as evidenced by the flattened smoke pouring from the liner's funnels, cause a postponement. (Michael V. Ralph collection.)

Left Tuesday, 2 April, is a fine, clear day. *Titanic* is shepherded through Victoria Channel on her way to Belfast Lough. (Authors' collection.)

Left Spectators line both sides of Victoria Channel to see the White Star liner off on her trials. Some record the scene with box cameras. (Public Record Office of Northern Ireland.)

Right *Titanic* enters the upper reaches of Belfast Lough. (David F. Hutchings collection.)

Right The full beauty of the vessel's sleek profile is seen for the first time as the tugs escort her into the ever-widening Lough. (Harland and Wolff Ltd.)

Left Not far from shore, the tugs get ready to cast off. *Titanic* prepares to proceed under her own power. (Private collection.)

Below far left Mid-way through the trials, builders' and owners' representatives gather for the first full meal served aboard *Titanic*. (Southern Newspapers plc.)

Below left Aboard on behalf of the owners is Harold A. Sanderson, board member of both IMM and Oceanic Steam Navigation Company. (Photo from *White Star*, by Roy Anderson.)

Below Trials completed, *Titanic* departs from Belfast about 8pm on 2 April. The morning of 3 April finds her well down the Irish Sea, when breakfast is served to all aboard. (THS/Vaughan Braatz collection.)

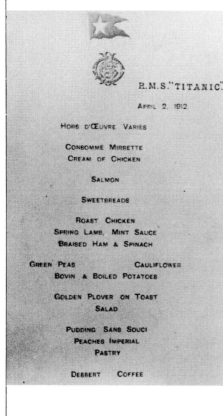

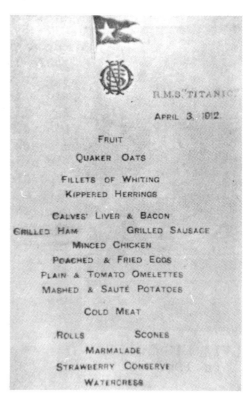

Chapter Five

SOUTHAMPTON

Located in Hampshire, 78 miles south-west of London, at the confluence of the Rivers Test and Itchen, Southampton has long been famous as a port. A situation very favourable to shipping and dry-docking operations is created by double tides, which maintain high water periods for two hours twice each day, and by a moderate tidal range. The nearby Isle of Wight protects the harbour from storms.

Southampton's origin is as ancient as the Roman occupation of Britain. The Roman settlement of Clausentum gave way to the Saxon village of Hamwih, which, in turn, became the fortified town of Suthamtune. By the early 15th century it had become an important trade centre, particularly for importing French and Spanish goods. From its West Quay, Henry V's troops embarked for the Battle of Agincourt, and the Pilgrim fathers' vessel *Mayflower* made its first departure.

With the expansion of other British ports, particularly London, Southampton's pre-eminence declined during the 16th and 18th centuries, to be revived in 1803 through the establishment of the Harbour Board, whose function was to expand docking facilities. In 1836 the Southampton Dock Company was formed and, with Parliamentary permission, constructed the Outer Dock (opened in 1843) and the Inner Dock (1851). The Itchen Quays, started in 1873 with the first phase completed in 1876, saw the Dock Company needing money to finance its expansion and maintain the upkeep of existing facilities. To this end, it borrowed £250,000 from the London & South Western Railway (LSWR), successor to the Southampton, London & Branch Railway, whose trains had run between Southampton and London since 1840.

The financial infusion permitted construction of the great 'Empress Dock', named by Her Majesty Queen Victoria on opening day, 26 July 1890. However, even this addition to its assets did not give the dock company the required financial flexibility. In November 1892 the firm sold its holdings to the railway company. With its large capital resources, the railway company could stabilize the financial condition of the docks' management and undertake modernization and new construction. The Itchen Quays were completed in 1895, and in 1902 the South Quay and Test Quays opened to shipping.

By 1906, most transatlantic lines were already using Channel ports. In addition, there was a considerable increase in continental destinations for passengers, rather than the UK ports which had so long prevailed. Early in 1907, White Star announced that it was transferring express passenger service from Liverpool, its home port since the company's founding, to Southampton. It established a secondary service from Liverpool, using *Baltic*, *Cedric*, *Celtic* and *Arabic*. *Oceanic*, *Majestic* and *Teutonic* were sent to Southampton. But it was *Celtic* which made the first White Star departure from the port, although under American Line charter. She departed on 4 May 1907 for New York.

To the new *Adriatic* went the first White Star-scheduled departure. Leaving Liverpool on her 8 May 1907 maiden voyage, she travelled to New York and, on her return, went to Southampton. Her subsequent departure for New York on 5 June 1907 marked the official inauguration of White Star's Southampton service.

For almost four years, White Star ships used Test Quay berths 36 to 41 for arrivals and departures, with *Oceanic*, *Teutonic*, *Majestic* and *Adriatic* maintaining weekly service to New York. In mid-1911, *Adriatic* was transferred to the Liverpool service, while *Teutonic* entered the White Star-Dominion route between Liverpool and Canada. With her 14 June 1911 maiden voyage departure *Olympic* marked the new White Star Dock's first official use and the start of a three-ship weekly service out of Southampton.

The White Star Dock* was as spectacular as the

---

*In 1922 the facility was renamed Ocean Dock.

giant vessels it was constructed to hold. Enclosing a water area of sixteen acres, open at the south to the River Test, the new dock was dredged to a depth of forty feet above mean tide to accommodate the giant liners in service and under construction. It contained a total of 3,806 feet of docking footage in six berths, and was 122 feet wide. Berths 43 and 44, a combined 1,476 feet in length, served the major liners. Passengers and express cargo were processed through two long, narrow one-storey sheds flanking the berths. The sheds' corrugated metal sides were painted green, matching the house colours of the owners, the London & South Western Railway.*

In 1836, when the dock company had been established, Southampton's population had been 25,534. With the port facilities' expansion, an influx began of dockers and other shore personnel involved with the loading, unloading, provisioning and

---

*This particular colour weathered in time to a dull, somewhat bluish-green.

repairing of ships. As more shipping companies made Southampton their port of call, increasing numbers of stokers and stewards, trimmers, greasers and deck hands, engineers, mates and masters came with their families to live in Southampton. By 1912 the city's population was 120,512.

They settled principally along the River Itchen's west bank, in communities named Portswood, Bevois Valley, Northam and Chapel. On the Itchen's east bank, their districts were Bitterne, Bitterne Park, Woolston and Sholing. To the west, Freemantle and Shirley. Here lived the men who served aboard the many vessels which had made Southampton the United Kingdom's premier passenger port and an important trade centre.

It was to this port city that *Titanic* came, fresh from her sea trials. As the sun rose at 5.31 am in the cool 45 degree temperature of 4 April, she stood gleaming, awaiting provisioning and staffing, and the start of her maiden voyage.

Below far left Southampton is an ancient city. The Bar Gate, one of the city's best-known antiquities, dates from medieval times. (Southern Newspapers plc.)

Below left Through the portals of West Gate marched troops of Henry V on their way to debark for France and the Battle of Agincourt. (Southern Newspapers plc.)

Above On this street in Northam, a Southampton district, lived many of the seamen who sailed on White Star ships. (*Daily Sketch.*)

Above right In preparation for the arrival of *Olympic*-class liners, the London and South Western Railway, owners of the Southampton Docks, constructed new deepwater facilities. (*Railway Magazine.*)

Right The new dock, named for the company whose ships it would berth, had a water area of 16 acres and was dredged to a depth of 40 feet. (*Railway Magazine.*)

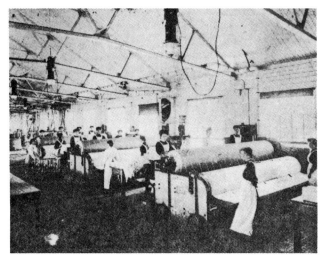

Above left To service its vessels, White Star constructed an extensive laundry facility. (*Southampton and District Pictorial.*)

Above The facility was located on the second floor of Harland and Wolff's Southampton works, adjacent to White Star Dock, and was able to finish vast quantities of soiled linen during the brief periods the Company's vessels were in port. (*Southampton and District Pictorial.*)

Left The laundry's equipment was of the latest design, and the entire facility could operate around the clock if necessary. (*Southampton and District Pictorial.*)

Below *Titanic*'s midnight arrival at Southampton is recorded in the log of the Southampton, Isle of Wight and South of England Royal Mail Steam Packet Co Ltd. Charges for the five tugs totalled more than £26. (*Red Funnel Group.*)

Chapter Six

PREPARATIONS

On 12 January 1912 British coal miners voted overwhelmingly to strike for a minimum wage. Their action had not yet commenced when on 20 February Prime Minister Asquith invited mine owners and the miners to discuss methods of averting the strike. The 22 February conference failed to effect an agreement, and the resulting strike closed practically all the country's coal mines.

Shipping companies were severely affected. One by one British freighters, coastal vessels and great liners returned to their home parts and were taken out of service, with no fuel to fire their boilers. Many owners took the opportunity to drydock their vessels. *Lusitania* went to Liverpool for maintenance and repairs. Drydocks at most ports were filled and booked well in advance.

The White Star Line announced that *Olympic*'s and *Titanic*'s usual 23-knot speeds would be reduced to twenty knots for the strike's duration to conserve coal and ensure that the vessels' schedules would be maintained.

At Southampton, berthing difficulties became so acute that ships were tied up in tandem. Between Test Quay berths 38 and 39, *Oceanic* and *New York* were moored side-by-side (*Oceanic* inboard, *New York* outboard, both facing down river), while at the new White Star Dock, across the water from Berth 44 where *Titanic* lay, the American Line's *Philadelphia* and *St Louis* and White Star's *Majestic* were tied up together.*

The coal strike was settled on 6 April, allowing the company to lift speed limitations on its liners. But there was not time for newly mined coal to be shipped to Southampton and loaded on *Titanic*. Coal from the five IMM ships in port and leftover coal from fuelling *Olympic* (which had departed from Southampton only hours before *Titanic*'s 3 April arrival) was sent rumbling down into *Titanic*'s capacious bunkers.

She had arrived with 1,880 tons of coal on board; to this was added 4,427 tons of 'pirated' fuel. The week in port consumed 415 tons for steam to operate cargo winches and to provide light and heat throughout the vessel.

Established on 6 October 1911, the British Seafarer's Union had enrolled more than 4,000 members by 12 April. Southampton-based shipping firms had recognized the union, which already had helped to arbitrate in several shipboard disputes. White Star now asked the union to supply the crew — seamen and stokers, trimmers and greasers — for *Titanic*. Other unions were represented among the crew: the National Sailors' and Firemen's Union of Great Britain and Ireland; the Dock, Wharf and Riverside Workers' Union; and the National Union of Stewards. (Deck officers were usually members of the Imperial Merchant Service Guild, while engineer officers were represented by the Marine Engineers' Association.)

Saturday 6 April was recruitment day for the majority of the crew. Union halls and the company's hiring hall were jammed. In addition to the 228 men from the British Seafarer's Union, the National Sailors' and Firemen's Union saw nearly 100 of its members signed on.

Sailing cancellations during the coal strike had caused widespread unemployment among Southampton's seamen. When the call went out for *Titanic*'s crew, there was an eager rush for berths. It would be good to get back to work, especially aboard a brand-new liner, and one commanded by E. J. Smith, a captain with whom the cream of Southampton seamen sailed.

And so they came to sign on, their precious seamen's books, the 'Certificate of Continuous Discharge', in their work-hardened hands: *Herbert Cave, Saloon Steward* (less than a month later a water-soaked passenger list recovered from his body

---

*On 10 April, the vessels' positions at Berth 46 were as follows: *Majestic*, inboard and facing towards land; in the middle, *St Louis*, facing towards the river; outboard and facing landwards was *Philadelphia*.

would provide the only clue as to which first class passenger had occupied what cabin); *Edward J. Buley, Able Seaman* (who, in order 'to better help his mother', had purchased his discharge six weeks before from His Majesty's Navy, where he had served aboard HMS *Dreadnought*); *William McQuillan, Fireman* (the only fireman who had come over from Belfast aboard *Titanic* on her sea trials); *John Coffey, Fireman* (for whom the green hills of Ireland would hold a special allure); *Charles Burgess, Baker* (destined to serve the sea longer than anyone else on board); *Frank M. Prentice, Kitchen Storekeeper* (among the crew, destined to live the longest); *Violet Jessop, Stewardess* and *John Priest, Fireman* (whose presences aboard *Olympic*, *Titanic* and *Britannic* are almost beyond belief*)...

Two others of the nineteen stewardesses were not unfamiliar with the rigours of the sea: Annie Robinson had been aboard the Canadian Pacific liner *Lake Champlain* when it had struck an iceberg. Kate Gold had been aboard *Suevic* when that vessel had run aground in 1907, and on *Olympic* during the *Hawke* collision.

On they came and signed: most from Southampton, but a sprinkling from Liverpool, London and Belfast. 'A British crew for a British ship.' Yet to come aboard were the postal clerks, the bandsmen and the à la carte restaurant staff. But by the end of that Saturday, with the coming of Easter Eve, most of the operating crew had been obtained. And with the promise of wages again, after the long coal strike, there were to be joyous celebrations of Easter in many homes the next day.

Not quite so joyous were *Titanic*'s senior officers. After arriving at Southampton from Belfast they discovered that they were to undergo realignment: to capitalize on his operational knowledge of the new class of ship, the company had assigned *Olympic*'s chief officer to *Titanic* for one voyage. The presence of Henry T. Wilde 'bumped' the *Titanic*'s previous chief, William M. Murdoch, to the position of first officer; former first officer Charles H. Lightoller moved to second officer, a place held previously by David Blair. Blair, better known as 'Davy', was forced to relinquish his berth. The remaining officers — Pitman (third), Boxhall (fourth), Lowe (fifth) and Moody (sixth) — were unaffected.

There was some confusion among the senior officers as to their new and untried responsibilities. 'But,' as now-second officer Lightoller said, 'a couple of days in Southampton saw each of us settled in our new positions and familiar with our duties.' Regular watches were assigned to all officers. During the day a senior and a junior were always on watch together, while at night two junior officers were in charge. When not on watch or otherwise required, officers could leave the ship for visits to Southampton. This usually occurred at night for, during *Titanic*'s days in port, there was much to do to prepare the vessel for its first voyage.

Although it would have brought favourable public reaction, White Star reluctantly was unable to permit visitors aboard *Titanic* while at Southampton; there simply was too much to do aboard the ship. The pinch of time taken to repair *Olympic* was now felt. Staterooms and public rooms were not finished; carpets were still being laid, paint applied, furniture fastened to decks, draperies hung, mattresses and bedding distributed, mirrors put into place.

Cutlery, tableware, dishes and glassware were arriving at the dockside in increasing amounts. All had to be taken aboard, counted, listed in department inventory books and stored. Breakages and shortages had to be reported and replacements quickly ordered.

General cargo began to arrive: ostrich plumes, shelled walnuts, cartons of books, straw goods, anchovies, butter, vinegar, preserves, cheese, cognac, velvet, hair nets; the red 25-horsepower Renault automobile belonging to one of the passengers; goat skins, jute bagging, mushrooms, olive oil; a quantity of rough oak beams, specifically noted on the stowage diagram as 'not to be taken for ballast'. All the variety of general cargo one would expect to be carried on a priority basis aboard a North Atlantic express passenger liner. The shippers frequently paid a premium rate for such transportation of their cargos. But they were compensated through lower insurance premiums, as the ships aboard which such cargo was carried were regarded as the safest of any in world trade.

On Good Friday, 5 April, the ship was 'dressed' — a sparkling rainbow of flags, pennants and burgees — arranged in established order, from the Pilot Jack at the stem to 'Burgee/3' (or 'A') at the stern; the Union Jack flew from the fore masthead and the stern flag staff, while the owner's white-starred red pennant fluttered from the main mast head. The handsome display was a salute to Southampton and its people. Since there could be no visitors to the ship this time, the flags were a sort of 'thank you' to those who would have to wait until *Titanic*'s return to see the wonders of her decks and interiors.

*Both Violet Jessop and John Priest were aboard *Olympic* when she collided with HMS *Hawke*. Each also survived *Titanic* and the loss of *Britannic*. In addition, Mr Priest survived the war losses of *Alcantara* and *Donegal*. He died of pneumonia in 1935. (It should be noted that the name of Frank 'Lucky' Tower, alleged in legend to have survived the sinkings of *Titanic*, *Empress of Ireland* and *Lusitania*, does not appear on the 'sign on list' for *Titanic*.)

The waterfront was deserted on Easter Sunday. Amid the liners and other vessels which rode quietly at their berths stood the great *Titanic*, dominating the river front skyline. All work aboard her stopped for the day. No smoke or steam rose from her funnels. The only signs of activity were the Blue Ensign at the stern flag staff and the sound of the ship's bell, ringing across the still harbour, marking the passage of the hours, the last quiet hours the ship would know . . .

Monday saw a resumption of the activity, somewhat hectic now, for there were fewer than three days before departure. Fresh supplies brought by train to the dock were transferred to the vessel's spacious refrigerators and store-rooms on G deck, aft:

Fresh meat	75,000 lb
Fresh fish	11,000 lb
Salt and dried fish	4,000 lb
Bacon and ham	7,500 lb
Poultry and game	25,000 lb
Fresh eggs	40,000
Sausages	2,500 lb
Sweetbreads	1,000
Ice cream	1,750 qts
Coffee	2,200 lb
Tea	800 lb
Rice, dried beans, etc	10,000 lb
Sugar	10,000 lb
Flour	200 barrels
Cereals	10,000 lb
Oranges	180 boxes (36,000)
Lemons	50 boxes (16,000)
Hothouse grapes	1,000 lb
Fresh milk	1,500 gals
Fresh cream	1,200 qts
Condensed milk	600 gals
Fresh butter	6,000 lb
Grapefruit	50 boxes
Lettuce	7,000 heads
Tomatoes	2¾ tons
Fresh asparagus	800 bundles
Fresh green peas	2,250 lb
Onions	3,500 lb
Potatoes	40 tons
Jams and marmalade	1,120 lb

Passengers would not be thirsty, either:

Beer and stout	20,000 bottles
Wines	1,500 bottles
Mineral waters	15,000 bottles
Spirits	850 bottles

Finally, the first and second class smoking rooms, and the two bars and general room provided for third class would be blue with tobacco smoke. Included in the ship's provision were 8,000 cigars.*

Now years had become weeks, weeks had become days, days had dwindled to hours. So little time remained before departure. Problems encountered during the trip from Belfast were being corrected, last-minute installations completed. Thomas Andrews had come over from the builders' yards and now worked tirelessly to ensure that when *Titanic* sailed she would represent the very best that Harland and Wolff could offer.

'Throughout the various days that the vessel lay at Southampton,' wrote his secretary, Thomas Hamilton, 'Mr Andrews was never for a moment idle. He generally left his hotel at about 8.30 for the offices, where he dealt with his correspondence, then went on board until 6.30, when he would return to the offices to sign letters . . .'

Andrews' activities, which typified the work so busily conducted throughout the liner, were further described: 'He would himself put in their places such things as racks, tables, chairs, berth ladders, [and] electric fans, saying that except he saw everything right he could not be satisfied. He was always busy, taking the owners around the ship, interviewing engineers, officials, managers, agents, sub-contractors, discussing with principals the plans of new ships, and superintending generally the work of completion. Now he was arranging for a party to view the ship, now writing a colleague . . .'

Few details escaped his attention, and he recorded his observations in notes and letters. He was concerned about the malfunction of a restaurant galley hot press. He agreed with the owner that the colouring of the private promenade's pebble dashing was too dark, and he approved a plan for staining green some wicker furniture on one side of the vessel. He noted that future attention be given to reducing the number of screws in stateroom hat hooks.

At last all appeared to be in order, even to Andrews' satisfaction. On the eve of sailing, he wrote to Mrs Andrews, 'The *Titanic* is now about complete and will I think do the old Firm credit to-morrow when we sail'.

---

*The provisioning list for *Titanic* has been lost. The preceding is a composite of several provisioning lists for *Olympic*, and represents what quite likely was in *Titanic's* larders when she sailed.

White Star Line

PALATIAL ROYAL MAIL STEAMERS
"OLYMPIC," 45,324 tons
AND
"TITANIC" 45,000 tons,
are the Largest Vessels in the World
(Fitted with Marconi Wireless Apparatus.)
"OLYMPIC" sails from Southampton and Cherbourg to New York regularly.
"TITANIC" sails from Southampton and Cherbourg on first voyage to New York April 10, 1912

White Star Line

LIVERPOOL, LONDON, SOUTHAMPTON. NEW YORK

Far left An advertisement for the *Titanic*'s maiden voyage.

Left Scandinavians are well-represented on *Titanic*'s passenger list. (Authors' collection.)

Far left The White Star Line aggressively seeks emigrants through its numerous agents. (Authors' collection.)

Right Good Friday, 12 April 1912. (Private collection.)

Left Multi-coloured flags flutter from *Titanic*'s lines as the ship is dressed for the enjoyment of Southampton's citizens. Good Friday was the only occasion on which *Titanic* was dressed. (Authors' collection.)

A Hampshire photographer visits *Titanic* and takes a series of pictures from bow to stern for his district newspaper.

Top left *Titanic*'s bow as seen from dockside. (*Hampshire Advertiser.*)

Top From above the officers' quarters, a view toward the fo'c's'le and across the River Test. (*Hampshire Advertiser.*)

Middle left The signal flags fly high over *Titanic*'s four massive funnels. (*Hampshire Advertiser.*)

Above The ship's deck cranes, the after docking bridge and the Blue Ensign are seen in this view looking towards land. (*Hampshire Advertiser.*)

Left Hawsers criss-cross at *Titanic*'s stern. (*Hampshire Advertiser.*)

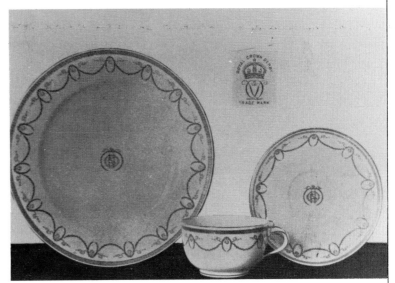

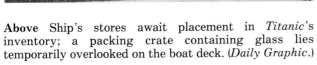

Above Ship's stores await placement in *Titanic*'s inventory; a packing crate containing glass lies temporarily overlooked on the boat deck. (*Daily Graphic*.)

Top right Also coming aboard at Southampton are dishes and crockery, perhaps in this typical White Star pattern of the period, for general dining room use... (Private collection.)

Middle right... as well as fine china for use in the à la carte restaurant. (Royal Crown Derby Porcelain Company.)

Right A view from the water shows a lack of activity aboard, suggesting the observance of Easter Sunday. (Private collection.)

Left Aft of *Titanic* are moored *Majestic, St Louis* and, unseen, *Philadelphia*, all stopped by Britain's coal strike. (Bob Forrest collection.)

Below left The shadow of the foremast falls across the bridge. *Philadelphia's* funnels can be seen on the left. (*Illustrated London News.*)

Below In an unusual view, *Titanic's* stern fills the landward portion of berths 43 and 44. (Bob Forrest collection.)

Above The ship's two wireless operators, John (Jack) Phillips (left) and Harold Bride pause for a smoke on the boat deck during the fine-tuning of the ship's radio apparatus. (Father Francis M. Browne, S.J. collection.)

Above right Passengers are not the only thing White Star seeks for *Titanic*'s voyage. But this call for cargo meets with a routine response. (THS.)

Right The only known picture of Captain Edward J. Smith standing on *Titanic*'s bridge is taken by a London photographer the day before the ship sails from Southampton. (*Daily Sketch*.)

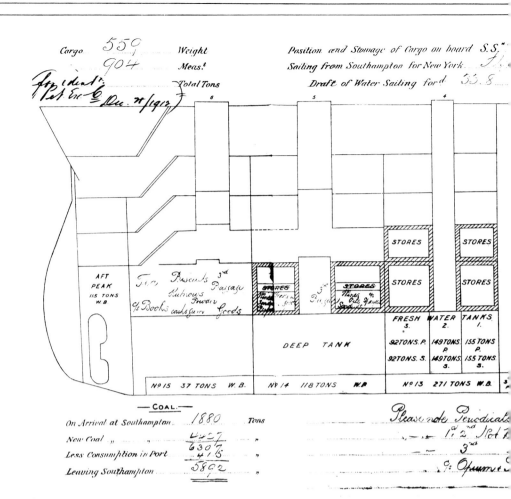

Right Second officer Charles Lightoller supervises completion of *Titanic*'s cargo stowage plan. The ship's cargo includes passenger William Carter's automobile (cargo hold two), cases of opium (the only contents of the specie room), and third class 'not wanted' luggage, stored in cold storage beef house number five and in hatch number six. The document tallies total cargo as weighing 559 tons; on the reverse side it records stowage of 11,524 separate pieces. The weight of coal leaving Southampton is noted as 5,892 tons. On the orlop deck in cargo hold one is 'a quantity of old oak beams'. A cautionary note states, 'This is cargo'. (National Archives.)

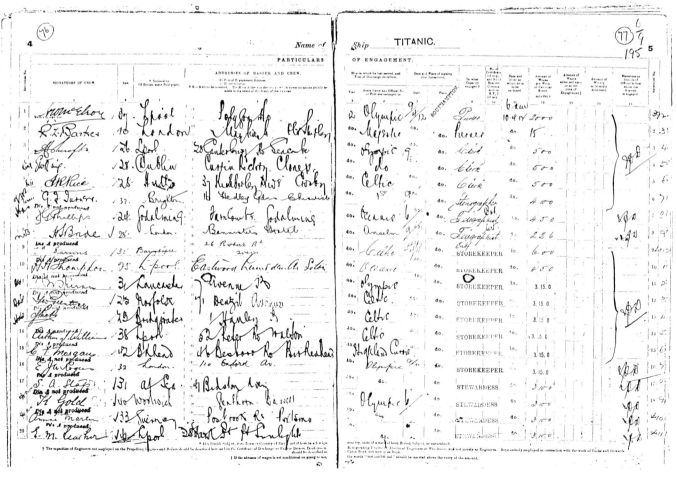

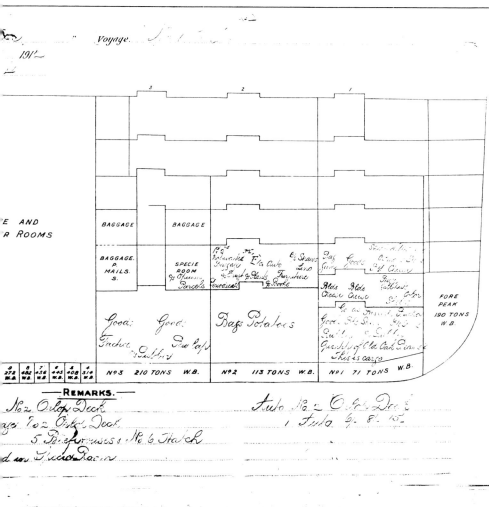

Below left and below Throughout the city of Southampton, company and union hiring halls are filled as members of the *Titanic*'s engine, deck and victualling departments sign on for the voyage. (Public Record Office.)

Overleaf Officers and department heads are hired by direct agreement with the company. No wage is listed for Captain Smith; as White Star's senior captain, his salary is $6,250 per year, plus an additional bonus of $1,000 if no ship under his command is involved in any accident during the year. (Public Record Office.)

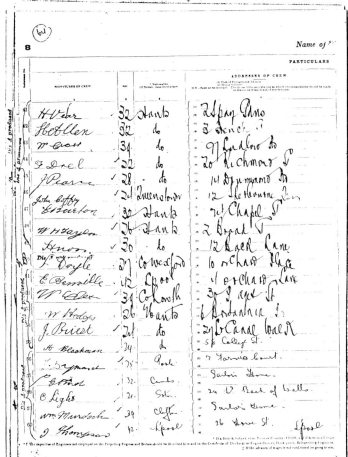

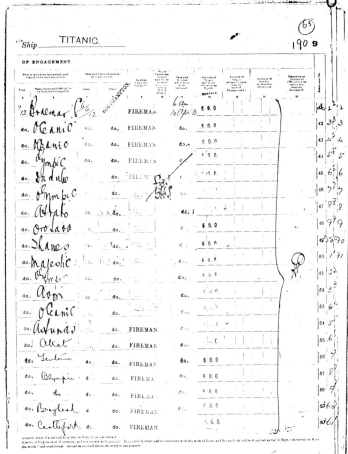

65

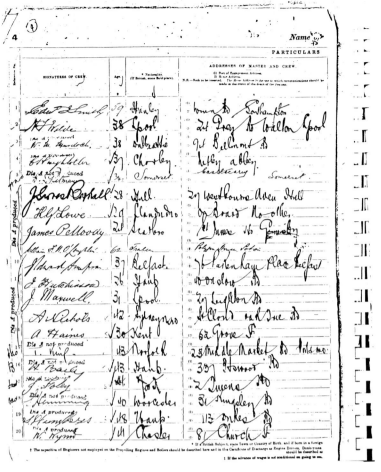

Trimmers, firemen, stewards and other members of *Titanic*'s crew sign on . . .

W. Binstead,
trimmer

A. Dore,
trimmer

G. Kearl,
trimmer

J. O'Connor,
trimmer

T. Preston,
trimmer

W.G. White,
trimmer

F. Long,
trimmer

C. Bennett,
fireman

B. Copperthwaite,
fireman

J. Chorley,
fireman

B. Cunningham,
fireman

A. May,
fireman

A.W. May,
firemen's messman

T. Hunt,
fireman

C. Painter,
fireman

A. Stanbrook,
fireman

W.H. Taylor,
fireman

E. Williams,
fireman

C.E. Andrews
steward

R. Butt
steward

W.E. Chiverton,
steward

G.B. Ede,
steward

E.S. Freeman,
steward

F. Hartnell,
steward

P. Henry,
steward

R.V. Jones,
steward

A. Lewis,
steward

E.H. Petty,
steward

T. Ryan,
steward

B. Webb,
steward

D.E. Saunders,
steward

F.G. Simmonds,
steward

F. Smith,
pantryman

F. Tamlyn,
steward

B. Thomas,
steward

Reginald Barker,
second purser

R.C. Bristow,
steward third class

George Dodd,
chief second steward

Ernest E.S. Freeman,
chief deck steward

Thomas Ford,
leading fireman

Preparations

Albert Haines,
boatswain's mate

W. Harder,
window cleaner

John Hardy,
chief second class steward

Charles Joughin,
chief baker

James W. Kiernan
chief third class steward

A. Maytum,
butcher

A. Nichols,
boatswain

C. Proctor,
chef

Cyril S. Ricks,
assistant storekeeper kitchen

T. Barker,
assistant butcher

Joseph T. Wheat,
assistant second steward

August H. Weikman,
barber

Fred Wright,
squash racquet court attendant

Miss Mary Sloan,
stewardess

Mrs Kate Gold,
stewardess

Mrs Snape,
stewardess

Chapter Seven

DEPARTURE

Wednesday, 10 April 1912. Sailing Day.

The sun rose over Southampton at 5.18 am to a generally fair morning with north-west to west winds, fresh and sometimes gusty. The temperature rose until, at noon, it stood close to fifty degrees. Soon after sunrise, members of the crew began to converge upon the docks. First in pairs or alone, then in small groups and, as the sun rose higher, in crowds. They came through Gate 4, down Central Road, and across the windswept railway tracks, bearing right on to Ocean Road and toward Berths 43 and 44. On they came, hordes of players filling a gigantic stage, the crew of *Titanic*.

Shortly before 7 am, Captain Edward John Smith, wearing a high bowler hat and a long overcoat, left Woodhead, his red brick, twin-gabled home on Winn Road in Southampton; he got into a waiting taxi and turned to wave good-bye to his wife Eleanor and twelve-year-old daughter Helen, who stood in the doorway. His ride from Westwood Park took him through the centre of Southampton and down the hill to the docks. Boarding the vessel at about 7.30 am, he went directly to his cabin to receive the sailing report from his chief officer, Henry Tingle Wilde.

Also boarding at about 7.30 am was Maurice Harvey Clarke, the Board of Trade's immigration officer. It was his function to clear *Titanic* under the Merchant Shipping Acts as an emigrant ship. During *Titanic*'s Southampton stay, he had been aboard several times inspecting such elements as the fresh water supply, food stowage, and sanitary arrangements for passenger and crew accommodations. His duty this sailing day was to oversee the crew muster, with the ship's officers and department heads assisting.

Except for Captain Smith, the officers had spent the night on board, keeping regular watches and supervizing the final night in port. Fourth Officer Boxhall had returned aboard at 11 pm the evening before, and all other officers and crew who were not earlier on watch were aboard by midnight. Captain

Smith now read and signed the last reports of the vessel's final day in port. Soon he would turn his attention to the documents and certificates necessary for clearing the liner.

Meanwhile, the crew poured up gangways and into the ship's interior, where they found their bunks, mess and general rooms, bathrooms and wash places. As they stowed their gear and sea bags, mates culled from other ships greeted one another with boisterous camaraderie. They were the best, and they knew it.

At 8 am the Blue Ensign was hoisted at the stern. Article 90 of the King's Regulations granted certain Royal Naval Reserve officers the authority to display the Blue Ensign aboard merchant vessels they commanded. While seven of *Titanic*'s eight officers were in the RNR (Pitman was not), only Captain Smith held a Blue Ensign Warrant, No 690. The company's red pennant went up the mainmast.

The crew had been directed by their petty officers to assemble on deck. Firemen alone gathered on one deck, the sailors on another, and stewards and cooks on a third deck. The ship's articles — the 'sign on lists' — were then produced for each department by White Star officials and the crew's names read out. Each member of the crew passed before a medical officer and by Captain Clarke, who assured himself that all particulars were correct. At the muster's completion, each department's papers were scrutinized by a company representative. A total head count was quickly made, and the number in each crew category quickly listed, the master list being brought to Captain Clarke.

While the compilations were being prepared, Captain Clarke fulfilled another statutory duty by ordering and witnessing the manning and lowering of two lifeboats under supervision of Fifth Officer Lowe and Sixth Officer Moody. Each, together with a bo'sun and seven seamen, entered a lifeboat — starboard boats 11 and 15 were used — and the boats were lowered to the water where they were pulled around the dock, hoisted back aboard and

replaced in the davits. The half-hour drill was over by 9.30 am, when the men were dismissed for breakfast. Crewmen on the 8-to-12 watch were ordered below. Their effort would supply the steam necessary for getting under way. The 12-to-4 watch were placed on standby, while those on the 4-to-8 watch were informally dismissed until half an hour before sailing. Many stokers and trimmers went ashore with, as shall be seen, some interesting results.

The muster showed several missing from each department, through either 'consent', or 'failed to join' (desertion). Company representatives had foreseen this contingency and had provided several additional men for each department to be present on a standby basis. The services of several being required, they signed on 'on board'. Should further substitutes prove necessary, those not selected were to wait on board until just before sailing so that each watch's full complement would be provided.

The muster lists were completed and handed over to Captain Clarke. Ship's surgeons William O'Loughlin and J. Edward Simpson repaired to the former's cabin with Board of Trade medical representatives to complete their reports on the crew's health. Captain Clarke, with Captain Benjamin Steele, White Star's marine superintendent at Southampton, proceeded to a bridge conference with Captain Smith and presented their own reports.

During crew muster, the officers had met on the bridge. Open at both sides, the navigating bridge's walls were lined with gleaming instruments and varied communications equipment. Three tall telegraphs with polished brass housings and repeater-annunciator dials transmitted speed and direction orders for engine room, docking and manoeuvring. They stood in a row along the forward bulkhead, below the fronting screen composed of alternately fixed and sliding glass panels.

The space was dominated at the centre by the compass binnacle, placed directly before the enclosed wheelhouse and containing the standard ship's compass. Four loudspeaker telephones were fitted. Activated by voice as well as by interrupter, each had a flag and an electric lamp to show which instrument was being activated. The teak grating floor was laid on top of the steel deck, and extended into the enclosed wheelhouse whose glass front looked out on to the compass binnacle. Also in the bridge shelter area were the watertight door control lever and alarm button, the submarine signal receiver and the helm indicator. The ship's two master clocks were placed in the adjacent chart room.

The senior officers — Wilde, Murdoch and Lightoller — submitted their reports to the Master. To Chief Officer Wilde had come the reports from the department heads: conditions of equipment,

completeness of stores, the status of public areas and staterooms and their readiness to receive passengers. First Officer Murdoch reported the vessel ready to sail: boatswain's parties were fully manned and standing by the moorings. Second Officer Lightoller reported that cargo was fully aboard, carefully and properly stowed, and that a duplicate of the manifest had been sent to Liverpool for dispatch aboard another ship to the company's New York office. First and second class passenger lists were complete, and a copy had been sent to the ship's print shop on D deck. Captain Smith was handed a copy, and scanned the list quickly, casually . . .

Allison. . .Astor. . .(Oh, yes. *The* Mr Astor. And his new wife.). . .*Butt* (Emissary and friend of President Taft.). . .*Carter* (The Carters of Philadelphia.). . .*Cardeza* (Also from Philadelphia. Heard they were in one of the two 'Millionaire Suites'.) *Dodge. . .Douglas. . .Futrelle* (The writer. Good mysteries.). . .*Harris* (The New York theatre man.). . .*Hays* (Grand Trunk Railway. Mr Ismay's guest.). . . Ah, yes, *Mr Ismay*. . .(He will probably be up here, on the bridge, soon. Heard his family was aboard, looking over the ship.). . .*Guggenheim*. . . *Roebling*. . .*Ryerson* (Hmm, five in the family.). . .*Straus* (A charming couple.). . .*Stead* (Old William T., himself. On the way to some sort of New York rally. Hope we'll have a chance to speak together during the crossing.). . . *Widener* (Philadelphia. George. Old P. A. B. Widener's son, and P. A. B. is on the board of the bank that owns the Company, the IMM, the White Star. . .)

A number of people would not be aboard *Titanic* on the maiden voyage. Almost fifty cancellations had been received by the ticketing offices. Some were for business reasons, others for personal or family reasons, several because travellers were unhappy with the location of their accommodation.

Henry Clay Frick, Pittsburgh steel magnate, engaged a suite in February 1912 but cancelled his booking when Mrs Frick sprained her ankle while visiting Madeira on a cruise aboard *Adriatic*. J. P. Morgan took over the booking but cancelled when business interests lengthened his stay abroad. The booking was then assumed by Mr J. Horace Harding and his wife, but the couple later transferred to the *Mauretania*. Mr George W. Vanderbilt, the American multi-millionaire, had telephoned from London on 9 April, cancelling his passage (or at least his and Mrs Vanderbilt's presence aboard). The couple's luggage was already aboard, having been forwarded in charge of their servant, Frederick Wheeler.* But Mr Vanderbilt's

*Mr Wheeler, himself booked as a second class passenger, stayed aboard to look after the luggage. He was lost in the sinking.

mother, Mrs Dressler, had requested the couple to cancel their passage. She had no actual premonition of misfortune, but simply an aversion to maiden voyages.

The Hon Robert Bacon, US Ambassador to France, had planned to board at Cherbourg with his wife and daughter. The delayed arrival of his successor, Myron T. Henrick, forced the Bacons to change their passage to yet another maiden voyage, that of the *France* on 20 April.

Captain Smith's perusal of the passenger list came to an abrupt but courteous end with the appearance on the bridge of Captains Steele and Clarke.

'Carry on, Mr Wilde,' said Smith as he guided his visitors across the navigating bridge to the chart room, where he accepted the muster list from Captain Steele. He scanned it, signed it and returned it to Captain Clarke for filing with the Board of Trade. He also handed to Captain Clarke the 'Report of Survey of an Immigrant Ship', a document prepared and required by the Board of Trade before a ship can leave port. Captain Clarke examined the report and noted where his Belfast counterpart, Francis Carruthers, had signed upon completion of sea trials on 2 April. It was Carruthers who issued the ship's certification to carry passengers, good for twelve months from that day.

Clarke signed the report in two places. He indicated he had observed and approved the boat drill carried out earlier that morning; he also signed the section indicating the amount of coal *Titanic* carried — 5,892 tons — '. . . sufficient to take the ship to her next coaling port'.

There was, however, a problem concerning the coal. In number 10 bunker on the aft, starboard side of number 6 boiler room, a coal fire had been smouldering since the ship left Belfast. Quite likely it had begun through the loading of coal without wetting it down. Regardless of cause, the fire burned. And the builders' men — the 'guarantee group' — were aware of the fire. They wished to examine the bulkhead and hull to determine whether they had been damaged by the fire's heat. Stokers were working the coal, playing hoses on it, and shovelling it away to get at the base of the pile, while the ship was at Southampton. Captain Smith had been assured by Chief Engineer Bell that the situation was under control, and that if there was damage — and he doubted there was — it would be confined to a small portion of the transverse bulkhead and would in no way damage the hull's soundness. On the chief engineer's assurance, Captain Smith assumed the risk. With the arrival on board of a full crew, extra men could be detailed to work out the burning coal. With the fuel removed, the fire would be extinguished, the bulkhead examined and secured. Smith made no mention of

the fire. If the Board of Trade inspector was aware of the condition, he made no mention of it in his public report.

Captain Clarke returned the certificate to Smith. There were further clearances to be signed at Cherbourg and Queenstown, where additional passengers would embark, before the document was to be forwarded to the original issuing office at Belfast.

As Marine Superintendent Steele prepared to leave, Smith handed him the 'Master's Report to the Company': 'I herewith report this ship loaded and ready for sea. The engines and boilers are in good order for the voyage, and all charts and sailing directions up-to-date. — Your obedient servant, Edward J. Smith'.

After Clarke's and Steele's departures, two new figures, dressed in civilian clothes, entered the bridge. Thomas Andrews and J. Bruce Ismay exchanged greetings and best wishes for a good voyage with Smith and Chief Officer Wilde before leaving the bridge. Each was to return to the area but one more time, almost exactly 96 hours later.

Illness had prevented Lord Pirrie, *Titanic*'s designer, from making the voyage. In his place, Andrews had boarded *Titanic* shortly after 6 am, and after a long and detailed inspection had held an informal muster of his own staff, the Harland and Wolff 'guarantee group'. These nine managers and apprentices had been selected for their knowledge of the ship's design and were aboard to assist the ship's own engineering staff in gaining detailed knowledge of the mechanical systems under actual operating conditions.

Andrews' cabin, A36, had been added during the last-minute modifications to the ship. Located on the port side of the after first class entrance, it did not appear on passenger agents' cabin lists or deck plans, and was thus unbooked. Since it was centrally located near entrances and corridors leading to all parts of the ship, it was an excellent place for Mr Andrews.

Ismay had come on board at about 9.30 am with his wife Florence and their three younger children, Tom, George and Evelyn. They had motored down in their big Daimler Landaulette from their London home at 15 Hill Street, in Mayfair. They had stayed overnight at the South Western Hotel, across from the docks, and from whose windows they could see *Titanic*'s four towering funnels. Mrs Ismay and the children were enthusiastic in their tour of the ship, especially in their examination of Mr Ismay's suite of rooms, B52, 54 and 56, with its own private promenade overlooking the liner's cliff-like port side.

Ismay greeted his secretary, W. H. Harrison, who would assist with IMM directors' meetings aboard *Titanic* in New York. Richard Fry, Ismay's

manservant, had come aboard earlier to unpack his employer's clothing, and was already settled down in cabin B102, across the hall from the suite. He was eagerly looking forward to the trip.

(Although travelling as 'Complimentary', paying no fare, both Harrison and Ismay held tickets — number 112059 and 112058, respectively; Fry travelled on Ismay's ticket and was not listed separately.) Also of unusual status were Marconi telegraphists Phillips and Bride. Although signed on as crew members and paid by the White Star Line, they were employees of the Marconi Company. They had temporarily left *Titanic* while the ship was tied up at Southampton. Phillips signed the ship's articles on 6 April when he returned briefly to check the spare parts supply. Bride signed on around 11.30 pm upon his 9 April return aboard ship.

Well before sailing time on 10 April the two men were up and about, testing and preparing their equipment. They arranged night watches by personal agreement: Phillips, the senior, was on duty between 8 pm and 2 am, while Bride, the junior, took the 2 am to 8 am watch. There was no regular duty rotation during the day: the men replaced one another to suit mutual convenience. But constant wireless watch was maintained.

Now, as the liner's departure preparations were completed, they made ready for the daily onslaught of personal communications directed to and from 'ADVISELUM', the wireless code word assigned to *Titanic* by the International Mercantile Marine for passengers' private or commercial messages.

Passengers were beginning to board in large numbers. The boat train carrying second and third class passengers had left London's Waterloo Station at 7.30 am and arrived at the dockside shortly before 9.30. Among those boarding through the second class entrance at C deck's after end were members of the ship's orchestra. The eight men, sailing as second class passengers under a contract provided by Messrs C. W. and F. N. Black of 14 Castle Street, Liverpool, were travelling collectively on ticket number 250654. Their cabin on E deck, aft on the starboard side, contained a separate room for their instruments.

(Occupying cabin E101, adjacent to the bandsmen's cabin, was a young lady, Edwina Celia Troutt, bearer of ticket number 34218, for which she had paid £10 10s. She was travelling with two friends, Miss Suzie Webber and Miss Nora Keane, but it was Edwina who was to charm generations of *Titanic* enthusiasts and historians with her lively and witty accounts of the voyage and its tragic end.)

Other second class passengers boarding included Benjamin and Esther Hart and their daughter Eva (ticket 13529, £26 5s); William H. Harbeck, an American film producer, who carried two Model 'A' Erneman cameras, two Jury's Kine 'Popular' cameras, and 110,000 feet of motion picture film (ticket 248749, £13); Mr and Mrs James V. Drew and their eight-year-old nephew Marshall (ticket 28220, £32 10s); C. Oldsworth, chauffeur to William Carter, whose 25 horsepower Renault car was stored in *Titanic*'s hold (ticket 248744, £13); 'Mr Hoffman and 2 children' — was it 'Mr Hoffman', and who were the '2 children'? (ticket 230080, £26); Mrs Allen O. Becker and three children, Marion, Richard and Ruth (ticket 230136, £39); Lawrence Beesley, a science master at Dulwich College in London (ticket 248698, £13); Father Thomas Roussell Byles, on his way to preside at his brother's New York wedding (ticket 244310, £13); Stanley Fox, a Rochester, New York businessman who was to become the centre of a bitter controversy (ticket 229236, £13). . .

Through the main second class entrance they streamed, and either walked down the red-carpeted stairway with its light oak railings, or took the birds' eye maple-lined elevator to their respective decks. Another entrance, aft of the main stairway, led to the after cabins and had no elevator; indeed, its centre was occupied by the slanted base of the mainmast, which was firmly embedded two decks below. Two additional second class entrances were located aft on E deck, port and starboard, just forward of the stores entrance.

Between 9.30 and 11 am third class passengers were also embarking through the aft entrance, near the stern on C deck, or via the forward gangway, which opened on to the narrow corridors of D deck near the bow. They were scanned intently by a medical officer, who also looked at their 'inspection card' which identified 'immigrant and steerage passengers'. British subjects were quickly passed, but aliens — predominantly Scandinavians — were examined more closely. The company had no wish to transport a passenger whose physical impairment would bar entry to the United States.

Leah Aks, with her ten-month-old son Filly, was on her way to join her husband in Norfolk, Virginia (ticket 392091, £9 7s); John and Annie Sage and their nine children were going to Jacksonville, Florida, where Mr Sage had just purchased a citrus farm (ticket 2343, £69 11s); Mrs Alma Paulsson and four children were joining Mr Paulsson in Chicago, Illinois (number 349909, £21 10s 6d); Leslie Williams and David Bowen, travelling together on ticket number 54636 (£16 2s), were both professional boxers from Wales (Williams a bantamweight and Bowen the Welsh lightweight champion), on their way to a series of prize fights with American pugilists; the Goodwin family, Fred and Augusta and their five children (including eighteen-month-old Sidney) were going to Niagara Falls, New York (ticket CA2144, £46 18s). . .

They passed through the steel-walled third class entrance, aft on C deck, catching a tantalizing

glimpse of the white-walled general room. Hurried along by stewards' gestures and urgings, they descended the steel stairways and entered the maze of corridors along which their small cabins were located. There seemed to be no regularity to the cabins' numbering and there were frequent pauses, questions, discussions with stewards (often accompanied by raised voices) and emphatic gestures. Up and down the veitchi-floored, steel-walled corridors the voices sounded, bringing the first presence of passengers to the ship's lower reaches: the shrill cries of children, the angry misunderstandings of adults, the confused murmurs and the subdued rush of third class passengers aboard *Titanic*.

The vessel's third class accommodation was arranged on four of *Titanic's* decks:

		Location	Number of berths	Section
Rooms	1-19*	E deck, forward	74	B
	19-103	F deck, forward	366	C,E,G
	104-126; 138-167	E deck, aft	172	M,Q
	127-137	D deck, aft	50	O
	168-202	F deck, aft	110	R
	203-221	G deck, aft	72	S
	224-260†	G deck, forward	150	F,D
Cabins (Alt 3rd)	G1-G40*	G deck, aft (forward of 203/221)	108	N
		Total	1,102	

Berths were thus provided in 296 cabins: 257 rooms which bore no deck designation in their numbering, and the 39 cabins on G deck aft, noted on plans as 'alternate second or third class, counted as third'.

Forward on G deck was accommodation originally planned as 'permanent third class open berths'. But in the final design the area contained separate, numbered rooms (224 to 260) with numbers 251 to 260 designated as 'portable 3rd, White Star pattern', a company system of partitions enclosing open space in steerage. Section 'A' on D deck, forward, was designated 'third class open space'.

Each passenger's ticket was stamped with the section letter. After being directed — and perhaps re-directed, several times — to the appropriate section, the passenger was shown to his or her berth. The considerable confusion among the 497 third class passengers boarding at Southampton may well be imagined.

*The number 13 was not used.
†Numbers 222 and 223 were omitted.

After the harassed stewards had helped their bewildered charges locate their berths, they turned to assist other incoming passengers. No one pointed the way to stairways, or described the complex combination of companionways and stairs which would lead to general rooms, dining saloons or the open deck. Left to themselves, passengers wandered about aimlessly, contributing to the confusion. Language differences added a further discordant note.

Now and then, someone would return triumphantly from an exploratory trek and lead the way for the others up a stairway to another corridor. Then another turn, and another. A stairway leading . . . down. Finally, a wire screen barrier labelled 'Second Class'. A shrug, a turn, and a retreat. Somewhere there was a stairway, somewhere an open room or a deck. Somewhere . . . Voices faded down the corridor, then died away, leaving only a distant murmur punctuated by children's cries.

Once steerage passengers located the upper regions, they found their smoking room and general room on C deck, near the stern. Just forward of these was the small well, designated 'Third class promenade'. They crowded the rail, pointing downwards and gesticulating as they observed other passengers boarding along the great ship's port side.

Suddenly, off to the landward side, the boat train for first class passengers appeared amid puffs of smoke, carefully winding its way across West Road, down the side of Central Road, and slowly turning slightly to the right to the track flanking White Star Dock. The boat train presented a colourful if clamorous appearance: it was pulled by a London and South Western Railway T9 locomotive in the company's green livery, a white disc at the left side of the boiler's front designating 'a mainline train, Waterloo to Southampton Docks'; the coaches were chocolate brown, with windows in the company's cream-coloured paint.

The train had departed from platform 12 at Waterloo at 9.45 am, amid a flurry of journalistic activity. Reporters and photographers from several newspapers were present to record the prominent passengers departing on *Titanic*'s maiden voyage. The 79-mile journey through Surbiton, Woking, Basingstoke, Winchester and Eastleigh ended with arrival at the dockside moments before 11.30 am.

Detraining at the dockside, first class passengers walked up the gently sloping gangway to the main entrance on B deck, amidships. Chief Steward Latimer and his staff were there to greet them and escort them to their cabins. Purser's clerk Ernest King found it a challenge to keep his records in order. The passengers were coming aboard so rapidly. . .

Mr and Mrs Isidor Straus		
Ellen Bird, Mrs Straus' maid		Ticket 17483 £221 15 7
John Farthing, Mr Straus' manservant	C55	
Col Archibald Gracie	C51	Ticket 113780 £28 10
Mr and Mrs Henry B. Harris	C83	Ticket 36973 £83 9 6
Mrs Ida Hippach, Miss Jean Hippach	B18	Ticket 111361 £57 19 7
Mr and Mrs John J. Astor		
Rosalie Bidois, Mrs Astor's maid		Ticket 17754 £224 10 6
Victor Robbins, Mr Astor's manservant	C62	
Miss Caroline Endres	C45	(Ticketed with Astors)
Mrs William Thompson Graham	C91	
Miss Margaret Graham	C125	Ticket 17582 £153 9 3
Miss Elizabeth W. Shutes	C125	

... And so it went. Clerk King flipped the ledger pages quickly as the passengers boarded, passed through the entrance and walked down the blue-carpeted corridors to their cabins. He had to hurry, for it was from his records that the ship's printer, Mr E. T. Corben, would prepare the passenger list.

Some time before the boat train's appearance, a distinguished figure climbed to the bridge and greeted the master. He was George Bowyer, a Trinity House harbour pilot, and as he stepped on to the steel deck the pilot flag, with its red-and-white horizontal stripes, was run up. 'Uncle George' Bowyer was well known to the *Titanic*'s officers. He had been a pilot at Southampton for more than thirty years and had handled the White Star liners since the company began using the port. He was the pilot aboard *Olympic* (with Captain Smith in command) during her September 1911 collision with HMS *Hawke*.

Bowyer now conferred with Smith about draughts, turning circles and manoeuvrability of the immense liner. He had already experienced a 'suction-attraction' problem with *Titanic*'s sister and did not wish for a similar occurrence with the new ship.

With the pilot's arrival, the ship's officers left for their respective departure stations and duties, in accordance with company regulations. Chief Officer Wilde was on the forecastle head, in charge of moorings and tugboat hawsers which were handled by the boatswain and his party. Second Officer Lightoller stationed himself at the after end of the forecastle, assisting Wilde.

First Officer Murdoch was at the stern, overseeing the handling by the boatswain's mate and his men of the mooring lines and tugboat hawsers there. Third Officer Pitman, on the docking bridge, passed along instructions to Murdoch in response to the bridge's telegraphed orders. On the navigating bridge, Fourth Officer Boxhall worked the engine room and docking bridge telegraphs, acting on orders from Smith and Bowyer. He also logged each command and manoeuvre. Fifth Officer Lowe, also on the navigating bridge, handled the ship's telephones. Sixth Officer Moody was at the gangway, and before the ship departed he would have a decision to make.

Moments before noon, Captain Smith gave an order to one of the quartermasters on the bridge. A faint smile played on the Captain's lips as the QM gave an overhead lanyard a steady downward pull. Outside, halfway up each of the two forward funnels, white gushes of steam flowed through the ship's huge whistles and hurled themselves into the warm spring air. *Titanic*'s triple-toned stentorian voice resounded throughout Southampton Harbour, announcing imminent departure.

As the Blue Peter was run up the foremast, the awesome voice spoke again. And yet again, in the traditional three salutes of departure.

Earlier that morning, following the crew muster, members of the 'black gang' — stokers and trimmers — whose watch would not start until 4 pm had gone ashore. Their destinations were the many public houses which lined Canute and Platform Roads, across from the dockyard. John Podesta, a surviving fireman, described his own experience:

'I got up on the morning of April 10th and made off down to the ship for eight o'clock muster, as is the case on all sailing days, which takes about an hour. As the ship is about to sail at about twelve o'clock noon most of us firemen and trimmers go ashore again until sailing time. So off we went [with] several others I knew on my watch, which was 4 to 8. My watch-mate, whose name was William Nutbean and I went off to our local public-house for a drink in the Newcastle Hotel. We left about eleven fifteen making our way toward the docks. Having plenty of time we dropped into another pub called the Grapes, meeting several more ship-mates inside. So having another drink about six of us left about ten minutes to twelve and got well into the docks and toward the vessel. With me and my mate were three brothers named Slade: Bertram, Tom and Alfred. We were at the top of the main road and a passenger train was approaching us from another part of the docks. I heard the Slades say, "Oh, let the train go by". But me and Nutbean crossed over and managed to board the liner. Being a long train, by the time it passed, the Slades were too late, and the gangway was down leaving them behind. So it seemed they did not have to go.'

The Slades, as well as stokers Shaw and Holden and trimmer Brewer, ran the length of the dock. The gangway had been detached and was being swung away when Sixth Officer Moody heard the men

shouting, 'Wait! Lower the gangway! We want to come aboard!' Moody paused a moment as the men came nearer. He could have held the gangway briefly until the tardy crewmen boarded. But he recalled the additional men still standing by, men whose services could be... relied upon. Moody ordered the gangway lowered, almost in the faces of the frustrated crew. Moody quickly passed the word, and Kinsella, Geer, Hosgood, Lloyd, Witt and Black stepped forward to sign on. The remaining standbys were dismissed by the junior engineering officer. But before they could depart — through E deck's after portside entrance, which had been held open for them — the liner had slipped her lines and drifted away from the dockside.

High above, on the navigating bridge, Pilot Bowyer's 'Make fast the tugs' was immediately passed to the officers at the forecastle and stern. Reports came back to the bridge, 'Tugs all fast'.

'Haul away. Easy,' came one order, with another issued to the quartermaster at the wheel. The tugs took up the slack on their hawsers. Mooring lines splashed away and were hauled back by dock hands, under the marine superintendent's watchful eye.

It was at this moment that H. G. Lloyd of Southampton, standing near the river end of the pier head, raised his camera and captured the scene on film. Viewing the photograph today, one can sense the excitement, smell the pungent odour of the good Welsh coal, see the drifting billows of smoke from the tugs' engines as they began to pull the liner away from the dock.

Down the dock's length, slowly...slowly...the great vessel was tugged to the River Test's turning circle, which formed the angle between the dock's waters and the sea channel's upper reaches. Having towed Titanic to the turning circle, the tugs again strained to manoeuvre the giant in a ninety-degree port turn, under Pilot Bowyer's orders. Barely minutes before, low tide had begun its flow and Titanic, drawing almost 35 feet of water, had to be handled with extreme caution. (It was to provide even this small margin of manoeuvrability that the vessel had been backed in to her berth during high tide on her 4 April arrival.)

Having completed her turn, Titanic stood poised for forward movment. Stoker John Podesta was still on deck, having been the last to board, just as the gangway was taken up. He heard the telegraph's jangle as it signalled 'Ahead slow', and felt the tremor as the two bronze wing propellers began to revolve.

The tugs slacked off. Vulcan, which had held the liner's after starboard quarter, dropped astern and moved to the port quarter. There, the door to the second class entrance on E deck stood open. The remnants of the standby crew, those whose services would not be required, waited to be taken ashore.

Titanic's bow began to cut through the water — slowly, almost imperceptibly at first, then faster through the flowing, incoming tide. Her propellers' first revolutions impeded a portion of the tidal flow and diverted it outward, towards both starboard and port. On the starboard side, the water swept harmlessly into the River Test. But on the port side, turbulence washed towards the nearby pierheads of the Test Docks. The passing Titanic's huge bulk made it impossible for the disturbed waters to find a ready outlet.

Still tied up at Berth 38 were Oceanic and New York, temporarily out of service since the coal strike. Moored in tandem, they faced downstream, with Oceanic inboard.

Water displaced by Titanic increased the volume of water under and around New York, with the result that the vessel was lifted from her normal position, her mooring ropes slackened. Then, as Titanic passed by, the water volume suddenly decreased in the American liner's vicinity, and she quickly reverted to her former position, bobbing, as it were, first up and then down.

The extreme movements caused too great a strain on the ropes, and they snapped with loud reports. Titanic's speed was increasing, and she was drawing water behind her with considerable force. New York's stern, now loose, began to arc toward the huge Titanic, passing broadside to her.

Said Captain Gale of the tug Vulcan:

'Someone sang out to me to get up and push the New York back, but such a thing was impossible. Had I got between the two ships we would almost certainly have been jammed. Instead, I turned the Vulcan round and got a wire rope on the port quarter of the New York. Unfortunately, that rope parted, but our men immediately got a second wire on board, and we got hold of the New York when she was within four feet of Titanic. Our movements were all the more trying because the broken mooring ropes from New York were lying in the water, and we stood a good chance of fouling our own propeller. Every rope on New York snapped, the stern lines being the first to go...'

The alert reactions of Captain Smith and Pilot Bowyer had also contributed to the prevention of a collision. At the first danger sign, the order 'Full astern' was given, and Titanic's forward movement was checked, then halted. Indeed, once the propellers' full backward force was felt, the vessel moved astern slightly, back toward the White Star Dock's entrance, her entire length moving past the New York's nearby stern. As an added precaution, Captain Smith quickly ordered the starboard anchor to be lowered within a few feet of the water. The bo'sun's party, under Lightoller's command, stood by to release the anchor instantly should it prove necessary.

Having fully broken loose, the wayward New

York drifted down river, controlled, now, by the tugs, which had managed to get additional lines aboard. But it was not until the vessel had drifted around the head of the Test Docks, ending up with her bow pointing towards the floating bridge across the River Itchen, that all of her forward movement ceased. She was temporarily moored there and *Titanic* was signalled to proceed.

(During this entire time there was fear that *Oceanic* also might break loose. Her lines held, although there must have been a tremendous strain on them. By the time *Titanic* had passed again, additional lines had been put on *Oceanic* so there would be no possible repetition of the incident.)

Her departure having thus been delayed by more than an hour, *Titanic* again moved towards the head of the ocean channel — a little more slowly, more cautiously than before — and made a smart starboard turn into Southampton Water. Twenty-four miles of sheltered water lay ahead before the English Channel was reached. Also ahead was the intricate reverse S-turn between Calshot Spit and the bank known as the Bramble. It was here that *Olympic* had collided with *Hawke* seven months earlier.

Titanic slowed for the manoeuvre. Under Bowyer's watchful eye and skilled appraisal, the turn was executed without incident and the great liner again picked up speed. It slowed once more, near the Nab Light Vessel, to drop Bowyer who, it might be imagined, mentioned in departing that he would see them all in a fortnight or so.

During the passage down Southampton Water, P. W. Fletcher, the ship's bugler, had passed from deck to deck sounding 'The Roast Beef of Old England', traditional meal call aboard White Star liners. A few hearty souls had remained on deck to watch the Isle of Wight slip past, and to observe the dropping of the pilot. But a majority had gone below to their first meal aboard the new ship. And it may have been that much dining saloon conversation concerned the near-accident and how skilfully it had been averted.

All pressures and exigencies of departure behind, *Titanic* again increased speed as she headed for a routine Channel crossing towards Cherbourg. By 3 pm on that 10 April, the afternoon sun began to cast lengthening shadows across the railings and through the liner's starboard portholes. The French tricolor fluttered from her foremast.

Surely this splendid afternoon was the zenith of *Titanic*'s proudest day, surely a day to remember.

Below *Titanic* at Southampton is ready to receive passengers and crew. (*Southampton and District Pictorial.*)

Overleaf Officers and crew members board *Titanic* early on sailing day and prepare for muster.

Charles H. Lightoller,
second officer

Joseph G. Boxhall,
fourth officer

James P. Moody,
sixth officer

Henry Ryland Dyer,
senior assistant fourth engineer

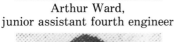
Arthur Ward,
junior assistant fourth engineer

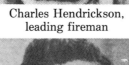
Charles Hendrickson,
leading fireman

James Taylor,
fireman

F. Fay,
greaser

J. Walpole,
head pantryman

J. Maxwell,
carpenter

Ernest W. King,
purser's clerk

F. Young,
fireman

Edward J. Buley,
able bodied seaman

W. Ennis,
Turkish bath steward

Alfred S. Alsopp,
junior electrician

William Beere,
sculleryman

Departure

W. Bott,
greaser

William Burke,
second saloon steward

John Charman,
saloon steward

Samuel Collins,
fireman

Alfred F. Evans,
lookout

E.W. Hamblyn,
bedroom steward

H. Johnson,
cook

Herbert Jupe,
assistant electrician

B. Noss,
fireman

W. Pryce,
saloon steward

H. Rudd,
storekeeper, engineering department

R.J. Sawyer,
window cleaner

Jonathan Shepherd,
junior assistant second engineer

Dr J. Edward Simpson,
assistant surgeon

James M. Smith,
junior fourth engineer

George Symons,
lookout

B. Terrell,
able bodied seaman

F. Terrell,
steward

T. Threlfall,
leading fireman

Walter Wynn,
quartermaster

WHITE STAR LINE.

Steamer *Titanic* Sailing 10th April 1912

CREW LIST.

No.		
1	Master	
7	Mates	
2	Surgeon	
7	Pursers or Clerks	
2	Carpenters	
1	Boatswains	
8	Boatwains' Mates and Quarter Masters	
39	Seamen, A.B.	
2	Ordinary *Window Cleaners*	
2	*Mess Room Stewards*	
2	*Masters at Arms*	
Total... 73		
28	Engineers, Ship	
8	„ Refrigerator and Electrical	
289	Engine Room Crew	
Total... 325		
2	Telegraphists	
471	Chief Steward and Staff	
20	Stewardesses	
1	Matrons	
Total... 494		
Grand Total... 892		

O & S 1998. (100-3-99).

Edw J Smith Master

Departure

Baptiste Allaria,
assistant waiter

Louis Crovelle,
assistant waiter

V. Gilardino,
waiter

Alfonsi Perotti,
waiter

E. Poggi,
waiter

Angelo Rotto,
waiter

Giovenz Salussolia,
glassman

Ercole Testoni,
assistant glassman

Ettera Valassori,
waiter

L. Zarracchi,
wine butler

Above Members of Gatti's staff for the à la carte restaurant also sign the ship's articles. (*Daily Mirror*.)

Left Following the crew's muster, Captain Edward J. Smith signs the muster list for the Board of Trade. (Public Record Office.)

Right The tickets for each class of *Titanic*'s passengers represent a contract for passage between the company and the purchaser. The first class ticket, printed on tan paper, provides for 20 cubic feet of luggage space. A separate sticker (folded back) notifies the purchaser of the company's limited responsibility for luggage carried. (National Archives.)

81

SECOND CLASS.

WHITE STAR LINE

ROYAL AND UNITED STATES MAIL STEAMERS.

256145

ISMAY, IMRIE & CO.,
1, COCKSPUR STREET, S.W.,
38, LEADENHALL STREET, E.C.
LONDON,
30, JAMES STREET
LIVERPOOL,
—
CANUTE ROAD, SOUTHAMPTON.

Agent at Paris—
NICHOLAS MARTIN, 9, Rue Scribe.

WHITE STAR LINE,
18, VIA ALLA NUNZIATA — GENOA.
21, PIAZZA DELLA BORSA — NAPLES.
84, STATE STREET — BOSTON.
9, BROADWAY — NEW YORK.
52, DALHOUSIE BUILDINGS — QUEBEC.
BELL TELEPHONE BUILDINGS,
118, NOTRE DAME STREET WEST, — MONTREAL.

JAMES SCOTT & CO., Agents,
QUEENSTOWN.

OCEANIC STEAM NAVIGATION COMPANY, LIMITED, OF GREAT BRITAIN.

PASSENGER'S CONTRACT TICKET.
(NOT TRANSFERABLE.)

BILL OF FARE.

JOSEPH BRUCE ISMAY,

SECOND CLASS.

WHITE STAR LINE.
— 256145 —
Oceanic Steam Navigation Company, Limited,
of Great Britain,

ISMAY, IMRIE & CO.,
30, JAMES STREET, LIVERPOOL,
CANUTE ROAD, SOUTHAMPTON.

Ship

Counterpart of Passenger's Contract Ticket.

CONTRACT TICKET.

JOSEPH BRUCE ISMAY,

WHITE STAR LINE

ROYAL AND UNITED STATES MAIL STEAMERS.

3136093

ISMAY, IMRIE & CO.,
1, COCKSPUR STREET, S.W.,
38, LEADENHALL STREET, E.C.
LONDON,
30, JAMES STREET
LIVERPOOL,
—
CANUTE ROAD, SOUTHAMPTON.

Agent at PARIS—
NICHOLAS MARTIN, 9, Rue Scribe.

WHITE STAR LINE
18, VIA ALLA NUNZIATA — GENOA.
21, PIAZZA DELLA BORSA — NAPLES.
84, STATE STREET, — BOSTON.
9, BROADWAY, — NEW YORK.
52, DALHOUSIE STREET, — QUEBEC.
BELL TELEPHONE BUILDINGS,
118, NOTRE DAME STREET WEST, — MONTREAL.

JAMES SCOTT & CO., Agents
QUEENSTOWN.

OCEANIC STEAM NAVIGATION COMPANY, LIMITED, OF GREAT BRITAIN.

THIRD CLASS (Steerage) PASSENGER'S CONTRACT TICKET.
(NOT TRANSFERABLE.)

BILL OF FARE.

JOSEPH BRUCE ISMAY,

SEE BACK.

3136093

WHITE STAR LINE.

LONDON CITY OFFICE.

Oceanic Steam Navigation Company, Limited,
of Great Britain,

ISMAY, IMRIE & CO.,
LIVERPOOL.

Ship

Counterpart of Steerage Passenger's Contract Ticket.

CONTRACT TICKET.

JOSEPH BRUCE ISMAY,

Left The second class ticket, printed on buff paper, contains a bill of fare... (National Archives.)

Below left... as does the third class (on white paper), which also shows a baggage allotment of 10 cubic feet. (National Archives.)

Right The boat train to Southampton departs from London's Waterloo Station, seen after its extensive 1911 renovation. (Authors' collection.)

Top far right Railway guards prepare to close carriage doors immediately prior to the departure of 'the first and last *Titanic* Special'. (Father Francis M. Browne, S.J. collection.)

Middle right At the start of his 79-mile journey to Southampton, Father Francis M. Browne leans from the corridor and snaps a view of the train winding its way out of the station. (Father Francis M. Browne, S.J. collection.)

Middle far right Also aboard the train is second class passenger Miss Lucy Ridsdale whose excess luggage requires payment of a surcharge. (National Archives.)

Right Stowage of cargo completed, documents listing its total value are filled out for company records. (National Archives.)

Departure

LONDON AND SOUTH WESTERN RAILWAY. (50)

EXCESS LUGGAGE TICKET. No. 7/ 6539

_____ o'clock Train ____10____ day of __April__ 191 2

From **WATERLOO** to _____

	Cwt.	Qrs.	Lbs.
Gross Weight ...	2	3	12
Weight Allowed ...	1	3	4
Excess Weight ...	1		8

Amount Received £ „ 2 „

Name of Passenger _____ Miss Lucy Ridsdale _____

_____ Booking Clerk.

THIS TICKET SHOULD BE DELIVERED UP BEFORE LEAVING THE RAILWAY.

WHITE STAR LINE.

FREIGHT LIST of S.S. "Titanic" Captain Smith from Southampton to New York. Sailed April 10th 1912

Left In *Titanic*'s post office (similar to those found on other transatlantic liners) the mail is already being sorted. (*Southampton and District Pictorial.*)

Middle left Hard at work in the forward, F deck sorting room are the British postal clerks James B. Williamson and John R. Jago Smith. (*Southampton and District Pictorial.*)

Bottom left Surrounded by his staff, head pantryman J. Walpole, seated, centre, will supervise distribution of food stores... (Authors' collection.)

Below... which will be used to prepare the passengers' first meals on board. (Authors' collection.)

Above right The boat train arrives, the passengers board, and are escorted to their cabins. On a passenger list for staff use later recovered from the body of steward Herbert Cave, some first class cabin assignments are indicated. (Public Archives of Nova Scotia.)

Above middle right The necessary clearance certificate for *Titanic*'s Southampton departure is executed by Board of Trade representative Captain Maurice Clarke. (Public Record Office.)

Above far right Trinity House pilot George Bowyer comes aboard shortly before departure. (Private collection.)

Right Several crew members depart or fail to join. Their replacements are signed on, 'on board'. (Public Record Office.)

Departure

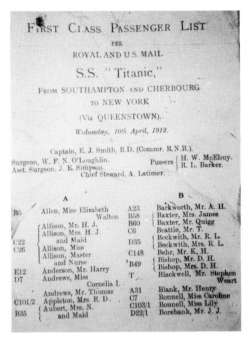

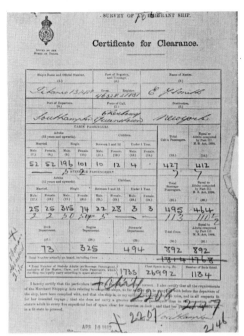

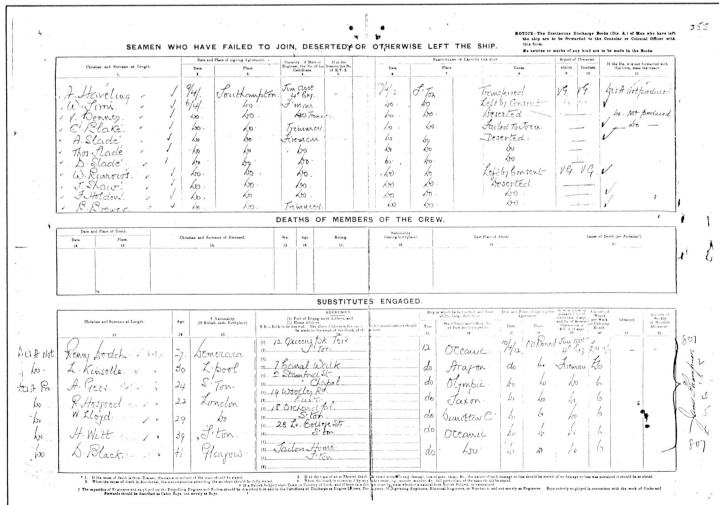

NOTICE—The Continuous Discharge Books (Dis A.) of Men who have left the ship are to be forwarded to the Consular or Colonial Officer with this form.

No entries or marks of any kind are to be made in the Books.

SEAMEN WHO HAVE FAILED TO JOIN, DESERTED, OR OTHERWISE LEFT THE SHIP.

Christian and Surname at length. 1		Date. 2	Place. 3	Capacity; if Mate or Engineer, the No. of his Certificate. 4	If in the Reserve the No. of R.V.Z. 4A	Date. 6	Place. 7	Cause. 8	Ability 9	Conduct 10	If the Dia. A is not forwarded with this form, state the reason 11
A. Haveling	✓	9/4/	Southampton	Sen Asst 4th Eng.		10/4	S. Ton	Transferred	VG	VG	Dis A not produced
W. Finn	✓	6/4/	do	Fireman		do	do	Left by Consent			do not produced
V. Denney	✓	do	do	do Trimmer		do	do	Deserted			
C. Blake	✓	do	do	Trimmer		do	do	Failed To Join	—	—	do
A. Slade	✓	do	do	Fireman		do	do	Deserted	—	—	✓
Thos Slade	✓	do	do	do		do	do	do	—	—	✓
D. Slade	✓	do	do	do		do	do	do	—	—	✓
W. Burrows	✓	do	do	do		do	do	Left by Consent	VG	VG	✓
J. Shaw	✓	do	do	do		do	do	Deserted			✓
F. Holden	✓	do	do	do		do	do	do	—	—	✓
B. Brewer	✓	do	do	Trimmer		do	do				

DEATHS OF MEMBERS OF THE CREW.

Date of Death. 12	Place. 13	Christian and Surname of Deceased. 14	Sex. 15	Age. 16	Rating. 17	Nationality (stating birthplace). 18	Last Place of Abode. 19	Cause of Death (or Fracture).

SUBSTITUTES ENGAGED.

Christian and Surname at Length. 21	Age. 22	Nationality. (If British, state Birthplace.) 23	ADDRESSES (1) Port of Engagement and Address, and (2) Home Address		Year 26	Ship in which he last served, and Year of Discharge therefrom	Date.	Place.		Amount of Wages per Calendar Month 30	Advances 31	Amount of Weekly or Monthly Allotment 32
Percy Dodd	27	Demerara	(1) 12 Queens Pk Terr, S. Ton		12	Oceanic	10/4/12	On Board	Sen Asst 4th Eng	£10.10	—	8/7
L. Kinsella	30	L'pool	(1) 7 Laurel Walk		do	Aragon	do	do	Fireman	£6		2
A. Geer	24	S. Ton	(1) 2 Stamford St. Chapel		do	Olympic	do	do	do	6		
R. Hosgood	22	London	(1) 19 Woolley Rd, Euston		do	Saxon	do	do	do	6		3
W. Lloyd	29	do	(1) 18 Orchard Pl. S. Ton		do	Dunottar C	do	do	do	6		5
H. Witt	39	S. Ton	(1) 28 L. College St. S. Ton		do	Oceanic	do	do	do	6		8/7
D. Black	41	Glasgow	(1) Sailors Home, S. Ton		do	do	do	do		6		

85

Insert At departure time, six tugs are ordered to manoeuvre *Titanic* from her mooring at Berth 44. (Red Funnel Group.)

Above As the last hawser securing *Titanic* to the land drops away, Southampton resident H. G. Lloyd captures the moment. The pilot flag flies from the portside halyard. (Russ Lownds Collection.)

Left 'Waving good-bye — stations and docks from the boat deck.' The gap between land and liner grows wider as Father Browne records the departure scene. (Father Francis M. Browne, S.J. Collection.)

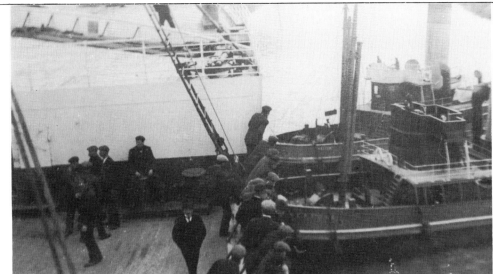

Top right Tugs strain to manoeuvre *Titanic* away from the dock... (Father Francis M. Browne, S.J. Collection.)

Middle right...and into the turning circle for her port swing into the River Test. (Father Francis M. Browne, S.J. Collection.)

Right Her turn completed, her propellers beginning to revolve, *Titanic* heads downstream. (Mariners Museum, Newport News, Virginia.)

Opposite page top left The tugs drop their lines, the great engines pick up their beat, and *Titanic* is under way. The open gangway door, aft, is for the debarkation of unsigned crewmen still aboard. (Mariners Museum, Newport News, Virginia.)

Opposite page top right A sudden interruption occurs when the nearby *New York* breaks her moorings. *Titanic*, engines full speed astern, comes to a halt near *Oceanic*'s bow. (*Daily Mirror*.)

Left But the *New York*'s stern continues to drift towards *Titanic*, and collision is averted only through the quick actions of Captain Smith and Pilot Bowyer, as well as Captain Gale of the tug *Vulcan*. (*L'Illustration*.)

This page above left From *Titanic*'s deck, Father Browne records the near-collision. (Father Francis M. Browne, S.J. collection.)

Above Her course reversed, *Titanic* drifts back towards the mouth of White Star Dock, as *New York* is manoeuvred to a temporary mooring in the River Itchen. (*Daily Mirror*.)

Insert Her safety from collision assured, *Titanic* continues on her way, making a starboard turn into the sea channel of Southampton Water. (Southern Newspapers plc.)

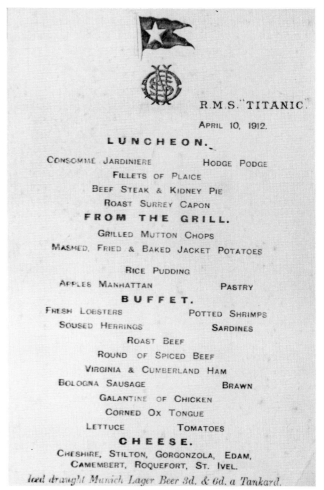

R.M.S. "TITANIC"

APRIL 10, 1912.

LUNCHEON.

CONSOMMÉ JARDINIERE   HODGE PODGE

FILLETS OF PLAICE

BEEF STEAK & KIDNEY PIE

ROAST SURREY CAPON

FROM THE GRILL.

GRILLED MUTTON CHOPS

MASHED, FRIED & BAKED JACKET POTATOES

RICE PUDDING

APPLES MANHATTAN   PASTRY

BUFFET.

FRESH LOBSTERS   POTTED SHRIMPS

SOUSED HERRINGS   SARDINES

ROAST BEEF

ROUND OF SPICED BEEF

VIRGINIA & CUMBERLAND HAM

BOLOGNA SAUSAGE   BRAWN

GALANTINE OF CHICKEN

CORNED OX TONGUE

LETTUCE   TOMATOES

CHEESE.

CHESHIRE, STILTON, GORGONZOLA, EDAM,
CAMEMBERT, ROQUEFORT, ST. IVEL.

Iced draught Munich Lager Beer 3d. & 6d. a Tankard.

Top left Seen from the after deck of the departing *Titanic, New York* has moved to a safe mooring. (Father Francis M. Browne, S.J. collection.)

Above The bugler's call resounds through the ship. Luncheon — the passengers' first meal is served. . . (Lloyd's of London.)

Middle left. . .as *Titanic* slows in her progress down Southampton Water so that unneeded crew may disembark aboard the tug *Vulcan*. (David F. Hutchings collection.)

Left The new liner passes the Isle of Wight on her way to the open sea. (Peter Pearce.)

Right *Titanic*'s decks seem deserted while passengers are sitting down to luncheon. (Smithsonian Institution.)

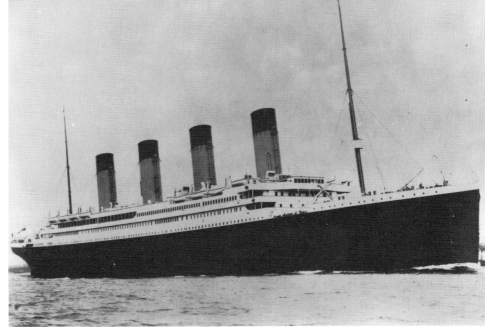

Middle right *Titanic* salutes a passing harbour craft as she sails down Southampton Water. (David F. Hutchings collection.)

Below Shortly after lunch is over, passengers — again on deck — watch as the boat approaches to take off pilot George Bowyer. (Father Francis M. Browne, S.J. collection.)

Chapter Eight

CHERBOURG

The 1907 inauguration of Southampton as its principal transatlantic port gave the White Star Line ready access to Cherbourg, France, due south and only 77 nautical miles from the English town. Cherbourg, too, was a deep water port, with a splendid harbour protected by a long sea wall. But while it did have a naval station and a small inner harbour for commercial coastal shipping, it lacked docking facilities for large ships. Passengers boarding liners in the roadstead had to be ferried out aboard tenders from the maritime land station. White Star's tenders, *Nomadic* and *Traffic*, had been built especially for use at Cherbourg, servicing *Olympic* and *Titanic*.

While the two giants were progressing at Harland and Wolff's Belfast yard, the construction of *Traffic* and *Normadic* also proceeded at the same yard. *Normadic* was launched on 25 April 1911. She was designed as a carrier of up to 1,000 first and second class passengers and their luggage. She had a gross tonnage of 1,273 and was 220.7 feet long.

Traffic, launched two days later, was somewhat smaller, with a length of 175.7 feet and a gross tonnage of 675. She accommodated 500 third class passengers and was fitted with heavy-duty conveyors for mails.*

Following *Titanic*'s launch on 31 May 1911, *Olympic* left Belfast for Liverpool for a two-day visit before going on to her maiden voyage departure from Southampton. Leaving Belfast the same day were *Nomadic* and *Traffic*, which proceeded directly to Cherbourg. There they performed their first service to *Olympic* on 14 June 1911, the first day of her maiden voyage. By 10 April 1912, the two tenders had met and served *Olympic* on each of her twelve subsequent Cherbourg visits. Now they were

to serve another liner on the first day, and at the first stop, of her own maiden trip.

At 9.40 am that morning, as the boat train was leaving London's Waterloo Station for *Titanic*'s Southampton departure, the *Train Transatlantique* was departing the Gare St Lazare in Paris for its own rendezvous with *Titanic* at Cherbourg's Gare Maritime. *Titanic*'s first Cherbourg visit was such an event that Nicholas Martin, manager of White Star's Paris office, made the trip with the passengers embarking at the French port. The fares from Paris were first class, 34s 3d (or $8.56); second class, 23s 7d ($5.90); third class 15s 11d ($4.10).

According to White Star company records, there would be 142 first class, 30 second class and 102 third class passengers.

When, after a trip of a little more than six hours, the train arrived at Cherbourg, the passengers received the disappointing announcement that embarkation aboard the tenders, scheduled for 4.30 pm, would be delayed at least one hour. *Titanic* had been involved in a near-mishap when leaving Southampton, and while she was not at all damaged, her departure had been delayed.

There was grumbling. But *c'est la vie*, what could one do? A stroll to the centre of town? A walk to the nearby Casino? A brief promenade along the Grande Jettée? There were few other attractions. And the tiny Gare Maritime was so uncomfortable. . .

There was confusion rather than grumbling among the 102 'Continental' passengers arriving at Cherbourg. They were Syrian, Croatian, Armenian and other Middle East nationals who, for reasons best known to their travel agents, had been routed from eastern Mediterranean ports via Marseilles to Paris and, now, to Cherbourg. Their travel arrange-

---

*In 1940, *Traffic* was scuttled at Cherbourg, but was raised and reconditioned by the German Navy. On 17 January 1941, while in action under Germany's flag, she was sunk by a British Royal Navy torpedo boat in the English Channel. *Nomadic* was to be broken up in 1970, but was instead sold for use as a floating restaurant and conference centre. Anchored on the River Seine in Paris, near the Eiffel Tower, she is the final remnant of the once-mighty White Star fleet.

ments called for departure via 'the first available ship', and they were surprised and pleased to find themselves about to board *Titanic*. But until the tardy liner arrived, there were pieces of luggage to protect, children to keep track of, and official announcements in a strange tongue to decipher.

The 'season' was now approaching its end, and in addition to the customary business travellers, there were many socially prominent passengers on the Cherbourg manifest. Among them were Mr and Mrs Thomas D. M. Cardeza (ticket number 17755, £512 6s); Mr Cardeza's valet, Gustave Lesneur, and Mrs Cardeza's maid, Anna Ward, were travelling on the same ticket. Mrs Charlotte Drake Cardeza was also accompanied by fourteen trunks, four suitcases and three crates of baggage, on which she would later place a value of £36,567 2s ($177,352.75) The Cardeza entourage was booked for suite B51, the three-room complex with its own promenade, on B deck's starboard side.

Among other first class passengers boarding at Cherbourg were Mr George Rheims (ticket 17604, £39 12s); Mr and Mrs Arthur Ryerson and their three children (ticket 17608, £262 7s 6d); Madame Leontine Aubert and her maid, Mlle Segesser (ticket 17477, £69 6s — Madame Aubert had declared while purchasing her ticket that she would take all her meals in the à la carte restaurant, and thus received a £5 rebate on her fare); department store magnate Emil Brandeis (ticket 17591, £50 9s 11d); Mr Benjamin Guggenheim and his valet, Victor Giglio (ticket 17593, £56 18s 7d); (Mr Rene Pernot, ticket 2131, £15 1s, Mr Guggenheim's chauffeur, travelled second class); 'Mr Morgan' (ticket 11755, £39 12s) and 'Mrs Morgan' and maid (ticket 17485, £56 18s 7d) were actually Sir Cosmo and Lady Duff-Gordon, the latter best known as dress designer 'Lucile'; Mrs James J. (Margaret) Brown, known to her friends as 'Molly' (ticket 17610, £27 14s 5d); 'Miss Rosenbaum' (ticket 17613, £27 14s 5d) was better known as Edith Russell.

Among the 30 second class Cherbourg passengers was 'Baron Alfred von Drachstedt', a passenger who would be dissatisfied with his second class accommodation, and who would go to the purser to arrange for a first class cabin. (He was thus assigned D38.) At a later date, he would admit to a United States court hearing a *Titanic*-related case that his name was actually Alfred Nournay. Other Cherbourg second class passengers may not have had as interesting a background as the 'baron', but they were just as real: Mr and Mrs André Mallet and their son, also named André; Mr and Mrs Joseph Laroche and their daughters Louise and Semorine; Mr and Mrs Nicholas Nasser, on their way to Cleveland, Ohio. Another second class passenger of more than passing interest was Samuel Ward Stanton, the well-known American marine

editor and illustrator. (Stanton was returning from Grenada, Spain, where he had been sketching the Alhambra for murals and other decorations he was to do for the new Hudson River Day Line steamboat *Washington Irving*.)

By 5.30 the passengers had re-assembled. Those not already aboard were conducted on to the tenders. The 172 first and second class passengers filled less than a fifth of the space on *Nomadic*, while *Traffic* was scarcely a quarter filled. There was, at least, room in which to await *Titanic*'s appearance beyond the breakwater.

After the late start, *Titanic*'s officers had not tried to make up the lost time. Her approach to Cherbourg was made as the lowering sun became an orange disc on the cloudless horizon. The French headlands were beginning to darken against the pale early evening sky. Speed was slackened as the distant breakwater with its beckoning lighthouse came into view. Ahead were the low shore of Cap de la Hogue and the purple height of Contentine.

The sky was awash with the red, blue and yellow of a fine spring sunset as *Titanic* moved slowly past the island fort and through the opening in the immense sea wall. The sky's yellow faded, red turned to rust and blue to purple as the two tenders came out from the shore. *Titanic*'s anchor was dropped in the roadstead at 6.30 pm.

Thirteen first class and seven second class passengers who were travelling only as far as Cherbourg prepared to disembark.* Cargo was unloaded: two cycles belong to Major G. I. Noel and his son, who were debarking; eight cases and a crated motor cycle consigned to Mr G. West; a canary, consigned to a Mr Meanwell, who had paid five shillings for its transport; yet another motor cycle, uncrated, this one consigned to a Mr Rogers.

Dusk descended as *Titanic* rode at anchor with all her lights aglow. As one observer said later, 'Perhaps then, more than at any other time, she was the lovely ship that people thought her to be. Her outline was etched clearly in light, with each porthole gleaming like a star, and the mast head lamps winking in the wavering breeze'.

Within ninety minutes, 22 passengers were taken ashore, 274 were taken aboard; Mr Meanwell's canary was on its way to its new Gallic home and all mails were transferred. At 8 pm, the tenders returning to shore, the *Titanic*'s windlass gear whirred and the clank of metal links sounded on the fo'c's'le as the great anchor was drawn up. Strident bells from the bridge ordered steam and the use of wing propellers for making a tight reverse turn.

By 8.10 pm the liner was under way, out of the

---

*Names of the 'cross Channel' passengers appear on no printed list, but are indicated on the Company's ticketing list.

Grande Rade, through the west passage and into the Channel. The engines' beat grew faster and deeper as the lights of Cherbourg dropped astern. The winking signal of the sentinel lighthouse disappeared beneath the horizon.

Across the Channel's southern reaches, around England's south coast, and into the lower reaches of St George's Channel, *Titanic* glided through the night on her passage from Cherbourg to Queenstown.

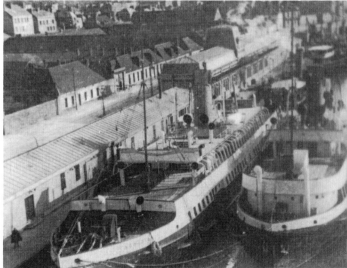

Inset At the end of *Titanic*'s Channel crossing lay the port of Cherbourg. (Authors' collection.)

Left Beyond the long jetty is the roadstead in which *Titanic* is to anchor. (Authors' collection.)

Below far left Transatlantic passengers arrive by train from Paris at the Gare Maritime, and embark aboard the tenders... (Authors' collection.)

Below left... *Nomadic* (left) and *Traffic*, which are moored alongside the Gare Maritime's pier. (Authors' collection.)

Top right First and second class passengers board *Nomadic*... (Authors' collection.)

Above right ... while third class step aboard *Traffic*; both tenders had been built especially for use with the new *Olympic* class liners. (Authors' collection.)

Right At 6.30 pm *Titanic* arrives at Cherbourg and drops anchor in the roadstead. (Bob Forrest collection.)

1ˢᵗ Voy. S.S. "Titanic" "   1ˢᵗ Voy. S.S. "Titanic" "

Names.	A.	C.	I.	No. of Contract Ticket.	No. of Continental Ticket.	Ocean Fare.	Inland Fare.	Forwarded to	No. of Inland Ticket.

Cross Channel Passengers

Names.				No. Contract	No. Cont.	Ocean	Inland	Forwarded	
Mr G Stevens				50	Southampton to Edinburgh				
" Brand				8	"	1 10			
" Collis				4	"				
Miss N Fletcher				405	"	1 10			
Maj G I Noel and Servt				48	Southampton to Queenstown	3			
Mr H Odell 6 adults				844	Queenstown Soton	24			
Mrs Cunningham 1 ad 2 ch				744	Edinburgh	3			
Miss Aby				45	"	1 10			
Mr Mrs J Farman				85	"	3			
Mr H Wollen				86	"	1 10			
Mr Mrs DB Edwards				87	Soton to Queenstown	3			
" C Nichols				103	"	4			
Mr Meanwell						5		1 Canary	
Maj Noel						5		2 Cycles	
Dr C West						4		8 Cases	
						10		1 Crated Cycle	
" Dulles				868		1 19 4		1 Dog	
" Harper				869		1 19 4			
Mr L P Smith	1			13695		60			
Mrs "	1								
Mr J Brennan	1			PC 14318		25 18 6			
	3					134 4 8			

Cross Channel Passengers

Names.	A	C	I	No. Contract	No. Cont.	Ocean	Inland	Forwarded	
Miss Kneese	1				Southampton to Edinburgh				
" Remesch	1			44		2			
Mr J de Grasse	1			651	"	1			
Miss Evans	1			88	"	1			
Rev H V Davies	1								
Miss H "	1			406	"	2			
" D Osborne	1								
Miss Tovey	1			516	"	2			
Mullen				404		1			
Rogers				144			10	Cycle	
				242164		29			
	8					38 10			

Left The list of passengers carried locally aboard *Titanic* shows 22 debarking at Cherbourg, and seven leaving at Queenstown. (National Archives.)

Below left While the cross-channel passengers disembark, 274 board from the tenders. (Painting by Ken Marschall; Richard Horline collection.)

Right All passengers having boarded, *Titanic* is cleared for departure from Cherbourg. At 8.10 pm the anchor is raised. (Public Record Office.)

Above far right *'Titanic*'s first sunrise' — Father Francis Browne is up at 6.45 am to record the opening moments of 11 April. (Father Francis M. Browne, S.J. collection.)

Right A lavish breakfast awaits first class passengers on the morning of April 11 . . . (Southampton City Museums.)

Far right. . . while in second class, an equally elaborate menu is served. The original menu is in postcard form, and has since been water damaged. (Southampton City Museums.)

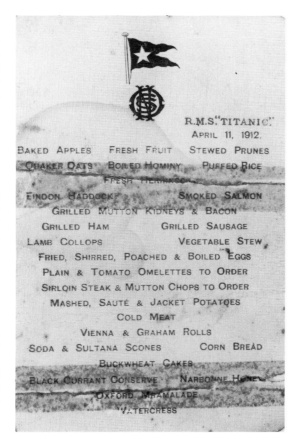

R.M.S. "TITANIC."
APRIL 11, 1912.

BAKED APPLES   FRESH FRUIT   STEWED PRUNES
QUAKER OATS   BOILED HOMINY   PUFFED RICE
FRESH HERRINGS
FINDON HADDOCKS   SMOKED SALMON
GRILLED MUTTON KIDNEYS & BACON
GRILLED HAM   GRILLED SAUSAGE
LAMB COLLOPS   VEGETABLE STEW
FRIED, SHIRRED, POACHED & BOILED EGGS
PLAIN & TOMATO OMELETTES TO ORDER
SIRLOIN STEAK & MUTTON CHOPS TO ORDER
MASHED, SAUTÉ & JACKET POTATOES
COLD MEAT
VIENNA & GRAHAM ROLLS
SODA & SULTANA SCONES   CORN BREAD
BUCKWHEAT CAKES
BLACK CURRANT CONSERVE   NARBONNE HONEY
OXFORD MARMALADE
WATERCRESS

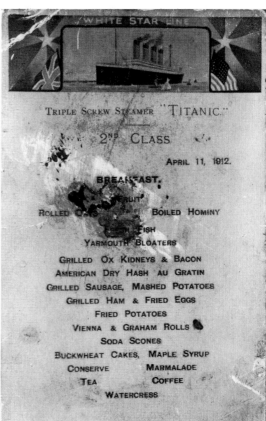

WHITE STAR LINE

TRIPLE SCREW STEAMER "TITANIC."

2ND CLASS

APRIL 11, 1912.

BREAKFAST.
FRUIT
ROLLED OATS   BOILED HOMINY
FRESH FISH
YARMOUTH BLOATERS
GRILLED OX KIDNEYS & BACON
AMERICAN DRY HASH AU GRATIN
GRILLED SAUSAGE, MASHED POTATOES
GRILLED HAM & FRIED EGGS
FRIED POTATOES
VIENNA & GRAHAM ROLLS
SODA SCONES
BUCKWHEAT CAKES, MAPLE SYRUP
CONSERVE   MARMALADE
TEA   COFFEE
WATERCRESS

Above The *Titanic* speeds towards Queenstown, and Father Browne photographs the waves curling off the liner's bows. (Father Francis M. Browne, S.J. collection.)

Above right First class passenger Master Robert Douglas Spedden, age six, spins his top on the after promenade deck as his father Frederick O. Spedden watches. (Father Francis M. Browne, S.J. collection.)

Middle right During his stroll, Father Browne pauses to photograph second class passengers enjoying the morning air from their own promenade. The sliding doors of the verandah and palm court are open. (Father Francis M. Browne, S.J. collection.)

Right During the morning, as she approaches Queenstown, Father Browne notes that '*Titanic* steers a very irregular course in order to test her compasses,' as evidenced by the ship's curving wake. (Father Francis M. Browne, S.J. collection.)

Chapter Nine

QUEENSTOWN

Departure's excitement had passed. The Channel crossing and the Cherbourg visit gave way to the first evening and night afloat. Passengers had time to examine the great new liner, to visit areas throughout the ship. The impressions of a first class passenger who travelled from Southampton to Queenstown were published in the *Belfast Telegraph* of 15 April 1912:

'"Look how that ship is rolling. I never thought it was so rough." The voice was a lady's, and the place was the sun deck [*sic*] of the *Titanic*. We had just got well clear of the eastern half of the Isle of Wight and were shaping our course down the English Channel toward Cherbourg.

'The ship that had elicited the remark was a large three-masted sailing vessel which rolled and pitched so heavily that over her bow the seas were constantly breaking. But up where we were — some 60 feet above the water line — there was no indication of the strength of the tossing swell below. This indeed is the one great impression I received from my first trip on the *Titanic* — and everyone with whom I spoke shared it — her wonderful steadiness. Were it not for the brisk breeze blowing along the decks one would scarcely have imagined that every hour found us 20 knots further upon our course.

'But other things besides her steadiness filled us with wonder. Deck over deck and apartment after apartment lent their deceitful aid to persuade us that instead of being on the sea we were still on terra firma. It is useless for me to attempt a description of the wonders of the saloon — the smoking room with its inlaid mother-of-pearl — the lounge with its green velvet and dull polished oak — the reading room with its marble fireplace and deep soft chairs and rich carpet of old rose hue — all of these things have been told over and over again, and only lose in the telling.

'So vast was it all that after several hours on board some of us were still uncertain of our way about — though we must state that with commendable alacrity and accuracy some 325 found their way to the great dining saloon at 7.30 when the bugle sounded the call to dinner. After dinner, we sat in the beautiful lounge listening to the White Star orchestra playing "The Tales of Hoffman" and "Cavalleria Rusticana" selections, and more than once we heard the remark, "You would never imagine you were on board a ship". Still harder was it to believe that up on the top deck it was blowing a gale.

'But we had to go to bed, and this reminds me that on the *Titanic* the expression is literally accurate. Nowhere were the berths of other days seen, and everywhere comfortable oaken bedsteads gave ease to the weary traveller.

'Then the morning plunge in the great swimming bath, where the ceaseless ripple of the tepid sea water was almost the only indication that somewhere in the distance 72,000 horses in the guise of steam engines fretted and strained under the skilled guidance of the engineers. After the plunge a half-hour in the gymnasium helped to send one's blood coursing freely, and created a big appetite for the morning meal.

'But if the saloon of the *Titanic* is wonderful, no less so is the second-class and in its degree the third-class. A word from the genial purser opened a free passage through all this floating wonder. Lifts and lounges and libraries are not generally associated in the public mind with second class, yet in the *Titanic* all are found. It needed the assurance of our steward guide that we had left the saloon and were really in the second class.

'On the crowded third-class deck were hundreds of English, Dutch, Italians and French mingling in happy fellowship, and when we wandered down among them we found that to them, too, the *Titanic* was a wonder. No more general cabins, but hundreds of comfortable rooms with two, four or six berths each, beautifully covered in red-and-white coverlets. Here, too, are lounges and smoking rooms, less magnificent than those amidships, to be sure, but nonetheless comfortable, and which, with the swivel chairs and separate tables in the dining-rooms, struck me as not quite fitting with my previous notion of steerage accommodation.

'And this morning, approaching Queenstown through the clear dawn, when the full Atlantic swell came upon our port side, so stately and measured was the roll of the mighty ship that one needed to compare the moving of the side with the steady line of the clear horizon.'

While passengers of all classes spent their first hours at sea inspecting and enjoying the comforts of the ship's public rooms, corridors, decks and staterooms, there were others with no time for enjoyment or rest. Trimmers, stokers and greasers in the bunkers and engine rooms; dining saloon and

bedroom stewards, polite and silent, performing their duties of service to passengers; cooks and bakers, dishwashers and scullerymen . . .

There was also little respite for the nine-member 'guarantee group' from Harland and Wolff's yard, headed by managing director Thomas Andrews. They continued to assist *Titanic*'s engineering staff with the vessel's pipes, ducts, heating and cooling machinery, plumbing, wiring — all the infra-structural systems which, during a first voyage, might require the special attention which a builder's representative could give. The shipyard had selected the best, all Belfast men, to form Andrews' group: William Henry Marsh Parr, assistant manager, electrical department; Roderick Chisholm, chief ship's draughtsman; Anthony ('Archie') W. Frost, outside foreman engineer; Robert Knight, lead-ing hand fitter engineer; William Campbell, joiner apprentice; Alfred Fleming Cunningham, fitter apprentice; Francis ('Frank') Parkes, plumber apprentice; and Ennis Hastings Watson, electrician apprentice.

Andrews, Chisholm and Parr travelled in first class; the others were on the second class passenger list. All were on 24-hour call at the request of the ship's various engineers. Perhaps a valve required clearing, or a kitchen sink drain unclogging. A section of pipe may have needed replacement and repainting; perhaps a malfunction of the ice machine or of one of the great sirocco fans in the engine room ventilators warranted attention.

The ship had been well constructed. There was not much for the Harland and Wolff men to do. But such as it was, their task assured the continued integrity of the builder's work.

Members of the ship's crew performed their appointed tasks, as well. Shift watches had been set for the engineering and engine room staffs: four hours on, four off for the stokers, trimmers and greasers; four hours on and eight off for the engineers (but they were 'on call' for four of their eight 'off' hours).

Assistant electrician George Ervine — at eighteen, the youngest of the engine room staff — had met his close companion and fellow assistant electrician Alfred Pirrie Middleton when they were working at Harland and Wolff, and neither would board the *Titanic* without the other. But both eventually applied to White Star, and received appointments aboard the vessel. Extracts of Ervine's last letter, posted to his mother at Queenstown, tell something of the voyage to that time:

'Yours received in Cherbourg, France yesterday evening. We have had everything working nicely so far, except when leaving Southampton.

'As soon as the *Titanic* began to move out of the dock, the suction caused the *Oceanic*, which was alongside her berth, to swing outwards, while another liner broke loose altogether and bumped into the *Oceanic*. The gangway of the *Oceanic* simply dissolved.

'Middleton and myself were on top of the after funnel, so we saw everything quite distinctly. I thought there was going to be a proper smash up owing to the high wind; but I don't think anyone was hurt.

'Well, we were at Cherbourg last night. It was just a mass of fortifications. We are on our way to County Cork. The next call then is New York . . .

'I am on duty morning and evening from 8 to 12; that is four hours work and eight hours off . . . (Have just been away attending the alarm bell.)

'This morning we had a full dress rehearsal of an emergency. The alarm bells all rang for ten seconds, then about 50 [*sic*] doors, all steel, gradually slid down into their places, so that water could not escape from any one section into the next.

'So you see it would be impossible for the ship to be sunk in collision with another . . .'

Up St George's Channel and approaching the Daunt Light Vessel which stood watch outside Cobh Harbour, *Titanic*'s course described a mighty arc as she swung in a long, gentle port turn. Slowing to a stop to pick up the pilot at the light vessel, she continued to the harbour opening at Roche's Point, her sounding line in constant use.

The telegraphs swung to 'stop', there was another clank of chain at the fo'c's'le, and a splash as the great anchor struck the water. *Titanic* stopped at 11.30 am, about two miles from land, and prepared to take aboard passengers and mails. Ferried out from the pierhead at the Queenstown railway station aboard the tenders *America* and *Ireland* came the 113 third class and seven second class passengers. Mails totalling 1,385 sacks were placed aboard. The tenders took about half an hour to make the trip from shore.

Mr H. Odell and his party ('6 adults', ticket number 84, £24) debarked, as did Mr E. Nichols. In Mr Odell's party was Francis M. Browne, a teacher at Belvedere College and a candidate for the priesthood. He had accepted Mr Odell's invitation to go on the first leg of *Titanic*'s maiden voyage, from Southampton to Queenstown. And as he left her to board the tender back to Queenstown, the 32-year-old teacher clutched the packet of exposed photographic plates, pictures he had taken during the preceding afternoon and earlier that morning around the liner's decks and public rooms.

Also boarding the tender, and mingling with the disembarking passengers, immigration authorities, reporters and visitors, was 24-year-old stoker John Coffey. When he signed on *Titanic*, Coffey had given his residence as 12 Sherbourne Terrace, Queenstown. It is not unlikely that his purpose in signing on had been to obtain free transportation home. He hid under some mail bags and awaited the tender's return to shore.

As the local passengers debarked, as John Coffey deserted, as authorities checked lists and immigration officer E. J. Sharpe certified the number of passengers aboard, third class passengers were conducted to their quarters. There was less hectic activity than there had been at Southampton or even at Cherbourg the night before. The stewards and attendants knew the ship's layout and their duties better than they had before; they, too, were in the process of 'shaking down', just as the ship was. And the passengers were more tractable, too: 'At least this lot spoke English,' one said.

'This lot' — Daniel Buckley, Katie Gilnagh, Ed Ryan; Nora O'Leary, Patrick O'Keefe, Mary and Kate Murphy; Margaret Rice and her five sons, Albert, George, Eric, Arthur and Eugene; John Kennedy; James Moran; Agnes, Alice and Bernard McCoy. Eugene Daly. . . Coming out on the tender, he had played lively airs on his Irish pipes. Now, as the ship's whistles sounded their three deep, mournful blasts of departure, Mr Daly took his place on the third class promenade, aft, and saluted the departing tenders — and his departing homeland — with the dirge, 'Erin's Lament'.

There was little overt sadness in the departure. There had, though, been a brief diversion several minutes earlier, when a stoker, black from his work at the furnaces, appeared at the top of the aft funnel, up the ladder for a breath of pure Irish air. An ill omen, some thought, but the sight was soon forgotten. At 1.30 pm, departure was imminent.

The starboard anchor came up, dripping. Once again, steam was fed into the engines. The great propellers began to turn as the liner began its majestic departure. From the tender's stern, Francis Browne took one last photograph. *Titanic* coursed past Roche's Point once again, outward bound. A brief stop to drop the pilot at the light vessel. A wide turn to starboard. The green fields and low hills of Ireland slipped past. In the sky the sun was beginning its decline. Encountering the Atlantic's heaving swells, *Titanic* turned, moving past the shore of southern Ireland.

The land, dark now in the lowering sun, was slipping astern when a French fishing trawler was sighted. She was so close to *Titanic* — even dangerously close — that she was splashed with the spray from the liner's bow. The fishermen cheered, and their salute was returned by *Titanic's* watch officer with a blast from the whistles.

With this encounter came the last sight of land. *Titanic* headed into the setting sun, leaving behind a golden wake which diminished, subsided, and became as one with the ocean's endless swells.

A view of Queenstown's waterfront from the cathedral esplanade shows the several docks from which tenders transported passengers out to vessels of various shipping lines, anchored beyond Roche's Point. (Authors' collection.)

Left White Star Line passengers frequently boarded tenders at Scott's Quay. St Coleman's Cathedral dominates the city's skyline. Not until 1914 would the cathedral's spire be completed. (Authors' collection.)

Below Anchoring two miles off Roche's Point about 11.30 am, *Titanic* awaits the arrival of passengers and mail. (Private collection.)

Left Half-hidden behind a mountain of mailbags and luggage trunks, the port doctor inspects emigrants boarding the tender. (Father Francis M. Browne, S.J. collection.)

Right Third class passengers in good health are issued with inspection cards permitting them to board *Titanic*. Once on the ship, their quarters' section letter and berth number are assigned and stamped in bold type on the ticket. (THS.)

Below The last mail sacks are hurried aboard. The final, reluctant farewells are spoken as the tenders are prepared for cast off. (*Cork Examiner.*)

Contract Ticket No. *35851*

INSPECTION CARD.
(Immigrants and Steerage Passengers.)

Port of Departure, QUEENSTOWN.

Date of Departure,

Name of Ship...... S.S. **TITANIC** 11th April 1912

Name of Immigrant...... *Gilnagh Kate*

Last Residence...... *Rhine*

Inspected and passed at

...AMERICAN...CONSULATE,

CORK, (QUEENSTOWN)

Passed at Quarantine, port of

......, U.S.

Passed by Immigration Bureau,

port of......

Q42

(Date.)   (Date.)

9

(The following to be filled in by ship's surgeon or agent prior to or after embarkation.)

Ship's list or manifest,...... No. on ship's list or manifest,......

Berth No. **Q 161**

Left Rounding the *Titanic*'s stern, the tender heads for the ship's side. A short time before, a stoker's blackened face, above the rim of the fourth funnel, had frightened many passengers. Apparently this photograph was taken by one of Father Browne's friends, identified only as 'McL', who went out to meet *Titanic*. (Father Francis M. Browne, S.J. collection.)

Left Confusion reigns when passengers, journalists and port officials crowd the rail as the tender reaches the liner's side. (*Cork Examiner.*)

Right Captain Smith peers down from the starboard bridge wing. (Father Francis M. Browne, S.J. collection.)

Journalists and photographers hastily record their impressions of the *Titanic*'s decks.

Above left Port side of the boat deck, looking forward: second class promenade in foreground, gymnasium windows and first class promenade towards the bow. (*Cork Examiner.*)

Left The third class promenade space, at the extreme stern, viewed from the aft end of the starboard boat deck. (*Cork Examiner.*)

Above Starboard side of boat deck, looking forward. (*Cork Examiner.*)

Right Passengers near the first class entrance observe the loading of mail from the tender *America*. Emergency boat No 2 is swung out, in keeping with company policy; lifeboat No 8 is closest to the camera. Officers' quarters are on the right. (*Cork Examiner.*)

Surveys 32.

SURVEY OF AN EMIGRANT SHIP.

ISSUED BY THE
BOARD OF TRADE.

No 408
13 APR 1912
BOARD OF TRADE, SURVEYORS OFFICE
QUEENSTOWN

Certificate for Clearance.

Ship's Name and Official Number. (1.)	Port of Registry, and Tonnage. (2.)	Name of Master. (3.)
Titanic 131428	*Liverpool* Gross Register 46328 21831	E. J. Smith.

Port of Departure. (4.)	Ports of Call. (5.)	Destination. (6.)
Southampton	Cherbourg and Queenstown	New York

CABIN PASSENGERS.

Adults (12 years and upwards).				Children.				Total Cabin Passengers. (15.)	Equal to Adults computed by Part III. M. S. Act, 1894. (16.)
Married.		Single.		Between 1 and 12.		Under 1 Year.			
Male. (7.)	Female. (8.)	Male. (9.)	Female. (10.)	Male. (11.)	Female. (12.)	Male. (13.)	Female. (14.)		
52	52	196	101	10	12	4	—	427	412
29	29	152	58	3	2	2	—	179	169½

STEERAGE PASSENGERS.

Adults (12 years and upwards).				Children.				Total Steerage Passengers. (25.)	Equal to Adults computed by Part III. M. S. Act, 1894. (26.)
Married.		Single.		Between 1 and 12.		Under 1 Year.			
Male. (17.)	Female. (18.)	Male. (19.)	Female. (20.)	Male. (21.)	Female. (22.)	Male. (23.)	Female. (24.)		
25	25	315	78	22	28	3	3	495	464
2	4	59	50	5				113	110

CREW.

Deck Department. (27.)	Engine Department. (28.)	Stewards' Department. (29.)	Total Crew. (30.)	Equal to Adults computed by Part III. M. S. Act, 1894. (31.)
73	325	494	892	892

Total Number actually on board, including Crew ... **2208** 2147

* Total Number of Statute Adults (as Steerage Passengers), exclusive of the Master, Crew, and Cabin Passengers, which the Ship can legally carry according to space allotted **1735** | Clear Space in Sq. Ft. **26992** | Number of Boats fitted. **1134**

I hereby certify that the particulars inserted in the above form are correct. I also certify that all the requirements of the Merchant Shipping Acts relating to emigrant ships, so far as they can be complied with before the departure of the ship, have been complied with, and that the ship is, in my opinion, seaworthy, in safe trim, and in all respects fit for her intended voyage; that she does not carry a greater number of passengers than in the proportion of one statute adult to every five superficial feet of space clear for exercise on deck; and that her passengers and crew are in a fit state to proceed.

Dated at *Queenstown*
this 11th day of *April* 19 12
E. J. Sharpe
Emigration Officer, or Assistant Emigration Officer.

(388s) (62345) Wt. 30276/150 3000 12-10 W B & L

pencilled notations on reverse:

cabin pass (1st + 2nd) 606
3rd ch (Emigrant) 710
Total 1316
892
Crew
Total Pass + crew 2208

Above After clearing *Titanic* for departure from Queenstown, the immigration officer, E. J. Sharpe, adds a pencilled notation on the clearance certificate's reverse side. His figure: 2,208 total passengers and crew. (Public Record Office.)

Opposite page Mr Sharpe also signs the final entry on the 'Report of Survey of an Emigrant Ship', which had been started by Mr Carruthers on the day of *Titanic*'s sea trials, 2 April. Captain Clarke had certified his observations at Southampton on sailing day. And now, the completed certificate is ready for forwarding to the Board of Trade surveyor's office. (Public Record Office.)

Right Preparations for departure are complete. Fourth Officer Boxhall (left) and Second Officer Lightoller prepare to close the gangway door for the last time. (*Cork Examiner.*)

M23780

REPORT OF SURVEY
OF

AN EMIGRANT SHIP.

No. 407
11 APR 1912
BOARD OF TRADE, SURVEYORS OFFICE
QUEENSTOWN

Name and official number.	Port of registry.	Tonnage. Gross. Net.	Single, twin, triple or quadruple screw. Registered horse-power.	Where and when built.
"Titanic" 131.428	Liverpool	41225 104*31	Triple Screw	Belfast 6-3-12

Date of expiration of passenger certificate.	Mean draught of water and freeboard.	Name and address of owner or agent.	Intended voyage.
2-4-13	34' 0" 31' 4"	Oceanic Steam Navigation Co. 30 James Street Liverpool	Foreign

MASTER AND OFFICERS.

Rank.	Name in full.	Number of certificate.	Grade.
Master ...	Edward John Smith	14102	Ex master
First Mate	Wm. McMaster Murdock	025,150	Ex Master
	Henry Tingle Wilde	027371	Ex masty
Second Mate	Chas. Herbert Lightoller	02/4706	Ex Master
First Engineer	Joseph Bell	19224	1st class
Second Engineer	Wm. Edward Farquharson	32833	1st Class

LIFE-SAVING APPLIANCES.

Description of boats and rafts.	No.	Cubic contents in feet.	No. of persons they will accommodate.	Materials.	Number under davits.	Are they so placed as to be readily got into the water?	Are they provided with the equipments required by the rules?
Boats, Section A.	14	9172	910	Wood	14	Yes	Yes
Boats, B.	✓						
Boats, C.	✓						
Boats, D.	2	648	80	Wood	2	Yes	Yes
Boats, E.	4		188	Wood with canvas		Yes	Yes
Life Rafts ...	✓						

Number of life belts.	Number of life buoys.	Is the ship supplied with all the life-saving appliances required by the rules?
3560	48	Yes

(322s) (61362) W1.27577/G.143. 1000 11-10 W B & L

EQUIPMENTS.

No. of compasses on board	Date of last adjustment	Number of chronometers	No. and description of fire pumps
4	2-4-12	2	3 Steam pumps

Description and state of distilling apparatus	No. of gallons of pure cold water that it is capable of producing in 24 hours	Quantity of fresh water in double bottom in gallons
Mess. Hocking & Co. New & in good condition	14000	That 1500 my tanks

SPACE AVAILABLE FOR PASSENGERS.

Area of passenger decks.	Total square feet.	Total number of adults.	Number of beds fitted.
On Saloon deck	1732	115	50
On Upper deck	7306	485	272
On Main deck	9861	655	466
On Lower deck	8093	480	346

REMARKS:—

REPORTS BY BOARD OF TRADE OFFICERS.

NOTE.—No Officer may certify to anything which he has not personally seen and examined, and then only if he is satisfied that it complies fully with the regulations. All words that do not apply should be struck out.

REPORTS.	Dates of inspection and signatures.
1. A passenger certificate is in force for this vessel, and no damage to the hull or engines has been reported since its issue. I am satisfied that the hull, boilers and machinery are in good condition and fit for the voyage.	Passenger Declaration for 12 months 6 days F. Carruthers 2-4-12 W. Sarrant 9/4/12
2. I have examined the distilling apparatus, which is in good working order and capable of producing 14000 gallons of cold water every 24 hours, and the engineers are competent to manage and repair it.	F. Carruthers 3-4-12
3. The fresh water on board is certified to amount to 200 500 gallons, and is contained in 7 tanks, and that portion in the double bottom complies with the regulations as to locking system, means of control and sub-division.	F. Carruthers 3-4-12
4. The coal on board is certified to amount to 5892 tons, which is sufficient to take the ship to her next coaling port.	M. H. Clarke 10-4-12
5. I have inspected the boats and their equipments, and have seen 16 swung out and lowered into the water. The lifebelts are in order and are conveniently placed. The distress signals and their magazine, and the other equipments, comply with the regulations and are to my satisfaction.	F. Carruthers 3-4-12
6. The various steerage compartments comply with the regulations as regards light, air and ventilation, and measurement for the numbers for which they are fitted. No cargo is stowed so as to affect the health or comfort of the steerage passengers.	F. Carruthers 3-4-12
7. I have inspected the provisions which are sufficient for 1150 adults; and the quality of the provisions and water for the passengers and crew is entirely to my satisfaction.	P. I. Attley 10/4/12
8. I have inspected the medical stores, and they comply both as to quality and quantity with the regulations, and are to my satisfaction.	

REPORTS—continued.

REPORTS	Dates of inspection and signatures.
9. I have inspected the crew and steerage passengers, and none of them appear to be by reason of bodily or mental disease unfit to proceed or likely to endanger the health or safety of the other persons on board.	P. I. Attley 10/4/12
10. I was on board this ship immediately before she sailed. I saw two boats swung out and lowered into the water. From the foregoing reports of inspection, and from what I saw myself, I was satisfied that the ship was in all respects fit for the intended voyage, and that the requirements under the Merchant Shipping Acts have been complied with.	M. H. Clarke 10-4-12
[Reports to be made when passengers are embarked at a port of call.]	Queenstown 11-4-12
I have inspected the steerage passengers, stores, medicines, etc., embarked here, and am satisfied that the regulations are complied with.	Concan Apre. 11th 1912
I have satisfied myself that everything on board this vessel is in order, and have issued the necessary certificate for clearance.	J. J. Sharpe.

Forwarded to the Board of Trade.

Signature William Tiller

Date 12th April 1912

The Assistant Secretary,
Marine Department, Board of Trade.

Above From the departing tender, Father Browne photographs the raising of the great starboard anchor from Queenstown Harbour. To the right of the anchor chain, the sounding line is continually in use. (Father Francis M. Browne, S.J. collection.)

Above right The starboard side of *Titanic* recedes as the tender draws away. (Father Francis M. Browne, S.J. collection.)

Top opposite page Anchor up, engines started, *Titanic* begins her majestic departure from Queenstown Harbour. . . (Father Francis M. Browne, S.J. collection.)

Top far right opposite page. . . and third-class passenger Eugene Daly, on the liner's stern, bids farewell to his homeland with the sorrowful sound of 'Erin's Lament', played on his pipes. (*Cork Examiner*.)

Right On a fine, brisk Irish afternoon, *Titanic* passes the Old Head of Kinsale on her way down St George's Channel to a rendezvous with the North Atlantic. (Painting by Ken Marschall; Dennis R. Kromm collection.)

Chapter Ten

AT SEA

Titanic was 'The Ship of Beauty' from the 15-foot teak pole atop each mast to the bilge keels running 294 feet amidships, port and starboard; from the 16-foot stem jackstaff to the 24-foot stern flagpole; between the 101-foot 6-inch forward mast and the 97-foot 5-inch main mast (both raked two inches per foot, the former containing a 50-foot iron ladder to the crow's nest). . .

The boat deck's first class entrance, with its linoleum-covered floor, Aeolian organ and six electric heaters. . . Oak panelled corridors leading to smoke room and lounge; revolving doors to keep out the sea's chill; mirrors, cut glass lighting fixtures, thick carpeting, draperies and furniture in a profusion of colours and textures. . . Suites of cabins in period decor. Broad decks open to the fresh ocean air; decks enclosed from spray and cold. Elevators for both first and second class passengers. . .

Second class corridors and public rooms: more luxurious, more comfortable than first class aboard many liners of a decade earlier. Oak panelling in the dining saloon and smoking room, sycamore in the library; mahogany furniture upholstered in green or red morocco leather, or tapestry, as in the library. Red-carpeted entrances, two-tone green carpeted corridors. Staterooms with white enamelled walls, moquette-covered mahogany furniture, linoleum on some floors, carpeting on others. Exotic birds eye curly maple panelling on corridor walls adjacent to the elevator and within it.

The third class public rooms: the bright, white-enamelled walls in the two F-deck dining saloons, with individual chairs instead of the customary benches. Two bars, one forward on D deck, the other adjacent to the C deck smoking room near the stern. The smoking room, oak panelled and framed, with teak tables and chairs and comfortable, contoured benches. The general room, similarly furnished, but with white enamelled walls panelled and framed in pine.

Filling the corridors and great public rooms were more than 1,300 passengers, who whiled away their time on board in many ways. There were few formal or organized activities. Dining hours were one of the few scheduled impositions on passengers' time: 8.30 to 10.30 am for breakfast, 1 to 2.30 pm for luncheon, 6 to 7.30 pm (perhaps a bit later) for dinner. The à la carte restaurant, with its light, fawn-coloured French walnut panelling and two-tone Dubarry rose carpeting, seated 137 diners at 49 tables. It was open from 8 am to 11 pm daily for first class passengers with more uncommon tastes. (White Star offered rebates to passengers who chose to eat all meals in the restaurant: $15 on tickets under $175, $25 on all others.)

Turkish and electric baths on F deck, forward, were open to ladies between 10 am and 1 pm, and to gentlemen from 2 to 6 pm. The purser sold tickets at the C deck enquiry office for $1 (four shillings). The swimming bath, measuring 32 feet by 13 feet by 6 feet deep, was open, free of charge, to gentlemen between 6 and 9 am and to ladies and gentlemen, respectively, during the day while the Turkish bath was open. There was a 25 cents (one shilling) charge for those not booking the Turkish bath.

They gymnasium, adjacent to the first class entrance on the boat deck, was open concurrently with the baths, and was open to children, only, between 1 and 3 pm.

Located forward on G deck, next to the post office, was the squash racket court. Tickets could be reserved at the enquiry office at 50 cents (two shillings) per half hour, which included equipment and the services of the professional, Fred Wright, if desired.

For the more sedentary, the library, on A deck adjacent to the main lounge was — like the lounge — open daily from 8 am to 11.30 pm. The verandah café and palm court, on A deck aft, could be opened to the air. But even while glass-enclosed, it provided a panoramic view of the passing, ever-changing sea.

Second class passengers lacked the privileged facilities afforded first class travellers, but they did not want for diversion, in any case. A well-stocked

library, aft on C deck, and a comfortable smoking room just above on B deck were flanked by covered deck space on which passengers could promenade.

Third class passengers had their own open deck spaces, forward and aft. Their 'general room' featured a piano. And individual tables and chairs were placed around the smoking room for card or domino games.

In all classes, each day passed leisurely with reading or writing, ship's orchestra concerts, smoking room card games and more active games on deck. There were no rigid routines, no formally-organized dances or balls, no general parties. Relaxation and individual pursuits — or those involving several good friends — marked the Atlantic crossing. Each morning, noon and night ship's bugler P. W. Fletcher summoned passengers to meals in the great dining saloons (532 seats in first class, 394 in second, and a total of 473 seats in the third class dining saloon's two compartments).

Contrary to popular belief, Captain Smith did not preside at the head of a large table filled with prominent and attractive passengers. Rather, he most frequently occupied a table for six at the forward end of the first class dining saloon's centre section. In thick weather or when entering or leaving port, he did not dine in public, preferring to take his meals on the bridge or in his own quarters, served by his personal steward, Mr J. A. Painton.

Reading, writing, card-playing... Dining, meeting with friends before and after meals in the luxurious reception room... Looking forward each day to the posting in the smoking room of the previous day's run (from one noon to the next): Thursday to Friday, 386 miles; Friday to Saturday, 519 miles; Saturday to noon Sunday, 546 miles. There was talk among passengers that on this maiden voyage the company wished to set a crossing record, and that additional boilers had been fired up early on Sunday morning, anticipating a swift dash to New York.

This, however, was not truly practicable to the company's needs. For to bring *Titanic* across in 'record time' would have meant arriving outside New York Harbour late on Tuesday night, 16 April. It would have been difficult, if not impossible, to dock the huge ship at night. In addition, the new liner's ceremonious welcome would have had to wait until daylight.

Twenty-four of 29 *Titanic* boilers were alight on Sunday. But it appears that the 'burst of speed', tentatively set for Monday, was only to allow the ship's own engineering staff and the builder's representatives to study the effect of an all-out, albeit brief, run. *Titanic* had never been truly tested at top speed. It was thought to be well over 22 knots, perhaps as high as 23. But certainly nothing near the record-holder *Mauretania*'s 26-knot pace!

At 75 revolutions per minute, the propellers drove *Titanic* through the smooth sea at 21½ knots, or almost 24½ land miles per hour. Friday and Saturday had been uneventful, typical days during a mid-April, North Atlantic crossing.

Wireless was standard equipment aboard most 1912 transatlantic passenger liners. Aboard *Titanic*, passengers sent their messages at the enquiry office at the starboard side of the forward first class entrance. The handwritten messages were paid for at the desk, at the rate of 12s 6d for the first ten words, and 9d for each additional word. Messages were sent by pneumatic tube to the wireless cabin, where the operator noted the word count and transmitted the message. At the end of the day a balance was struck between the wireless operators and the purser's clerk regarding the total number of commercial words sent.

Incoming messages were handwritten by the receiving operator and typed on a Marconi form by the relief operator before being sent by pneumatic tube to the enquiry desk. Upon receipt at the desk, they were dispatched by bell boy to the addressee, in one of the public rooms, or the passenger's cabin. Messages regarding navigation were taken directly to the bridge, a few steps down the corridor on the port side of the officers' quarters.

On each day, as on all days at sea except Sunday, Captain Smith made a thorough inspection of the vessel, as required by White Star Line rules. A little after 10 am, resplendent in full dress uniform, wearing his Transport Medal and Royal Naval Reserve Decoration, he received in his quarters the chief engineer, purser, assistant purser, surgeon and chief steward. At 10.30 am, after listening to reports based on their department inspections an hour earlier, Smith led the entire entourage through corridors and public rooms of all classes: kitchens, pantries, dining saloons, hospitals for passengers and crew, barber's shops, baker's shop, bars...

The impressive group of uniformed officers strode throughout the ship, examining, observing, noting cleanliness, condition, performance. From deck to deck, downward to the great storage rooms, cargo spaces and engine rooms — where the captain was attended by the chief engineer alone. Back, then, through third class quarters and up to the open decks where winches, cranes and ventilators were examined, tested... Back to the bridge, to Captain Smith's quarters, where comments and suggestions were exchanged and orders issued.

Their part in the daily inspection completed, the department heads returned to their duties. Captain Smith convened his officers and conferred with them, discussing the inspection's results and the day's navigation details.

Titanic had received many wireless messages of congratulation and good wishes for a successful

maiden voyage: on Friday morning, the *Empress of Britain*, eastbound from Halifax to Liverpool; and during the afternoon, the French Line vessel *La Touraine*, bound from New York to Le Havre. Each 'greeting' had also contained advice of ice. But this was not uncommon during an April crossing.

At about 11 pm on Friday, *Titanic's* wireless apparatus ceased to function. The problem appeared to be in one of the secondary circuits, and Phillips and Bride toiled through the early morning hours to trace the trouble. Between 4.30 and 5 am on Saturday, the difficulty was discovered and repaired. There was no further malfunction of the apparatus.

Friday thus passed on Saturday. All along the North Atlantic lanes, eastbound and westbound, vessels were encountering ice near the parallel of 41° 50′ North latitude: *President Lincoln, Saint Laurent, East Point, Avala...*

Some reported the danger by wireless. Others — having no wireless — could not report until their arrival in port. *Manitou*, the Anchor Line's *California, Corby, Minnesota...* And on Saturday: *Borderer, Hellig Olav...* Into Sunday: *Montcalm, Canada, Mount Temple, Corinthian, Corsican...*

'Ice between 41° and 42° North, and between 49° and 50° West... Field ice, some growlers, some bergs...'

But on Saturday, Captain Smith also received some good news from chief engineer Bell: the fire which had burned continuously in boiler room number 6 since *Titanic's* sea trials almost two weeks earlier finally had been extinguished shortly after noon. It appeared that the captain would be spared the indignity of calling for the New York City Fire Department's assistance upon arrival, as he might have been considering. Saturday became Sunday.

Sunday, 14 April. The day passed from dawn to dusk to dark. The minutes ticked on...

9 am*: A message was received in the wireless room from *Caronia*, eastbound, New York to Liverpool via Queenstown: 'Captain, *Titanic* — West-bound steamers report bergs, growlers and field ice in 42° N, from 49° to 51° W, April 12. Compliments, Barr'. The message was delivered to the bridge, to Captain Smith, who posted it for his officers to read and note.

10.30 am: Divine Service was held in the first class dining saloon. Passengers from all classes attended, those from third class eyeing with awe the room's luxurious decor. Captain Smith led the service, not from the Church of England's Book of Common Prayer, but from the company's own prayer book. The ship's orchestra provided music and accompaniment to the hymns. The service concluded at about 11.15 with the singing of the fine old hymn, 'Oh God, our Help in Ages Past'.

12 noon: In accordance with company rules, the liner's great whistles and the telegraphs between engine room and navigating bridge were tested. Assembled on the wing of the navigating bridge were the ship's officers, sextants in hand, to 'shoot the sun' and calculate the vessel's position. Shortly afterwards, their determination was logged, and then posted in the several main companionways and smoking rooms. 'Since noon, Saturday, 546 miles.'

1.42 pm: A wireless message from *Baltic*, eastbound from New York to Liverpool via Queenstown: '... Greek steamer *Athenai* reports passing icebergs and large quantities of field ice today in latitude 41° 51′ N, longitude 49° 52′ W... Wish you and *Titanic* all success. Commander.' The message was delivered to Captain Smith as he conversed with J. Bruce Ismay. Smith handed the copy to Ismay, who put it in his own pocket. Later, Ismay showed the message to several passengers. It was not until 7.15 pm, when Captain Smith asked for its return, that the message was posted in the chart room.

1.45 pm: A private message from the liner *Amerika* to the United States Hydrographic Office at Washington, DC, was received and relayed by *Titanic's* wireless operator: '*Amerika* passed two large icebergs in 41° 27′ N, 50° 8′ W on April 14'. Since the message concerned navigation, it should have been sent to the bridge for attention. It was not.

5.30 pm: A change in air temperature was now noted by passengers taking walks on the decks. The temperature appeared to be dropping rapidly, and many passengers left the decks for the comfort of the warm, inside rooms. Between 5.30 and 7.30 pm, the air temperature dropped ten degrees, to 33 degrees F.

5.50 pm: Captain Smith's instructions in the night order book called for the ship's course to be altered at this time from S 62 W to S 85 W. (The normal time for the turn would have been about 5.20 pm. The delay had the effect of placing *Titanic* on a course slightly to the south and west of what would have been her normal course, and was thought by the bridge officers to represent a precautionary move by the captain to avoid the ice about which he had been warned.)

6 pm: Second officer Lightoller relieved chief officer Wilde on the bridge.

7.15 pm: With knowledge of the approaching ice-field, first officer Murdoch ordered lamp trimmer Samuel Hemming to secure the forward fo'c's'le hatch to prevent the light's glow from interfering with the crow's nest's ice watch.

7.30 pm: A wireless message from *Californian* to *Antillian* was overheard by *Titanic*: 'To Captain,

*All times, throughout, are *Titanic's* time, unless otherwise specified.

114

Antillian: Six-thirty pm, apparent ship's time; latitude 42° 3′ N, longitude 49° 9′ W. Three large bergs 5 miles to the southward of us. Regards. Lord.' Harold Bride took the message to one of the officers on the bridge. (Later he could not recall to whom he delivered it.) Captain Smith was not advised personally of this latest ice message; he was in the à la carte restaurant, enjoying dinner at a party given by Mr and Mrs George D. Widener, whose other guests included the Thayers, the Carters, Major Butt and their own son, Harry.

7.30 pm: Lightoller, as officer of the watch, took a stellar observation, then gave the data to fourth officer Boxhall to work out. After plotting the ship's position, Boxhall appended his memorandum to the navigation chart. Later, around 10 pm, Captain Smith entered the 7.30 pm position on the chart itself.

8.30 pm: The Reverend E. C. Carter organized and conducted a hymn sing, which began at this hour in the second class dining saloon. To piano accompaniment, more than 100 passengers sang hymns until well past ten o'clock. More than one passenger who attended later recalled one particular hymn, 'Eternal Father, Strong to Save', with its refrain, 'O hear us when we cry to Thee for those in peril on the sea'.

8.40 pm: Ship's carpenter J. Maxwell was ordered by Lightoller to look after the ship's fresh water supply and to advise chief engineer Bell to do the same, as the water was about to freeze.

8.55 pm: Captain Smith excused himself from the Wideners' party. He went directly to the bridge and, finding Lightoller on duty, engaged him in conversation, as described later by Lightoller:

'We commenced speaking about the weather. He said, "There is not much wind". I said, "No, it is a flat calm". I said that it was a pity the wind had not kept up with us whilst we were going through the ice region. Of course he knew I meant the water ripples breaking on the base of the berg. . . I remember saying, "Of course there will be a certain amount of reflected light from the bergs," with which the Captain agreed. Even with the blue side toward us, we both agreed that there would still be the white outline. . .'

9.20 pm: Captain Smith retired. His last words to Lightoller were, 'If it becomes at all doubtful let me know at once. I shall be just inside'.

9.30 pm: Lightoller sent a message to the crow's nest to 'keep a sharp lookout for ice, particularly small ice and growlers' until daylight.

9.40 pm: A message was received in *Titanic*'s wireless room. 'From *Mesaba* to *Titanic*. In latitude 42° N to 41° 25′, longitude 49° W to longitude 50° 30′ W, saw much heavy pack ice and great number large icebergs, also field ice, weather good, clear.' The message never reached *Titanic*'s bridge. Harold Bride had turned in to take a nap, and senior Marconi operator Jack Phillips was alone on duty, extremely busy with commercial traffic to the Cape Race shore station.

10 pm: Lightoller was relieved on the bridge by first officer Murdoch. He made his rounds of the ship before going to his own cabin to sleep. Lookouts Symons and Jewell were relieved in the crow's nest by Fleet and Lee; before they departed, Symons passed the word received earlier from Lightoller, to keep a careful lookout for ice and growlers.

10.30 pm: Eastward bound from Halifax, the freighter *Rappahannock* emerged from her passage through an extensive ice-field, during which she had sustained rudder damage. Her acting master, Albert E. Smith, seeing *Titanic*'s lights abeam, contacted her and sent a message by Morse signal lamp: 'Have just passed through heavy field ice and several icebergs'. After a moment, *Titanic* acknowledged, 'Message received. Thank you. Good night.'

10.55 pm: Stopped in ice at least nineteen miles north of *Titanic*'s course, the master of the freighter *Californian* asked his radio operator to notify ships in the vicinity of the ice. Cyril Evans called up *Titanic* and was in the middle of his message, 'We are stopped and surrounded by ice,' when *Titanic*'s operator abruptly broke in with, 'Keep out! Shut up! You're jamming my signal. I'm working Cape Race.' Evans ceased his transmission and tuned in to listen to *Titanic*'s Cape Race traffic. He then turned off his station and went to bed, as usual, at 11.30 pm. It had been a long day for *Californian*'s sole wireless operator. . .

Sunday at sea. A routine Sunday during a mid-April North Atlantic crossing, typical, except for ice warnings and falling temperatures. Yet even these were not uncommon for the season.

Time ran on. The sound of seven bells marked 11.30 pm. Sunday was almost over. The minutes passed. . .

Above left Flanking the main third class entrance, C deck aft, are doors to the general room (left) and smoking room. (*Olympic*; Authors' collection.)

Above Patterned linoleum adds brightness to the third class smoking room, whose oak panelling and teak furniture are enjoyed by the men. (*Olympic*; Authors' collection.)

Left White-painted pine contributes a light, airy look to one of the two third class dining rooms on F deck. (*Olympic*; Shipbuilder.)

WHITE STAR LINE
Specimen Third Class Bill of Fare
Subject to Alteration as Circumstances Require

	Sunday	Monday	Tuesday	Wednesday	Thursday	Friday	Saturday
Breakfast	Quaker Oats and Milk Smoked Herrings and Jacket Potatoes Boiled Eggs Fresh Bread and Butter Marmalade, Swedish Bread Tea and Coffee	Oatmeal Porridge and Milk Irish Stew Broiled Sausage Fresh Bread and Butter Marmalade, Swedish Bread Tea and Coffee	Oatmeal Porridge and Milk Ling Fish, Egg Sauce Fried Tripe and Onions Jacket Potatoes Fresh Bread and Butter Marmalade, Swedish Bread Tea and Coffee	Quaker Oats and Milk Smoked Herrings Beefsteak and Onions Jacket Potatoes Fresh Bread and Butter Marmalade, Swedish Bread Tea and Coffee	Oatmeal Porridge and Milk Liver and Bacon Irish Stew Fresh Bread and Butter Marmalade, Swedish Bread Tea and Coffee	Quaker Oats and Milk Smoked Herrings Jacket Potatoes Curried Beef and Rice Fresh Bread and Butter Marmalade, Swedish Bread Tea and Coffee	Oatmeal Porridge and Milk Vegetable Stew Fried Tripe and Onions Fresh Bread and Butter Marmalade, Swedish Bread Tea and Coffee
Dinner . .	Vegetable Soup Roast Pork, Sage and Onions Green Peas Boiled Potatoes Cabin Biscuits, Fresh Bread Plum Pudding, Sweet Sauce Oranges	Barley Broth Beefsteak and Kidney Pie Carrots and Turnips Boiled Potatoes Cabin Biscuits, Fresh Bread Stewed Apples and Rice	Pea Soup Fricasse Rabbit and Bacon Lima Beans, Boiled Potatoes Cabin Biscuits, Fresh Bread Semolina Pudding Apples	Rice Soup Corned Beef and Cabbage Boiled Potatoes Cabin Biscuits, Fresh Bread Peaches and Rice	Vegetable Soup Boiled Mutton and Caper Sauce Green Peas, Boiled Potatoes Cabin Biscuits, Fresh Bread Plum Pudding, Sweet Sauce	Pea Soup Ling Fish, Egg Sauce Cold Beef and Pickles Cabbage, Boiled Potatoes Cabin Biscuits, Fresh Bread Cornaline Pudding Oranges	Bouilli Soup Roast Beef and Brown Gravy Green Peas, Boiled Potatoes Cabin Biscuits, Fresh Bread Prunes and Rice
Tea	Ragout of Beef, Potatoes and Pickles Apricots Fresh Bread and Butter Currant Buns Tea	Curried Mutton and Rice Cheese and Pickles Fresh Bread and Butter Damson Jam Swedish Bread Tea	Haricot Mutton Pickles Prunes and Rice Fresh Bread and Butter Swedish Bread Tea	Brawn Cheese and Pickles Apples and Rice Rhubarb Jam Currant Buns Tea	Sausage and Mashed Potatoes Dry Hash Apples and Rice Fresh Bread and Butter Swedish Bread Tea	Cod Fish Cakes Cheese and Pickles Fresh Bread and Butter Plum and Apple Jam Swedish Bread	Rabbit Pie Baked Potatoes Fresh Bread and Butter Rhubarb and Ginger Jam Swedish Bread.

SUPPER—Every Day.—Cabin Biscuits and Cheese.   Gruel, Coffee.

Fresh Fish served as substitute for Salt Fish as opportunity offers

Kosher Meat Supplied and Cooked for Jewish Passengers as desired

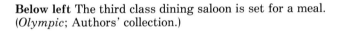

Below far left Third class passengers' meals are hearty and nourishing. (*Olympic*; Cropley Collection, Smithsonian Institution.)

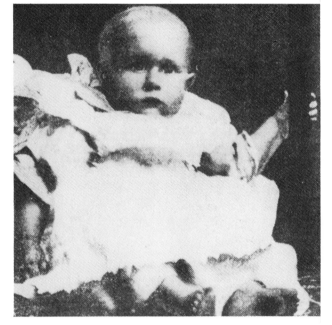

Below left The third class dining saloon is set for a meal. (*Olympic*; Authors' collection.)

Above Among those enjoying the *Titanic*'s superior third class accommodation are (left to right) Eileen and Neal McNamee, Patrick O'Keefe and August Wennerstrom. . . (Authors' collection.)

. . . and the Goodwin family **below** including 18-month-old Sidney **right**. The entire family was lost. (*Daily Mirror*.)

Third class passengers could pay less than $20 for their fares. Travelling in third class on *Titanic* are (Row 1) John Garfirth, Frederick Goodwin, John Sage and Miss Stella Sage. (Row 2) Travelling second class, Charles V. Clark, Mrs Ada Clark, Frederick J. Banfield and Robert Phillips. (Row 3) Miss Alice Phillips and Harry Rogers. (Authors' collection.)

Below left Waygood's hoist serves the ship's galleys, bringing foodstuffs from stores on G deck to preparation areas in the D deck galleys. (*Olympic*; Harland and Wolff Ltd.)

Above right Second class passengers would sit down to luncheon here during *Titanic*'s first full day at sea on 12 April. (Southern Newspapers Ltd.)

Above far right First and second class galleys have been combined to provide a full range of services. (*Olympic*; Authors' collection.)

Right Chief Marconi operator John ('Jack') Phillips is busy sending passengers' messages in the ship's wireless room on the boat deck, forward. (Marconi Company Ltd.)

Middle far right He uses the finest available equipment, similar to that found in another transatlantic liner of the period. (Marconi Company Ltd.)

Far right The wireless set's design, including this multiple tuner, enables him to keep in touch with ships and land stations 500 miles or more away. (Authors' collection.)

Far left The Canadian Pacific liner *Empress of Britain*, eastbound from Halifax to Liverpool, sends a greeting to the new White Star liner at 11 am on 12 April. (Authors' collection.)

Left At 12 noon each day, Commander Smith and all officers not on watch step to the bridge wing to 'shoot the sun' with their sextants, establishing the ship's position. (*Olympic*; Harland and Wolff Ltd.)

Middle far left The second class entrance on B deck aft is pierced by the mainmast. (*Olympic*; Barrie Rogers Davis collection.)

Middle left Forward of the mainmast on B deck is another second class entrance, with elevator. The lobby area, panelled in birds eye curly maple. . . (*Olympic*; Barrie Rogers Davis collection.)

Bottom far left. . .leads to the smoking room on the left. (*Olympic*; National Maritime Museum, Greenwich.)

Bottom left The second class smoking room is panelled in oak. A patterned floor covering is added later. (*Olympic*; Harland and Wolff Ltd.)

Top right School teacher Lawrence Beesley enjoys good reading in the second class library, panelled in sycamore. Outside, while he reads, children play on the covered promenade deck. (*Olympic*; Harland and Wolff Ltd.)

Middle right The second class dining saloon on D deck, looking forward. . . (*Olympic*; Barrie Rogers Davis collection.)

Right. . .and looking aft. The room, panelled in oak, seats 394 diners. (*Olympic*; National Maritime Museum, Greenwich.)

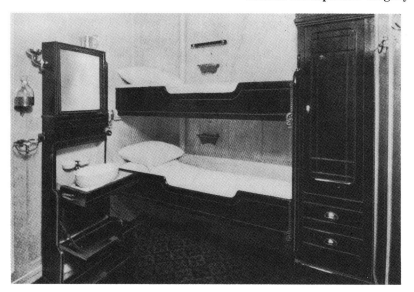

Left Accommodation for second class passengers ranges from this two-berth cabin on D deck. . . (*Olympic*; Barrie Rogers Davis collection.)

Middle left. . .to this four-berth cabin, also on D deck. (*Olympic*; Barrie Rogers Davis collection.)

Bottom left The French liner *La Touraine*, eastbound from New York to Le Havre, is in wireless communication with *Titanic* on 12 April. (Authors' collection.)

Below At 8 pm Captain Coussin sends an ice warning, to which Captain Smith responds. (Private collection.)

Above right In second class cabins on E deck. . . (*Olympic*; National Maritime Museum, Greenwich.)

Above far right. . .passengers prepare to retire after a pleasant day at sea. (*Olympic*; National Maritime Museum, Greenwich.)

Right Among those travelling second class are (Row 1) Elizabeth Hocking, her son George, her daughter Nellie and Henry P. Hodges. (Row 2) E. A. Sjostedt and Leonard Hickman (Row 3) Lewis Hickman his brother (yet another brother was also on board) and Charles Williams, the English racquets champion. . .

Far right. . .and John Harper, pastor of the Walworth Road Baptist Church, London, travelling with Nina Harper, his daughter and Jessie Leitch, his niece. (*Daily Mirror*.)

Above left Dawn, Saturday, 13 April: *Titanic* races westward. (Painting by Ken Marschall; Rustie Brown Collection.)

Above At 10 am, Captain Smith inspects the vessel from bridge to keel. He is seen on board *Adriatic*, about three years earlier, conducting a similar inspection. (Authors' collection.)

Middle left Deck chairs line the port side of the promenade (A) deck. The view forward, aboard *Olympic*, closely resembles that on *Titanic* except for the absence of the latter's glassed-in screen. (Private collection.)

Left Looking forward, down B deck's port side, there is insufficient space for deck chairs, but plenty of sunlight through the large windows in this first class area. (*Olympic*; Harland and Wolff Ltd.)

Top At 9 am on 14 April, the Cunarder *Caronia*, westbound, reports ice seen two days earlier. (Authors' collection.)

Above At 1.42 pm, *Baltic*'s captain relays a warning of ice seen earlier that day by the Greek steamship *Athenai*, a message retained by J. Bruce Ismay until 7 pm. (Authors' collection.)

Top right The first class menu for *Titanic*'s last luncheon features cockie leekie soup and grilled mutton chops. (Southampton City Museums.)

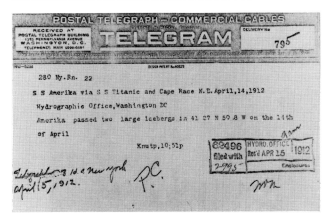

Middle right and right 1.45 pm: *Titanic* relays a message from the German steamer *Amerika* to the Hydrographic Office in Washington describing ice south of *Titanic*'s course. Even though it concerns navigation, the message is not brought to the bridge. (Authors' collection and National Oceanic and Atmospheric Administration.)

Extensive facilities provide first class passengers with many opportunities for physical activity. After a workout on gymnasium apparatus. . . (Harland and Wolff Ltd.)

Below . . .including a ride on an electric camel. . . (*L'Illustration*.)

Below right . . .one could take refreshing plunge in the pool. . . (Private collection.)

Bottom right . . .or relax in the Turkish bath. (Authors' collection.)

Left The first class barber's shop on C deck also sells souvenirs of the voyage. (*Olympic*; National Maritime Museum, Greenwich.)

Below left Green wicker decorates the port side verandah and palm court. Through the folded-back revolving door, the first class smoking room is visible. (*Olympic*; Harland and Wolff Ltd.)

Below third left The Café Parisienne on B deck's starboard side is a popular gathering place for young people throughout the day. (Harland and Wolff Ltd.)

Bottom left A men's public lavatory on A deck forward unabashedly displays its plumbing. (*Olympic*; Harland and Wolff Ltd.)

Below First class cabins include some of the best afloat. Cabin A21 is one of the more modest accommodations. . . (*Olympic; Shipbuilder.*)

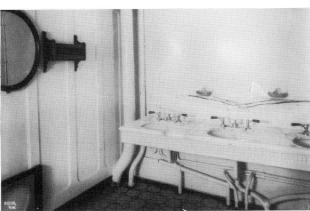

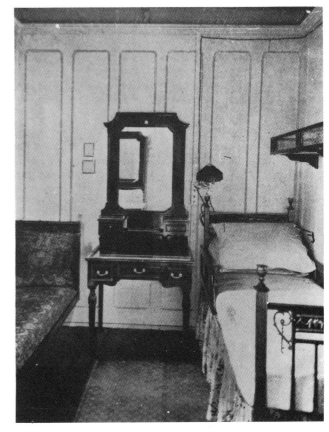

Left Perhaps the most palatial passenger accommodation on any liner, the starboard suite B51, 53 and 55 has its own private promenade. . . (Private collection.)

Middle left. . .and a luxurious sitting room augments its two bedrooms, private bath and trunk room. (*L'Illustration*.)

Bottom left A corresponding suite on the port side, B52, 54 and 56, occupied by J. Bruce Ismay, also has its own private promenade. (Harland and Wolff Ltd.)

The special B-deck suites are decorated by Messrs A. Heaton and Company, and feature a variety of period furniture and architectural designs.

Top right First class stateroom B57. (Harland and Wolff Ltd.)

Top far right First class stateroom B58. (Harland and Wolff Ltd.)

Middle right First class stateroom B59. (Harland and Wolff Ltd.)

Middle far right First class stateroom B60. (Harland and Wolff Ltd.)

Right First class stateroom B63. (Harland and Wolff Ltd.)

Far right First class stateroom B64. (Harland and Wolff Ltd.)

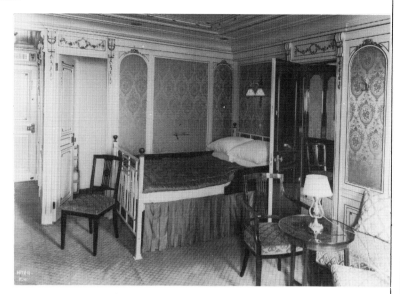

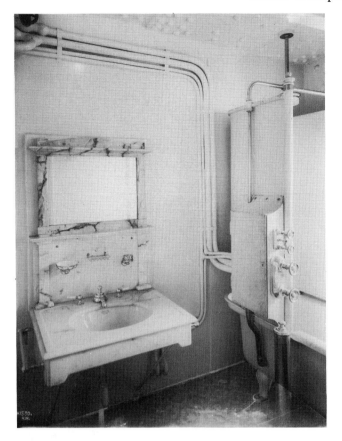

Left A marble wash basin and a cabinet shower are hallmarks of first class private bathrooms of the highest order. (*Olympic*; Harland and Wolff Ltd.)

Below left Simplicity denotes another private first class bathroom. A steward's call button is always nearby. (*Olympic*; Harland and Wolff Ltd.)

Below C deck has its share of period rooms, as this Louis XVI stateroom on *Olympic* demonstrates well. (Harland and Wolff Ltd.)

From bow to stern, C deck staterooms offer something for everyone.

Top right First class stateroom C9; (*Olympic*; *Shipbuilder*.)

Top far right First class stateroom C15. (*Olympic*; *Shipbuilder*.)

Middle right First class stateroom C67. (*Olympic*; *Shipbuilder*.)

Middle far right Parlour of suite C62. (*Olympic*; *Shipbuilder*.)

Bottom right First class stateroom C98. (*Olympic*; *Shipbuilder*.)

Bottom far right First class stateroom C117. (*Olympic*; *Shipbuilder*.)

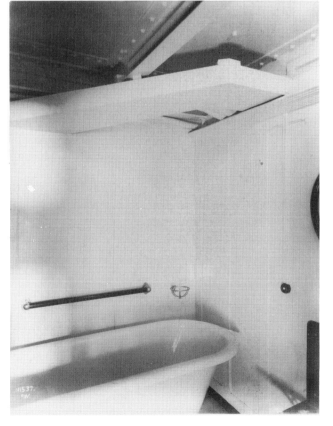

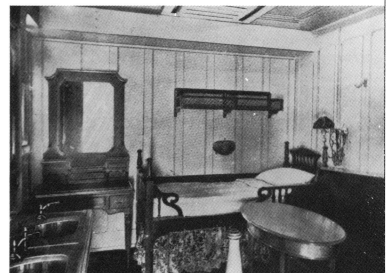

Right P. W. Fletcher, the ship's bugler, plays 'The Roast Beef of Old England' to summon all passengers to another sumptuous feast. (Authors' collection.)

Far right The final second class dinner features four main courses from which to choose. (Lloyd's of London.)

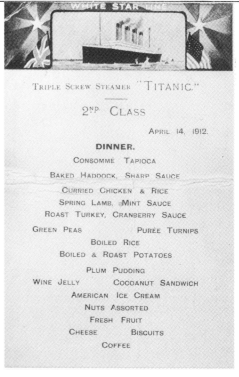

WHITE STAR

TRIPLE SCREW STEAMER "TITANIC."

2ND CLASS

APRIL 14, 1912.

DINNER.

CONSOMMÉ TAPIOCA

BAKED HADDOCK, SHARP SAUCE

CURRIED CHICKEN & RICE
SPRING LAMB, MINT SAUCE
ROAST TURKEY, CRANBERRY SAUCE

GREEN PEAS PURÉE TURNIPS
BOILED RICE
BOILED & ROAST POTATOES

PLUM PUDDING
WINE JELLY COCOANUT SANDWICH
AMERICAN ICE CREAM
NUTS ASSORTED
FRESH FRUIT
CHEESE BISCUITS
COFFEE

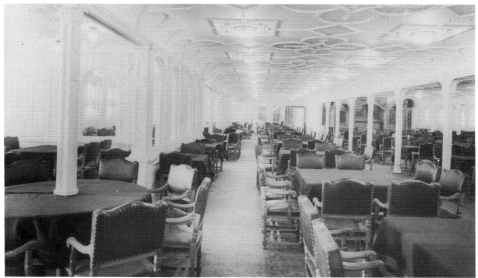

The first class dining saloon seats more than 500 people amid Jacobean splendour. (*Olympic*; Harland and Wolff Ltd.)

Right as dinner begins, the ship's orchestra, resplendent in their blue tuxedos, serenade the passengers with a varied repertoire of musical selections. (Authors' collection.)

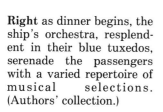

WHITE STAR LINE

MUSIC

REPERTOIRE.

Overtures.

1 Il Barbiere di Siviglia	...	Rossini
2 Zampa	...	Herold
3 Semiramide	...	Rossini
4 La Gazza ladra	...	"
5 Muta di Portici	...	Auber
6 Italiana in Algeri	...	Rossini
7 Tancredi	...	"
8 Guglielmo Tell	...	"
9 Morning, Noon and Night in Vienna		Suppè
10 Pique Dame	...	"
11 Poet and Peasant	...	"
12 Raymond	...	A. Thomas
13 Martha	...	Flotow
14 Agnes	...	F. Paer
15 The Bohemian Girl	...	Balfe

Operatic Selections, etc.

16 The Quaker Girl	...	Monckton
17 The Girl in the Train	...	Leo. Fall
18 Samson and Delilah	...	St. Saëns
19 Madame Sherry	...	K. Hoschna
20 Cadix	...	Valverde
21 Aida	...	Verdi
22 Thaïs	...	Massenet
23 The Chocolate Soldier	...	O. Strauss
24 Cavalleria Rusticana	...	Mascagni
25 Mignon	...	Thomas
26 Un Ballo in Maschera	...	Verdi
27 Pagliacci	...	Leoncavallo
28 Orphée Aux Enfers	...	Offenbach
29 Madam Butterfly	...	Puccini
30 The Dollar Princess	...	Leo Fall
31 A Waltz Dream	...	O. Straus
32 Miss Hook of Holland	...	Rubens
33 The Merry Widow	...	Lehar
34 Our Miss Gibbs	...	Monckton
35 The Arcadians	...	"
36 The Belle of Brittany	...	Talbot
37 Havana	...	Stuart

Right J. Bruce Ismay indicates the table preferred by Captain E. J. Smith (centre) and his own table (at top). . . (National Archives.)

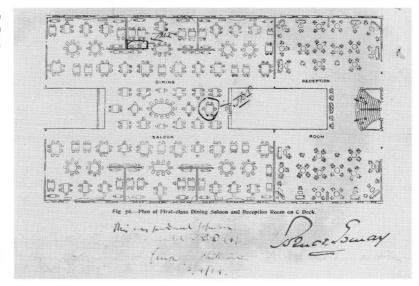

Below . . .next to the partition (rear, centre) forming a side alcove. (*Olympic*; Authors' collection.)

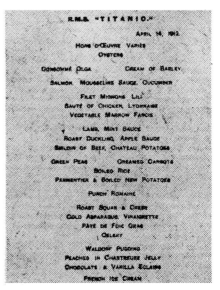

Above right Four hours before disaster, first class passengers enjoy a fine repast. . . (*Daily Mirror.*)

. . .as the orchestra's beautiful music continues under Wallace Hartley's baton. (THS.)

2

38 Dear Little Denmark	*Rubens*
39 The Fair Co-ed	*Luder*
40 The Grand Mogul	"
41 The Gay Musician	*Julian Edward*
42 A Trip to Japan	*Klein*
43 His Honour the Mayor	*Julian Edward*
44 The Red Mill	*V. Herbert*
45 The Prima Donna	"
46 The Three Twins	*Karl Hoschna*
47 The Prince of Pilsen	*Luder*
48 It Happened in Nordland	*V. Herbert*
49 Neptune's Daughter	"
50 Faust	*Gounod*
51 Carmen	*Bizet*
52 Il Trovatore	*Verdi*
53 Rigoletto	"
54 La Traviata	"
55 Puritani	*Bellini*
56 La Sonnambula	"
57 Lucia di Lammermoor	*Donizetti*
58 La Favorita	"
59 Tosca	*Puccini*
60 La Bohéme	"
61 The Mikado	*Sullivan*
62 Pirates of Penzance	"
63 Iolanthe	"
64 A Princess of Kensington	*E. German*
65 Merrie England	"
66 Tom Jones	"
67 Manon Lescaut	*Puccini*
68 Les Contes D'Hoffman	*Offenbach*
69 Mefistofele	*Boïto.*
70 Tannhauser	*Wagner*
71 Lohengrin	"
72 The Girls of Gottenburg	*Caryll & Monckton*
73 Haddon Hall	*Sullivan*
74 The Gondoliers	"
75 Recollections of Gounod	*Godfrey*
76 Sullivan's Melodies	"
77 The Maid and the Mummy	*A. Aarons*
78 Love's Lottery	*Julian Edwards*
79 M'lle Modisté	"
80 Miss Dolly Dollars	"
81 Wonderland	"

3

82 The Princess Beggar	*A. G. Robyn*
83 The Geisha	*Jones*
84 San Toy	"

Suites, Fantasias, etc.

85 Peer Gynt Suite	*Greig*
86 Three Dances: "Henry VIII"	*E. German*
87 Three Dances: "Nell Gwyn"	"
88 Three Dances: "Tom Jones"	"
89 The Rose	*Myddleton*
90 The Thistle	"
91 The Shamrock	"
92 American National Airs	*Tobani*
93 Plantation Songs	*Chtsam*
94 Canadian Songs	*Retford*
95 Tosti's Popular Songs	*Godfrey*
96 Popular Songs	*S. Adams*
97 Reminiscences of the Savoy	*M. Moore*
98 Reminiscences of Wales	*Godfrey*
99 Reminiscences of All Nations	"
100 National Anthems, Hymns, etc., of all Nations.	

Waltzes.

101 Love and Life in Holland	*Joyce*
102 Partners Galore	*G. V.*
103 The Druid's Prayer	*Davson*
104 Vision of Salome	*Joyce*
105 Remembrance	"
106 Beautiful Spring	*Lincke*
107 Wedding Dance	"
108 Comedie d'Amour	*G. Colin*
109 Valse Septembre	*F. Godwin*
110 Mondaine	*Bose*
111 Réve d'Artiste	"
112 Swing Song	*Hollaender*
113 Sphinx	*Popy*
114 Songe d'Automne	*Joyce*
115 La Lettre de Manon	*Gillet*
116 Cecilia	*Pether*
117 Apach's Dance	*Offenbach*
118 Verschmähte Liebe	*P. Lincke*
119 Lysistrata	"
120 Luna	"

Left In the à la carte restaurant, Captain E. J. Smith dines with the Wideners and their party. (*Olympic*; Harland and Wolff Ltd.)

Middle left At 7.30 pm, the Leyland Line freighter *Antillian* receives an ice report from its fleet mate *Californian*; *Titanic*'s operator overhears it, and Harold Bride delivers the message to the bridge. (Authors' collection.)

Bottom left As dinner comes to a close, some first class passengers retire to the reception room for their after-dinner coffee. An Axminster carpet and wicker furniture add to the decor. (*Olympic*; Authors' collection.)

Top right Many ladies go to the Georgian-style reading and writing room on A deck. (*Olympic*; THS/Allan C. O'Malley collection.)

Top far right Others adjourn to the Louis Quinze lounge, with its comfortable green colour scheme and always-intriguing bookcase. (*Olympic*; Bob Forrest collection.)

Middle right At 9.40 pm, the liner *Mesaba* warns *Titanic* of an extensive ice field in the immediate vicinity. The message is not taken to the bridge. (Authors' collection.)

Middle far right Forty-five minutes later, at 10.25, the Allan liner *Parisian*'s wireless operator Sutherland sends *Titanic* a position report, then goes off the air until 8 am the next morning. (Authors' collection.)

Right Men in first class could enjoy a late-night cigar or drink in the Georgian smoking room, aft on A deck. . . (Byron Collection, Museum of the City of New York.)

Far right. . . where they are surrounded by the finest mahogany, mother-of-pearl inlay work and stained glass windows. (*Olympic* [just prior to scrapping]; THS.)

By now, many first class passengers have gone to their cabins. They include (Row 1) Christopher Head, Mrs Nelle Snyder and Mrs George M. Stone. (Row 2) Frank Carlson, Adolphe Saalfield and Walter M. Clark and (Row 3) Robert W. Daniel.

Below left As the three first class elevators whisk passengers to their staterooms. . . (Olympic THS.)

Below. . .the clock's allegorical figures of Honour and Glory crown another hour of Time under the great wrought iron and glass dome above the forward first class entrance. It is 11 pm and lights in many public rooms are extinguished. A quiet calm, broken only by occasional footsteps and the distant throb of the engines, envelopes the ship. (J. Welton Smith collection.)

Chapter Eleven

DISASTER

Seven bells. . .

When lookouts Frederick Fleet and Reginald Lee had come on duty at 10 pm the sky was cloudless and the air clear. Now, at around 11.30 pm, just half an hour before they were to be relieved, a slight haze had appeared, directly ahead and about two points on either side. High in the crow's nest, fifty feet above the fo'c's'le deck, the two men strained their eyes to see what might lie through and beyond the mist.

Suddenly — his training causing his reflexes to function instinctively — Fleet gave the warning bell three sharp rings ('Object directly ahead') and immediately reached across the crow's nest to the bridge telephone, in its compartment on the starboard side. He rang its bell urgently.

'Are you there?'

'Yes. What do you see?'

'Iceberg right ahead.'

'Thank you.'

Fleet replaced the telephone and gripped the crow's nest rail. At first sight the object was a dark mass. Even now, as it approached through its enveloping haze, it had no white. Now it was just off the bow, higher than the fo'c's'le head but not so high as the crow's nest. . .a great black mass. . .

The two men felt the vessel's veering to port and each sensed rather than actually felt the impact with the berg. As the ice moved along the ship's starboard side they looked down on to its irregular top and saw white for the first time, a sort of fringe around its top. And as the berg, still clad in haze, moved down the vessel's length and passed by, only then did the other side appear to be white. And it was the white side which was visible as the ice drifted away from the liner, moving astern, seemingly surrounded by its own peculiar light.

Fleet turned to Lee. There had been such little noise, only the brittle smash of ice fragments hitting the forward deck area. 'That was a narrow shave.' Neither man realized the severity of the encounter.

On the bridge, the sound of three bells from the crow's nest instantly alerted the men on duty. The telephone was answered immediately by sixth officer Moody, junior officer of the watch. Moody's 'Thank you' to Fleet was followed in the same breath by his report to Murdoch, repeating the message, 'Iceberg right ahead!' Murdoch, too, reacted instinctively: he rushed to the telegraph to order the engines stopped and reversed, calling at the same moment to quartermaster Robert Hichens, 'Hard-a-starboard'. Quickly he glanced at a set of printed instructions posted near the helmsman: 'In case of emergency, to close watertight doors on tank top, press bell; push for 10 seconds to give alarm; then move switch to "on" position and keep it there. . .' He then reached for the lever which electrically activated the doors.

Hichens responded immediately to Murdoch's command. He spun the wheel hard over, until it could turn no more. The great ship began to swing, and had already moved two points to port* — a deflection southward of west which, if it had been completed, would have been a forty-degree turn — when the impact occurred.

Between sighting and collision it had taken little more than half a minute. Prompt action by officer of the watch Murdoch had prevented a head-on collision with the berg's mass. But a granite-hard spur projecting from its main bulk struck *Titanic*'s underbelly on the starboard side about twelve feet above the keel, scraping and bumping along a jagged, irregular 300-foot length, opening to the sea's inrush the forepeak, number one hold, number

---

*Prior to a 1928 international agreement, the words 'port' and 'starboard' when used for steering orders referred to the direction the tiller, or wheel, was to be turned: 'Port' meant 'Port the tiller', with the rudder and ship's head going to starboard, and vice versa. Today, the words 'right' and 'left' are used, as are the directions of intent for the turns.

two hold, number three hold, number six boiler room, and poking about six feet beyond the bulk-head of number five boiler room.

Fourth officer Boxhall, on his way from his quarters to the bridge, heard the crow's nest's three warning bells. Approaching the bridge, he heard Murdoch's order to the quartermaster and the clamour of the engine room telegraph's bells. Entering the bridge area, Boxhall noticed the telegraph indicating 'Full Speed Astern', and he saw Murdoch pulling the lever which closed the water-tight doors. With the others he felt the long, grinding sensation of impact as the liner continued its slow port turn. Glancing to his side, Boxhall saw Captain Smith.

'What have we struck?' the commander demanded of Murdoch.

'An iceberg, Sir. I hard-a-starboarded and reversed the engines and I was going to hard-a-port around it, but she was too close. I could not do any more. I have closed the watertight doors.'

'The watertight doors are closed? And have you rung the warning bell?'

'Yes, Sir.'

Captain Smith and first officer Murdoch walked quickly to the starboard bridge wing, peering aft, looking for the berg.

Returning inside, the commander ordered Boxhall to inspect the forward area, below, and report back to him as quickly as possible. Boxhall departed and the captain laid his hand on the engine room telegraph's handles, moving them to 'Half Ahead'. He then dispatched standby quartermaster Alfred Olliver to take a message to chief engineer Bell. When Olliver returned, the engines were stopped again, this time for good.

If his own men were prompt in reporting to him, chief engineer Bell already knew what was happening. While standing at the forward, starboard side of number six boiler room, leading stoker Frederick Barrett had just received the order to 'Stop!' and was issuing his own order to shut down the dampers. He heard the impact's crunching and then a sound like thunder rolling forward towards him. Water suddenly appeared — so quickly that Barrett had no idea *how* — pouring through a gash in the ship's side about two feet above the stokehold floor and about two feet in front of where Barrett stood. He barely had time to run towards the bulkhead between boiler room number six and number five, aft, when the watertight door began to descend.

Only James Hesketh, the engineer on duty, and George Beauchamp, a stoker, were able to get through the door before it closed. Barrett used the emergency escape ladder.

Boxhall returned to the bridge after a fifteen-minute tour. During the examination he, himself, had seen no damage above F deck, but he had been told by postal clerk John Smith that water was coming in the lower mail sorting room, and that mail sacks were being moved to the deck above. On his way back to the bridge, Boxhall alerted second officer Lightoller and third officer Pitman (each of whom had, a few minutes earlier, stepped on deck to see why the ship had stopped, and had then returned to his respective cabin to await orders); on being alerted to the condition by Boxhall, each man hurriedly presented himself to Captain Smith on the bridge.

Boxhall was detailed by the commander to work out the ship's position. He moved quickly to the navigation room and began pouring over the chart. Noting the appended ice warnings from earlier wireless traffic, he spotted the position he had worked out earlier from the 7.30 pm stellar observation, which Captain Smith had entered on the chart around 10 pm.

Since 5.50 pm the ship had been on a course of South 86 West true. (The steering compass course was North 71 West, a deflection of two points from the standard compass reading of North 73 West, but this was a known factor for which thorough compensation had been made.)

Using the ship's course, the 7.30 pm stellar observation and *his own estimate* of the ship's speed at 22 knots, Boxhall worked out a position based on dead reckoning.* He hastily scribbled his findings on a scrap of paper, hurried out on to the bridge and gave the paper to Captain Smith.

41° 46′ N, 50° 14′ W.

The captain himself took the position to the wire-less room several minutes after midnight. Handing the paper to wireless operator Phillips, he ordered a call for assistance.

CQD. . . CQD. . .

The first twenty minutes after the collision set the stage for the drama which ensued. Just as a kaleido-scope exhibits an endless variety of symmetrical forms, so did activities aboard *Titanic* between 11.40 pm 14 April and 2.20 am 15 April offer an infinite variety of human emotions and behaviour. . .

---

*If Boxhall failed to take into account the one-knot southerly current through which *Titanic* was passing, an error of four miles in latitude could have entered his figures. During the eight-to-midnight watch, the ship's clocks were set back 23 minutes to compensate for west-ward progress. Did he remember to include this time change in gauging the distance travelled? And the ship's speed was 21½ knots, not the 22 which Boxhall estimated. These elements, combined in an extremely rough estimate, might approximate an actual position four miles south and six miles east of his calculated position.

Disaster

Sunday, 14 April 1912 — 11.40 pm. (Atlantic Mutual Insurance Company.)

From the crow's nest, lookout Frederick Fleet **below** glimpses the approaching iceberg, rings the warning bell three times and telephones the bridge: 'Iceberg right ahead'. Later he sketches his impression of the berg's initial appearance. (*Daily Sketch*/THS/ Authors' collection.*)

*All plan sections are the authors' copyrighted work. (See end papers for full plans.)

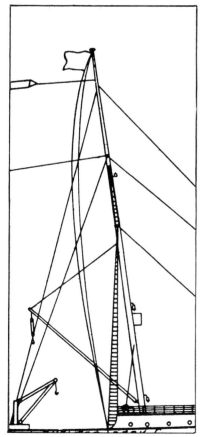

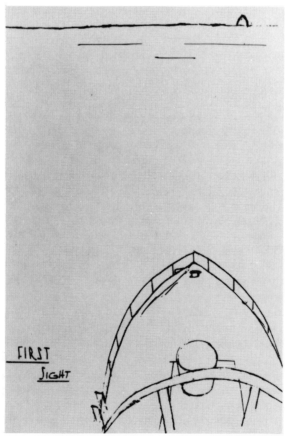

FIRST SIGHT

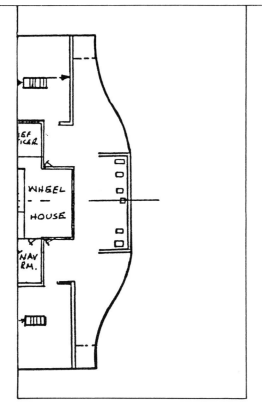

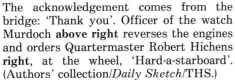

The acknowledgement comes from the bridge: 'Thank you'. Officer of the watch Murdoch **above right** reverses the engines and orders Quartermaster Robert Hichens **right**, at the wheel, 'Hard-a-starboard'. (Authors' collection/*Daily Sketch*/THS.)

IMPACT

Disaster

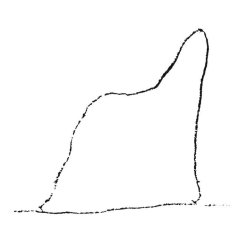

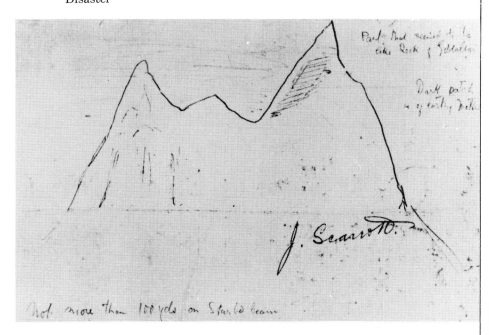

Frederick Barrett
leading stoker

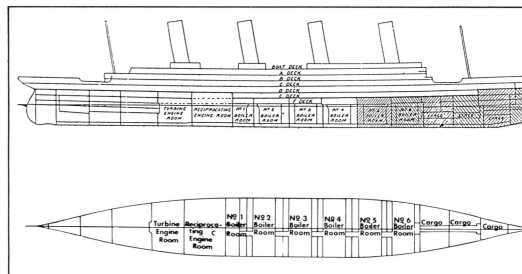

Above The huge liner swings two points to port before a spur from the passing berg tears a 300-foot-long hole in her starboard side. Leading fireman Frederick Barrett is astonished to see water pouring through a gash in the side of boiler room 6. The watertight door between boiler room 6 and 5 is quickly closed in front of him, and he uses an emergency ladder to escape the now-flooding compartment. (*Daily Mirror.*)

Top right Second class passenger Lawrence Beesley, reading in his cabin D56 before retiring, notices nothing more than what seems to be an extra heave of the ship's engines and a slight dancing movement of his bunk mattress. (*Illustrated London News.*)

Centre right Colonel Archibald Gracie, unable to see anything wrong from the boat deck, decends to the first class entrance hall. He encounters his friend, James Clinch Smith, who shows the colonel a small piece of ice from the berg. Gradually, the story of the collision spreads among passengers. (Authors' collection.)

142

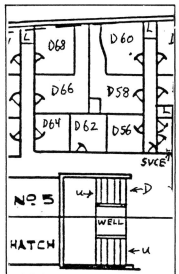

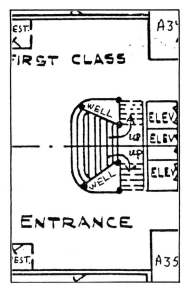

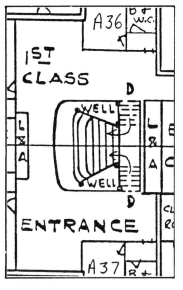

Harland and Wolff managing director Thomas Andrews **bottom left** has spent much of the evening in his cabin, A36, pouring over the ship's plans and noting possible modifications based on his observations so far during the voyage. He is so absorbed that he does not notice the collision or the cessation of forward movement.

A knock at the door. Andrews is asked to come to the bridge. Upon his hurried arrival, Captain Smith asks him to accompany him on a tour of the ship. Using the crew's companionways to avoid disturbing passengers, the two men inspect the ship's forward area. Within ten minutes they are back on the bridge.

They confer briefly. During the first ten minutes since the collision, water has risen fourteen feet above the keel, forward. The first five compartments are filling and the water's weight has already begun to pull the bow down. The watertight bulkhead between boiler rooms 6 and 5 extends only as high as E deck. When the bow sinks lower, the water from boiler room number 6 will flow into number 5. This will draw the bow even lower, and the water will flow into number 4, then 3, 2 . . .

The ship is doomed.

Captain Smith hesitates before asking the inevitable question, 'How long have we?'

Andrews jots a few figures on a scrap of paper before answering. 'An hour and a half. Possibly two. Not much longer.'

Captain Smith does not hesitate now. 'Uncover the boats. . .'

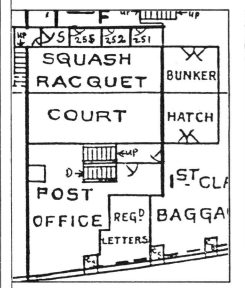

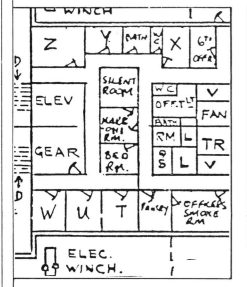

James B. Williamson,
postal clerk

John R. Jago Smith,
postal clerk

Oscar S. Woody,
postal clerk

John George Phillips,
senior wireless operator

Harold Sydney Bride
junior wireless operator

Above By 11.55 pm, fifteen minutes after the collision, the post office on G deck, forward is already flooding. The five postal clerks — three American, two British — struggle through two feet of water to transfer 200 pouches of registered mail to the sorting room on F deck. (*Southampton and District Pictorial*/ Washington, DC *Evening Star*.)

Above and left A few minutes after midnight, Captain Smith hurries from the bridge to the wireless room, where he hands to chief telegraphist John George Phillips the ship's position, worked out moments earlier by fourth officer Boxhall. 'You had better get assistance,' the Captain says. Second telegraphist Harold Sydney Bride rises from the instrument. He had just relieved Phillips, but now Phillips sits down and prepares to send the distress call. (Marconi Marine Ltd/Private Collection.)

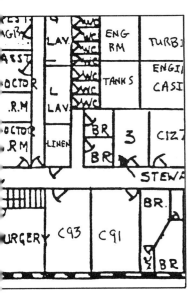

Margaret Graham,
first class passenger

Ernest W. King,
purser's clerk

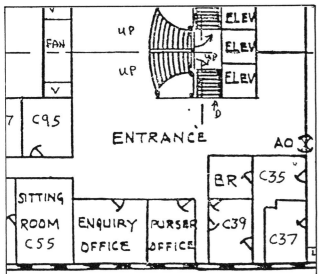

Above Nineteen-year-old Margaret Graham is in cabin C91 with her governess, Miss Elizabeth W. Shutes. At about 12.10 am, seeing a ship's officer in the corridor, Miss Shutes asks if there is any danger. The officer responds, 'No,' but she hears him say, down the hall, 'I think we can keep out the water a bit longer'. Margaret is nibbling a chicken sandwich. Her hand begins to shake so badly that the chicken keeps falling out of the sandwich. (*Daily Sketch.*)

Left Many of the ship's passengers, some still dazed from their sudden awakening, line up at the counter of the purser's office to claim their valuables. The air is one of urgency, but there is no confusion as the staff, including purser's clerk E. W. King, distribute the valuables.

Occasionally a passing friend exchanges good-natured jibes with members of the line. A number of passengers are still not aware of the danger and, in spite of the stewards' continued urgings, make no preparations to leave the ship. (*Daily Mirror.*)

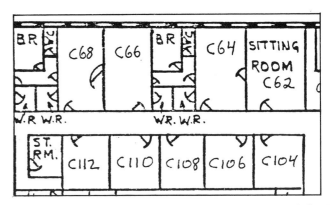

Bottom and above Other passengers, more aware of the emergent condition, do prepare to leave. In cabin C104, Major Arthur Peuchen dresses warmly and leaves quickly. Remaining behind on the cabin table is a tin box containing securities valued at more than $300,000. (*Philadelphia Inquirer.*)

Frederick Wright,
sports instructor

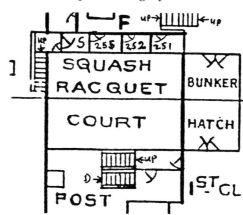

J. Maxwell,
carpenter

James P. Moody,
sixth officer

W. Ennis,
bath steward

By 12.25 am, the order has been passed to load the lifeboats. Colonel Archibald Gracie, in search of extra blankets for the boats, encounters squash rackets instructor Fred Wright on the stairway at C deck. 'Hadn't we better cancel that appointment for tomorrow morning?' the colonel asks jocularly. Wright replies in the affirmative. What he does not tell Gracie is that the squash rackets court on G deck is already flooded to the ceiling. (*Daily Mirror*.)

Brooke Webb,
smoke room steward

Reginald Barker,
second purser

John Charman,
saloon steward

Percy C. Taylor,
cellist, orchestra

Theodore Brailey,
pianist, orchestra

George Krins,
violist, orchestra.

Crewmen of *Titanic* struggle through the first hour following the collision to determine the extent of the damage, prepare boats for launching and calm passengers' fears.

146

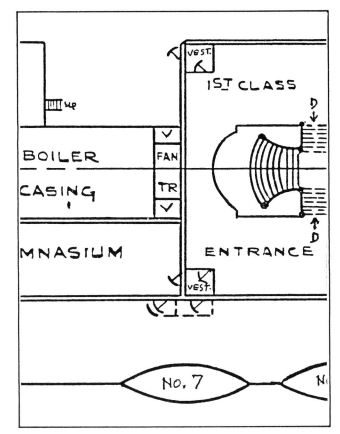

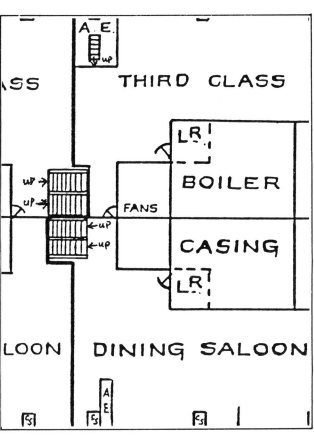

Miss Dorothy Gibson

Pierre Marechal

James R. McGough

William T. Sloper

Archie Jewell

Gus Cohen

At 12.45 am, boat number 7 is lowered without confusion. Although having a capacity of 65, it has only 28 people in it. As the boat stands off, its stunned passengers spend more than ninety minutes watching *Titanic* slowly sink.

Among the first class passengers aboard: Miss Dorothy Gibson, model and actress (*Morning Telegraph*.) Mr Pierre Marechal, French aviator (*Daily Sketch*.) Mr James R. McGough, Philadelphia banker (*Philadelphia Public Ledger*.) Mr William T. Sloper (*Hartford Times*.) Look-out Archie Jewell helps to man the boat.

About an hour after the collision, third class passenger Gus Cohen passes the third class dining saloon. He observes many gathered there in prayer, a number with rosaries in their hands. (Private collection.)

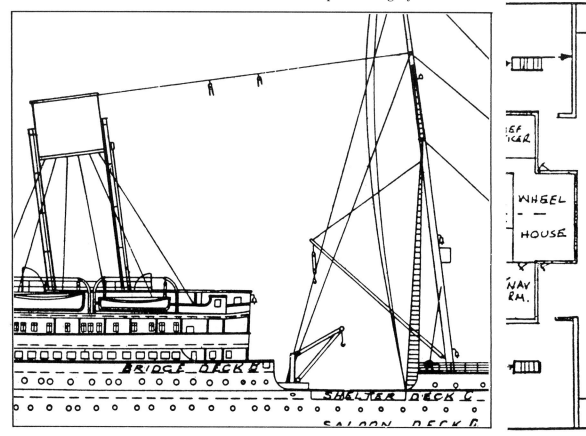

Mrs Eleanor Widener

At about 12.45 am, under fourth officer Boxhall's direction, quartermaster George Thomas Rowe begins firing distress rockets from the socket mounted on the bridge rail at a 20-degree angle. Each socket distress rocket shoots upward to a height of 800 feet before exploding with a thunderous report and scattering twelve brilliant white stars. Altogether, eight rockets are fired at about five-minute intervals. Rowe leaves the bridge at 1.25 am.

During this period, Boxhall observes a vessel approach *Titanic* to within five or six miles. He sees her green (starboard) and her red (port) lights at first, as though the vessel is approaching head on. Not much later he views the red light, and two mast-head lights, with his naked eye. From the distance between masthead lights, he judges the vessel to be a four-masted steamer. With quartermaster Rowe, Boxhall tries to reach the passing vessel with the Morse lamp. But the vessel passes, turning very slowly until only her stern light is visible, and then vanishes.

Mrs Marion Thayer

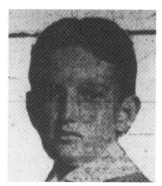

Jack Thayer

148

Disaster

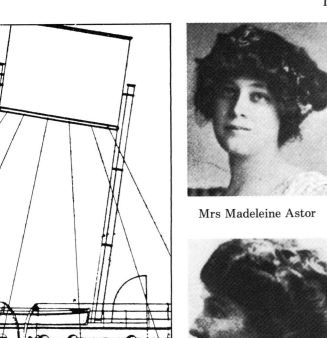

Mrs Madeleine Astor

Mrs Lucile Carter

When second officer Lightoller lowers port boat number 4 from the boat deck to the promenade deck at 12.45, he intends to load passengers through the windows in the promenade deck's forward screen. The windows, however, are closed. Lightoller sends someone down to crank them open and goes on loading other boats from the boat deck. Meanwhile, a group of women, children and maids assemble on the promenade deck. They can see the lowered boat outside the windows, but have no way of boarding.

Finally, Lightoller finishes loading the other boats and returns to number 4. The windows are now open and the boat is pulled inboard by a wire hawser. The women are assisted into the boat after more than an hour's wait.

And they are people not accustomed to waiting: Mrs George Widener (Eleanor), Harry Widener, Mrs John Jacob Astor (Madeleine), Mrs John B. Thayer (Marian), Jack Thayer, and Mrs William E. Carter (Lucile).

By 12.45 am, boiler room number 5 is almost empty. The stokers have been sent to their boat stations. But leading fireman Fred Barrett and a few others have stayed behind to help junior assistant second engineers Herbert Harvey and Jonathan Shepherd in operating the pumps. Shepherd has fallen into an open manhole and has broken his leg. He has been carried to a pump room at one end of the boiler room and is made comfortable while others go about their work until given orders from the bridge to report to boat stations.

Barrett and Harvey stay behind to continue manning the pumps, and it looks for a while as though their efforts are succeeding. Suddenly, without warning, the bulkhead between boiler rooms 6 and 5 gives way with a tremendous inrush of icy sea water.

Harvey orders Barrett up the escape ladder. The water is bursting upward as Barrett, clambering up the ladder, turns to see engineer Harvey, in the murky metal cavern far below, running towards where his fellow-engineer Shepherd lies helpless. Before he can reach his friend, Shepherd is engulfed by the surging water. (*Marine Engineer.*)

Jonathan Shepherd,   Herbert Harvey,
junior assistant second engineers

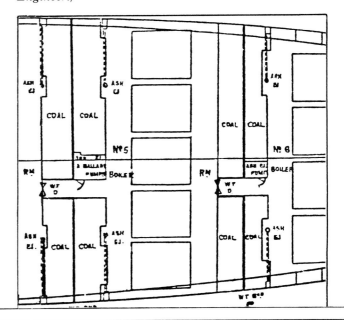

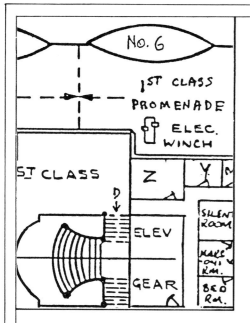

Turrell Cavendish,
first class passenger

Portside boat number 6 is lowered at about 12.55 am. As the boat is loading, Mr Turrell Cavendish brings his wife to the deck's edge and exchanges a lingering last kiss with her before assisting her into the boat.

Less formal is the arrival aboard of Denver socialite Margaret 'Molly' Brown. She is walking away from the deck area when strong arms seize her and drop her four feet into the descending boat.

As the boat is lowered in a series of jerks, the passengers see there is but one man in it. Their shouted appeals for aid result in first class passenger Major Arthur Peuchen being permitted by second officer Lightoller to slide down the falls to assist.

The boat is in the charge of quartermaster Robert Hichens, whose behaviour afloat — particularly his reluctance to return to pick up survivors, and his cavalier attitude toward female passengers — will be much criticized. Hichens will not be censured for his alleged actions. As number 6 reaches the water, it carries 28 passengers and crew. (Library of Congress/*Daily Mirror*.)

Mrs Turrell Cavendish,
first class passenger

Margaret 'Molly' Brown,
first class passenger

J. Bruce Ismay assists in loading boat 5 with women and children from the large crowd gathered nearby. Among them is first class passenger Marguerite Frolicher, age 22. When the boat is nearly full, no more women can be found, and third officer H. J. Pitman permits several men to get in, including tennis star Karl Behr.

As boat 5 creaks down towards the flat sea, the pace is too slow for overly anxious Bruce Ismay. 'Lower away! Lower away!' he cries again and again, waving one arm in a giant circle.

Fifth officer Lowe, supervizing the boat's lowering, can tolerate this no more. 'If you'll get the hell out of the way I'll be able to do something! You want me to lower away quickly? You'll have me drown the whole lot of them!' Ismay, crushed, leaves, and number 5's progress resumes.

But its problems are not yet over. First class passenger Dr H. W. Frauenthal decides the time is right to join his wife in the boat, and with his brother, jumps into the boat as it is lowered away. In doing so, he dislocates two ribs of Mrs Annie May Stengel, already in the boat, and knocks her unconscious.

Later, passenger Edward P. Calderhead is transferred in mid-ocean to lifeboat 7. (*Daily Sketch/Philadelphia Bulletin*/Arnold Watson collection.)

Mrs Annie May Stengel,
first class passenger

Edward P. Calderhead,
first class passenger

Karl Behr,
first class passenger

Miss Marguerite Frolicher,
first class passenger

Harold G. Lowe,
fifth officer

When boat 3 is loading, first officer Murdoch instructs able-bodied seaman George Moore to jump in the boat and pass the ladies in. When there are no more ladies, men passengers are accepted.

Gentlemen passengers help the ladies board, then stand back, not boarding themselves. Among these heroes are Messrs Hays, Davidson, Roebling and Howard B. Case, the London manager of the Vacuum Oil Company.

Six-year-old Robert Douglas Spedden boards with his mother and father. Later, in the boat, as the sun comes up and the extent of the ice-field can be seen, little Douglas will exclaim, 'Oh, Muddie, look at the beautiful North Pole with no Santa Claus on it!'

There are 32 on the boat, including eleven crewmen. (Lloyd's *Deathless Story/Daily Sketch*.)

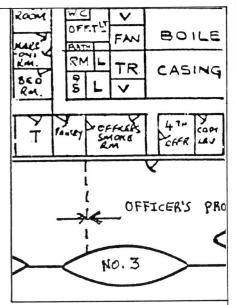

Howard B. Case,
first class passenger

Robert Douglas Spedden,
first class passenger

Samuel Collins,
crewman

First officer William Murdoch is in charge of lowering emergency boat number 1, forward on the starboard side. After seeing whether he and his wife might board boats 7 and 3, Sir Cosmo Duff-Gordon approaches Murdoch and asks, 'May we get in that boat?' 'With the greatest pleasure,' replies Murdoch, who hands Lucille and Miss Francatelli, her secretary, into the boat. He then allows several American men to board. The boat's capacity is forty. It leaves *Titanic* with twelve aboard, seven of whom are crew.

It is not unlikely that Murdoch sends the boat away thinking it will afford a means of saving many lives of those in the water after *Titanic* sinks. No seaman in the boat is willing to assume this responsibility, however, and none of the passengers thinks to remind the crew of it.

Below (Lest the moral of the under-filled boat be lost to its readers, a London newspaper prints a diagram of boat number 1, carefully delineating the position of each of its occupants.) (Private collection/*Daily Sketch/Daily Mirror*.)

Sir Cosmo Duff Gordon

Lady Duff Gordon

George Symons,
boat 1's helmsman

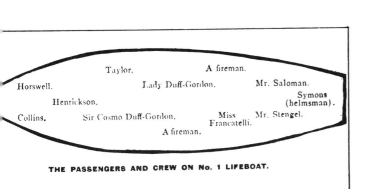

THE PASSENGERS AND CREW ON No. 1 LIFEBOAT.

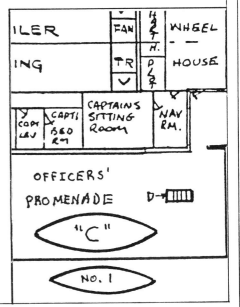

151

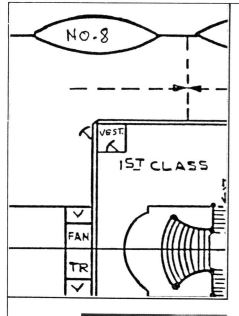

NO. 8

VEST.

1ST CLASS

FAN

TR

Miss Ellen Bird,
first class passenger

Isidor Straus,
first class passenger

Mrs Ida Straus,
first class passenger

Around 12.30 am, as the first lifeboats are being prepared, word comes down from the bridge that only women and children are to be loaded.

Together on deck at this time are Isidor and Ida Straus and their friend, Colonel Archibald Gracie. Gracie recalls Mrs Straus, when asked to join a group preparing to board a boat, stating emphatically, 'No! I will not be separated from my husband. As we have lived, so will we die. Together'. Mr Straus is equally emphatic when it is suggested that, because of his age, no one would object if he is allowed to accompany his wife: 'No. I do not wish any distinction in my favour which is not granted to others'.

Mr and Mrs Straus sit down on steamer chairs on the glass-enclosed A deck and watch the hectic activity stirring around them.

At 12.50 am while portside boat number 8 is loading, the Strauses are seen on the boat deck encouraging Mrs Straus's maid, Ellen Bird, to enter the boat. After the maid is safely aboard, Ida and Isidor leave the deck and go below to meet their fate together.

When all passengers and crew are aboard, the boat carries only 28.

Thomas Jones, AB helps to load boat 8. At the American Senate's inquiry, he is asked, 'Can you give me the names of any passengers on this boat?'

The witness responded, 'One lady — she had a lot to say and I put her to steering the boat'.

Lucy-Noel Martha, Countess of Rothes, is at the tiller all night, staunch and steadfast, steering steadily for what all believe is a ship's masthead light not ten miles away. As the countess steers, her cousin Gladys Cherry pulls an oar. (*New York News*/Private Collection.)

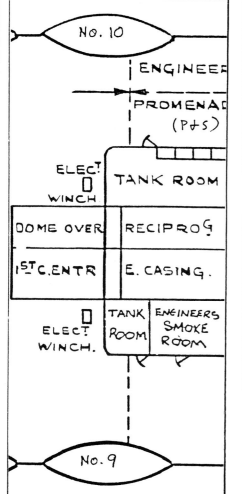

NO. 10

ENGINEER

PROMENAD
(P+S)

ELECT
WINCH.

TANK ROOM

DOME OVER

RECIPROG

1ST C. ENTR

E. CASING.

ELECT
WINCH.

TANK
ROOM

ENGINEERS
SMOKE
ROOM

NO. 9

Mrs May Futrelle,
first class passenger

Jacques Futrelle,
first class passenger

Lowered to the boat deck's edge, boat 9 is filled almost to capacity. There are at least 56 on board, including two or three men who enter the boat when no other women come forward. Loading is halted when an elderly lady raises a great fuss and refuses to board. She pulls away from the solicitous crew and goes below.

By now, the ship has developed a noticeable list and, after a French lady falls and slightly injures herself trying to enter the boat, Purser Herbert McElroy stations three men in the boat to assist the women in bridging the widening gap between boat and ship.

Novelist Jacques Futrelle escorts his wife to the boat, and encountering reluctance on her part to leave him, says, 'For God's sake, go! It's your last chance! Go!' After further indecision, Mrs Futrelle's choice is made for her as an officer forces her into the boat.

Once afloat, there is difficulty in following the officer's instruction to pull clear. For a while, it appears that no one has a knife with which to cut loose the oars' lashings. (*Daily Mirror*/*Philadelphia Inquirer*.)

As *Titanic* sinks by the bow, the firing of distress rockets continues, with no discernible results. Boats are now more fully loaded. (Painting by Michael V. Ralph.)

Mrs Emma Schabert, first class passenger

Filled from A deck, boat 11 is overloaded at least five beyond its rated capacity. At least seventy are jammed in, more than in any other boat. Among those on board is first class passenger Mrs Emma Schabert.

The problems of boat 11 continue: Upon reaching the water, it is almost swamped by the fat jet of water from the ship's pump discharge. The after block of the tackle gets jammed. (Second officer Lightoller later noted that 'The sea was so flat that when the boats were lowered we had to overhaul the tackles to unhook them because there was not the slightest lift on the boat to allow for slacking and unhooking.')

In the crowded conditions, tempers flare, and some women complain about having to stand, while others register protests about the men's smoking. (Kyrill Schabert — Michael Findlay collection.)

By 1.25 am there is little doubt that the remaining boats will have to take aboard many more than those which have been lowered earlier.

Starboard boat 13 is lowered at 1.25 with 64 aboard — mainly second and third class women and children. It is first brought to the level of A deck, and after all women in view are boarded, men are permitted to enter. Among them are Lawrence Beesley and Dr Washington Dodge, who had seen his wife and son off earlier in boat 7.

Nearing the water, number 13 encounters a great volume of water being discharged from the ship's side. Fortunately, the occupants' shouts to 'cease lowering' are quickly heeded, and they are able to push away from the rushing stream.

Reaching the sea, they are unable to detach the falls — again because the sea is so calm there is no lift to the boat. They drift aft, still attached, coming directly under boat 15, which begins its descent about thirty seconds after number 13. Once again the occupants of number 13 shout for relief, and once again the response of the men on deck is swift. The lowering of number 15 is stopped instantly, and those aboard boat 13 are able to cut the falls and drift out from underneath. (Private collection/Mr and Mrs Arthur Dodge/*Daily Sketch*/*Sphere*.)

Lawrence Beesley, second class passenger

Dr Washington Dodge, first class passenger

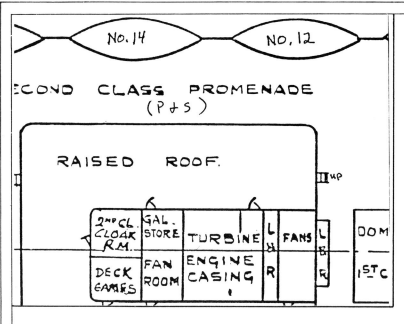

SECOND CLASS PROMENADE
(P & S)

RAISED ROOF.

| 2ND CL. CLOAK RM. | GAL. STORE | TURBINE | | FANS | | DOM |
| DECK GAMES | FAN ROOM | ENGINE CASING | L H R | | L B R | 1ST C |

Margaret Devaney,
third class passenger

Harold G. Lowe,
fifth officer

Joseph Scarrott,
able-bodied seaman

Benjamin Guggenheim,
first class passenger

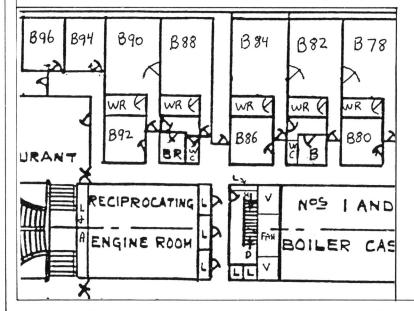

B96	B94	B90	B88	B84	B82	B78
		WR	WR	WR	WR	WR
		B92		B86		B80
URANT			BR WC		WC B	
	RECIPROCATING				NOS 1 AND
	ENGINE ROOM			FAN	BOILER CAS

Second officer Charles Lightoller supervizes the lowering of boat 12 at 1.25 am with forty women and children. Chief officer Henry T. Wilde passes the boat's passengers along.

At first manned only by able-bodied seaman Frederick Clench, the boat is later placed in charge of able seaman John Poigndestre. As the boat descends, a male passenger jumps into the boat as it passes B deck.

Once it reaches the water, there is again difficulty in unhooking the falls. Passenger Margaret Devaney lends a pocket knife to seaman Poigndestre, who cuts through the ropes.

The partially filled boat is rowed off, and after the sinking is tied to boats 4, 10, 14 and collapsible D. Fifth officer Lowe then transfers all passengers out of boat 14 to allow him to return for those in the water. Additional passengers come to boat 12 from collapsible D and overturned collapsible B.

When boat 12 arrives alongside *Carpathia* she is overloaded, with at least seventy on board. (Mrs George A. Landsberg — Michael Findlay collection.)

By 1.30 am panic has begun among some of the passengers. While portside boat 14 is being lowered with almost sixty on board, a group of unruly passengers crowds the rails and threatens to jump in the heavily-loaded boat. To frighten them away, fifth officer Lowe fires three shots down the ship's side, with no intent to cause injury. The warning is successful, and the boat reaches the water without further incident.

As number 14 stands off about 150 yards from the sinking liner, Lowe herds five boats (4, 10, 12 and collapsible D, as well as his own 14) together and transfers passengers from the latter into the other boats, distributing them as evenly as possible. In the confusion, families and loved ones are separated from one another.

Transfer completed, Lowe and four volunteer crewmen, including seaman Joseph Scarrott, row back to where *Titanic* has since sunk, to pick up survivors. They rescue only three, one of whom, William F. Hoyt, dies shortly after being brought aboard.

Still later, after *Carpathia* is sighted, Lowe has a sail up on number 14 and is sailing smartly toward the rescue ship when he encounters collapsible A, almost swamped. Hastily he transfers its twenty men and one woman to boat 14, in which they arrive at *Carpathia*'s side. (Private collection.)

As the inevitability of the evening's outcome becomes increasingly apparent, those for whom there will be no place in the boats begin to comtemplate and to act. Smelting magnate Benjamin Guggenheim and his manservant Victor Giglio leave the boat deck and return to their cabins, B82-84 and B86, respectively. There, they change into evening dress, Guggenheim shedding the heavy sweater-and-lifebelt combination proffered by his steward, Henry Etches. 'We've dressed up in our best and are prepared to go down like gentlemen,' he explains. (*New York Times*.)

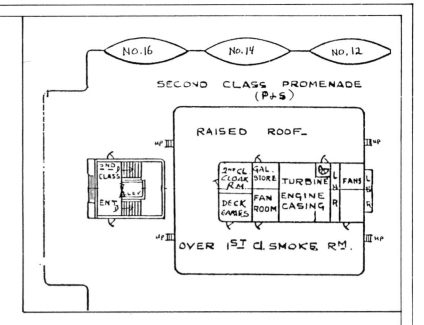

Boat 16 is lowered at 1.35 am with more than fifty on board. Among them are three stewardesses, including Violet Jessop and Elizabeth Leather. Jessop will repeat the evacuation experience less than five years later when *Titanic*'s sister ship *Britannic* sinks in the Aegean Sea. Mrs Leather offers to assist in rowing *Titanic*'s boat 16 — not because she has to, but because doing so will keep her warm. (Arnold Watson collection.)

Following his encounter with fifth officer Lowe during the lowering of boat 5, Bruce Ismay quietly resumes assisting with the loading of passengers. By 1.40 am most of the forward boats have gone, and the crowd has moved aft. Englehardt collapsible C has been attached to the davits vacated by boat 1. When no one responds to chief officer Wilde's repeated calls for women and children to come forward, he orders the boat to be lowered away. Ship's barber August H. Weikman and the others in boat C observe Ismay and William E. Carter step into the boat as it leaves the deck. The ship's list causes the boat to swing against the liner's hull, and there is fear that the protruding rivet heads will damage the canvas-sided craft. Hands and oars are used to push the boat bodily away from the ship. Collapsible C is the last starboard-side boat launched. (*White Star* by Roy Anderson /*Philadelphia Bulletin*.)

Miss Violet Jessop, stewardess   August H. Weikman, barber

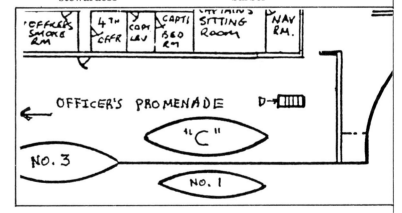

After seeing to the boats' provisioning, and helping to get several of them away (including his own assigned boat, number 10), chief baker Charles Joughin retires to his cabin on E deck at 1.45 for some liquid fortification: a half-tumbler full of whisky. He sees Dr William O'Loughlin rummaging about, perhaps with the same goal in mind. Joughin returns to the boat deck, then, believing all boats gone, descends to B deck where he tosses about fifty deck chairs overboard through the large ports, in preparation for his own escape. (*Daily Mirror*.)

J. Bruce Ismay, first class passenger   Charles Joughin, chief baker

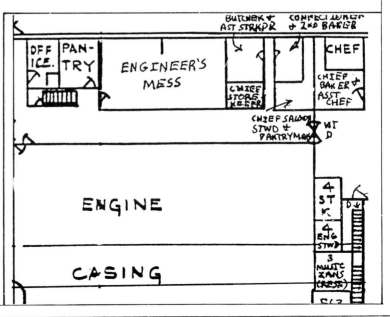

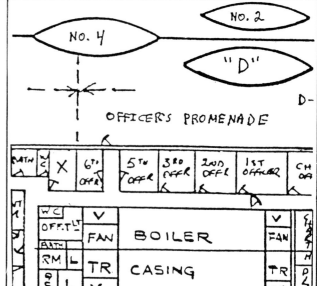

At last, difficulties are overcome, and after an hour's wait, the loading of boat 4 begins while emergency boat 2 is also prepared for lowering. Crowds have moved aft, away from the ever-rising water. Boat 2 is lowered at 1.45 with 25 on board a craft built for forty. (Painting by Ken Marschall; Dennis R. Kromm collection.)

Harry E. Widener,
first class passenger

George D. Widener,
first class passenger

John B. Thayer,
first class passenger

John and Madelene Astor,
first class passengers

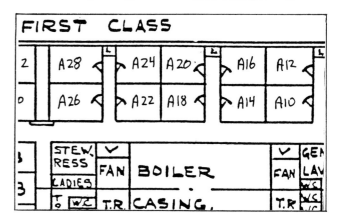

With one foot in boat 4, the other in the window sill, second officer Lightoller begins to load. John Jacob Astor assists Madelene through the window frame and into the boat. He asks if he may join his wife, saying she is 'in delicate condition'. When he is told he may not, he kisses her goodbye and returns to B deck. Arthur Ryerson sees his wife and two daughters in, then overrules Lightoller's statement that thirteen-year-old Jack Ryerson cannot go.

George Widener and his son Harry see Mrs Widener into the boat and step back. John B. Thayer and son 'Jack' escort Mrs Thayer into the boat. The men stand quietly together as the boat is lowered away at 1.55 with more than forty women and children aboard. Upon reaching the water, fifteen feet below, it is discovered that the boat lacks sufficient seamen to man it. Quartermaster W. J. Perkis is ordered down the falls to assist, and several other men drop into the boat as well. Seven additional men are pulled out of the water by the women and crew; two later die from exposure. (Private collection/*Daily Mirror/Philadelphia Public Ledger*.)

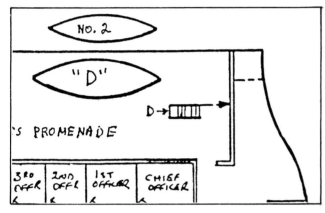

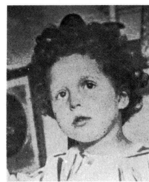
Michel Navratil,
second class passenger

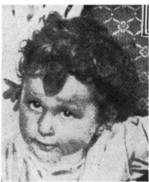
Edmond Navratil,
second class passenger

Henry B. Harris,
first class passenger

Hokan Björnstrom-
Steffanson,
first class passenger

All boats away on the port side, collapsible D is fitted into boat 2's davits, and quickly filled. The fo'c's'le head is just going under water. (Painting by Ken Marschall; Charles Heebner collection.)

With more than 1,500 still on board, and just 47 available spaces in collapsible D, Lightoller instructs the crew to lock arms and form a circle around the boat. Only women and children are permitted to pass through the circle.

Second class passenger 'Mr Hoffman' carries his two sons, Michel and Edmond, to the ring and hands them off. 'Mr Hoffman' is, in fact, Michel Navratil, and he has kidnapped the children in an effort to rescue a faltering marriage.

Theatre impressario Henry B. Harris escorts his wife to the circle, then steps back.

Third class passengers Frank Goldsmith and his mother Emily bid a tearful farewell to Mr Goldsmith and family friend Tom Theobald, and enter the boat.

At 2.05, collapsible D begins its downward journey. The sea is pouring on to the forward end of A deck as *Titanic*'s tilt grows steeper.

As the boat passes them in its descent, Hugh Woolner and Hokan Björnström-Steffanson decide to jump for it. Steffanson leaps and lands upside-down in boat D's bow. Woolner follows and ends up folded over the gunwale before being pulled all the way in. (*Daily Sketch/Harper's/Arnold Watson Collection/Authors' collection.*)

Left Emily and Frank Goldsmith, third class passengers

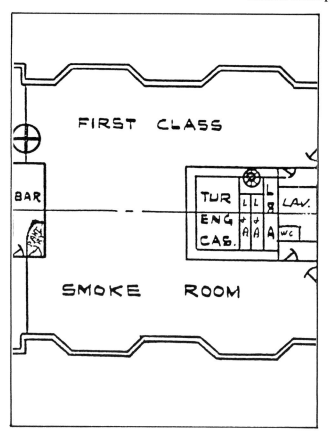

Archie Butt,
first class passenger

Arthur Ryerson,
first class passenger

At 2 am, Archie Butt and Arthur Ryerson adjourn to the first class smoking room with Francis D. Millet and Clarence Moore. The four sit at their usual table and play one last hand of cards together while awaiting the end. Ten minutes later, they leave.

A steward sees Thomas Andrews alone, in the same room, with his lifebelt lying on a table. *Titanic*'s designer is lost in thought, arms folded across his chest, staring at the painting above the fireplace. It is Norman Wilkinson's work, 'Plymouth Harbour'. (*Philadelphia Public Ledger*/Authors' collection.)

At 2.05 Captain Smith goes to the wireless cabin and releases Phillips and Bride, who have been toiling ceaselessly since the collision to bring aid. Phillips continues to work while Bride gathers their papers before they leave.

Captain Smith leaves and, on his way forward, tells several of the crew, 'It's every man for himself,' before returning to the bridge of his last command. As the cold waters of the Atlantic thunder in, he sees for the last time the familiar company notice to commanders, with its bright red underlining, posted on the wheel-house wall. There is time, too, to think of his beloved wife Eleanor and his young daughter Helen. He is alone when the bridge is inundated. (National Archives.)

WHITE STAR LINE.

The Managers are desirous of impressing upon Commanders the importance of strictly adhering to the Company's Regulations, and attention is particularly called to the following points:—

1.—The vital importance of exercising the utmost caution in Navigation, *safety outweighing every other consideration*.

2.—*Over-confidence*, a most fruitful source of accident, should be especially guarded against.

3.—It cannot be too strongly borne in mind that any serious accident affects prejudicially not only the welfare of the Company, but also the prospects and livelihood of the Commanders and Officers of the Ships; and, as every consideration is shown to those placed in positions of responsibility, the Company relies upon faithful and efficient service being given in return, so that the possibility of accidents may be reduced to a minimum. The Company assumes the entire risk of insurance on its vessels, their freights, and on a considerable portion of the cargoes carried by them; whilst the large sum which is paid annually to its Officers as a bonus for absolute immunity from accidents is additional evidence of anxiety to subordinate all other considerations to the paramount one of *safety in navigation*.

4.—No thought of making competitive passages must be entertained, and time must be sacrificed or any other temporary inconvenience suffered, rather than the slightest risk should be incurred.

5.—Commanders should be on deck and in full charge during Thick Weather, in Narrow Waters, or when near the Land. A wide berth must be given to all Headlands, Shoals, and other positions of Peril; cross bearings must be taken wherever possible, *and the use of the ordinary deep sea lead* not neglected when approaching land in thick or doubtful weather, more particularly in view of the fact that signals on shore are not always reliable.

6.—The attention of Commanders is particularly directed to Articles 16 and 23 of the "Regulations for preventing Collisions at Sea," viz:—

Article 16.—Every Ship shall, in a Fog, Mist, Falling Snow, or Heavy Rain Storms, go at a moderate speed, having careful regard to the existing circumstances and conditions.

Article 23.—Every Steam Ship, which is directed by these rules to keep out of the way of another vessel, shall, on approaching her, if necessary, slacken her speed, or stop or reverse.

7.—The Regulations as to Inspection of Watertight Doors, and Fire and Boat Drill are to be carefully observed; Rigid discipline amongst Officers maintained and the Crew kept under judicious control. Convivial intercourse with Passengers is to be avoided.

8.—It is expected that all details connected with the working of the Steamers will be mastered by the Commanders, and any suggestions tending to improvement are invited, and will receive every consideration.

Liverpool, Jan. 1st, 1901.   MANAGERS.

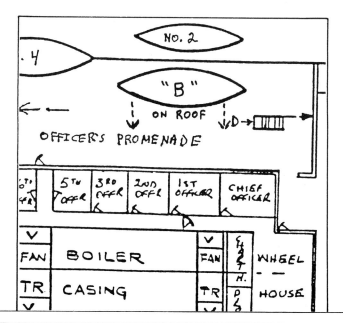

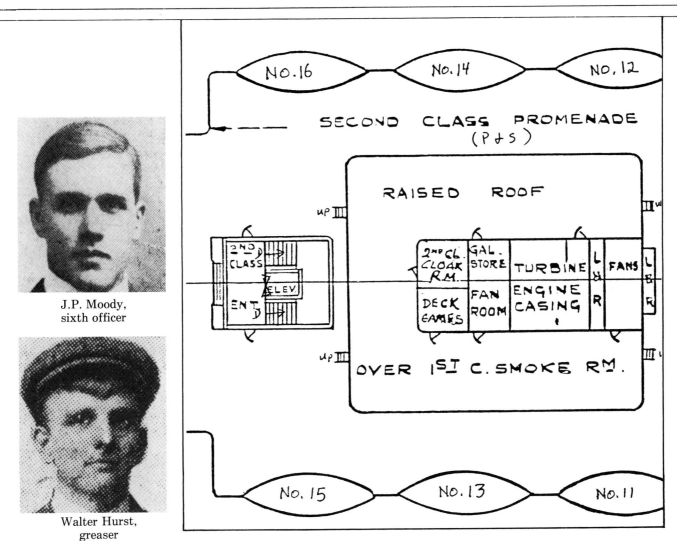

J.P. Moody,
sixth officer

Walter Hurst,
greaser

Efforts to prepare collapsible B **below left** for launching end abruptly. There simply is no more time. At 2.10 the ship's bow plunges and those struggling to launch the boat, including sixth officer Moody, second officer Lightoller and greaser Walter Hurst suddenly find themselves in the water. The wave carries the unlaunched boat over the deck's edge and it floats upside down. *(Daily Mirror.)*

Father Thomas R. Byles recites the rosary, hears confessions and gives absolutions to more than 100 passengers, mainly second and third class, now gathered on the after end of the boat deck **above**. (Authors' collection.)

Father Thomas R. Byles,
second class passenger

Wallace H. Hartley,
bandmaster

Similar thoughts inspire the ship's orchestra leader. As the water begins its inexorable climb up the slanting boat deck, bandmaster Wallace Hartley, outside the gymnasium, taps his bow and ends the ragtime that has served so well to lift people's spirits during the evening. He chooses as the orchestra's final piece 'Nearer, My God, to Thee'.* (Robert DiSogra Collection.)

*While some survivors recall hearing the hymn 'Autumn', 'Nearer, My God, to Thee' is easier to play, and was musicians' traditional hymn at the funeral of a union colleague. It was the late King Edward VII's favourite hymn, and in an interview not long before *Titanic*'s sailing, Hartley had said it would be the hymn he would select for his own funeral.

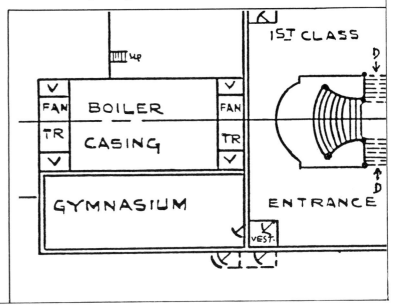

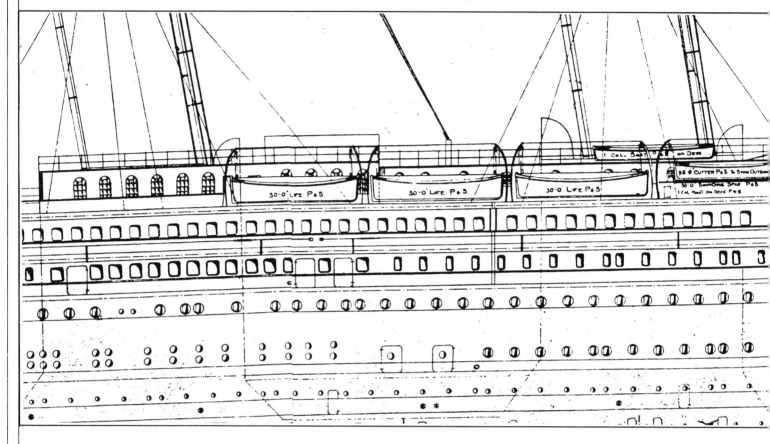

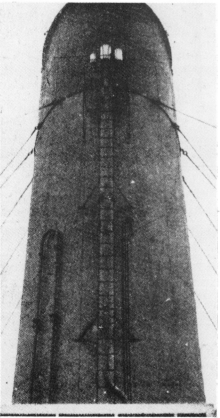

Archibald Gracie,
first class passenger

The rapidly rising water catches Archibald Gracie and many others on the boat deck. Gracie jumps with the wave, as one would do at the seashore, and the water carries him to the roof of the officers' quarters near the base of the second funnel. As he clings to an iron railing, the ship sinks beneath him, and Gracie is pulled under water. Swimming furiously, he manages to reach the surface where he makes for overturned collapsible B. (*The Truth About the Titanic*.)

Charles D. Williams,
first class passenger

As the liner's stern angles upwards, the forward funnel's stays can no longer stand the extra strain on them. A guywire on the starboard side snaps, followed almost at once by the portside stay. The giant funnel topples forward in a cloud of soot and sparks, flattening the starboard bridge wing and striking the water, its wash pushing collapsible B away from the ship. Scores of swimmers are crushed, among them first class passenger Charles D. Williams of Philadelphia. (Mrs R. Norris Williams — Michael Findlay collection.)

The stern lifts clear out of the water as the passengers move further aft. All boats are now gone, and more than 1,500 people remain on board. (*Daily Sphere.*)

An ever-increasing roar is heard by those in the boats as everything movable in the ship breaks loose and plunges towards the now-submerged bow. The ship's lights, kept on by the heroic efforts of the engineers, go out, flash on once more, then are extinguished for good. *Titanic* is visible only as a silhouette against the starlit sky. (Painting by Ken Marschall; Joseph Ryan collection.)

The ship achieves a completely perpendicular position, and remains there for several moments. She then settles back slightly, and slides to the bed of the North Atlantic 13,000 feet below. It is 2.20 am. (*Daily Graphic*.)

Rosa Abbott,
third class passenger

Richard Norris Williams,
first class passenger

Collapsible A had become badly tangled in its lashings on the roof near the forward funnel. As *Titanic* sank, the boat broke loose and floated away. Now, in the 28-degree water, any refuge is sought, and swimmers make for the boat, which is half-submerged with its canvas sides not pulled up. More than two dozen are soon on board, including tennis star R. Norris Williams and third class passenger Rosa Abbott (the only woman on board). Algernon H. Barkworth, a Yorkshire justice of the peace, bobs alongside in his great fur coat, put on over his lifebelt. As the dangerously overloaded craft wallows off, its freezing passengers begin reciting the Lord's Prayer in unison. Just before dawn, they are plucked from their precarious situation by fifth officer Lowe in boat 14. (Arnold Watson collection/Mrs R. Norris Williams—Michael Findlay collection/Lloyd's *Deathless Story of the Titanic*.)

Algernon H. Barkworth,
first class passenger

Mrs J. Stuart White,
first class passenger

Aboard boat 8, Mrs J. Stuart White tries to help. She shows an inexperienced crewman how to row, then uses her cane with its built-in electric light to spot other lifeboats nearby, and signal as needed. (Mr Harry S. Durand—Michael Findlay collection.)

Mrs Ida Hippach,
first class passenger

Miss Jean Hippach,
first class passenger

In crowded boat 4, Jean Hippach and her mother Ida watch a sky filled with shooting stars. Jean cannot recall ever having seen so many. They are not so bright as *Titanic*'s distress rockets had been. (Authors' collection.)

162

Chapter Twelve

CALIFORNIAN AND OTHERS

For Dundee, in Scotland, 26 November 1901 was a proud day. A vessel, number 159, was launched at that date by the Caledon Shipbuilding and Engineering Company Ltd, whose success, it was hoped, would enable the city to become a major shipbuilding centre. The steamer had a gross tonnage of 6,223 and a net of 4,038 tons. She was 446 feet in length at the waterline, 447 feet 6 inches between perpendiculars, 53 feet 6 inches wide, and had a moulded depth of 34 feet 8 inches. Her cavernous holds were designed primarily for cotton carrying — a trade for which her owners Frederick Leyland and Co Ltd (the Leyland Line), had become well known.

During construction the vessel had her upper bridge deck lengthened to include nineteen state-rooms. Although certified for 47 passengers, the normal number carried was 35. Passenger accommodation was on the vessel's port side; starboard quarters were for ship's officers, engineers and stewards. Her full crew complement was 55: ordinary crew were housed in quarters under the forecastle head.

The passengers' dining saloon was handsomely finished in Hungarian ash and satinwood with teak frames, and upholstered in moquette. The smoking room was panelled in oak, upholstered in embossed leather and had rubber floor tiling. There was electric lighting throughout the ship. Dundee's new pride bore her name in nine-inch brass letters, according to builder's specifications, on each bow and at the stern — *Californian*.

While *Californian* was under construction, Frederick Leyland and Company Ltd was acquired by the Morgan interests during formation of the International Mercantile Marine. To put *Californian* to best use within the combine, additional passenger cabins were added.

After sea trials on 23 January 1902, *Californian* loaded for her maiden voyage. Departing from Dundee on 31 January, she arrived at New Orleans, Louisiana, USA, on 3 March. The return trip to Liverpool, her company's home port, was completed on 21 March. In April the vessel was chartered by the Dominion Line, another IMM member, and sent from Liverpool to Portland, Maine. After the last of five Dominion Line voyages was completed in December 1902, the steamer reverted in January 1903 to her original owner.

Between her maiden voyage in 1902 and the spring of 1912, *Californian* had four masters. Stanley Lord, her fourth captain, had been in command less than a year. Born in Bolton, near Liverpool, in 1877, Lord had gone to sea as a cadet in 1891 in the barque *Naiad*; he served as second mate aboard the *Lurlei* and in 1897 began his service with the West India and Pacific Steam Navigation Company. When the Leyland Line purchased the company in 1900, Lord stayed on as an officer. He passed for master in February 1901 and for extra master three months later. In 1906 he received his first Leyland command, *Antillian*, which was followed by commands of *Louisianian*, *William Cliff* and, in 1911, *Californian*.

The voyage preceding the April 1912 crossing had not been an auspicious one. *Californian* had left New Orleans with a load of cotton on 20 February 1912. On her arrival at Le Havre, in France, on 20 March it was found that 55 bales of her cargo had been sea-damaged and 567 bales were 'country damaged' — a total of 622 damaged bales, not a happy report for Captain Lord to file with the owners.

Californian departed from Liverpool for Boston, Massachusetts, with a general cargo on 5 April 1912. By 14 April her noon position, by observation, was 42° 05′ N, 47° 25′ W. Her course was altered during the afternoon so that longitude 51° West could be crossed at latitude 42° North on account of ice reports received on 9 and 13 April.

Two sun observations taken at 5 pm and 5.30 pm*

---

*All times are *Californian*'s apparent time, which was twelve minutes earlier than the *Titanic*'s apparent time.

showed *Californian* to be sixty and 64 miles, respectively, ahead of her dead reckoning position. At 6.30 pm three large icebergs were seen drifting south of the ship. At 7.30 pm Lord ordered a wireless message to be sent to *Antillian*: '6.30 pm apparent ship's time, latitude 42° 5′ N, longitude 49° 9′ W, three bergs five miles southwards of us. Regards, Lord.' (Lord was subsequently told by his wireless operator that a routine exchange of signals with *Titanic* indicated that she, also, had received the ice message sent to *Antillian*.)

At 7.30 pm chief officer G. F. Stewart took a stellar observation on the Pole Star and reported to Captain Lord a latitude of 42° 5½′ N. Knowing that his ship was heading towards ice, Lord doubled his look-outs at 8 pm and moments later took charge of the bridge himself, third officer Groves also being on duty. Lord reported the weather as calm, clear and starry. At 10.15 there was a brightening along the western horizon. Lord concluded this 'glow' to be caused by ice and at 10.21 rang the engine room, ordering full speed astern and the helm put hard-a-port. The ship swung around to ENE by compass (NE true) and surged to a stop.

Californian was stationary, surrounded by loose ice, about half a mile from the edge of a low ice-field. Lord calculated the vessel's location, based on a course S 89 W (true), 120 miles from the noon position, and on the 7.30 pm stellar observation. He logged *Californian*'s position as 42° 5′ N, 50° 7′ W.

At 10.30 pm, as he was leaving the bridge, Captain Lord pointed out to the third officer a light to the eastward. Lord thought it was an approaching vessel; Groves thought it was a star. Going down to the saloon deck Lord sent for chief engineer W. S. A. Mahan and asked him to keep steam up during the night in case they should begin bumping into ice.

Lord also pointed out to Mahan the light he had seen earlier, which now appeared to be a steamer approaching from the south and east. Leaving the saloon at 10.55 pm the captain encountered the wireless operator and asked if he knew of any other vessels in the vicinity. 'Only the *Titanic*,' was the response. 'That's not *Titanic*,' Lord said. 'She's a vessel close to us in size. You'd better contact *Titanic*, however, and let her know we're stopped in ice.' Wireless operator Evans immediately went to send the message.

The vessel approached *Californian* from the east and got closer all the time. When Lord first sighted her, he could see only the masthead light and what appeared to be white deck lights. By 11.30 pm he could see the green (starboard) side light, and estimated the ship's distance at about five miles.* He

---

Californian's bridge, 49 feet above the waterline, permitted an observer to see eight miles to the horizon.

asked third officer Groves, officer of the watch, to try to contact the ship by Morse lamp, and heard the lamp clicking away, but there was no response from the other vessel.

Twenty-nine-year-old Ernest Gill, on *Californian*'s crew list as a fireman, came off his 8-to-12 watch and went on deck shortly after midnight. He looked over the rail and saw off the starboard side '. . . a very large steamer, about ten miles away. I watched her for a full minute'. Going below, Gill reported the sighting to his bunk mate, saying he had seen the big vessel 'going full speed'.

Unable to sleep, Gill left his bunk and went on deck again about 12.30 am. He had been there about ten minutes when he saw a white rocket, '. . . about ten miles away on the starboard side. I thought it must be a shooting star. In seven or eight minutes I saw distinctly a second rocket in the same place . . . It was not my business to notify the bridge or the lookouts . . . I turned in immediately after'.

Fireman Gill did report later that while he could see the stars spangling out from the rockets, he observed no Morse signalling from the vessel, nor could he hear any noise such as escaping steam, the concussion of exploding distress rockets, or anything of the sort, though conditions were ideal for doing so.

When second officer Herbert Stone came on watch shortly after midnight, he was detained briefly at the wheelhouse door by Captain Lord, who pointed out a steamer a little aft of *Californian*'s starboard beam. The captain also showed Stone the dense ice to the south, and asked to be advised if the vessel came any closer. He told Stone he would be resting on the chart room settee, and then left the bridge.

Stone took over the watch at about eight minutes past twelve from third officer Groves, who reported *Californian*'s heading as east-northeast and that the vessel was swinging; he also called Stone's attention to the ship off the starboard beam.

To Stone, the vessel appeared to be south-south-east and dead abeam, starboard of *Californian*. He observed one masthead light and a red side light, as well as one or two indistinct lights, resembling portholes or open doors, around her decks. He also judged her to be a small tramp steamer about five miles off.

Groves had reported on his fruitless attempt to contact the steamer with the Morse lamp. After taking the watch, Stone tried, at about ten minutes past midnight, to contact the vessel, again without success.

Apprentice James Gibson came on watch. About five minutes after Stone, Gibson also tried to signal the steamer with the Morse lamp. He thought at first that he received a response, but observed through binoculars that it was the flicker of what seemed to be a masthead oil lamp.

Captain Lord, meanwhile, was resting in the chart room. At 12.35 am he whistled up the speaking tube to inquire if the vessel had moved. Stone advised him it had not and that repeated attempts to call it up had failed.

At about 12.45 am, *Californian's* time, Stone observed a flash of light in the sky. In his own words:

'...just above that [nearby] steamer. I thought nothing of it, as there were several shooting stars about, the night being fine and clear with light airs and calms. Shortly after, I observed another [light] distinctly over the steamer; in fact, it appeared to come from a good distance beyond her. Between then and about 1.15 I observed three more, the same as before, and all white in colour ...'

At 1.15 am Stone whistled down the speaking tube to advise Captain Lord of the rockets he had seen. Lord, answering from his own cabin, inquired if the rockets were private signals, to which Stone responded, 'I don't know. But they are all white'. The captain ordered Stone to keep signalling the nearby vessel and '... when you get an answer let me know by Gibson'. Stone continued using the Morse lamp but with no response. The captain returned to the chart room settee.

Californian continued to swing through south, and by 1.50 was heading west-south-west. The other ship had a bearing of south-west-by-west, and by 2 am had begun to steam away, bearing SW½ W. Her red (port) light became invisible, and only her stern light could be seen.

As ordered, Stone sent Gibson to the chart room to report to the captain.

According to Gibson, he roused the drowsy master, told him of the other ship's departure and how it still had not returned the signals from their own Morse lamp. Gibson also said he told Captain Lord about the sighting of distant rockets, eight altogether. Gibson stated that the captain had acknowledged his report with 'All right', and then inquired about the rockets. 'Are you sure there were no colours in them?' He then asked what time it was. Gibson returned to the bridge and reported his conversation to officer of the watch Stone.

But Lord was unaware of Gibson's visit. In a sworn affidavit, he stated, 'I have recollection between 1.30 and 4.30 of Gibson opening the chart room door and closing it immediately. I said: "What is it?" *but he did not reply*'. [Authors' italics.]

In what surely must be one of history's most poignant ironies, *Californian's* wireless operator also was asleep and his receiver inactive during the momentous hours of *Titanic's* sinking.

Evans had turned in at 11.30 pm, having been on duty alone since 7 am. At about 12.15 am third officer Groves came to the wireless cabin to listen to traffic. Evans was half asleep, and did not advise Groves that the mechanical signal detector needed winding. Groves, though wearing the set's headphones, was unable to hear any wireless signals.

And that night there were many signals...

New York time	*Titanic* time* (approximate)	Communication
10.25 pm	12.15 am	*La Provence* receives *Titanic* distress signals.
10.25 pm	12.15 am	*Mount Temple* hears *Titanic* sending CQD. Says require assistance. Gives position. Can not hear me. Advise my captain his position 41.46 N, 50.24 W.
10.28 pm	12.18 am	*Ypiranga* hears CQD from *Titanic*. *Titanic* gives CQD here. Position 41.44 N, 50.24 W. Require assistance (calls about ten times).
10.35 pm	12.25 am	CQD call received from *Titanic* by *Carpathia*. *Titanic* says, 'Come at one. We have struck a berg. It's a CQD, OM. Position 41.46 N, 50.14 W'.
10.35 pm	12.25 am	Cape Race hears MGY, (*Titanic*)[†] give corrected position 41.46 N, 50.14 W. Calling him; no answer.
10.36 pm	12.26 am	MGY (*Titanic*) says CQD. Here corrected position 41.46 N, 50.14 W. Require immediate assistance. We have collision with iceberg. Sinking. Can hear nothing for noise of steam. Sent about fifteen to twenty times to *Ypiranga*.
10.37 pm	12.27 am	*Titanic* sends following: 'I require assistance immediately. Struck by iceberg in 41.46 N, 50.14 W'.
10.40 pm	12.30 am	*Titanic* gives his position to *Frankfurt*, and says, 'Tell your captain to come to our help. We are on the ice'.
10.40 pm	12.30 am	*Caronia* sends CQ message to MBC (*Baltic*) and CQD: MGY (*Titanic*) struck iceberg, require immediate assistance.
10.40 pm	12.30 am	*Mount Temple* hears MGY (*Titanic*) still calling CQD. Our captain reverses ship. We are about fifty miles off.

*Approximate time on *Californian* would be twelve minutes earlier.

[†]A three-letter code indicated each wireless station, whether ashore or on board ship.

10.46 pm	12.26 am	DKF (*Prinz Friedrich Wilhelm*) calls MGY (*Titanic*) and gives position at 12 am 39.47 N, 50.10 W. MGY (*Titanic*) says, 'Are you coming to our?' DFT (*Frankfurt*) says, 'What is the matter with u?' MGY (*Titanic*) 'We have collision with iceberg. Sinking. Please tell captain to come'. DFT (*Frankfurt*) says, 'OK, will tell'.	11.25 pm	1.15 am	*Baltic* to *Caronia*, 'Please tell *Titanic* we are making toward her'.
			11.30 pm	1.20 am	*Virginian* hears MCE (Cape Race) inform MGY (*Titanic*) 'that we are going to his assistance. Our position 170 miles north of *Titanic*'.
10.48 pm	12.38 am	*Mount Temple* hears *Frankfurt* give MGY (*Titanic*) his position, 39.47 N, 52.10 W.	11.35 pm	1.25 am	*Caronia* tells *Titanic*, '*Baltic* coming to your assistance'.
10.55 pm	12.45 am	*Titanic* calls *Olympic* SOS.	11.35 pm	1.25 am	*Olympic* sends position to *Titanic* 4.24 am GMT. 40.52 N, 61.18 W. 'Are you steering southerly to meet us?' *Titanic* replies, 'We are putting the women off in the boats'.
11 pm	12.50 am	*Titanic* calls CQD and says, 'I require immediate assistance. Position 41.46 N, 50.14 W'. Received by *Celtic*.			
11.03 pm	12.53 am	*Caronia* to MBC (*Baltic*) 'SOS, MGY (*Titanic*) CQD in 41.46 N, 50.14 W. Wants immediate assistance'.	11.35 pm	1.25 am	*Titanic* and *Olympic* work together.
			11.37 pm	1.27 am	MGY (*Titanic*) says, 'We are putting the women off in the boats'.
11.10 pm	1 am	MGY gives distress signal. DDC (*Cincinnati*) replies. MGY's position 41.46 N, 50.14 W. Assistance from DDC not necessary, as MKC (*Olympic*) shortly afterwards answers distress call.	11.40 pm	1.30 am	*Titanic* tells *Olympic*, 'We are putting passengers off in small boats'.
			11.45 pm	1.35 am	*Olympic* asks *Titanic* what weather she had. *Titanic* replies, 'Clear and calm'.
11.10 pm	1 am	*Titanic* replies to *Olympic* and gives his position as 41.46 N, 50.14 W, and says, 'We have struck an iceberg'.	11.45 pm	1.35 am	*Baltic* hears *Titanic* say, 'Engine room getting flooded'.
			11.45 pm	1.35 am	*Mount Temple* hears DFT (*Frankfurt*) ask, 'Are there any boats around you already?' No reply.
11.12 pm	1.02 am	*Titanic* calls *Asian* and says, 'Want immediate assistance'. *Asian* answered at once and received *Titanic*'s position as 41.46 N, 50.14 W, which he immediately takes to the bridge. Captain instructs operator to have *Titanic*'s position repeated.	11.47 pm	1.37 am	*Baltic* tells *Titanic*, 'We are rushing to you'.
			11.50 pm	1.40 am	*Olympic* to *Titanic*, 'Am lighting up all possible boilers as fast as can'.
11.12 pm	1.02 am	*Virginian* calls *Titanic* but gets no response. Cape Race tells *Virginian* to report to his captain the *Titanic* has struck iceberg and requires immediate assistance.	11.50 pm	1.40 am	Cape Race says to *Virginian*, 'Please tell your captain this: The *Olympic* is making all speed for *Titanic*, but his (*Olympic*'s) position is 40.32 N, 61.18 W. You are much nearer to *Titanic*. The *Titanic* is already putting women off in the boats, and he says the weather there is "calm and clear". The *Olympic* is the only ship we have heard say, "Going to the assistance of the *Titanic*". The others must be a long way from the *Titanic*.'
11.20 pm	1.10 am	*Titanic* to MKC (*Olympic*) 'We are in collision with berg. Sinking head down; 41.46 N, 50.14 W. Come soon as possible'.			
11.20 pm	1.10 am	*Titanic* to MKC (*Olympic*), captain says, 'Get your boats ready. What is your position?'	11.55 pm	1.45 am	Last signals heard from *Titanic* by *Carpathia*, 'Engine room full up to boilers'.

11.55 pm	1.45 am	*Mount Temple* hears DFT (*Frankfurt*) calling MGY (*Titanic*). No reply.
11.57 pm	1.47 am	*Caronia* hears MGY (*Titanic*) though signals unreadable still.
11.58 pm	1.48 am	*Asian* heard *Titanic* call SOS. *Asian* answers *Titanic* but receives no response.
Midnight	1.50 am	*Caronia* hears *Frankfurt* working to *Titanic*. *Frankfurt* according to position 172 miles from MGY (*Titanic*) at time first SOS sent out.
12.05 am	1.55 am	Cape Race says to *Virginian* 'We have not heard *Titanic* for about half an hour. His power may be gone'.
12.10 am	2 am	*Virginian* hears *Titanic* calling very faintly, his power being greatly reduced.
12.20 am	2.10 am	*Virginian* hears 2 V's signalled faintly in spark similar to *Titanic*'s, probably adjusting spark.
12.27 am	2.17 am	*Virginian* hears *Titanic* call CQ but unable to read him. *Titanic*'s signals end very abruptly, as power suddenly switched off. His spark rather blurred or ragged. Called MGY (*Titanic*) and suggested he should try emergency set, but heard no response.
12.30 am	2.20 am	*Olympic*, his signal strong, asked him if he had heard anything about MGY (*Titanic*). He says, 'No. Keeping strict watch, but hear nothing more from MGY (*Titanic*)'. No reply from him.
12.52 am		*Carpathia* sends message to *Olympic* giving the official time the *Titanic* foundered in 41.46 N, 50.14 W, as at about 2.20 am.

The manual *Distinguishing Night Signals of Steamship Lines* listed private signals registered by the Board of Trade pursuant to the Merchant Shipping Act of 1894. In its 28 pages were descriptions of signals generated through various pyrotechnic lights, rockets and Roman candles for commercial shipping companies and yacht clubs to facilitate night identification of owners and, in some instances, specific routes of vessels.

The final entry on the 1904 edition's last page was as follows:

'The Board of Trade have also approved the use of a rocket throwing out one white star by British fishing vessels when urgently requiring the aid of one of His Majesty's cruisers employed in protecting the fisheries.'

In 1912 there were many vessels, particularly smaller craft such as might be employed in fishing or commercial sailing, which did not have wireless equipment. Their masters had to rely upon flag hoists by day and pyrotechnic signals by night. Such a vessel was the Norwegian *Samson*, a wood sailing barque owned by the Acties-Saelfaenger Dpsk Co of Trondhjeim, Norway, under the command of Captain C. I. Ring. On the night of 14-15 April 1912, the 148-foot vessel, of 506 gross tons, appears to have been in the vicinity of the position where *Titanic* was in her death throes.

In a sworn statement shortly before his death in 1962, *Samson*'s chief officer, Henrik Naess, said that he saw the rockets fired by *Titanic*, that he and his ship were within eyesight of the liner. Naess was part of an expedition that had taken the vessel into the forbidden sealing grounds off the North American coast. He knew that they had been spotted in these illegal areas, and in his statement said that on sighting the rockets he thought they may have been signals to heave to and be searched.

A cache of seal pelts would have been difficult to explain to any authority. To give assistance would have exposed the presence of the cargo. So *Samson* steamed away.

Twenty miles or more to the northwest, Captain Stanley Lord dozed while his officers and men kept watch through the long, cold night, out of sight and unaware of the drama unfolding.

At 4.30 am, near daybreak, *Californian*'s captain was awakened by chief officer G. V. Stewart, then officer of the watch. Upon reaching the bridge, Captain Lord was for a time undecided whether to push through the ice or to seek a clearer passage to the south. As daylight came, he saw clear water to the west and at 5.15 am ordered the engines on stand-by.

About this time the chief officer remarked that there appeared to be a steamer, a four-masted vessel with a yellow funnel, bearing south-south-east from *Californian*. He expressed concern that the vessel might be in distress, perhaps with a broken rudder, and that the second officer had told him she had fired several rockets during his watch.

Captain Lord ordered wireless operator Cyril Evans to find out the vessel's name and whether she required assistance. Evans quickly turned on his set and gave a 'CQ', — 'All stations, someone answer'. His first response was from DFT (the *Frankfurt*), who asked, 'Do you know that the *Titanic* has sunk during the night, collided with an iceberg?' As Evans was thanking *Frankfurt* for the news, MGN (*Virginian*) entered the traffic, and it was from her that MWL (*Californian*) received the official news of

167

Titanic's loss, along with the position.

Evans wrote the message, with the position, on a slip of paper and handed it to chief officer Stewart, who took it at once to Captain Lord on the bridge. Lord calculated the position — 41° 46′ N, 50° 14′ W, — to be S 16 W, about 19½ miles from *Californian's* estimated position. Lord immediately ordered *Californian* under way.

A look-out, Benjamin Kirk, was given a pair of binoculars, placed in a coal basket and hauled high up to the main truck with instructions to keep a sharp watch for survivors, wreckage or boats. Following courses between south and south-west, and pushing through field ice at no more than six knots, *Californian* reached open water about 6.30 am and proceeded at full speed — seventy revolutions, about 13½ knots — southward, down the icefield's western edge.

Around 7.30 *Mount Temple* was passed, stopped in the wirelessed position of the disaster. There was no sign of wreckage in this location. *Californian* continued south, soon passing a pink-funnelled, two-masted ship heading north, the *Almerian* (another Leyland vessel, but one having no wireless).

Shortly after passing *Almerian*, *Californian* sighted *Carpathia* to the south-south-east, on the icefield's eastern side. Confirming by wireless that it was indeed *Carpathia*, and that she was at the disaster site picking up survivors, Lord continued steering south until *Carpathia* was almost abeam, then altered his own course and sped through the ice, stopping alongside *Carpathia* at about 8.30 am.

At about 12.05 am, after receiving from Captain Smith *Titanic's* position worked out by fourth officer Boxhall, senior Marconi operator Jack Phillips **above left** sits down at the wireless and calls 'CQD'. (Marconi Company.)

Above He sets the frequency on the multiple tuner to 600 metres... (Authors' collection.)

Left ... and adjusts the spark gap for maximum range before transmitting the distress signal... (Authors' collection.)

... which hurtles out into space through the *Titanic*'s immense antenna. (Authors' collection.)

Below *Titanic* is not alone in the North Atlantic that night. (United States Hydrographic Office.)

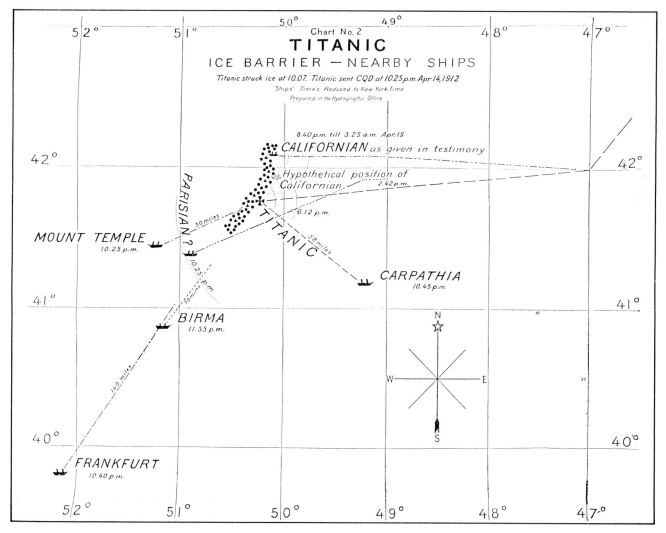

Chart No. 2

TITANIC

ICE BARRIER — NEARBY SHIPS

Titanic struck ice at 10.07. Titanic sent CQD at 10.25 p.m. Apr.14, 1912

Ships' Times Reduced to New York Time

Prepared in the Hydrographic Office

8.40 p.m. till 3.25 a.m. Apr.15

CALIFORNIAN *as given in testimony*

Hypothetical position of Californian. 2.42 p.m.

6.12 p.m.

PARISIAN ?

50 miles

TITANIC

MOUNT TEMPLE
10.25 p.m.

10.25 p.m.

5.8 miles

CARPATHIA
10.45 p.m.

70 miles

BIRMA
11.55 p.m.

N

W — E

S

140 miles

FRANKFURT
10.40 p.m.

Left *La Provence* is the first vessel to receive *Titanic*'s call for help. (Mariner's Museum, Newport News, Va.)

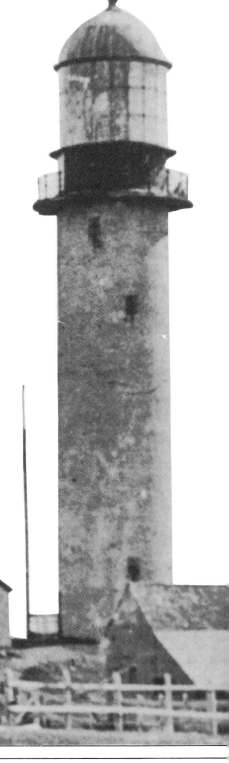

Above Forty-nine miles to the west, *Mount Temple* hears the distress signal at almost the same time. *Titanic*'s operator can barely hear *Mount Temple*'s response due to the roar of steam escaping from *Titanic*'s boiler exhausts. (Mariner's Museum, Newport News, Va.)

Below At the same time, the operator at the Cape Race, Newfoundland, land station picks up *Titanic*'s transmission which erroneously gives her position as 41° 44′ N, 50° 24′ W. (Canadian Marconi Company.)

Three minutes later, the wireless operator aboard the Hamburg-America liner *Ypiranga* logs the same position, reported by Cape Race, repeated ten times by *Titanic*. By 12.25 am *Titanic*'s distress call, received by *Carpathia*, contains the position actually worked out by Boxhall, 41° 46′ N, 50° 14′ W. (Authors' collection.)

Northwards across the ice field, at least nineteen miles from Boxhall's position, the Leyland Line freighter *Californian* **right** is stopped half-a-mile from ice directly in her path — ice which her master feels will be dangerous to traverse in the dark. (Private collection.)

Her sole radio operator, Cyril Evans, as is his custom, has shut down his station and retired for the night. (*New York American*.)

Cyril Evans   Ernest Gill   Charles V. Groves

Bottom Shortly after midnight, from *Californian*'s after deck... (Scottish Record Office.)

...stoker Ernest Gill comes off duty, stops for a cigarette, and sees off to starboard what he thinks are the lights of a large passenger ship. He does not inform the officer of the watch because, he feels, it is not his duty. (*Boston Journal*.)

Earlier, during his watch on the bridge, Charles V. Groves had seen the light of a vessel to starboard, and had tried unsuccessfully to signal it. In the third officer's opinion, the ship is nothing more than a small tramp steamer. (*Daily Sketch*.)

Stanley Lord,
Californian's captain

Harold T. Cottam,
Carpathia's wireless
operator

The *Californian*'s master, Stanley Lord, also had seen the vessel's light and, before going below, tells Groves to continue signalling. (*Washington Evening Star.*)

Top Fifty-eight miles to the southeast is the Mediterranean-bound Cunarder *Carpathia*. (Private collection.)

Preparing for bed, her wireless operator Harold Cottam struggles with a knot in his shoelace. As he does so, he hears *Titanic*'s distress call and immediately informs Captain Arthur Rostron. (*Daily Mirror.*)

Above Seventy miles to the southwest, the Russian-Asiatic liner *Birma*... (Mariner's Museum, Newport News, Va.)

...intercepts the distress call. Her operators log the wireless traffic flashing among the responding vessels. The first message gives *Titanic*'s position. (*Sphere.*)

Left *Titanic* (MGY) quickly responds to *Birma* (SBA) regarding the nature of the difficulty. (Frank P. Aks.)

172

Right *Birma* advises *Titanic* she is on the way. (*Sphere*.)

Second right *Frankfurt* (DFT) breaks in asking for more details. (Frank P. Aks.)

Third right *Birma*'s operator dutifully responds. (Frank P. Aks.)

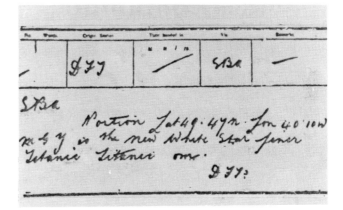

Below But time is growing short for *Titanic*. Her operators try the new signal for distress, SOS. (*Sphere*.)

Bottom right By 1.30 am, desperation is apparent in *Titanic*'s transmission. (*Sphere*.)

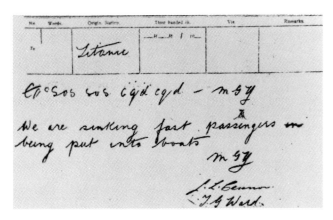

Left Among vessels with wireless receiving the *Titanic*'s calls for help are the White Star liner *Celtic*. . . (Authors' collection.)

. . .the North German Lloyd's *Prinz Friedrich Wilhelm*, 170 miles due south. . . (Michael V. Ralph collection.)

. . .and the Allan Line's *Virginian*, 170 miles north. (Authors' collection.)

Bottom left Responding to *Titanic*'s call at about 1 am, the Anchor-Donaldson Line's *Saturnia*, westbound from Glasgow to New Brunswick, turns and steams towards the sinking ship. However, she is forced to stop within six miles of the distress position when she encounters heavy ice. (Authors' collection.)

Top right At 1.25 *Olympic*, 512 miles to the west, asks, 'Are you steering southerly to meet us?' *Titanic*'s operator can only reply, 'We are putting the women off in boats'. (Authors' collection.)

Above right Allegedly nearby, but apparently not aware of the unfolding disaster because she has no wireless, is the Norwegian sealing vessel *Samson* (Authors' collection.)

Top far right Out of Gloucester, Massachusetts, the fishing schooner *Dorothy Baird* is also in the vicinity, as reported by the Wilson's and Furness-Leyland freighter *Etonian*. (Typical Gloucester schooner; Arnold Watson collection.)

Right One of the last vessels to hear *Titanic*'s distress call is the Leyland freighter *Asian*. She is unable to divert her course because she is proceeding to Halifax with the disabled tanker *Deutschland* in tow. Along with *Virginian, Asian* hears the final transmission from *Titanic*... two faint-sounding V's at 2.17 am. (Mariners Museum, Newport News, Va.)

Awakened at 4.30 am to determine the status of a nearby vessel, visible in the early morning light, *Californian*'s wireless operator is quickly advised by *Frankfurt* of *Titanic*'s loss. Once notified, Captain Lord immediately sets *Californian*'s course toward the reported disaster site. Under way by 5 am, the ship proceeds several miles through heavy ice to the ice field's western side and steams down its length. *Carpathia* comes into view to the east, and *Californian* again crosses the ice barrier to reach *Carpathia*'s side at 8.30. (*Harper*'s.)

Chapter Thirteen

RESCUE

With the International Mercantile Marine's formation in 1902, American financial interests dominated the North Atlantic trade. It appeared that the Cunard Line would have to join the Morgan combine to survive. However, to preserve representation of British ships and a British company on the North Atlantic, the government advanced to Cunard, through a low-interest loan, the cost of building two large and fast liners, on condition that the company remain a purely British concern. Cunard applied the loan to construction of *Lusitania* and *Mauretania*, which both entered service in 1907.

Five years earlier in 1902, Cunard had built *Carpathia* for its Liverpool—New York run, a liner, it was hoped, that would operate in close competition with IMM's ships. Constructed by C. S. Swan & Hunter Ltd, with engines by the Wallsend Slipway and Engineering Co Ltd, both of Newcastle, *Carpathia* was of 13,603 gross and 8,660 net tons. Her dimensions were 540 feet long by 64.5 feet wide. As completed, her accommodation was for 204 second and 1,500 third class passengers, 486 of the latter being housed in rooms, the remainder in dormitories.

Launched on 6 August 1902, *Carpathia* underwent sea trials from 22-25 April 1903. On 5 May she set out on her maiden voyage from Liverpool to Boston via Queenstown and back. After one return visit to Boston, *Carpathia* was placed on the Liverpool—New York service for which she was planned.

In 1903 the Cunard Line became official agents for Hungarian emigration, and in November *Carpathia* was diverted to take up the route between New York and Trieste, service she shared with the ageing *Aurania* (1883). Cunard was quickly able to assign other liners to the Trieste route, and in the spring of 1904 *Carpathia* returned to her Liverpool—New York service. During 1905 her accommodation was modified to house 100 first class, 200 second class and 2,250 third class. She re-entered service employed almost exclusively between New York, Trieste and other Mediterranean ports.

Arthur Henry Rostron* was born at Bolton, near Liverpool, in 1869.[†] Educated at Bolton Public High School, he joined the training ship *Conway* at the age of seventeen and served for two years as a cadet. Afterwards he spent several years in sailing vessels and steamers trading to various parts of the world. He joined the Cunard Company in 1895 as fourth officer of *Umbria* and, except for a brief leave to take qualifying drill in the Royal Naval Reserve, he never left the company's service until his retirement in 1931.

He was second, first and chief officer aboard many Cunard ships during the early 20th century: *Etruria, Servia, Ultonia, Saxonia, Pannonia, Ivernia* and *Campania*. It was on 26 April 1907, while chief officer of *Campania*, that Rostron sighted off the Irish coast near Cork a long-necked object which he sketched as it moved, turning its head from side to side. Rostron stated at the time — and never subsequently denied — that what he saw and sketched was a sea serpent.

However imaginative the young officer may have been, it did not interfere with his progress in the company's service. In 1907 he was given his first command, the cargo ship *Brescia* in the Mediterranean trade. Subsequent commands were *Ivernia, Pavonia, Saxonia* and *Pannonia*. In January 1912 he assumed his sixth command . . . *Carpathia*.

On Thursday, 11 April 1912 at noon, *Carpathia* departed Pier 54 at the foot of West Street in New York. The day was clear, with bright sunshine and

---

*In April and May 1912 newspaper accounts of the disaster, and even in a 1931 history of the Cunard Line, his name is spelled 'Rostrom', but *Rostron* it undeniably is.

[†]Stanley Lord, master of *Californian*, was born in Bolton in 1877.

moderately cool temperatures. The 743 passengers (128 first, 50 second and 565 third class) were glad to be on their way to the Mediterranean's warm and sunny ports. The weather turned cloudy after the vessel left New York. Cool air turned to cold, and by Saturday there was rain. Sunday, however, dawned bright and clear. At 10.30 am, Captain Rostron conducted Divine Service. The entire crew attended and, according to first class passenger Mrs James Fenwick, it was 'most impressive'.

Twenty-one-year-old wireless operator Harold Thomas Cottam was tired. He had been on duty all day, since 7 am that Sunday, 14 April. Except for a brief meal break around noon he had been hard at work in the wireless 'shack', a white-painted structure atop the deck house containing the second class smoking room, aft of the funnel. As was customary on all but the largest liners in 1912 he had no relief operator. He had no stated duty hours aboard *Carpathia*, but was supposed to be available during daylight hours to handle commercial traffic from and for passengers.

Now it was midnight and, as was his personal custom, he was preparing to retire. The minutes passed, and normally Cottam would have been in bed. But he was waiting for confirmation of an earlier communication with the Allan liner *Parisian*. As he undressed he kept the earphones on his head, waiting to hear from the other ship. ('A minute more . . . No, a few minutes more. . .') He removed his jacket and bent over to unlace his boots, still wearing the 'phones.

Not receiving word from *Parisian*, Cottam again sat down at his set and switched frequency to the Cape Cod land station. He planned to listen for a few minutes for news items or messages of general interest, then switch back to see if *Parisian* was trying to reach him. He heard Cape Cod transmitting commercial messages for *Titanic* and jotted down three or four, planning to forward them in the morning.

Then, ready to retire except for a knot in one shoelace, and half-an-hour past his regular bed time, almost idly and of his own accord he called *Titanic*:

MPA *(Capathia)*: 'I say, old man, do you know there is a batch of messages coming through for you from MCC (Cape Cod)?'

MGY *(Titanic)*: (Breaking in) 'Come at once. We have struck an iceberg. It's CQD, old man. Position 41 46′ N, 50 14′ W'.

MPA: Shall I tell my captain? Do you require assistance?'

MGY: 'Yes. Come quick.'

Scarcely pausing to put on his jacket against the night's chill, Cottam ran forward to the bridge. He burst in and blurted out the distress message he had just received to the officer of the watch, first officer H. V. Dean. Dean moved quickly. Propelling Cottam in front of him he rapidly descended the steep steps to the captain's cabin.

Captain Rostron had just gone to bed. He was not yet asleep when Dean and Cottam entered abruptly, without knocking. Irritated by the untoward intrusion Rostron demanded to know the reason. Dean stood by as Cottam reported to the captain: 'Sir, I have just received an urgent distress call from *Titanic'*. Captain Rostron sat up. '. . . She requires immediate assistance.' Rostron's feet were on the floor. '. . . She has struck an iceberg and is sinking. Her position is 41° 46′ North, 50° 14′ West.'

Rostron was hastly dressing. 'Are you certain?'

'Yes, sir.'

'Absolutely certain?' (Perhaps Rostron was remembering the sea serpent.)

'Yes, sir.'

Captain Rostron strode to the chart room and examined the navigation chart. Rapidly he determined *Carpathia's* position and its relative distance from the position of *Titanic's* distress call The distance — 58 miles — and the course — North 52 degrees West — were quickly calculated.

The bo'sun's mate passed the chart room window, on his way to supervize the watch crew wash down the decks. Rostron called the man and directed him to get all the ship's boats ready for lowering. *Carpathia*, he explained, was in no danger. They were hurrying to assist another vessel. Rostron then sent for chief engineer Johnson, who quickly reported to the bridge. Johnson was told to put on extra stokers and make all speed possible. Next, the captain sent for the ship's doctors, three of them — English, Italian and Hungarian. To each he assigned a post of duty.

To the officers now assembled on the bridge, Rostron issued a series of orders to cover all contingencies during the recovery of survivors. Chief steward Hughes and chief purser Brown were instructed to have all their men at the gangway to receive survivors from *Titanic*. ('Titanic?' There was a murmur of astonishment as the assemblage heard for the first time the name of the ship they were rushing to aid . . .)

The entire crew of *Carpathia* was to be called and served coffee. Then tea, coffee and hot soup were to be prepared for survivors coming aboard. Blankets were to be readied. All public rooms on the ship, all officers' cabins — including the captain's — were to be given up to *Titanic*'s people. *Carpathia*'s steerage passengers were to be placed in one section of the third class quarters and the vacant berths given to people from *Titanic*'s steerage.

Whilst these orders were being carried out quickly and quietly, Harold Cottam sat in the wireless shack, crouched over his apparatus, with a member of the stewards' staff assisting as a messenger. Each bulletin went straight to the bridge where

Captain Rostron was directing preparations. The news from *Titanic* was not good.

At 12.50 am, *(Titanic's* time), to *Olympic:* 'I require immediate assistance.'

At 1.10 am, to *Olympic:* 'We are in collision with berg. Sinking head down. Come as soon as possible. Get your boats ready.'

At 1.25 am: 'We are putting the women off in small boats.'

1.35 am: 'Engine room getting flooded.'

1.45 am: 'Engine room full up to the boilers . . .'

This was the last *Titanic* signal Cottam heard directly.

During this time, Rostron was issuing additional instructions from his post on the bridge: All gangway doors to be opened; powerful lights to be hung at the gangways and strung over the sides; a chair to be slung at each gangway to help in getting the sick and injured aboard; canvas bags to be ready to haul children up. Pilot ladders and side ladders, blocks and lines of various kinds to be placed where they would be of help to the small boats and the people in them; oil to be poured down the forward lavatories to make the water alongside the ship as smooth as possible . . .

At 2.30 chief officer Hankinson reported everything in readiness.

Carpathia's normal top speed was 14½ knots. With the urgency of the situation, the engine room crew worked up the speed to almost 17½ knots. The liner's frame shuddered, the engine bed plates vibrated as the engines strained to meet the demand for speed . . . more speed . . .

Passengers on *Carpathia* began to sense that something was happening. They noticed the pronounced vibrations of the engines, the stirring of stewards in the corridors, and the drop in cabin temperatures as steam from radiators was diverted to drive the vessel. Bells rang at stewards' stations as passengers demanded information. Cabin doors opened and heads peered out into the corridors. But Captain Rostron had ordered stewards into each corridor, politely but firmly to ask all passengers to return and remain in their cabins. The decks, companionways and public areas were to be kept clear of passengers so that the crew could complete preparations to receive survivors.

Carpathia sped through the smooth sea. The night was clear and fine, the sky thick with stars. The air was keenly cool. As Captain Rostron later described the situation:

'More and more now we were all keyed up. Icebergs loomed up and fell astern; we never slackened, though sometimes we altered course suddenly to avoid them. It was an anxious time with the *Titanic's* fateful experience very close in our minds. There were seven hundred souls on *Carpathia;* these lives, as well as all the survivors of *Titanic* herself, depended on a sudden turn of the wheel.'

Shortly after 2.30 am ship's time a green flare was sighted suddenly, far ahead. In a few seconds it disappeared. At 3 am, Rostron ordered rockets fired at fifteen-minute intervals to let survivors know help was approaching. The company's night signals* were also displayed.

By 3.35 *Carpathia* was almost to the position where *Titanic,* if afloat, would be seen. But there was only a vast emptiness.

Occasionally green lights could be glimpsed, but they were so low in the water that they could only be from small boats. Captain Rostron put the engines on 'stand by' to alert engineers for possible instant action. At 4 o'clock the engines were stopped.

About 300 yards directly ahead a green light shone, low in the water. A small boat. Rostron ordered 'dead slow ahead' and sounded the liner's whistle to let those in the boat know they had been seen. He wanted to take the boat on the port or lee side. But a large iceberg drifted lazily across the liner's bows. The ship had enough way to swing around, and the first of *Titanic's* boats moved slowly towards *Carpathia's* starboard side.

From the boat, a voice hailed: 'We have only one seaman in the boat and can't work very well'.

Carpathia inched forward. The lifeboat was alongside.

'Stop engines.'

Lines were thrown and made fast. At 4.10 the women from boat 2 began climbing aboard through the shelter deck's open gangway. There were only 25 in a boat with capacity for 40. Also aboard was fourth officer Boxhall, who had been ordered to take charge of the boat's all-female complement.

Captain Rostron sent word asking Boxhall to report to him on the bridge. Still wet and shivering uncontrollably — from emotion as much as cold — Boxhall told Rostron in a broken voice that *Titanic* had sunk at 2.20 am.

It had been difficult to keep news of the rescue from *Carpathia's* passengers. Now it was impossible. What had began as rumour became fact. A few passengers who were able to elude the watchful stewards came on deck; now there were more and more. They pressed against the railings.

In the early dawn's half light the pathetic fleet of *Titanic* lifeboats appeared, strung out in a ragged line, barely moving through the ice-strewn sea. In the first rays of the rising sun they homed in on *Carpathia*, which moved slowly, gently through the

---

*The Cunard Company's night signal, for use on the high seas, as registered on 12 June 1874, consisted of the display of a blue light and two roman candles, each throwing out six blue balls to a height not exceeding 150 feet.

ice, cruising from boat to boat, gathering in the pitiful cargoes of chilled and frightened passengers and crew.

There was ice all around: growlers, barely out of the water; sheets and broken pieces of floe ice; dozens of large bergs, some over 200 feet high, first pink in the dawn's light, then gold in the rising sun, some resembling full-rigged ships.

With look-outs posted at the forepeak and in the crow's nest on the forward mast, *Carpathia* dodged through the ice, pausing to take aboard survivors, then moving dead slow ahead to the next lifeboat.

Many women were hauled aboard in slings and bo'sun's chairs, children in canvas ash bags; the men, crew and passengers alike, climbed wearily up the ladders and netting slung over the side. As they reached the deck they were taken below where nourishment and warmth awaited them.

One after another the boats arrived, a sad flotilla — all that remained of a mighty liner which, not five hours earlier, had been in the midst of her maiden voyage. At 6.15 am, collapsible C with Bruce Ismay aboard, came up. At 7 am, boat 14 with collapsible D in tow . . .

(During the night, fifth officer Lowe had transferred twelve men and one woman — third class passenger Rosa Abbott — from half-swamped boat A to boat D. Leaving three bodies aboard the soggy collapsible, Lowe opened the boat's seacocks before casting it adrift. Boat D was taken in tow by boat 14 and, to assist the oarsmen, Lowe raised boat 14's mast and sails. The boats approached *Carpathia* in a manner which one onlooker later described as resembling 'a ruddy regatta'.)

Boat 9, boat 4 . . . by 8 am, boat 6.

A breeze had sprung up and the water was getting choppy. Aboard the overturned boat collapsible B, second officer Lightoller was having difficulty keeping the craft afloat. Moving at his command, those aboard leaned in unison to the left, then to the right, then back to the left to maintain a precarious balance. The boat was very low in the water and Lightoller was afraid searchers aboard *Carpathia* would not see it. He tried to attract attention with repeated blasts on his pocket whistle. Finally, *Carpathia* wheeled ponderously and headed toward them. Slowly. . . slowly. . . The small boat was almost swamped by the rising waves. Soon, though, they were alongside the tall, cliff-like sides and all were taken aboard quickly, including the body of one who had died during the night.

Lightoller himself was the last up the ladder, the final *Titanic* survivor to board *Carpathia*.

There was silence as the survivors boarded — heavy, oppressive silence broken only by the shuffle of feet on the wooden decks and the shrill squeal of the block and tackle hauling up the bo'sun's chairs. There were no shouts of greeting or recognition, no cries of grief or loss. Many women believed their husbands had been saved by other ships. Even when the dreaded realization of widowhood swept over them their grief was inward and personal. Sobs were muffled.

Some went directly to the solitude of cabins. Bruce Ismay, in shock, was taken to Dr McGee's cabin; the doctor ordered that the stricken man be treated in seclusion. Madelene Force Astor was escorted to the infirmary by Gottlieb Rencher, *Carpathia*'s senior hospital attendant.

With the last survivor aboard, the disaster's immensity began to emerge. Of *Titanic*'s 2,227 crew and passengers there were but 705 living survivors aboard *Carpathia*. Lost were 1,522 — a chilling, mind-numbing figure.

Carpathia circled the area, vainly searching for possible additional survivors. Captain Rostron arranged to have a service in the first class saloon, conducted as the ship passed over the spot where *Titanic* sank, as nearly as could be calculated; a service, as he said, of respect to those who were lost and of gratitude for those who had been saved.

Among the woman survivors, muted grief gave way to sobs of anguish. Men stood during the service with tears streaming down their drawn faces. Bravery gave way to fatigue. Babies cried in hunger and confusion; small children whined fretfully or played unconcernedly. Gradually the survivors drifted away. Some went to cabins where double and triple occupancy was the rule. Others found rest on cots and mattresses hastily placed throughout the ship's public rooms. Survivors from *Titanic*'s third class were directed to *Carpathia*'s steerage. But regardless of their destination, cabin or steerage, each was cared for with tenderness and solicitude by *Carpathia*'s passengers and crew.

While the last lifeboat was being taken aboard, *Californian* arrived from the icefield's western side. Speeding through ice at considerable risk to his own vessel, Captain Lord signalled that he wished to communicate with *Carpathia*. There was little to say. It appeared there were no more survivors in the vicinity. The sea was rising and Captain Rostron wished to be on his way. Thirteen of *Titanic*'s lifeboats had been taken aboard* There appeared nothing else left to do.

Rostron ordered *Carpathia* to make one final turn about the wreck site. There was very little wreckage: some deck chairs, pieces of small furniture, a few lifejackets . . . A single body, head half-submerged.

---

*Seven were carried in *Carpathia*'s davits, six on chocks at the forecastle head. Boats 4, 14 and 15 and collapsibles B, C and D were cast adrift and sank quickly. Collapsible A had already been set adrift by fifth officer Lowe.

Leaving *Californian* to search for any survivors on rafts or wreckage, at 8.50 am Rostron ordered *Carpathia* to head west, away from the ice. But a tremendous ice-field that stretched to the horizon soon blocked their passage. Great bergs thrust out of the pack ice, itself six to twelve feet above the water line. For nearly four hours *Carpathia* sailed around the pack, logging some 56 miles, before getting to clear water.

One by one the ships which had diverted towards the disaster site returned to their normal courses: *Baltic, Olympic, Frankfurt. Mount Temple,* which was still at the western edge of the ice-field, turned and headed west again.

There remained one sad duty to perform. Three men who had survived to reach *Carpathia*'s deck succumbed to shock and exposure, expiring shortly after they were taken aboard. Seaman W. H. Lyons, age 26; bedroom steward S. C. Siebert, age 29; and an unidentified fireman, of whom no record was preserved. A third class passenger, Edward Lindley, had been taken aboard, dead, from collapsible A.*

At 4 pm, *Carpathia*'s engines were stopped and her flag lowered to half-mast. It was windy and quite chilly; passengers were below. Rev Father Roger B. T. Anderson, an Episcopal monk, who earlier had headed the memorial service, now read the burial service. As he pronounced the beautiful benediction, members of *Carpathia*'s crew gently picked up each body, lifted it over the side, and committed it to the deep.

A respectful moment of silence followed. Then, as Lawrence Beesley said, 'When it was over the ship steamed on again to carry the living back to the land'.

Shortly after coming aboard and lodging in Dr McGee's cabin, Bruce Ismay was visited by Captain Rostron, who suggested that Ismay notify White Star's New York office about the disaster. Ismay scribbled a note on a scrap of paper and handed it to the captain:

'Deeply regret advise you *Titanic* sank this morning after collision with iceberg, resulting in serious loss of life. Full particulars later. Bruce Ismay.'

The message, addressed to P. A. S. Franklin, United States vice president of the IMM, was taken by Rostron to the radio shack for transmission. After consultation with *Titanic*'s officers, Ismay dispatched a second message to Franklin. It had already been decided in a conversation with Captain Rostron that *Carpathia* was to take the survivors to New York. Now Ismay, in agreement with his officers, requested by wireless that the White Star liner *Cedric*, then at New York, be held until the

Carpathia's arrival. In that way, the crew could be trans-shipped to England with minimal discomfort and displacement.

'Very important you should hold *Cedric* daylight for *Titanic*'s crew. Answer. YAMSI.'

('YAMSI' was Ismay's personal signature, used only on his private messages.)

During the morning, even as *Carpathia* was skirting the ice-field searching for open water, a roster of survivors was carefully compiled. *Carpathia*'s chief purser, E. G. F. Brown, and second purser, P. B. Barnett, prepared and checked the list of surviving passengers. *Titanic*'s second officer Lightoller prepared the list of deck and engine department survivors (seamen, stokers, trimmers and greasers), while chief second class steward John Hardy compiled those from the victualling department (cooks, stewards and messmen).

The lists were re-checked carefully before being taken to wireless operator Harold Cottam for transmission. He was exhausted, for he had had no sleep for more than 24 hours. In response to an inquiring message from *Olympic*, he had snapped, 'I can't do everything at once. Patience, please'. He did manage to transmit a brief account, concluding with 'Please excuse the sending, but am half asleep'.

When the survivor lists arrived, Cottam was overwhelmed. He began sending names to *Olympic*, which relayed them to Cape Race. He was close to collapse from the strain. *Titanic*'s own junior wireless operator was in *Carpathia*'s hospital suffering from frostbite and injured feet. In response to appeals from Cottam and Rostron, Bride agreed to be carried to the wireless shack where he began assisting the exhausted Cottam.

Absorbed as they were in transmission of survivors' names, Cottam and Bride ignored all inquiries from newspapers and requests for particulars from private sources. Even an inquiry from United States President William Howard Taft regarding his personal friend Archie Butt remained unanswered. The operators were simply inundated by the responsibilities and requirements of their task.

On Wednesday morning, *Carpathia* ran into a heavy fog and was forced to reduce her speed. The mournful sound of the liner's fog whistle set everyone's nerves on edge. Despite the speed reduction, the liner was able to cover 168 miles between 4 am and 4 pm at a rate of fourteen land miles per hour. The US Navy scout cruiser *Chester* had been despatched from near Nantucket Island at President Taft's request, to assist with transmis-

---

*Lawrence Beesley, in *The Loss of the SS Titanic*, mentions burial of eight bodies. Colonel Archibald Gracie, in *The Truth About the Titanic*, describes four bodies, as does Mrs James A. Fenwick, a *Carpathia* passenger.

sion of the survivors' lists. Bride later complained, 'If the *Chester* had had a decent operator I could have worked with him longer, but he got terribly on my nerves with his insufferable incompetence'.

(Surely not incompetent was a young wireless operator working at the private station atop New York City's Wanamaker's Department Store. Twenty-one-year-old David Sarnoff was tuned in to marine wireless traffic early on the morning of Sunday, 15 April, when he caught the first signals of the disaster being transmitted and relayed through the ether. He remained steadfastly at his station — MHI — listening and recording all the messages he could hear. It was from this principal source that many newspapers and wire services obtained their first accurate news of the disaster. Young Sarnoff went on to become one of the century's outstanding industrialists in the field of communications.)

At 1.20 am on Monday, 15 April, Carr Van Anda, managing editor of the *New York Times,* was handed the first wireless bulletin describing *Titanic*'s CQD and request for assistance. After telephone calls to *Times* correspondents in Montreal and Quebec, and to White Star's New York office, Van Anda and his staff assembled coverage based on fact, file material and a brilliant flash of journalistic intuition. The early morning edition of the *New York Times,* hitting the streets as other newspapers merely were printing copies of the bulletin, was a reporting triumph, and did much to kindle early public interest in the disaster.

The tragic news gripped the world's attention. During Monday and Tuesday, newspapers' special editions followed one after another, each revealing additional details of the wreck and the people aboard. Early editions relied on known facts — and few they were: names of millionaires and other famous people known to be aboard; scant data about the vessel itself, its immense cost and luxurious furnishings; accounts of historic sea wrecks. In some less ethical cases, the absence of hard information prompted editorial invention. In other cases, the vagaries of wireless reception caused outright falsehood to be published as fact.

White Star offices on both sides of the Atlantic were besieged. In the New York offices at 9 Broadway, company officials, aware only that the ship was in distress and not yet cognizant of the disaster, attempted to buoy the spirits of those making enquiries. At one point, a special train, with Pullmans for first class passengers and day coaches for second and third class passengers, was ordered to be made up and despatched via the New York, New Haven and Hartford Railroad to Halifax, Nova

Scotia where, it was anticipated, *Titanic*'s passengers would be safely landed.

However, as one wireless bulletin followed another and confirmation of the awful loss was received at last, over the signature of Bruce Ismay himself, officials were forced to confess that the ship had indeed been lost, and with it a large number of passengers.

By 17 April most survivors' names were known, having been received from *Carpathia* and relayed first by *Olympic* and then by *Chester* to land-based telegraphists who then flashed the news to an eagerly expectant public.

At the New York Maritime Exchange's request, flags of all shipping in New York Harbour were half-masted on Wednesday in honour of *Titanic*'s dead. Delayed by fog and rainy weather, *Carpathia* was expected to dock at Cunard's Pier 54 around 9 pm on 18 April. The sense of shock and loss prevailed as New York prepared to receive survivors.

Government representatives and the press made extensive plans to greet the survivors. The function of the former was to minimize survivors' exposure to curiosity, the function of the latter to maximize it.

General Nelson H. Henry, Surveyor of the Port, issued orders that only closest relatives — father, husband or son; mother, wife or daughter — would be admitted to the pier, and not more than two would be allowed for each expected survivor. He had forty inspectors on his staff, and each request for a pier pass was verified carefully.

The United States Secretary of the Treasury, in a telegram to New York Surveyor of Customs Loeb, suspended all customs regulations involved in landing survivors and examining their luggage. Federal immigration officers waived the usual examination of steerage passengers.

New York City's Mayor Gaynor and Police Commissioner Waldo jointly planned precautions on and near the pier. Under Inspector George McCluskey's direction, 150 foot patrolmen, twelve mounted police and 25 detectives would man barricades and cordon off the Fourteenth Street area as far east as Eighth Avenue to all but authorized pedestrian and vehicular traffic. Police Lieutenant Charles Becker* headed a squad of strongarm men to prevent pickpockets and petty thieves from operating.

Now, as the cool, rainswept dusk gathered, police began erecting a series of ropes dotted with green lanterns, for 75 feet on either side of the pier's main entrance. No one had been permitted on the pier since the previous day, and as *Carpathia*'s arrival

---

*Less than three months later, on 15 July 1912, the murder of gambler Herman Rosenthal led to Lieutenant Becker's conviction for heading an underworld gang specializing in graft and corruption. Becker subsequently was executed for Rosenthal's murder.

hour drew near, passes of all those attempting to enter were scrutinized carefully. Few newspapers applying for passes had been issued one. At the request of John Pierpont Morgan and the Astor, Guggenheim and Thayer families, reporters were kept outside, in front of the pier and in hotels on adjacent side streets, where many newspapers had set up direct telephone links to their main offices.

The United States Treasury Department had no reluctance about having reporters accompany the boats which were to bring officials out to *Carpathia* for boarding prior to docking. It was left to the Cunard Line to issue a firm injunction forbidding the boarding of *Carpathia* prior to her docking by anyone other than designated officials.

Thus, *Carpathia*, having passed the Ambrose Light Vessel, was confronted with a flotilla of small craft, each carrying reporters shouting questions through megaphones at *Carpathia*'s passengers who lined the rails, peering down at the newspaper people in the early evening gloom. While some reporters shouted their questions, others fired off magnesium flares and flash powder, attempting to photograph the dramatic scene.

In spite of the injunction, some reporters had bribed their way aboard the pilot vessel *New York*. As *Carpathia* slowed to take aboard the pilot, several reporters attempted to climb the pilot's ladder. They were rebuffed by third officer Rees, who had to manhandle them away from the vessel's side. (One reporter did manage to elude Rees and board *Carpathia*. He was apprehended immediately and taken to Captain Rostron, who restricted the man to the bridge, on his honour. It is to the reporter's credit that he did not leave the bridge until after *Carpathia* docked. He later filed a story told from his unique vantage point.)

As *Carpathia* proceeded into the harbour she was buffeted by strong winds and heavy rains. Thunder and lightning rolled across the sky as the liner slowed off the Staten Island quarantine station, barely stopping to take aboard the port doctor Joseph J. O'Connell, who arrived alongside on the *Governor Flower*.

Long having outdistanced the newspaper boats, *Carpathia* crossed the upper bay — the Statue of Liberty off her port side illuminated only briefly by the lightning flashes — and passed the Battery at Manhattan's southernmost tip. Here, in silence, more than 10,000 people had gathered, standing in the heavy downpour to watch *Carpathia* pass.

On up the North River (as the Hudson is known in the West Side pier area), her silhouette standing out against the distant New Jersey waterfront's lights, the ghostly lightning still affording flickering glimpses of her funnel and superstructure, *Carpathia* approached the Cunard pier at Fourteenth Street. Onlookers gasped in surprise as she turned in a great circle towards the New Jersey shore, then wheeled again and stopped at a point opposite the White Star Line piers 59 and 60, at the foot of West Nineteenth and West Twentieth Streets. It was dark on the river, and a misty rain was falling. But flashes of lightning revealed to those on shore the *Titanic*'s lifeboats, manned by crewmen, being lowered from *Carpathia*'s davits. The Merritt & Chapman tug *Champion* stood by, and four *Titanic* boats were lowered to her deck, while seven were lowered into the water, where *Champion* took them in tow. Two boats remained on *Carpathia*'s forward deck.

Champion, the lifeboats close behind her, proceeded to the bulkhead between piers 58 and 59. As the boats were set free from the tow, they were secured to the bulkhead; the boats lowered to the water were also secured, under the supervision of Osborne B. Thomas, International Mercantile Marine's dockmaster in New York.

As *Carpathia* docked five blocks to the south, *Titanic*'s boats, once again afloat, bobbed slowly in the silent black water.*

After dropping the boats, *Carpathia* proceeded at an almost painfully slow pace to Pier 54. By 9.30 the liner had been warped into the pier's north side, her departure point eight days earlier. The crowd inside the pier stirred expectantly as the forward and aft gangways were lowered. Conversation subsided to a quiet murmur. Outside in the misty streets the vast throng of spectators became silent and, as though they, too, wished to become part of the drama, strained against police lines.

Portable wood fences had been set up to clear

---

*During Thursday night, souvenir hunters ravaged the lifeboats. Many of the wood markers bearing the name 'SS Titanic' were pilfered, as were many of the wood White Star pennant markers. On Friday morning, guards were assigned to keep curiosity seekers from the boats. The name *Titanic* was sanded from the remaining markers. Also on Friday morning, the two boats left aboard *Carpathia* were rowed over from Pier 54.

The boats remained afloat until Saturday, 20 April, when they were hoisted to the second floor loft between piers 58 and 59. They were carefully chocked and covered with tarpaulins. On 16 May the boats were joined by collapsible A, which had been picked up at sea on 13 May by *Oceanic*, and brought to New York.

Regarded as *Titanic*'s only physical assets (prepaid freight and passenger tickets being the only other tangible assets), the boats were evaluated for salvage by surveyors assigned by the United States District Court. Their appraised value, $4,520 (about £930) was part of the $96,000 (nearly £19,800) turned over to the British Admiralty Court, representing the total amount of salvage realized from *Titanic*.

spaces at the foot of each gangway and to provide a path to the door. Relatives and friends of survivors pressed forward as the first of *Titanic*'s passengers began descending the gangways. Many were ill clad, wearing only such clothing as had been provided and altered by the kind women passengers aboard *Carpathia*. Welcomed by tears and hugs of joy, the survivors headed to the street exit where a line of cars waited to whisk them to their homes or to hotels provided by the White Star Line. Some were assisted to ambulances which departed for St Vincent's and St Luke's Hospitals.

As the survivors began to appear at the pier's front entrance, they were greeted by clamorous reporters and by many explosions of photographers' magnesium flares. Confused, bewildered, exhausted, many were utterly oblivious of the shouted questions and the reporters who crowded in from all sides.

One by one the passengers departed: Bruce Ismay was driven to the Ritz-Carleton Hotel. Mrs John Jacob Astor was met by her stepson Vincent Astor, a nurse and two doctors, and taken by limousine to the family's Fifth Avenue home.* William T. Sloper was met by his father and taken to the Waldorf Hotel for a rest before proceeding to their Connecticut home. Major Arthur Peuchen also stopped at the Waldorf en route to Toronto, while 'a downtown hotel' provided shelter for actress-model-socialite Dorothy Gibson and her mother.

Around 11 pm the third class survivors began to emerge from the aft gangway. Much of the crowd had dispersed by now and there were no reporters outside the pier. Many of the 174 survivors were destitute. Having lost all in the wreck, they had no resources for the basics of existence. The White Star Line and numerous municipal and private relief services provided temporary assistance and, for many, transportation funds to relatives in distant cities, when needed. The debarking third class survivors presented a formidable task for the Women's Relief Committee and the American Red Cross.

(In contrast, several first class survivors departed from New York aboard private trains for home. At Grand Central Station, a special train awaited Mrs Charles Hays, widow of the president of the Grand Trunk Railroad. Others taking the private rail route included the Thayers (son John B. Jr; his mother; and her maid, Margaret Fleming), and Mrs George D. Widener and her maid, Emily Geiger. Each train departed Jersey City, New Jersey, before 11 pm and arrived at various destinations near Philadelphia, Pennsylvania, around 12.30 am. The Pennsylvania Railroad also provided a nine-car train without charge for any survivor wishing to travel to Philadelphia or points west. The railroad had a representative at *Carpathia*'s pier, and eight taxi-cabs to convey passengers to Pennsylvania Station on the other side of Manhattan.)

Last to disembark from *Carpathia* were *Titanic*'s crew. Taken off at the aft gangway they passed through the echoing, now dark and empty pier, and were led down a narrow stairway at the pier's edge to where the United States Immigration Service tender *George Starr* was moored. Rather than march the 214 crew through the streets and risk exposing them to the probing questions of newspaper reporters who might be lurking there, the company transported them aboard the tender, northward six blocks to Pier 60 at the foot of West Twentieth Street.

(Most crew had lost their identification papers. Until the men and women could be examined thoroughly, to land them might violate United States immigration regulations. Water transportation prevented this possibility.)

After debarking, the crew were marched across the pier's reception area, from which all but company employees had been cleared, to Pier 61, where the vessel *Lapland*, owned by the Red Star Line (part of the IMM) was moored. *Titanic*'s 210 crew members boarded and were assigned cabins in *Lapland*'s third class area, with first class accommodation for the four surviving officers. A meal was then served to them in the first class dining saloon.

The *Titanic*'s story is full of contrasts: of sound and silence, of light and darkness, of joy and sadness. There is no sadder silence nor deeper darkness than the early morning hours of 19 April. Her passengers having disembarked from another ship, her crew resting fitfully aboard yet another vessel, her boats heaving gently up and down in the tidal swell of a strange port, the very name *Titanic* appeared likely to pass from the pages of history. There was so little left of her. Soon passengers and crew would disperse, the small boats would disappear. Soon the name *Titanic* would no longer be spoken. And her memory would fade, to be remembered by a few, perhaps. At this sad, dark hour *Titanic* appeared destined for oblivion.

Or so it seemed. . .

Aboard *Carpathia*, in contrast, as she lay moored at Pier 54, all was jubilation. While grieving for the lost, *Carpathia*'s passengers were happy that they had been able to contribute so directly to the survivors' rescue.

The passengers were encouraged to go ashore while the liner was cleaned and restocked with food

---

*Young Vincent Astor had wished to take his stepmother off *Carpathia* at Quarantine, using the family yacht *Noma*. He abandoned this plan after consulting with White Star officials.

and provisions. The turnaround was to be so rapid that there was no time to launder *Carpathia*'s linen. The entire linen supply of *Saxonia*, a Cunarder docked nearby, was raided and transferred to *Carpathia*.

Cunard refused all White Star's offers of payment. The rescue was a humanitarian service, and no money could be accepted for such an act. Indeed, Cunard added to the costs it had already incurred by giving a month's wages to every crewman who had participated in the rescue.

While *Carpathia* was still at sea before reaching New York, *Titanic* survivors formed a committee to collect funds from among their group for distribution to *Carpathia*'s crew. Committee members were Dr H. W. Frauenthal, who acted as treasurer; Mrs J. J. ('Molly') Brown, Mrs William Bucknell and Mrs George Stone. (Both Mrs Astor and Mrs Widener declined to contribute to the fund. They expressed sympathy for the cause but preferred to defer their contributions to a later date and 'in their own way'.)

When *Carpathia* reached New York, the amount of $4,360 (nearly £900) was distributed among the crew. Captain Rostron was given $500 (£100) while the remainder of the officers and crew received amounts varying from $100 (£20) to each officer and the chief engineer; $50 (£10) to each of the three surgeons; and so on, down to $10 (£2) each to the 47 seamen and $5 (£1) to each of the 49 firemen.

The fund eventually exceeded $15,000 (£3,000) and was turned over for safekeeping to J. P. Morgan & Company, Mr Morgan himself taking personal charge of the money.

At the time of the rescue *Carpathia* had aboard 743 passengers (128 first, 50 second and 565 third class). While at New York from 18-20 April, twelve first and four second class passengers left the ship, four additional first and four second class passengers came aboard, so when she again departed from New York at 4 pm on Saturday 20 April, *Carpathia* carried 735 passengers (120 first, 50 second and 565 third class).

Although he — and the company — were anxious to get back to sea, Captain Rostron spent most of the in-port period preparing his report to the company* and appearing at the first session of Senator Smith's investigating committee. As a result of these commitments, the captain had no time to go to the Custom House to clear his ship. A sympathetic surveyor, however, saw that the necessary papers were delivered to the pier.

Fifteen minutes before sailing time, Harold Bride, *Titanic*'s junior wireless operator, was carried ashore on the shoulders of two *Carpathia* officers. Bride had been almost constantly on duty since boarding the ship from the overturned collapsible and now, totally exhausted, he was taken to nearby St Vincent's Hospital for treatment of crushed and frostbitten feet.

While *Carpathia* was completing her interrupted voyage, yet another survivors' committee was formed to prepare a suitable reward for the gallant captain and his crew. Frederick Seward was the committee's chairman, and its members were Mrs J. J. Brown, H. B. Steffanson, F. O. Spedden, J. G. Frauenthal, Karl H. Behr and George A. Harder. Using the funds, whose collection had begun aboard *Carpathia* during the return to New York, and which had now been augmented with additional contributions, the committee had purchased a silver loving cup for presentation to Captain Rostron, and had struck commemorative medals for each of the 320 crewmen aboard at the time of the rescue.

Carpathia made her first return visit to New York on 29 May. After all passengers had disembarked, the committee assembled on deck and presented the loving cup to Captain Rostron. A standby crew of replacements who hadn't been aboard on 15 April was placed on duty at all essential posts. At 10 am 260 crew members who had participated in the rescue assembled in the first class dining saloon. The men formed two lines, each department's officers in front and the men at the rear, and were handed their medals personally by Captain Rostron.

Six gold medals were presented to Captain Rostron, Chief Engineer Johnson, First Surgeon Frank McGee, First Purser E. G. F. Brown, Chief Steward Hughes and Second Engineer Marshall. Silver medals went to the junior officers, while the crew received bronze medals. Sixty medals were sent to crew who had left the roster, forwarded to their homes by the purser.

Though the ceremonies were over, and though gratitude had been expressed and honours bestowed, there were reactions of a more solemn nature: of bereaved families; of shock and disbelief; of investigative bodies formed to find out how and *why*. . .

In the disaster's aftermath, reaction set in, reaction which was to change the way people thought about the sea and the ships that sailed on it. . .

---

*Rostron concludes his report (which is dated 'R.M.S. *Carpathia*, April 19') with the words, 'Saved. . .Total 705 souls'. During the Mersey hearings, it was said that an additional six names had been added to Captain Rostron's report 'by the Purser'. The Board of Trade accepted the figure of 711 as the correct number of survivors. But Rostron, even in a second report, made for the historic record and, dated April 27, 1913, did not modify his own figure; the number of 705 survivors appears to be correct.

Newlyweds James and Mabel Fenwick begin a three-month honeymoon trip to Europe. They have chosen the Cunard Line's *Carpathia*, and have booked cabin A21 for the voyage. They are to have a front-row seat to history. (Mr and Mrs George A. Fenwick.)

Top right The *Carpathia* departs from New York's Pier 54 on 11 April with some 700 passengers. Fortunately, she is not filled to capacity. (Robert DiSogra collection.)

Above right Loved ones wave farewell through the giant doors in adjacent Pier 56's southern side as *Carpathia* begins her voyage. (Mr and Mrs George A. Fenwick.)

Centre right As must all newly embarked passengers, the Fenwicks unpack their luggage. . . (Mr and Mrs George A. Fenwick.)

Right . . .consult the passenger list to see whether any acquaintances are on board. . . (Mr and Mrs George A. Fenwick.)

Below . . .and arrange to hire deck chairs for the voyage. (Mr and Mrs George A. Fenwick.)

CUNARD LINE
Cabin Baggage
Stateroom _A 21_
On S.S. _Carpathia_ Sailing _____
Passenger's Name _Fenwick_

LIST OF

SALOON PASSENGERS

PER

S. S. "CARPATHIA,"

COMMANDER A. H ROSTRON, R.D.. R.N.R.

Surgeon—FRANK E. McGEE   Purser—E. G. F. BROWN, R.N.R.
Chief Steward—E. H HUGHES   Asst. Purser—P. B. BARNETT

From New York to Gibraltar, Genoa, Naples, Trieste and Fiume, April 11th, 1912.

Rev. R. B Anderson
Mr. J. A. Badenock

Mr. A. Bernard
Miss M. R. Birkhead
Miss S. Birkhead
Mr V. Biaggi
Mrs. Biaggi
Miss Marie Buon
Mr. H. B Burke

Mrs. Wilson M. Carr
Mrs. L. Catty
Miss Catty
Rev. Prof. G. Clements
Dr. S. Coit
Capt. Chas. F. Crain, U.S.A.
Mrs. Crain
Miss Elizabeth Crain

A 573
CUNARD S.S. CO. Ltd.
R.M.S. CARPATHIA.
RECEIVED FOR
(HIRE)
DECK CHAIR.
4/- or 1 Dollar.

A 574
CUNARD S.S. CO. Ltd.
R.M.S. CARPATHIA.
RECEIVED FOR
(HIRE)
DECK CHAIR.
4/- or 1 Dollar.

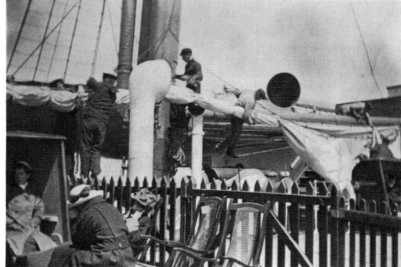

Harold Thomas Cottam,
Marconi operator

Far left The first days pass with the usual shipboard activities, such as deck quoits... (Mr and Mrs George A. Fenwick.)

...taking pictures of obliging crew members... (Mr and Mrs George A. Fenwick.)

...and observing daily maintenance routines. (Mr and Mrs George A. Fenwick.)

Shortly after midnight on 15 April, the shipboard routine comes to an abrupt end. In *Carpathia*'s wireless shack **bottom far left** located aft on the roof of the second class smoking room... (*New York Times*.)

...Marconi operator Harold Thomas Cottam is startled to receive a distress call from the stricken *Titanic*. He immediately notifies Captain Rostron who plots the famous rescue course of North 52 West. Four hours later, after a dash through ice-filled waters, *Carpathia* arrives at a spot near the distress position. (Mr and Mrs Arthur Dodge.)

Awakened by a man's voice crying, '*Titanic*'s going down', Mrs Fenwick hastily dresses and takes her camera on deck. **Top right** Her first view is of the wide expanse of ice nearby. (Mr and Mrs George A. Fenwick.)

Right She photographs the thrilling view of a nearby twin-peaked iceberg towering more than 75 feet above the green water. (Mr and Mrs George A. Fenwick.)

Far right above Suddenly, in the distance, a small boat under sail approaches *Carpathia*. It is *Titanic*'s lifeboat 14, under fifth officer Lowe's command. (Mr and Mrs George A. Fenwick.)

Right As the boat nears *Carpathia*'s side, Lowe reefs the sail, and it is now clearly seen that he has another boat (collapsible D) in tow. The photograph **right** was marked for identification during a subsequent American court proceeding. (National Archives.)

Left The overcrowded collapsible D draws near *Carpathia*'s gangway door. Among the passengers on board are Mrs Henry Harris and the Navratil children. (National Archives.)

Middle left Boat 6, with Molly Brown, Mrs Candee and Major Peuchen aboard, comes into view. . . (National Archives.)

. . .and approaches *Carpathia*'s side. (National Archives.)

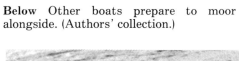

Below Other boats prepare to moor alongside. (Authors' collection.)

Top left As the boats reach the safety of *Carpathia*'s side, passengers await their turn to disembark. Lifebelts have been discarded in the bottom of the boat, and oars lie abandoned on the thwarts. (Mr and Mrs Arthur Dodge.)

Above *Titanic*'s boats are hoisted to the forward deck, where they are drained of water and placed in chocks. (National Archives.)

At about 8.30 am *Californian* appears from the west and signals that she wishes to communicate with *Carpathia*. In one of maritime history's most dramatic photographs, **middle left** Mrs Fenwick records the arrival, with *Californian*'s crew very much visible on her decks. (Mr and Mrs George A. Fenwick.)

Left Leaving *Californian* to complete a thorough search of the area, *Carpathia* proceeds toward New York, encountering the Russian-Asiatic liner *Birma* about noon. (Mr and Mrs George A. Fenwick.)

William H. Lyons,
able seaman

Far left At Captain Rostron's request, Episcopal priest the Rev Roger Anderson conducts a service in memory of the dead and thanks for the living in *Carpathia*'s first class saloon. (*Daily Mirror*.)

Above *Titanic*'s survivors and lifeboats crowd the forward deck. (*Harper*'s.)

At 4 pm, while most passengers are below decks, *Carpathia* stops for a few moments to permit burial of three *Titanic* crewmen and one passenger. Among the crew is able seaman William H. Lyons, age 26. (*Cork Examiner*.)

The following day, *Titanic*'s survivors appear on deck to relax as much as they are able. (*Harper*'s.)

The good women from among *Carpathia*'s passengers work together to make and alter clothing for *Titanic*'s women survivors. (*Illustrated London News*.)

Right Some survivors lie in the sun, seeming almost too exhausted to move. In the centre, young Gershon (Gus) Cohen dozes. . . (*New York Journal*.)

. . .while other passengers queue up for meals. . . (Mr and Mrs George A. Fenwick.)

Below . . .in *Carpathia*'s third class dining saloon. (Ken Marschall Collection.)

Below right Passengers receiving meals in the second class dining saloon do not have to queue up, but two seatings are necessary to accommodate the unexpected guests. (Ken Marschall Collection.)

Bottom During the return to New York, second class passenger Lawrence Beesley poses while wearing a bathrobe borrowed from Mr Fenwick. He is joined by two *Titanic* survivors. (Mr and Mrs George A. Fenwick.)

Bottom right A lone third class woman survivor joins several members of *Titanic*'s crew on deck. (*Daily Mirror*.)

191

Right Few survivors manage to send personal messages, for *Carpathia*'s wireless is busy sending official survivor lists. (Mr and Mrs Arthur Dodge.)

Below A group of survivors poses for a souvenir snapshot. Dr Frank McGee obliges by taking the picture. Survivors nearby express indignation when the group's leader requests his companions to 'Smile, please'. The subjects are the sole occupants of emergency boat 1, capacity forty; the people requesting the photograph are Sir Cosmo and Lady Duff-Gordon, seen in the back row with Lady Duff-Gordon's secretary, Miss Francatelli. (*Daily Mirror*.)

Below right Other group photographs involve people who are more heroic. Captain Rostron directs the arrangement of his officers for a group portrait. (Mr and Mrs George A. Fenwick.)

Bottom Crew from another area pose, too, somewhat less formally. (Private collection.)

THE WESTERN UNION TELEGRAPH COM

25,000 OFFICES IN AMERICA.   CABLE SERVICE TO ALL THE WOR

RECEIVED AT S. P. Depot, 3rd & Townsend Sts. Tel. Sutter 43

S.S.Carpathia.April. 17-12.

Harry.W.Dodge,

Pacific Hardware and Steel Co.,San Franci

All safe .Notify Mother and Vida.

Father.

2.39pm

In preparation for future reunions, survivors exchange their business cards with one another. (Mr and Mrs Arthur Dodge.)

Top right As the world watches and waits, *Carpathia* passes Fire Island, less than 58 miles from her New York City pier. (*Harper*'s.)

Middle right Although New Yorkers are not to be allowed on Pier 54, a city newspaper provides them with a vicarious experience through a cutaway diagram illustrating the pier's layout. (*New York Evening Journal*.)

Right As *Carpathia* passes the Sandy Hook pilot's station, she is surrounded by boats hired by the press and curiosity seekers. *Titanic* survivors crowd the rails for the long-awaited first view of New York. (*Harper*'s.)

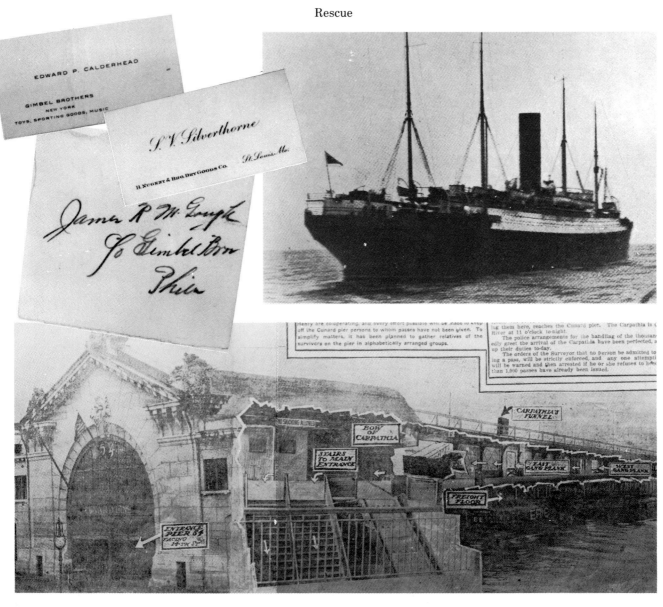

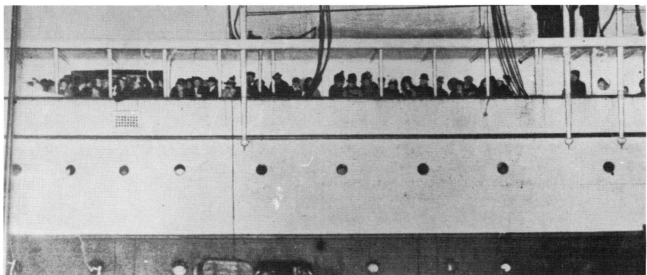

Left To everyone's surprise, *Carpathia* steams past her own pier, northward to White Star's piers 58 and 59. There, the unloading of *Titanic*'s thirteen lifeboats, some temporarily stowed in *Carpathia*'s davits, begins. (*Popular Mechanics*.)

Middle left The Merritt and Chapman tug *Champion* (right) takes the boats in tow as they clear *Carpathia*'s side. (*Harper*'s.)

Bottom left The last two lines of first class passenger Mrs H. W. Cassebeer's landing card reflect the suspension of the usual customs formalities. Even the steerage passengers are permitted to bypass the rigours of an Ellis Island inspection. (Bob Forrest collection.)

Below Outside Pier 54, police have strung ropes to clear spaces for the departing survivors. Reporters and the merely curious vie for space against the ropes. (*Harper*'s.)

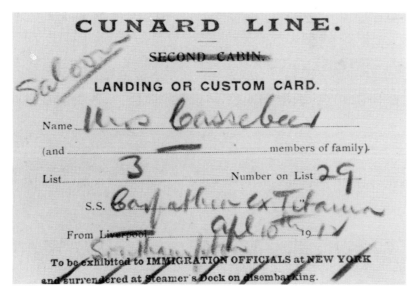

Top All eyes turn as the first survivors leave the pier for New York hotels. (Private collection.)

Above A woman identified as Mrs Jacques Futrelle is escorted to a waiting car by Robert Norton (right), a reporter for the *Boston Post*. (*Harper*'s.)

Right Among the last to be brought ashore is Harold Bride, *Titanic*'s surviving wireless operator. Suffering from severely frostbitten and smashed feet, he is carried down the gangway to a waiting wheelchair. His fatigue — from assisting *Carpathia*'s Harold Cottam with the transmission of survivors' names — is apparent on his face. (*Philadelphia Bulletin*.)

Newspaperman William Randolph Hearst's self-professed interest in the average person manifests itself in one of the few photographs **above** taken of third class survivors upon their New York arrival. At St Vincent's Hospital for a check-up are (from left) Mrs Agnes Sandstrom and children Margaret, four, and Beatrice, sixteen months; Mrs Maria Bickstrom and infant; Mrs Nadia Naked and child (the caption explained that Mrs Naked had lost six male cousins in the disaster); Mrs Lannons Bscheer and infant; and Mrs Louise Towna and her daughters Mariana and Therese. George and Kirk Towna, her sons, sit before the group. (Third class names, often due to linguistic difficulties or simple haste, are recorded very inaccurately in published passenger lists, as well as newspaper renderings: Marie *Backstrom* is on one published list, but her child is not. Mrs Naked is shown with but one child; published lists indicate two children saved, and a different first name. Mrs Bscheer and infant do not appear in the published lists at all. Mrs Towna and her children were known, in fact, as the Thomas family.) (*New York Evening Journal*.)

Left Unable to speak any English, their father Michel Navratil lost, four-year-old Michel Junior and two-year-old Edmond quickly become known as the '*Titanic* orphans'. Until their identity can be ascertained, they reside at the New York home of another survivor, Margaret Hays, under the watchful ministrations of the Children's Aid Society. (*Harper*'s.)

The sorrowful expressions on these third class passengers' faces confirm the ordeal they have survived. From left, Mrs Baum (no such name appears on published passenger lists); Mrs Leah Aks and ten-month-old son Frank ('Filly'), with whom she was reunited on the *Carpathia*; Mrs Jane Quick and daughters Vera and Phyllis. (*New York American.*)

As the last of the 705 survivors leave the *Carpathia*, the only tangible sign of their presence is a stack of lifejackets on one of the hatches. (*Daily Sketch.*)

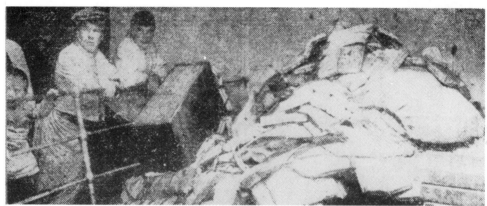

There were other souvenirs, as well. Before *Carpathia*'s arrival in New York, honeymooners James and Mabel Fenwick find an unusual remembrance in the form of a four-inch-square hardtack biscuit from one of *Titanic*'s lifeboats. (Mr and Mrs George A. Fenwick.)

Workmen are put to work on Saturday 20 April sanding off the remaining *Titanic* nameplates from the thirteen recovered boats. Souvenir hunters had emptied the boats of much of their equipment and markers during the night of 19 April. Once the workmen are finished, the boats are hauled up to the second floor loft between piers 58 and 59, from which point they disappear into history. (*Daily Sketch.*)

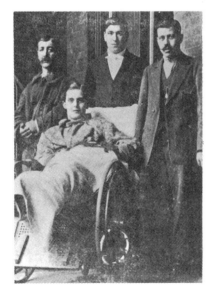

Above left Left with little more than the clothes on their back *Titanic*'s surviving crew are given new clothing at the Institute of the Seaman's Friend in New York. (*Daily Mirror*.)

Above The Institute, located at 507 West Street, across from Pier 54, then holds a memorial service in memory of the lost. (Authors' collection.)

Middle left The detained crew, some now wearing their somewhat ill-fitting clothing, gather on the steps of the Seaman's Friend building. (Authors' collection.)

Far left Others must spend time recuperating at New York's St Vincent's Hospital. Stoker John Thompson, coal passer William McIntyre and passenger Emilio Pella gather around waiter Thomas Whiteley, in the wheelchair. (Authors' collection.)

Left One week after her rescue, third class passenger Sarah Roth (left) marries Daniel Iles in New York. Her bridesmaid, Emily Badman (right) is also a survivor of *Titanic*. (*New York Tribune*.)

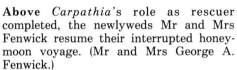

Above *Carpathia*'s role as rescuer completed, the newlyweds Mr and Mrs Fenwick resume their interrupted honeymoon voyage. (Mr and Mrs George A. Fenwick.)

Above right Re-stocked with linen and supplies borrowed from the Cunarder *Saxonia*, the *Carpathia* is moments away from leaving her New York pier for the second time. (*Popular Mechanics*.)

Middle right As the liner turns out into the North River, the bugler of the *Saxonia* salutes her with a rendition of 'Auld Lang Syne'. (Library of Congress — Bain Collection.)

Right Again heading westward, *Carpathia*'s crew is asked to assemble. From the bridge, Captain Arthur Rostron thanks the ship's company for the self-sacrificing manner in which they cared for *Titanic*'s survivors. He expresses his pride at being commander of such a fine crew, and later distributes funds collected by the survivors in gratitude for the kindness they received. (*Daily Sketch*.)

Top left Slowly, shipboard routine returns. Emigrants have hung their laundry on the ship's rails as they enjoy the sun on the Mediterranean route. (Mr and Mrs George A. Fenwick.)

Top The heroic captain modestly poses before one of *Carpathia*'s boats, now back on its chocks. (Mr and Mrs George A. Fenwick.)

Middle left One week after her fateful rush to *Titanic*'s side, *Carpathia*'s menus feature the usual selection of good food. (Mr and Mrs George A. Fenwick.)

Middle, previous page And the nightly dance programmes, suspended for the duration of the rescue voyage, resume. (Mr and Mrs George A. Fenwick.)

Bottom, previous page The Fenwicks leave the ship at Genoa. Mabel Fenwick takes one last photograph by which to remember *Carpathia*. (Mr and Mrs George A. Fenwick.)

Top, this page *Carpathia*'s crew do not forget *Titanic*'s victims. At the liner's first post-disaster arrival at Trieste, her football team plays a match with a Hungarian team, the proceeds going to the Titanic Relief Fund. (*Daily Mirror*.)

Middle On 29 May, during the liner's next visit to New York, Denver socialite Margaret ('Molly') Brown presented a loving cup and special commemorative medals to Captain Rostron.

Right The dramatic rescue of *Titanic*'s passengers and crew by *Carpathia* is permanently recorded in the 1912 edition of *Trans-Atlantic Passenger Movements* with a unique listing. (Frank O. Braynard collection.)

NEW YORK—LIVERPOOL.

N. Y. Arrival	Westbound I	II	III	STEAMER	N. Y. Departure	Eastbound I	II	III	Dept.
Jan. 2	59	74	185	Saxonia	Jan. 6	19	49	101	7
" 4	335	226	217	Lusitania	" 10	377	222	427	7
				Ivernia	" 13	18	14	89	6
" 15	84	233	299	Franconia					
" 21	95	124	216	Carmania	" 27	160	115	249	11
" 29	160	285	394	Laconia					
Feb. 5	31	116	317	Cameronia					
" 10	65	246	285	Campania	Feb. 14	29	84	200	9
" 18	70	372	279	Carmania					
" 24	311	428	900	Lusitania	" 28	316	160	387	14
Mar. 2	83	275	540	Campania	Mar. 6	91	117	324	3
" 8	245	275	933	Mauretania	" 13	245	130	384	5
" 15	362	328	1076	Lusitania	" 20	287	174	634	5
" 24	93	374	618	Campania	" 27	61	115	289	8
" 29	339	325	1032	Mauretania	Apr. 3	305	154	490	13
Apr. 7	175	298	1623	Caronia	" 10	117	128	451	1
" 14	96	366	933	Carmania	" 17	102	151	361	31
" 18	201	118	179 (207 crew)	Carpathia ex Titanic.					
" 19	238	296	942	Mauretania	" 24	465	291	677	25
" 28	96	368	1004	Caronia	May 4				

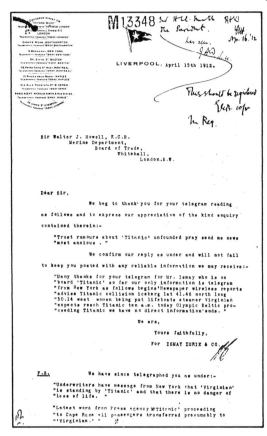

Liverpool, April 15th, 1912

Sir Walter J Howell, K.C.B.

  Marine Department,

    Board of Trade,

      Whitehall,

        London. S.W.

Dear Sir,

    We beg to thank you for your telegram reading as follows and to express our appreciation of the kind enquiry contained therein:-

    "Trust rumours about 'Titanic' unfounded pray send me news most anxious."

    We confirm our reply as under and will not fail to keep you posted with any reliable information we may receive:-

    "Many thanks for your telegram for Mr. Ismay who is on board 'Titanic' so far our only information is telegram from New York as follows begins 'Newspaper wireless reports advise Titanic collision iceberg at 41.46 north long 50.14 west women being put lifeboats steamer Virginian expects reach Titanic ten a.m. today Olympic Baltic proceeding Titanic we have no direct information' ends."

                We are,

                Yours faithfully,

                For ISMAY IMRIE & CO.

P.S. We have since telegraphed you as under:-

"Underwriters have message from New York that 'Virginian' is standing by 'Titanic' and that there is no danger of loss of life."

"Latest word from Press agency is 'Titanic' proceeding to Cape Race all passengers transferred presumably to 'Virginian'."

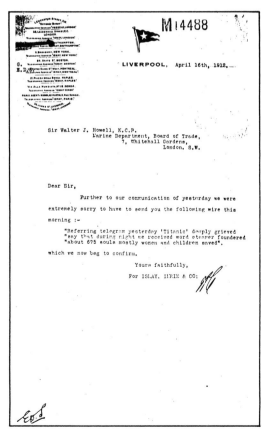

Liverpool, April 16th, 1912.

Sir Walter J. Howell, K.C.B.

  Marine Department, Board of Trade,

    7, Whitehall Gardens,

      London. S.W.

Dear Sir,

    Further to our communication of yesterday we were extremely sorry to have to send you the following wire this morning:-

    "Referring telegram yesterday 'Titanic' deeply grieved to say that during night we received word steamer foundered about 675 souls mostly women and children saved".

which we now beg to confirm.

                Yours faithfully,

                For ISMAY IMRIE & CO.

Chapter Fourteen

AFTERMATH

One of Mr Ismay's first thoughts following his rescue by *Carpathia* was a notification to the company: 'Deeply regret to advise *Titanic* sunk this morning, 15th, after collision with iceberg, resulting serious loss of life; further particulars later. Bruce Ismay'.

Though Captain Rostron himself endorsed the transmission, Marconi operator Cottam did not send the message until 17 April. It was received in New York at 9 am that same day.

The world learned quickly of the disaster, though it might not have been through Mr Ismay. And the world quickly reacted.

In America, the word was received directly, by Mr Sarnoff and his apparatus atop the Wanamaker Department Store; by way of Marconi's land station at Cape Race and, somewhat later, from Cape Cod, Siasconsett and Sea Gate. In England the news came via wireless messages relayed eastwards from ship to ship to the great receiving station at Poldhu, in Cornwall; then by way of cable messages sent to London from Montreal, Halifax and New York.

Press services — Reuters in Europe, the Associated Press in New York — picked up the story and sent it on its way. The messages arrived and departed by landline, cable and wireless — a flow which brought news to first an incredulous and then a shocked world.

On the morning of 15 April, while it was still dark, crowds began to gather in London and New York. First revealed by rumour, then by stunning, confirmed fact: '*Titanic* Strikes Iceberg. Sinking At The Head. Women and Children Being Put Off in Boats. Rescue Ships On The Way. No Word From *Titanic* for Last Two Hours. . .'

Rumour begat rumour. At Southampton, home of a majority of *Titanic*'s crew, excited family members and friends gathered before the White Star offices in Canute Road. Company officials advised them to be calm and have patience, that at the moment all appeared well. *Virginian*, it was said, was well on her way to the stricken vessel, and it

was planned to have her tow *Titanic* to Halifax. *Titanic*'s own sister, *Olympic*, was in communication, and White Star's *Baltic* was also on the way to assist.

The *Southern Daily Echo*, Southampton's evening newspaper, was likewise reassuring in its lead story:

'The White Star liner *Titanic*, the world's largest and most luxurious vessel, which left Southampton on Wednesday last with over 2,500 souls on board, collided with an iceberg last evening in mid-Atlantic. For some hours great anxiety prevailed, but fortunately more reassuring tidings reached us this afternoon, when all passengers were reported to be safe. . .'

The balance of the half-page article described icebergs and listed the prominent men and women known to be aboard.

By 16 April's evening edition, the frightful news was known and confirmed.

'Rarely, if ever, in the history of the port, have such scenes been witnessed as were seen outside the offices of the White Star Line in Canute Road this morning, when the following brief but pregnant message was posted:-

'"Titanic foundered about 2.30 am April 15th. About 675 crew and passengers picked up by ships' boats of Carpathia and Californian. Remaining and searching position of disaster. Names of those saved will be posted as soon as received."

'Dismay and incredulity struggled for the mastery of the faces in the anxious crowd as regulated by the police they pressed forward to read the fateful bulletin, for the ambiguity of the message, and the absence of any direct mention of loss of life still held out hopes which the more optimistic eagerly clutched at. It was a grim and silent crowd, nearly entirely composed of men, that waited patiently in the roadway to hear the latest tidings. Ninety-five per-cent of the members of the crew of Titanic are members of the newly-formed British Seafarers' Union, and there were many tearful enquiries at the offices of the Union at Terminus Terrace. A rumour that a tramp steamer had reached Halifax with a number of survivors of the liner on board, raised drooping hopes a little, but did little to dispel the gloomy forebodings that

gripped every heart. Many of the crew have wives and large families, and almost everyone seemed to have a husband, father, brother, son or sweetheart aboard the doomed vessel.'

Southampton quickly became a city of mourning. Flags flew at half-mast and crowds gathered on almost every street corner to discuss the fearful event. In Southampton's Northam and Shirley districts, nearly every able-bodied man followed the sea.

York Street is the centre of Northam. Most of the trimmers and stokers lived along this street. Knots of anxious women could be seen up and down its length. The dismal scene was repeated throughout the city: Northam Road, Cable Street, McNaughton Street, Russell Street. . .

The crew members' names were the last to be posted. Waiting gave way to anxiety and then to hysteria as the women, the families, waited. It was the *not knowing* that was unbearable. . .

At New York, the scene was the same. As bulletins began appearing in newspaper office windows, or on large overhead billboards, crowds gathered to watch each posting of the latest news. At first there was confidence. A special train was being ordered to pick up survivors at Halifax. And just as quickly, confidence faded and died as the truth became known.

Among the many bulletins received by wireless and cable at New York, the final three are perhaps the most pointed:

'April 15, 11.30 am — Allan Line steamer *Parisian* reports by wireless that steamer *Carpathia* is in attendance on steamer *Titanic* and has picked up twenty boats of passengers. *Baltic* is turning to give assistance and steamer *Olympic* will reach the scene between three and five o'clock today to render assistance.'

'April 15 — An official message received via the cable ship *Minia* off Cape Race says that steamers are towing *Titanic* and endeavouring to get her into shoal water near Cape Race for the purpose of beaching her.'

'April 15 (via Reuter) — The *Titanic* sunk at 2.20 this morning.'

Outside the White Star Line's New York office at 9 Broadway, opposite Bowling Green Park, crowds began to assemble during Monday's morning hours. Many were clerks and messengers, loiterers with little to do. But as the day wore on they were joined by businessmen and people of a more affluent mien. Much of their interest was in the latest news regarding the rescue; but no little interest was also shown in the men and women who arrived to determine directly from company officials the status of family members.

Inside the offices, with White Star personnel having only a knowledge of the disaster but, as yet, no survivors' names, all was chaos at first. To the

company's recently appointed New York press representative, David Lindsey, fell the trying task of facing reporters who stormed the offices in search of news. Mary Downey, office telephone operator, was on duty during the developing situation's early stages; she stayed at her post for many long hours, politely and patiently handling the huge backlog of calls. After only a few hours' rest, she returned to the switchboard and remained there until *Carpathia*'s arrival.

The news received thus far, while not boding well for the ship itself, was not entirely negative as far as the passengers were concerned. Vice president Philip A. S. Franklin allayed fears and appeared optimistic. To the assembled reporters he stated, 'We place absolute confidence in *Titanic*. We believe the boat is unsinkable'. But as the hours passed, even Franklin began to wear a worried expression. Yet he maintained his confident appearance before the rich and famous — and their representatives — who came to 9 Broadway: Mrs Benjamin Guggenheim; Madelene Astor's father, W. H. Force; even the mighty J. P. Morgan, who wished to see for himself how things were going.

Afternoon and early evening editions of many New York newspapers also reflected faith. If their headlines did not flatly state 'All Saved', at least they were not negative: '*Titanic* Under Tow of *Virginian*. On Way to Halifax'.

Even the insurance market demonstrated its trust in *Titanic*'s invincibility. Re-insurance rates, which had soared earlier to fifty or even sixty per cent dropped back to fifty, forty-five, thirty before settling at twenty-five per cent.

Ismay's message, despatched from *Carpathia* around 10 am (ship's time) on 15 April, had not yet reached the company's offices. It remained for messages relayed by *Olympic* to tell the story:

'New York, April 15, 8.20 pm (Reuter) — The following statement has been given out by the White Star officials:- Captain Haddock of the *Olympic* sends a wireless message that the *Titanic* sank at 2.20 am (Monday) after all the passengers and crew had been lowered in lifeboats and transferred to the *Virginian*. The steamer *Carpathia* with several hundred passengers from *Titanic* is now on her way to New York.'

The optimism lasted for less than half an hour.

'New York, April 15, 8.45 pm (Reuter) — The following dispatch has been received here from Cape Race:- The steamer *Olympic* reports that the steamer *Carpathia* reached *Titanic*'s position at daybreak but found no boats, only wreckage. She reported that the *Titanic* foundered at about 2.20 am in lat 41 46, long 50 14. The message adds:- All the *Titanic*'s boats are accounted for. About 675 have been saved of the crew and passengers. The latter are nearly all women and children. The Leyland liner *Californian* is remaining and searching the vicinity of

the disaster. The *Carpathia* is returning to New York with the passengers.'

The White Star Line could no longer withhold the dreaded news, news of which it had been aware since receiving Haddock's message at 6.16 pm New York time. The reason for the apparent delay was stated by Franklin during the American Inquiry:

'At about 6.20 or 6.30 pm April 15 the following telegram was handed to me by Mr Toppin, my assistant:

"*Carpathia* reached *Titanic*'s position at daybreak. Found only boats and wreckage. *Titanic* had foundered about 2.20 am in 41.16 [*sic*] north, 50.14 west. All her boats accounted for. About 675 souls saved, crew and passengers, latterly nearly all women and children. Leyland Line SS *California* [*sic*] remaining and searching position of disaster. *Carpathia* returning to New York with survivors; please inform Cunard. Haddock."

'Immediately that telegram was received by me it was such a terrible shock that it took us a few minutes to get ourselves together. Then at once I telephoned, myself, to two of our directors, Mr Steele and Mr Morgan, Jr, and at the same time sent downstairs to the reporters. I got off the first line-and-a-half, where it said: "The *Titanic* sank at two o'clock am" and there was not a reporter left in the room — they were so anxious to get out and telephone the news.'

In England, the news was equally slow in arriving and, at first equally confusing. Since most wireless traffic was directed to New York, British newspapers received the news via cable, after it had been codified and edited by their North American correspondents. Thus, the story which emerged throughout the United Kingdom was less fragmented than the North American — particularly New York — versions had been.

As in New York, throngs of anxious relatives besieged Oceanic House, White Star's London office, in Cockspur Street, near Trafalgar Square. And as in New York, they were greeted with the appalling news: 'Yes, the *Titanic* has sunk. Yes, there has been loss of life. We shall post the names as they are received'.

London newspapers waxed editorially about 'speed' and 'luxury' (both 'excessive'); they mourned the loss of passengers and crew, and rejoiced for the 705 who had been saved.

King George V and Queen Mary expressed deep sorrow in their telegram:

'Sandringham,
Tuesday, 6.30 pm

The Managing Director,
White Star Line,
Liverpool

The Queen and I are horrified at the appalling disaster which has happened to the Titanic and at the terrible loss of life.

We deeply sympathise with the bereaved relatives, and feel for them in their great sorrow with all our hearts.

George RI'

The press had already raised the question of insufficient lifeboats. In an exclusive interview with London's *Daily Mail*, The Right Hon Alexander M. Carlisle, late general manager of Harland and Wolff (he had retired in 1910), who had partly designed *Titanic*, stated unequivocally that the Board of Trade's archaic regulations had been the basis for the inadequacy. Carlisle said he had advocated forty boats in *Titanic*'s original design, but because Board of Trade regulations did not require more than sixteen, his own suggestion had been ignored. As it was, White Star had provided twenty boats, more than the outdated regulations called for. But lifeboat rules specified the same for a ship of 50,000 tons as they did for one of 10,000.

Concerning this point there was to be much discussion.

And as in New York, there was an immediate effort to establish a relief fund* for the destitute among survivors and the families of those lost. The London Lord Mayor's Fund received donations through the willing efforts of all the metropolitan newspapers; boxes for cash deposits were placed strategically throughout the city and money also arrived from the Mayor's Funds of many cities throughout the United Kingdom.

One city, however, collected its own fund for disbursement to its own sufferers. Now that the immense loss of life among the crew was known (only 214 saved out of 907 aboard), Southampton was a stricken city. The sad scenes are drawn no more graphically than in the reports of an unknown London *Daily Mail* 'stringer'. In dispatches on 22 and 23 April this unnamed writer painted word pictures of tragedy and despair, of lost homes and

*In Great Britain, money subscribed to the Titanic Relief Fund exceeded £413,200. Distribution was administered by the Mansion House Committee, formed in March 1913. Proceeds were still being distributed, under special circumstances, more than fifty years later.

The Mayor's Fund, under sponsorship of New York Mayor Gaynor, received donations from all over the country, the total, administered by the American Cross, reaching $161,600 (£33,319). The Red Cross distributed an additional $100,000 (£20,618) collected by the New York

American newspaper and the (New York) Women's Relief Committee.

Distributions of funds in the United States were for relief of survivors' immediate needs; those of the British funds took the form of long-range 'annuity' payments, in addition to meeting pressing needs.

dreams, of women whose men would never return: husbands, sons, brothers, fiancés. . .

The first survivor lists were posted on 17 April. In the ever-changing crowd outside the Canute Road offices were young women with babies in their arms, babies who laughed and crowed in the sunlight while their mothers grieved with eyes which had known no sleep through the night. There were old women, some crying quietly, others seeking to comfort sobbing daughters. . .

'Later in the afternoon hope died out. The waiting crowds thinned, and silent men and moaning women sought their homes. In the humbler homes of Southampton there is scarcely a family that has not lost a relative or friend. Children returning from school appreciated something of the tragedy, and woeful little faces were turned to the darkened, fatherless homes.'

On Thursday, 18 April the reporter viewed York Street through the eyes of one of its female residents whose husband, fortunately, had been aboard *Olympic*. She told a doleful story of the women along her street who had lost loved ones:

'Mrs May, across the way, lost her husband and eldest son. The son was married a year ago and his wife had a baby six weeks ago. . .

'Mrs Allen, around the corner, lost her husband George. And the young girl there in black, the one on this side, is Mrs Barnes. She lost her brother. The woman going into the shop is Mrs Gosling. She lost a son. And Mrs Preston, of Prince Street, a widow, she lost a son, too.'

[The reporter continued:] 'Crossing the road I had a talk with the elder Mrs May, a slight, pale woman with dark sorrowful eyes. She asked eagerly for news, but when I had none to give, she sighed and the corner of her apron went to her eyes. "Yes, it's true," she said in a weary voice. "Husband and son have gone and left eleven of us. It was the first time that Arthur and his father had been at sea together, and it wouldn't have happened if Arthur hadn't been out of work because of the coal strike. He tried to get a job ashore but failed, and he had his wife and baby to keep. So he signed on aboard the *Titanic* as a fireman. His father shouldn't have been on the *Titanic*, but a bad leg kept him from going on his own ship, the *Britannia*. Now they're gone and there are eleven of us. The eldest boy, nineteen, makes a few shillings a week by odd jobs. My own youngest baby is six months old."

'At dawn today there was a large crowd of men and women outside the White Star offices in Canute Road. The offices had remained open all night, and there were watchers who had seen the sun set and sun rise waiting and hoping throughout the night. In the afternoon the crowd increased. As each inquirer left the office he or she did not go immediately away, but stayed with the waiting crowd as if seeking consolation in common sorrow.'

By Friday, 19 April, the distress among families was worsening. In the reporter's words:

'I have spent the day in widows' houses, houses without food or fuel and in some cases without furniture. I have seen women fainting and heard children crying for food. During the coal strike many breadwinners were out of work, furniture was sold and pawned, and numerous families received notices to quit [the premises]. Then came the *Titanic* and firemen, trimmers and greasers who had known no work for many weeks eagerly joined the big ship to save their homes. Today hundreds of women are clamoring for food themselves and milk for their babies.

'Many women who wait for hour after hour outside the White Star offices pathetically cling to the hope that their men, being in the four-to-eight watch, have escaped in one of the boats. The twelve-to-four watch was the death watch. One drooping woman was leaning on a bassinet containing two chubby babies, while a tiny mite held her hand. "What are we waiting for, Mummy? Why are we waiting such a long time?" asked the tired child. "We are waiting for news of father, dear," came the choked answer, as the mother turned away her head to hide her tears.'

Southampton was not alone in its grief. The observance of a grieving nation's symbolic mourning was the Service to the Memory of the Dead held on Friday, 19 April at London's St Paul's Cathedral. The warm spring sunlight was a striking contrast to the cool semi-darkness of the great church's interior. Thousands crowded into the service, while thousands more, unable to gain admittance, filled the streets outside.

Among those present was Alexander Carlisle, who fainted during the service. Another congregation member was Mr Stanley May, who had travelled aboard *Titanic* from Southampton to Queenstown. In a strange occurrence — for the coincidence was not yet known — the final hymn of the service was the same which had concluded the Sunday night hymn sing aboard *Titanic*: 'Eternal Father, Strong to Save'. And once again, the refrain, this time in sad reflection, 'O Hear us when we cry to Thee for those in peril on the sea'.

Back in New York, J. Bruce Ismay was not precisely in peril on Friday, 19 April. But he was in danger of becoming the symbol of everything preventable regarding *Titanic* and the disaster. In its search for a scapegoat, the American press selected Ismay and his escape from the sinking ship on which to vent their collective spleen. In what must be the nadir of yellow journalism, William Randolph Hearst's *New York American* published an Ismay photograph, around whose borders were ringed photographs of women who had lost male family members. The caption, 'J. Brute Ismay' reflected an almost-studied denial of fact.

As Lord Mersey subsequently stated, 'Mr Ismay, after rendering assistance to many passengers, found C collapsible, the last boat on the starboard side, being lowered. No other people were there at the time. There was room for him and he jumped in. Had he not jumped he would merely have added one more life, namely his own, to the number of those lost'.

Ismay's 30 June 1913 resignation from International Mercantile Marine's presidency was misinterpreted by many to have resulted from the vilification he received after *Titanic*'s loss. But as early as January 1912 Ismay had voiced his intent to resign his position in favour of Harold Sanderson. One reason for travelling to America aboard *Titanic* had been to discuss his forthcoming resignation with bankers and IMM board members on that side of the Atlantic.

In the inquiry conducted in the name of the United States Senate, Ismay conducted himself with dignity. He answered plainly the myriad questions put to him, displaying in his responses the knowledge of the company and its operations for which he was so respected among his colleagues.

Friday, 19 April — the first day of the United States Senate Inquiry, chaired by Michigan's Senator William Alden Smith. The inquiry was to begin on a note of anticipation, and it would end on a note — for some — of uncertainty.

The dates of *Titanic*'s future sailings appear in a *New York Times* advertisement on the day she sank. (*New York Times*.)

Personal reactions are immediate. Even as *Olympic* rushes to aid *Titanic*, names of known survivors are posted, and friends write to express their concern. (Mr and Mrs Arthur Dodge.)

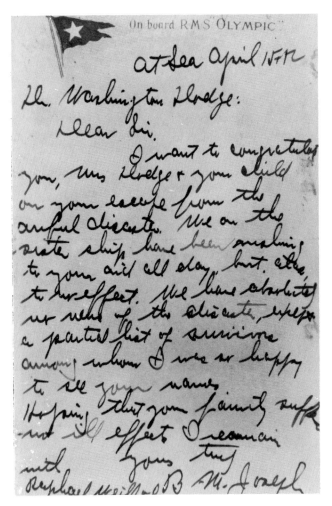

207

HYDROGRAPHIC OFFICE,
WASHINGTON, D. C.

DAILY MEMORANDUM

N-8.

No. 1013.   April 15, 1912.

N O R T H   A T L A N T I C   O C E A N

OBSTRUCTIONS OFF THE AMERICAN COAST.

Mar. 28 – Lat 24° 20', lon 80° 02', passed a broken spar projecting about 3 feet out of water, apparently attached to sunken wreckage.––EVELYN (SS) Wright.

OBSTRUCTIONS ALONG THE OVER-SEA ROUTES.

Apr 7 – Lat 35° 20', lon 59° 40', saw a lowermast covered with marine growth.––ADRIATICO (It. ss), Cevasco.

ICE REPORTS.

Apr 7 – Lat 45° 10', lon 56° 40', ran into a strip of field ice about 3 or 4 miles wide extending north and south as far as could be seen. Some very heavy pans were seen.––ROSALIND (Br ss), Williams.

Apr 10 – Lat 41° 50', lon 50° 20', passed a large ice field a few hundred feet wide and 15 miles long extending in a NNE direction.––EXCELSIOR (Ger ss), (New York Herald)

COLLISION WITH ICEBERG – Apr 14 – Lat 41° 46', lon 50° 14', the British steamer TITANIC collided with an iceberg seriously damaging her bow; extent not definitely known.

Apr 14 – The German steamer AMERIKA reported by radio telegraph passing two large icebergs in lat 41° 27', lon 50° 08',––TITANIC (Br ss).

Apr 14 – Lat 42° 06', lon 49° 43', encountered extensive field ice and saw seven icebergs of considerable size.––PISA (Ger ss).

J. J. K N A P P

Captain, U. S. Navy,
Hydrographer.

Above left Before *Titanic*'s loss is known, the United States Hydrographic Office issues an early statement on the incident. (National Archives.)

Top As the first bulletins are posted outside New York newspaper offices. . . (Private collection.)

Above . . .crowds gather in the street exclaiming as each new detail appears. . . (Private collection.)

Left. . .and the sound of newsboys' voices fill the streets with the latest headlines about the disaster. (Private collection.)

Right The city's newspapers find it difficult to keep up with the rapidly changing developments in the North Atlantic. (*New York Evening Sun.*)

The Evening Sun.

WALL STREET
NIGHT EDITION

WALL STREET
NIGHT EDITION

PRICE ONE CENT.

NEW YORK, MONDAY, APRIL 15, 1912.

VOL. XXVI. NO. 25.

TITANIC'S PASSENGERS ARE TRANSSHIPPED

RESCUE BY CARPATHIA AND PARISIAN; LINER IS BEING TOWED TO HALIFAX AFTER COLLISION WITH ICEBERG

Baltic, Virginian, Olympic and Other Ships at or Near the Scene---Summoned by Urgent Wireless Calls for Help.

BIGGEST LINER IN CRASH OFF GRAND BANKS

She Carried Over 1,400 Passengers, Many of Prominence—White Star Offices Here Get Message from the Olympic Telling of Rescue.

THE TITANIC U...

The Evening Sun.

FINAL EDITION
INCLUDING FULL TRANSACTIONS

FINAL EDITION
INCLUDING FULL TRANSACTIONS

NEW YORK, MONDAY, APRIL 15, 1912.

PRICE ONE CENT.

VOL. XXVI. NO. 25.

ALL SAVED FROM TITANIC AFTER COLLISION

RESCUE BY CARPATHIA AND PARISIAN; LINER IS BEING TOWED TO HALIFAX AFTER SMASHING INTO AN ICEBERG

Baltic, Virginian, Olympic and Other Ships at or Near the Scene---Summoned by Urgent Wireless Calls for Help.

...CH OFF GRAND BANKS

...Many of Prominence—White ...Message from the ...Rescue.

THE TITANIC UNDER WAY.

FRED MERKLE
QUITS THE GIANTS

The Evening Sun.

WALL STREET
NIGHT EDITION

WALL STREET
NIGHT EDITION

PRICE ONE CENT.

NEW YORK, TUESDAY, APRIL 16, 1912.

VOL. XXVI. NO. 26.

HOPE FOR MORE TITANIC SURVIVORS FAINT; CARPATHIA ONLY SHIP ON HAND IN TIME.

CAPTAIN OF ALLAN LINER REPORTS THAT HE ARRIVED TOO LATE TO RESCUE ANY FROM TITANIC---PERHAPS 1,400 LOST

Many Men of Great Prominence Are Among the Missing —Col. John Jacob Astor Probably Lost—His Wife Is Rescued—Bruce Ismay Was Saved.

SAVED ARE MOSTLY WOMEN AND CHILDREN

Delayed Message From the Carpathia, Which Is Coming to This Port, Tells of the Rescue of About 800—Hope That Virginian Saved Some Is Destroyed.

WRECKED IN GREATEST OCEAN DISASTER.

THE ILL-FATED TITANIC AND H...

The Evening Sun.

FINAL EDITION
INCLUDING FULL TRANSACTIONS

FINAL EDITION
INCLUDING FULL TRANSACTIONS

NEW YORK, TUESDAY, APRIL 16, 1912.

PRICE ONE CENT.

VOL. XXVI. NO. 26.

ONLY ABOUT 800 RESCUED FROM TITANIC; VIRGINIAN HAS NO SURVIVORS OF WRECK

CAPTAIN OF ALLAN LINER REPORTS THAT HE ARRIVED TOO LATE TO RESCUE ANY FROM TITANIC---PERHAPS 1,400 LOST

Many Men of Great P...

WRECKED IN GREATEST OCEAN DISASTER.

THE ILL-FATED TITANIC AND HER COMMANDER

...DS OF DISASTER

MARQUARD ON

The Evening Sun.

WALL STREET
NIGHT EDITION

WALL STREET
NIGHT EDITION

NEW YORK, WEDNESDAY, APRIL 17, 1912.

PRICE ONE CENT.

VOL. XXVI. NO. 27.

NAMES OF ALL FIRST AND SECOND CABIN SURVIVORS HAVE BEEN SENT IN, REPORTS CRUISER CHESTER

THRONGS LAY SIEGE TO WHITE STAR LINE OFFICE FOR WORD FROM THE SEA

The President's Brother, Henry W. Taft, Calls Personally to Seek News of Major Archibald Butt.

MEN AND WOMEN SHOW HEAVY STRAIN

Long Vigil Stimulated by Hopes That Federal Cruisers Will Relay Assuring Messages From the Carpathia.

PASSENGER ON OLYMPIC SENDS STORY OF VAIN RUSH TO THE RESCUE

The Hundreds on Titanic's Sister Ship Stunned by the News and Voyage Proceeds in Gloom.

A FEW MORE NAMES OF SURVIVORS

Marconi Message Received from Carpathia, via S. S. Francenia Gives Number of Rescued as 700.

BRINGING SURVIVORS TO NEW YORK THE CUNARDER CARPATHIA WHICH IS BELIEVED TO HAVE ALL SAVED FROM THE TITANIC.

HER AND VOKES

HEARD TITANIC CALL

TALKING TO

Left Inside White Star's New York offices at 9 Broadway, the scene is one of frenzied anguish. . . (*New York World*.)

. . .while outside the news-hungry crowd fills the pavement and overflows the kerbs. . . (*Independent*.)

. . .across the street into Bowling Green Park. (*Washington Evening Star*.)

Bottom left In *Titanic*'s home port, crowds assemble in Canute Road outside White Star's Southampton offices, seeking news. (*Southampton and District Pictorial*.)

Top right When the news finally arrives, it is not good. The crowd's mood becomes one of despair. (*Daily Sketch*.)

Above right By 19 April, anxious faces are watching the names of the rescued crew. . . (*Daily Mirror*.)

Top far right. . .being posted outside the White Star offices at Southampton. (Lloyd's *Deathless Story*.)

Wives and family members await news of loved ones. As the hours pass, their hopes dim. (*Daily Mirror/Southampton and District Pictorial*.)

Right and far right Sometimes the news is good and bad simultaneously. Mrs Hurst of 15 Chapel Road receives word of her husband (lost) and her brother-in-law (saved). (Private collection.)

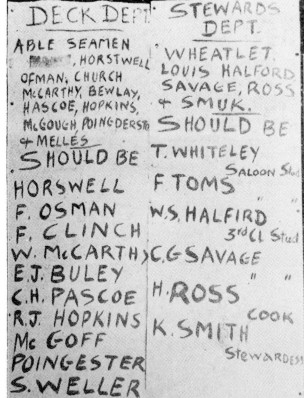

DECK DEPT. | STEWARDS DEPT.

ABLE SEAMEN
, HORSTWELL
OFMAN, CHURCH
McCARTHY, BEWLAY,
HASCOE, HOPKINS,
McGOUGH, POINGDERSto
& MELLES
SHOULD BE

HORSWELL
F. OSMAN
F. CLINCH
W. McCARTH,
E.J. BULEY
C.H. PASCOE
R.J. HOPKINS
McGOFF
POINGESTER
S. WELLER

WHEATLET,
LOUIS HALFORD
SAVAGE, ROSS
& SMUK.
SHOULD BE
T. WHITELEY
    Saloon Stud
F TOMS
W.S. HALFIRD
    3rd Cl Stud
C.G SAVAGE
    " "
H. ROSS
    Cook
K. SMITH
    Stewardess

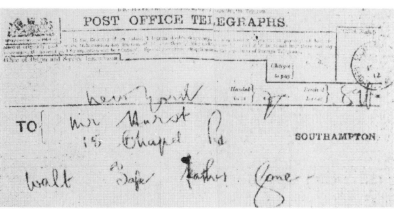

POST OFFICE TELEGRAPHS.

TO   Miss Hurst
      15 Chapel Rd   SOUTHAMPTON

Walt   Safe Father Gone

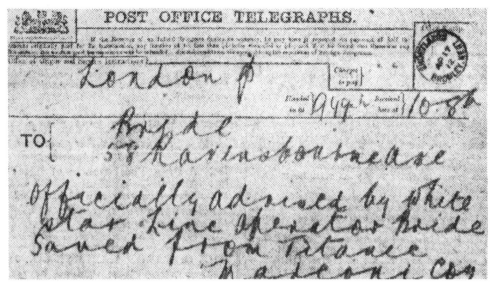

Left At Shortlands, Kent, the father of wireless operator Harold Bride receives word of his son's safety from his son's employer, the Marconi Company. (*Daily Mirror*.)

Top right Tragedy devastates the May family of 75 York Street. Mrs May, the mother of eight children, has lost her husband and eldest son. The son, himself married, leaves a widow and six-week-old child. (*Daily Sketch*.)

Bottom left Entire streets in the city of Southampton are filled with sorrow as in one house after another the sad news arrives. (Lloyd's *Deathless Story*.)

Middle left Other notifications are grim and final. Third class steward Sidney Sedunary's watch is recovered and returned to the grieving family. (Southern Newspapers plc.)

Middle right Many other Southampton families have lost relatives in the disaster. Every one of these children from the Northam School has lost at least one family member. (*Southampton and District Pictorial*.)

Right News of the disaster is no less shocking to the people of London... (Private collection.)

Far right...who crowd Oceanic House, White Star's offices in Cockspur Street. (*Illustrated London News*.)

Above far right Worried relatives and friends enter the London offices to scan the lists of survivors posted inside. (*Daily Graphic/Daily Mirror*.)

146 ft. HIGH

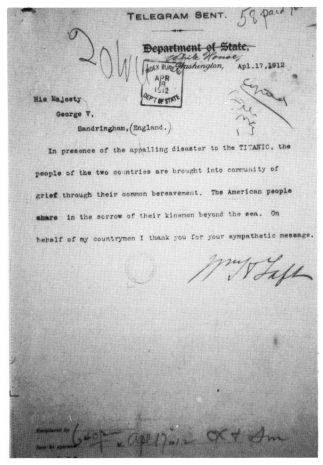

Newspapers try to give their readers an impression of the lost *Titanic*'s tremendous size. (*Daily Mirror*.)

The President of the United States, William Howard Taft, extends the condolences of the American people to 'their kinsmen beyond the sea', in his personal message to His Majesty King George V. (National Archives.)

In a letter dated 16 April, Sr Guglielmo Marconi mentions to his wife that he, too, had planned to be aboard *Titanic*. (Marconi Company Ltd.)

214

5 ft. HIGH

185 ft. HIGH

Funds to relieve financial hardship are quickly begun. . . (*Daily Graphic*.) **Right** In London, the Lord Mayor's Fund. . . (*Daily Graphic*.)

Below. . .receives contributions from many sources. . . (*Daily Sketch*.)

Below right. . .while at Southampton, proceeds from the fund are distributed to the needy widows of lost crewmen by Henry Bowyer, the city's mayor. (*Daily Mirror*.)

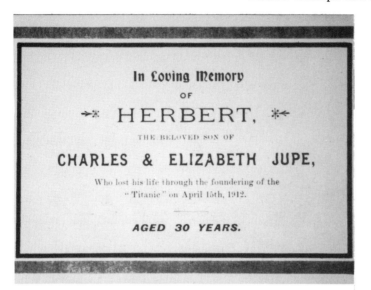

In Loving Memory
OF
HERBERT,
THE BELOVED SON OF
CHARLES & ELIZABETH JUPE,
Who lost his life through the foundering of the
"Titanic" on April 15th, 1912.

AGED 30 YEARS.

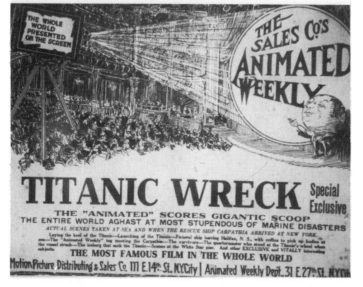

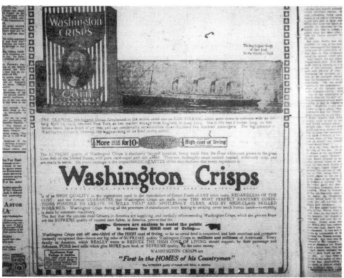

Far left Sorrow is personal and private, as reflected in this memorial card for a member of *Titanic*'s engineering staff. (Public Archives of Nova Scotia.)

Left Others try to capitalize on public interest generated by the disaster. (Mr and Mrs Arthur Dodge.)

Bottom left The comparatively new art of cinematography contributes its full share of exploitation. (*Morning Telegraph*.)

Middle far left When original footage is not available, exhibitors resort to animated film. (*New York Tribune*.)

Bottom far left Even food companies take advantage of the catastrophe to rouse public interest in their product. (*New York Tribune*.)

Right An unexpected reaction is the strike of *Olympic*'s black gang on 24 April, just prior to sailing. The men refuse to work aboard a liner carrying insufficient lifeboats. Mr Lewis, a Seafarers' Union official, boards the ship to negotiate a settlement. (*Daily Mirror*.)

Below The desertion of 285 crew members causes a cancellation of *Olympic*'s voyage. While the vessel lies off the Isle of Wight, passengers on deck await settlement of the matter. (*Daily Mirror*.)

Right Meanwhile, other shipping lines demonstrate their concern for safety by publicly testing their lifeboats. At Southampton, *Philadelphia* of the American Line lowers her boats to confirm their seaworthiness. (*Daily Sketch*.)

This page In the days following the disaster, editorial cartoons bring home to the public the moral impact of the great loss. (Authors' collection.)

Above right In one of the first concrete attempts to improve maritime safety, the US Navy scout cruiser *Birmingham* is ordered to patrol the area off the Grand Banks and to report twice daily on ice conditions. She departs from Philadelphia for a two-week tour of duty, beginning 19 May. (*National Archives*.)

Right and left below Another vessel, White Star's *Oceanic*, has already located a hazard to navigation: *Titanic*'s collapsible A, found drifting at position latitude 47° 01′ N, longitude 30° 56′ W. Three bodies found in the boat are buried at sea and the boat is brought back to New York on *Oceanic*'s upper deck. (*Southampton and District Pictorial/Daily Sketch*.)

On *Oceanic*'s return from New York, she carries as passengers Michel and Edmond Navratil, now reunited with their mother Marcelle. (*Southampton and District Pictorial*.)

'Lolo' and 'Momon' are glad to be going home at last. (*Southampton and District Pictorial*.)

Aftermath

Chapter Fifteen

THE AMERICAN INQUIRY

At almost the same moment that *Carpathia* docked at 9.35 pm on 18 April, United States Senator William Alden Smith arrived at Pier 54. A member of the Senate Committee on Commerce, he had been appointed by his fellow Senators to chair a subcommittee to investigate *Titanic*'s loss. Senator Smith had achieved his appointment by introducing a resolution he had framed himself to initiate the investigation.

After a hurried conference with President Taft and a brief meeting with Attorney General Wickersham (who confirmed the subcommittee's authority to subpoena British subjects while they were in United States territory), Smith departed from Washington on the 3.30 pm train to New York, the *Congressional Limited.*

Arriving too late to meet the incoming *Carpathia* as she came up the bay, Smith boarded at the pier and was directed to the surgeon's cabin, where Bruce Ismay awaited an appropriate moment to disembark. Pushing past Phillip Franklin, IMM's vice president, the Senator conferred for almost half an hour with the stricken Ismay. Then, after pausing briefly to observe *Titanic*'s third class passengers being examined by immigration authorities, Smith left the ship. At the pier's entrance he stopped to tell newspaper reporters he foresaw no difficulties or obstacles raised by the White Star Line or British authorities which would impede his investigation.

The remainder of the '*Titanic* Subcommittee' of the Committee on Commerce had been selected more for political balance than maritime expertise. Its members included six Senators: George C. Perkins, California; Jonathan Bourne, Jr, Oregon; Theodore Burton, Ohio; Furnifold M. Simmons, North Carolina; Francis G. Newlands, Nevada; and Duncan U. Fletcher, Florida.

The hearings occupied seventeen days between 19 April and 25 May. At first in New York, then in Washington, and then back in New York the subcommittee examined 82 witnesses on various phases of the disaster. Among those testifying were 53 British subjects or residents, and 29 citizens or residents of the United States. Testimony of twelve witnesses concerned telegraphic and wireless traffic.

Hastily assembled, with no members having any comprehensive knowledge of ships or shipping, the subcommittee plodded through witness after witness. Sometimes its questions — almost all of them posed by Senator Smith — were piercing and analytical; at other times they were needless and, indeed, heedless of a witness's emotions or (as in Harold Bride's case) physical well-being.

Senator Smith had a personal axe to grind. He was a vehement opponent of the Morgan interests — the very J. P. Morgan whose International Mercantile Marine owned the White Star Line, *Titanic*'s operator. But throughout the hearing Smith maintained an air of objectivity which made the summary of his findings acceptable to many.

Smith hoped to obtain for his American constituency recompense, or at least the right to sue, through establishing a knowledge of negligence by *Titanic*'s owner and operators. If Ismay was concealing such knowledge, the IMM, the despised Morgan combine, could be sued under the provisions of the Harter Act. A response to the 1898 *La Bourgogne* disaster, the law stated that if a company owning a steamship had privity of negligence aboard, the individual passengers or their surviving kin could sue the company for damages. Though *Titanic* had been a British ship she had been owned by an American trust, indictable under the Harter Act.

Throughout the first day's hearings, in the East Room of New York's Waldorf-Astoria Hotel, Smith jabbed again and again at a weary though dapper Ismay. Again and again the Senator failed to elicit knowledge of negligence, just as he was to fail in his subsequent questioning of company officers and ship's crew.

On Saturday morning, 20 April, federal subpoenas were served on 29 *Titanic* crew members

before they could leave aboard the *Lapland*, which departed for England at 10 am. The crewmen had complained bitterly of being held as virtual prisoners aboard *Lapland* since *Carpathia*'s docking. Yet, fewer than half of the 210 crew survivors went to a memorial service held at 507 West Street, the Institute of the Seaman's Friend Society, during the afternoon of 19 April, which all were free to attend.

After *Lapland* was well away, it was discovered that five of the crew whose testimony was needed had left without being subpoenaed. Senator Smith made a hasty call to the Brooklyn Navy Yard, and a wireless message was sent to *Lapland* to stop and await a boarding party. A federal marshal was despatched by tug, in pursuit of *Lapland* and the crew witnesses. His mission was successful, and five more men were detained to give testimony.

Ismay asked to leave, to return to England where he felt his services were needed. Though Ismay had already testified, Senator Smith declined his request, stating the possibility of future questioning.

Sunday, 21 April was a travel day. The sub-committee would sit at Washington, DC, commencing Monday. During Sunday, the Senators and their staffs, *Titanic*'s officers and crew, White Star and Marconi Company officials, attorneys, journalists — all travelled to the nation's capital aboard various trains. Subcommittee members took an early train, while officers and crew did not arrive until 6 pm. They were quartered at the Continental Hotel at government expense. Both crew and officers complained: the former because they had to 'double up' in the rooms (a strange complaint from men accustomed to crews' quarters aboard ships of the period); the officers' complaints were based on their enforced proximity to the crew's rooms. The officers were subsequently moved to rooms on a different floor. As a result of their complaints, the crew were moved on Monday to the Hotel National, which provided less elegant, but separate, rooms for each man.

The sessions of Monday and Tuesday, 22 and 23 April, were jammed with spectators and reporters. Each session's start was delayed until sergeants-at-arms could establish order in the hearing rooms. During Monday's hearing, fourth officer Boxhall neatly and patiently described the boats' loading and also made the first official mention of the 'mystery ship'. On Tuesday, look-out Fleet and quartermaster Hichens described their parts during the disaster's first moments.

An interesting point as to why the boats left *Titanic* half-filled was developed by fifth officer Lowe during Wednesday's session: officers in charge of loading the lifeboats were not confident that the boats, filled to their rated 'sea capacity', would reach the water without breaking in two during lowering from the weight of passengers.* What the officers did think — wrongly as it turned out — was that the half-filled boats would stand by to pick up survivors through lower gangway doors, or those who had jumped into the water. The hypothetical 'lowering capacity' was ignored, of course, during the lowering of the last several boats.

On Tuesday, Mr Ismay had once again requested to return to England or, failing that, at least to New York, where he could look after company business. The request was denied by Senator Smith, an action which resulted in the appearance of Ismay and his attorney Charles Burlingham at Smith's office at 10 am on Wednesday, 24 April. Even this direct appeal was refused. Ismay, following this latest confrontation, composed and sent a letter to Senator Smith in which he presented the unfairness of his being kept long after his usefulness to the subcommittee had expired.

Senator Smith, in a somewhat belligerent response, wrote immediately to Mr Ismay that he could tolerate no outside or individual interference with his pursuit of the truth and that he was '. . sure the message would be received in the same spirit in which it was written'. Mr Ismay seethed. Mr Ismay remained in Washington.

Reactions of the British press to the conduct of Senator Smith's hearings were starting to become known in America. There was mounting indignation regarding the proceedings' legality, as well as attacks on the Senator's personal integrity. 'A parody of judicial inquiry', said the London *Daily Express*, which also called Senator Smith 'asinine'. Other newspapers derided the hearings' validity and the qualifications of the subcommittee's members. Smith's treatment of Bruce Ismay did not go unnoticed, although Ismay's status as hero or scapegoat was yet to be decided in his own country.

Senator Smith dismissed the criticisms as based on inaccuracies and half-truthful data British reporters had transmitted by cable to their home offices. As the days passed, many editors in America and even some in England came to Smith's defence: how else, they asked, were the *facts* to be made known? How else could the circumstances and conditions under which the disaster took place be put on public record?

---

*Edward Wilding, naval architect for Harland and Wolff, testified at the subsequent British inquiry that *Titanic*'s boats had been test-lowered at the yard, carrying the equivalent weight of a full complement of passengers. The test — actually of the new Welin davits — and its results were not made known to *Titanic*'s officers.

The spirit of the American inquiry, the querulous British reaction and the investigation's function are contained in a *New York Herald* editorial:

'Nothing has been more sympathetic, more gentle in its highest sense than the conduct of the inquiry by the Senate committee, and yet self-complacent moguls in England call this impertinent... This country intends to find out why so many American lives were wasted by the incompetency of British seamen, and why women and children were sent to their deaths while so many in a British crew have been saved'.

Having failed to establish responsibilities under the Harter Act's provisions, Senator Smith was now, it appears, trying to establish a moral responsibility on which judgements might be based.

The crewmen were enjoying their Washington stay, although officers were increasingly annoyed about having to remain. The hotel rate for the crew was $2.50 (10 shillings) per day, while the daily witness fee was a mere $3 (12 shillings). Though the men had been guests of various city organizations, they lacked for pocket money. A visit to the Washington lodge of the Benevolent and Protective Order of Elks was marked by a testimonial, signed by all crew attending. They had a bus tour of the capital city and were prominent among congregations at several churches' Sunday services.

Senator Smith, who by now knew all the men by their first names, was able to get their fee raised to $5 (£1) a day on 25 April. But two days later, several crewmen augmented their meagre financial condition by appearing in two performances at the Imperial Theatre, a local music hall. There, they related in their own words to rapt audiences their roles in *Titanic*'s high drama. The theatre's management proudly boasted that 'The crew will receive the entire proceeds from the first show'. It is not a matter of record how much the men received.

Thursday, 25 April was spent interrogating 23 of *Titanic*'s crew. The men were heard separately by individual subcommittee members, Smith himself interviewing Hains, Hemming and Evans at 10 pm to wrap up the day's activity.

Three members of *Californian*'s crew testified before the Senators on 26 April: her master, Captain Stanley Lord; wireless operator Cyril Evans; and a crewman described variously as 'deck hand', 'donkeyman', and 'assistant engineer' — although his name appears on the crew list as a fireman — Ernest Gill.

Gill appeared first and swore that the affidavit he had given on 24 April at Boston was his, and was true. In it, Gill recounted his observation of a large ship near *Californian*, and what appeared to be two rockets, fired from a distance of about ten miles.

Witness Stanley Lord testified regarding *Californian*'s position and the repeated, unsuccessful attempts to contact a nearby vessel with the Morse lamp.

The final *Californian* crewman, Cyril Evans, testified regarding the wireless traffic between himself and *Titanic*'s operator, and confirmed, casually, at the end of his testimony, that the ship's apprentice had informed Captain Lord *three times* about the rockets seen by Gill and other *Californian* crewmen.

Titanic's officers and crew were permitted to depart on Monday, 29 April. They immediately travelled to New York, where they awaited *Adriatic*'s 2 May departure for Liverpool. Detained for one more day at Washington by Senator Smith, Bruce Ismay was finally released from American jurisdiction on 30 April. He, too, went to New York where he immediately boarded *Adriatic* for the return to England.*

The remaining days wrapped up loose ends. Regarding an offer of payment for Harold Bride's exclusive story, Guglielmo Marconi testified that he authorized the wireless man to accept payment from *any* newspaper, not specifically the *New York Times*.

Resolved, too, was the *Asian* incident (a merging of two wireless messages causing the erroneous report that 'Titanic in tow, on way to Halifax...'); and the reason for the delay of the transmission of Ismay's 15 April message. (*Carpathia*'s wireless operator, overwhelmed by the sudden strain placed on him and his equipment, confused Ismay's message with an almost-identical one sent to the Cunard office by Captain Rostron, and did not transmit Ismay's message until 17 April.)

Subsequent testimony of passengers and others associated with the disaster confirmed and put on public record what was already known: there was an inadequate number of lifeboats.

On 18 May, the next-to-last day of the hearings, Captain John J. Knapp of the United States Hydrographic Office testified. He proved with charts and authority-laden testimony that the ship seen by *Titanic* could have been no other than *Californian* and that the ship seen by *Californian* (the steamer which, in the eyes of Captain Lord and

---

*On the 2 May voyage, *Adriatic* also carried to England a thirty-foot model of *Titanic*, carefully crated. Built by the White Star Line at a cost of more than £3,000, the model was intended for display at the company's New York office but had been recalled, for obvious reasons.

At some point during its handling the model was damaged: a vertical crack appeared, from keel to upper deck, in the same location on the model as the hole torn by the iceberg above the keel of the *Titanic*. Also, it is reported that while there were davits for twenty lifeboats on the model, only twelve boats were shown.

several officers, was a small vessel about five miles away) could not possibly have been any other than *Titanic*.

Travelling to New York on 19 May, Senator Smith visited *Olympic* at her pier, interviewed her captain, Herbert J. Haddock, and visited the engine room and stokehold, where stoker Frederick Barrett dramatically demonstrated to the Senator where he had been standing when the iceberg pierced *Titanic*'s hull. Senator Smith returned to Washington to prepare his report to the full United States Senate.

The report summarized the subcommittee's investigations, interviews and interrogations. After establishing *Titanic*'s ownership and the structure of IMM White Star's parent company, the report went on to describe the ship, sea trials, Board of Trade certification and the composition of her passenger list. The ship's voyage prior to striking ice was described in detail including weather conditions, speed, and ice warnings received by *Titanic*. Paragraphs describing the collision, damage and flooding were followed by summaries of the wireless distress calls, first press reports and vessels in the vicinity of the sinking site.

Captain Lord, master of *Californian*, was soundly condemned for his apparent negligence in failing to respond to what were apparently distress signals from *Titanic*. In the report's most strongly worded section, Senator Smith set the tone for the years of controversy which followed.

The *Titanic*'s lifeboats' capacities, their loading and lowering, and conduct of crew and passengers while afloat were summarized, as were the commendable actions taken by Captain Rostron as he drove *Carpathia* through the ice to rescue survivors.

More than two pages of the report described discrepancies in wireless and telegraphic services during the hours following the disaster. The possibility of censorship by Captain Rostron was dismissed, as was any nefarious reason for the delay of Ismay's 15 April message. However, *Carpathia*'s wireless operator and the surviving operator from *Titanic* (unnamed in the summary) were rebuked mildly for making arrangements to sell stories of their experiences.

A summary of the recommendations, while brief, contained suggestions for changes in structure and lifeboat capacity for vessels licensed to carry passengers from American ports, and further recommended that all foreign flag vessels be similarly modified or lose their passenger licences. Adequate manning of boats and boat drills for passengers were recommended. The necessity for regulation of radiotelegraphy was strongly stated, including 24-hour manning of equipment, action against amateurs' interference, reliable auxiliary power sources, and maintenance of all messages' secrecy.

It also contained a suggestion that the firing of rockets or Roman candles on the high seas for any other purpose than as a distress signal be stopped, thus putting to an end the colourful practice of night recognition signals. Two excellent exhibits augmented the summary: an alphabetical list of *Titanic*'s crew and a similar passenger list, separated by class. Each indicated 'saved' or 'lost' for each entry.

The report was nineteen pages long and exhibits occupied another 44 pages. It was ordered to be printed on 28 May 1912, only three days after the final depositions had been obtained, and summarized 1,145 pages of testimony and affidavits. Altogether the investigation had cost the American taxpayers $6,600 (£1,360). Roughly, the breakdown was: $3,300 (£680) for stenographic services; $1,100 (£227) for witnesses' mileage; and $2,200 (£453) for housing *Titanic*'s officers and crew at Washington.

After its approval by the subcommittee, the report was submitted to the entire United States Senate on 28 May. Speaking with calmness and deliberation, Senator Smith presented the report and summarized its contents in an eloquent speech more than two hours long. At its close, he called for three pieces of legislation: the first, a joint resolution with the House of Representatives, to strike a medal for presentation by the President of the United States to Captain Arthur Rostron, on behalf of the American people.

The second was Senate Bill 6976, known later as the Smith Bill, calling for an examination and re-evaluation of existing statutes of marine legislation. The third was a joint resolution for a maritime commission to investigate the laws and regulations regarding construction and equipment of all ocean-going vessels.

Smith and his speech were badly received by some of the British press. He was referred to as an 'ass', and his speech as 'shoddy eloquence', 'Bombastic', 'Grotesque', 'A violent, unreasoning diatribe'. All these, and more, were heaped upon Smith and the colleagues who had permitted his seemingly grotesque excesses. Other British newspapers and magazines, while not exactly praising the Senator, did admit that his investigation had served the necessary function of preserving testimony while it was still fresh in the witnesses' minds.

American papers were almost unanimous in their acceptance of the report. Many recognized the value of recording the facts, while some actually expressed surprise at the Senator's ability to generate such a document. As might be expected, Smith generally fared far better with the American press than with its British counterpart.

While the American investigation into the disaster's causes was being conducted, far to the

north in the Atlantic Ocean off Canada's eastern shore, one of the disaster's effects was being diligently pursued. The cable ship *Mackay-Bennett*, out of Halifax, was searching for bodies of *Titanic*'s victims. The results, though not so far-reaching as Senator Smith's enquiry, were equally dramatic.

Far left Senator William Alden Smith of Michigan heads the subcommittee of the Committee on Commerce investigating *Titanic*'s loss. (*Illustrated London News*.)

He is assisted by six other senators, including Theodore Burton of Ohio **middle left** and Duncan U. Fletcher of Florida **left**. (*Philadelphia Public Ledger*.)

Hearings begin at the Waldorf-Astoria Hotel in New York. Bruce Ismay is the subcommittee's first witness. (Library of Congress.)

Above As stenographer Charles McKinistry records every word, Bruce Ismay responds to a senator's questioning. Reporters crowd into the hearing room. (Authors' collection.)

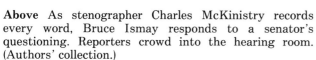

Above middle Captain Arthur Rostron leaves *Carpathia*, amid the feverish work needed to resume her interrupted voyage, to give testimony before Senator Smith's subcommittee in New York. (Authors' collection.)

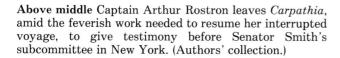

Top right Second officer Charles H. Lightoller describes the details of *Titanic*'s voyage and evacuation for the senatorial subcommittee. (*New York American.*)

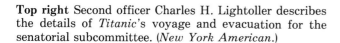

The packed hearing room listens to every word of testimony. *Carpathia*'s wireless operator Harold Cottam (1) and Guglielmo Marconi (2) await their turns to give evidence. Representative Hughes (3), Bruce Ismay (4), Senator Smith (5) and P. A. S. Franklin (6) follow the proceedings. (*Illustrated London News.*)

As his employer Guglielmo Marconi watches, Harold Bride (to the right of, and slightly below centre) gives evidence about the ice warnings and wireless communications. He has had to be carried into the room, still suffering from frost-bite and injury to his feet. *Carpathia*'s wireless operator Cottam is in the centre of the crowd standing. (Authors' collection.)

There are many questions for *Titanic*'s surviving wireless operator, but as Bride (right) continues to give evidence, Marconi is pleased by the man's fortitude. (*Philadelphia Inquirer.*)

Left The inquiry shifts to Washington, DC on 21 April, and three of White Star's principals arrive in the Nation's capital: P. A. S. Franklin, IMM's vice president; company attorney Charles Burlingham; and managing director Bruce Ismay. (Private collection.)

Below left With interested spectators forming a backdrop, testimony resumes in the crowded confines of Senator Smith's office. Major Arthur Peuchen, right facing camera, listens to the evidence. (Private collection.)

Fourth officer Joseph Groves Boxhall describes details of *Titanic*'s navigation. (*Halifax Morning Chronicle*.)

Harold Godfrey Lowe, *Titanic*'s fifth officer, doesn't think much of Senator Smith or the inquiry itself. 'Ice' is his laconic reply to Senator Smith's query regarding the composition of icebergs. (*Halifax Morning Chronicle*.)

Below left Toronto's Major Arthur Peuchen describes in calm detail the circumstances surrounding his being ordered to assist in the manning of lifeboat 6. (*Halifax Morning Chronicle*.)

Below middle Between sessions, *Titanic*'s crew have little to do while they await Senator Smith's summons to testify. (*New York Times*.)

Below The crew descend the steps of the Capitol Building after having given evidence. (*Philadelphia Inquirer*.)

Top right The detained men willingly pose for a group portrait. In the front row, from left, are Ernest Archer, able seaman; Frederick Fleet, look-out; Walter Perkis, quartermaster; George Symons, look-out; and Frederick Clench, able seaman. In the back row, Arthur Bright, quartermaster; George Hogg, look-out; George Moore, saloon steward; Frank Osman, able seaman; and Henry Etches, bedroom steward. (Private collection.)

Joseph G. Boxhall

Harold G. Lowe

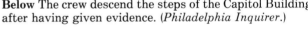

Arthur G. Peuchen

Above right The photograph is soon incorporated into a scheme to raise money for the destitute crew during their Washington stay. The men's pay ended when *Titanic* sank, in accordance with British regulation of the time. (*Washington Evening Star.*)

Above A pensive Bruce Ismay, his testimony apparently concluded, his several requests to return home refused, awaits Senator Smith's next request. (Private collection.)

Above right Ismay leaves the Senate hearings in the company of P. A. S. Franklin and attorney Charles Burlingham on 30 April, in time to board *Adriatic*, in New York, for home. His enforced stay in America has lasted two full weeks. (*Illustrated London News.*)

Right As one of its recommendations, Senator Smith's subcommittee proposes — and the United States Congress unanimously agrees — to the commissioning of a one-thousand-dollar gold medal for *Carpathia*'s Captain Arthur Rostron. It is presented to the heroic master in July 1912 by President William Howard Taft, in the name of the American people. (*Popular Mechanics.*)

Chapter Sixteen

HALIFAX

For 705 of *Titanic*'s people, joyous reunions with loved ones had been made possible by *Carpathia*'s 58-mile dash. In the port cities of New York, Plymouth, Southampton and Liverpool, families were together again at last, the ordeal now a haunting memory.

The collective emotions and involvement of another city in particular had risen and fallen repeatedly as conflicting elements of *Titanic*'s drama were played out in the North Atlantic. That city was Halifax, Nova Scotia.

Early wireless messages, garbled and transposed*, had expressed the likelihood, indeed the near certainty, that all passengers and crew were safe, and would be brought to Halifax. Newspapers reported that White Star's agents there had received orders to send salvage tugs to the liner's side. The immigration bureau of the Canadian Department of Commerce was sending inspectors to expedite the landing of survivors. Halifax officials prepared for the unexpected diversion of the world's largest liner and her passengers to their port.

Within hours, however, early optimism had turned to despair as the wireless messages took on an increasingly sombre tone. By 10 pm local time on 15 April, the truth was known in Halifax. Welcoming plans were cancelled.

But Halifax still was to have a role in the sad dénouement now unfolding. Even as the Cunarder *Carpathia* headed for New York, White Star had contacted its Halifax agents, A. G. Jones and Company, and through them had chartered the Commercial Cable Company's cable ship *Mackay-Bennett* for a difficult assignment: to search thoroughly the area where *Titanic* had sunk and, whenever possible, to recover the bodies of passengers and crew.

There were preparations to be made. The White Star agents contracted with John Snow and Company Ltd, the province's largest undertaking firm, to oversee the arrangements. In view of the numbers expected, Snow asked for and received the assistance of nearly every embalmer in Nova Scotia, New Brunswick and Prince Edward Island. More than forty members of the Funeral Directors' Association of the Maritime Provinces were soon on their way to Halifax. Among them was Annie F. O'Neill, of St John's, New Brunswick, who was assigned to embalm the women and children.

At the Halifax waterfront, tons of ice were poured into *Mackay-Bennett*'s cable tanks and holds. Embalmers' tools and supplies were stowed. More than a hundred plain wood coffins were brought on board the vessel, moored to her usual pier near Upper Water Street. Captain F. H. Lardner supervized the loading uneasily. Undertakers from the group assembled by Snow, and headed by chief embalmer John J. Snow, Jr, came on board. From Halifax's All Saints Cathedral came Canon Kenneth O. Hind, who joined the ship just prior to departure, which was at 12.35 pm on Wednesday, 17 April. The all-volunteer crew was paid double wages for the grim days that lay ahead.

Mackay-Bennett steamed out of the harbour at full speed, seemingly ignored by the citizenry at large. Within ninety minutes of her departure, she was forced to reduce speed for some five hours due to fog and bad weather. At noon, on Saturday, 20 April, the ship's wireless operator sent out a request for all ships which had seen wreckage or bodies to communicate with her.

Soon a message came in from the North German Lloyd liner *Rhein*, to the effect that they had passed wreckage and bodies in latitude 42° 01' N, longitude 49° 13' W. As *Mackay-Bennett* made for that position, the liner *Bremen* reported three large

---

*A query from *Baltic*, 'Are all *Titanic* passengers safe?' and a message from *Asian* stating she was towing the disabled tanker *Deutschland* to Halifax were merged and misread ashore as '*Titanic* passengers safe; being towed to Halifax'.

icebergs and bodies at latitude 42° 00' N, longitude 49° 20' W. The two adjacent sightings seemed conclusive. After passing numerous towering icebergs, Lardner's ship arrived in the area at 8 pm on Saturday, too late to begin searching. They stopped and drifted. During the middle watch, bodies and extensive wreckage were sighted.

At daylight, the *Mackay-Bennett's* boats were lowered, and in spite of the heavy seas, 51 bodies were recovered. The fourth body found was that of a little blond-haired boy, perhaps two years old, the only child recovered. Just four women were recovered on this first day. Once aboard the cable ship, the *Titanic's* people were treated with dignity and respect; a carefully-planned procedure was followed.

As each body was recovered, a piece of canvas with a stencilled number on it was attached. In a ledger book, a descriptive entry was made on the numbered page corresponding to the assigned number. Hair colour, height, approximate weight and age, obvious markings such as scars or birthmarks, and other details of physical description were recorded. With a witness present in each case, a full inventory of the deceased's pockets, money belt, jewellery, and clothing was compiled in meticulous detail. Addresses on letters, names on passports, numbers of passage tickets, legends on key tags, descriptions of personal photographs found in billfolds — all were recorded to assist in identifying the deceased either on board or, later, ashore. Personal property was placed in canvas bags, each bearing the number corresponding to its contents' owner.

At 5 pm, the day's work drawing to a close with the end of daylight, the boats were hauled back aboard. John Snow and his assistants embalmed twenty bodies, a further six being left for the following morning. At 8.15 pm Canon Hind officiated at a moving burial service on the forecastle deck. Some 24 bodies, mostly of crew, none identified, all badly disfigured by sea life, were committed to the deep.

Sunday, 21 April was observed as a day of rest and remembrance aboard *Mackay-Bennett*. Recovery operations resumed at 5.30 on Monday morning, amid an enormous quantity of wreckage. The cable ship came upon collapsible B, bottom up, its side smashed in. There was a brief but futile effort to pick it up before the more pressing work began.

The ship recovered 27 bodies, Colonel John Jacob Astor among them. As one unidentified crewman observed, 'Everybody had on a lifebelt and bodies floated very high in the water in spite of sodden clothes and things in pockets. Apparently people had lots of time and discipline must have been splendid, for some had on their pyjamas, two or

three shirts, two pairs of pants, two vests, two jackets and an overcoat. In some pockets a quantity of meat and biscuits were found, while in the pockets of most of the crew quite a lot of tobacco and matches, besides keys to the various lockers and stateroom doors were found'.

After steaming for nineteen miles in and out of a line of wreckage, *Mackay-Bennett* came upon additional victims as light was fading. A buoy was dropped to mark the spot where tomorrow's work would begin. The day closed as Saturday had, with Canon Hind presiding as fifteen were committed to the sea, 'some of them very badly smashed and bruised', according to the crewman.

Identifications of some victims completed, their names were sent ashore via wireless on 22 April. Since the *Mackay-Bennett* lacked a powerful set, the Cunarder *Laconia* assisted with the transmission as she passed through the area on her way from Liverpool to New York. Several other passing ships advised the *Mackay-Bennett* via wireless of further sightings of victims and debris. The crew of the Leyland Line's *Winifredian* (on charter to the Atlantic Transport Line) spotted the body of a man dressed in evening clothes, floating about 25 miles from *Titanic's* distress position. There was heavy ice in the area, and with *Mackay-Bennett* notified, *Winifredian's* crew made no efforts to recover him.

Wednesday, 23 April arrived with the cable ship embedded in a fog so dense that visibility was less than one ship's length. It was impossible to search further. The bodies brought aboard on Tuesday were searched, tagged, and stored away. There were no burials to perform.

By this point, supplies had begun to run low. *Mackay-Bennett* sent a message to the Allan liner *Sardinian* early in the morning. 'Recovering bodies of *Titanic*. Will be passing. Can you let us have all the canvas and burlap you can spare?' Several hours later, the two ships met cautiously in the fog, and a small boat was despatched to the cable ship with the needed materials.

Wireless reports continued. The *Royal George* reported passing an empty lifeboat, drifting and in good condition. *Mackay-Bennett's* response included a mention that some eighty bodies were now on board. The schooner *Banshee* reported a huge wreckage field, which included 'a considerable amount of white woodwork and framing, amongst which was a cabin door and its adjoining partition'. Her crew also saw the bodies of two men alongside their ship; both were dressed in grey overalls and seemed to be sailors. The *Cestrian* had reported a large amount of wreckage, too, consisting of deck fittings, bedding, life preservers and chairs.

At about midnight the fog finally lifted, and Captain Lardner set a course for the wirelessed positions where additional victims might be found.

At 4.30 am on Thursday, yet another body was found, a prelude to what was to be a most arduous day for *Mackay-Bennett's* crew, and especially for the undertakers. During the fourteen hours that followed, 87 additional victims were recovered, searched, and tagged. All were kept on board.

By now, it was apparent that the facilities and men on *Mackay-Bennett* were being severely taxed. Captain Lardner had sent a message to White Star's New York office, saying, 'Heavy southwest squall has interfered with operations. Fifty bodies recovered. All not embalmed will be buried at sea 8 pm with divine services. Can only bring embalmed bodies to port'. The captain's concern was apparent.

Acting on instructions from P. A. S. Franklin, the Halifax agents, A. G. Jones and Company, on 21 April chartered a second vessel, *Minia*, owned by the Anglo-American Telegraph Company Ltd. Captain W. G. S. DeCarteret had orders to go to sea by 4 pm on 22 April. But John Snow and Sons did not have the requisite number of coffins on hand, since *Mackay-Bennett* had taken a hundred of them. Mr Snow immediately communicated with the James Dempster Company Ltd, which kept its factory running through the afternoon and evening to supply the coffins. The Reverend H. W. Cunningham, of St George's Church in Halifax, and undertaker H. W. Snow came up the gangway. It was nearly midnight on 22 April when *Minia* departed from Halifax. Stowed on board were 150 coffins and twenty tons of ice, along with ten tons of iron grate bars. Coffins were placed in the forward hold, while the ice went into *Minia's* main cable tank, on top of 100 miles of cable there had not been time to remove.

She arrived at the disaster site at about 12.45 am on Friday, 26 April. The crew retired for what they knew would be a challenging day ahead. At 6.15 am, the *Minia* sent a supply of embalming fluid across by lifeboat, and the two ships then began searching together. By noon, they had found fourteen more bodies, and these were placed aboard *Mackay-Bennett*, which then departed for Halifax, having on board all that could be looked after.

Mackay-Bennett's crew had found 306 bodies; of these, 116 had been buried at sea, too badly decomposed to be brought into port. The cable ship returned with 190 victims on board, almost twice as many as there were caskets available.

As she steamed toward Halifax, relatives and friends of those lost in the tragedy already were arriving. An information bureau was established at the Halifax Hotel, where loved ones could obtain the latest news about recoveries and movements of *Mackay-Bennett*, and *Minia*, which was continuing the search.

By evening, she had recovered eleven bodies. Early the next morning the search resumed, but a northerly gale with a dense fog prevailed, and only one body was recovered. On the 28th, again only a single victim was located. Thick weather returned on the 29th.

On the 30th, Captain DeCarteret sent a message to the White Star Line: 'Believe late northerly gales have swept bodies into Gulf Stream and carried them many miles east. Searched along longitude 48.20 between latitude 41.20 and 41.50 and recovered only one body, making total 14, two being unknown were buried. Believe those on board mostly crew'.

A young *Minia* crewman, Francis Dyke, temporarily serving as a wireless operator, found time to compose a letter to his mother. Dated 27 April, at 2.20 am, the letter explained the feelings of those involved with the solemn task:

'My Darling Mother,
'I expect you will surprised to receive this written on this [telegram] paper, but I am on watch now in the wireless room [and] thought it a good opportunity to write...
'We began the search yesterday + the first we picked up was C. M. Hayes [*sic*] of G. Trunk Rail. It was no trouble to identify him as he had a lot of papers on him + a watch with his name on.
'We picked up 10 more bodies yesterday (waiters + sailors). All those who are identified are embalmed and packed in ice + are to be sent to N. York. I can tell you none of us like this job at all but it is better to recover them and bury them properly than let them float about for weeks. The Revd. Cunningham came out with us to bury those not identified. When we passed over the spot where the T. sank he held a short service in the saloon, which I thought very nice of him. I expected to see the poor creatures very disfigured but they all look as calm as if they were asleep. Mack and I have had to keep 6 hours watches all this trip, so as to keep in touch with all ships + give them news — it is difficult to keep awake all night but I am getting used to it now...'

Meanwhile, in Halifax, authorities characteristically had preparations well in hand. As the *Mackay-Bennett* drew closer to her home port, employees of A. G. Jones, supplemented by White Star staff from New York, worked with city officials, Snow's personnel, officers from HM Naval Dockyard, harbour police and others to ensure a dignified, carefully controlled arrival.

It had been decided that the *Mackay-Bennett* would not dock at her own pier with its limited space, but would, instead, sail about a mile further up the harbour, towards the Narrows and Bedford Basin, to dock at the Royal Canadian Naval Dockyard's north coaling wharf number 4. The location, heavily guarded and surrounded by the dockyard's concrete wall, would permit better crowd control and ensure some privacy for the proceedings.

A transfer company was hired to bring the off-loaded coffins from the wharf to the Mayflower Curling Rink on Agricola Street, which had been set up as a temporary morgue. Each horse-drawn hearse would be permitted to carry a maximum of ten coffins, in view of the steep route along North Street from the dockyard to the curling rink.

Clergymen in the city's churches requested during their 28 April services that people keep away as much as possible from the area during the coffins' transfer, set for some time on the 30th. The medical examiner and the deputy registrar of deaths would be stationed at the dockyard wharf to issue immediately the requisite certificates of death and burial permits.

Normally the site of spirited curling contests, the Mayflower rink now was scarcely recognizable. At its western end, behind a wooden partition, 34 benches were set up where the embalmers were to work. The bodies, when prepared, would be brought out to the main rink, where 67 canvas-enclosed cubicles had been set up.

Each enclosed an area large enough to accommodate three coffins. At the rink's eastern end, the observation room, normally used as a place for watching the curlers, was to be used as a viewing area, from which friends of the deceased could observe the bodies being brought out from the embalming room. The loved ones would then be escorted to the cubicles, where positive identification would be attempted.

Arrangements were made with shipping and railroad companies for the carriage of coffins; those caskets leaving with friends could be carried in the baggage car on payment of a regular first class fare. Coffins also could be sent by express on payment of two first class fares.

American Consul Ragsdale suspended the usual formalities governing transfer of bodies to the United States.

Further plans were announced: bodies would be kept at the Mayflower rink for up to two weeks to give maximum opportunity for loved ones to claim them. Further description of all bodies would be recorded, and, where bodily features were distinguishable, photographs would be taken of the deceased. The records and photographs were to be retained, and the body's location after burial noted, so that exhumation, if desired at any time in the future, could be done without possibility of error.

At 9.30 am on Tuesday, 30 April, the *Mackay-Bennett* arrived. Past Chebucto Light marking the boundary of Halifax Harbour, she slowly steamed, her mainmast flag fluttering at half-staff. The harbour, usually filled with bustling craft, was silent and empty. On past McNab's Island, past Point Pleasant Park at the southern tip of Halifax. Another mile, and a pause at Georges Island, where port physician W. D. Finn and various police officials boarded and the formalities were accomplished. The imposing Citadel, the huge fortress high on top of the hill dominating mid-city, stood impassively as the proceedings unfolded below.

As the vessel drew close to the dockyard, those assembled — a few dockyard officials, some relatives and friends of the victims, several reporters, police — could see Canon Hind on the bridge with Captain Lardner. *Mackay-Bennett's* crew lined the rails and on the stern could be seen the piled coffins. A large tarpaulin covered the foredeck. Beneath it, and in the hold, were bodies for whom no coffins had been available. As the ship was sighted down the harbour, canvas curtains shielding the waiting coffins and the embalmers' tents on the pier were lowered, and twenty sailors from the Canadian cruiser *Niobe,* in the yard for repairs, snapped to attention as guards.

Docking was quickly effected. Those on shore stood silently, and removed their hats. A canvas-covered gangway was put in place, and White Star Line officials and other authorized persons went aboard. Again there was only silence, punctuated now and then by the slow tolling of the city's church bells. The flags of every city building were at half-mast.

The first bodies to be taken ashore were those from the foredeck: crew for whom there had been no embalming or other preparation. The *Mackay-Bennett's* crew carried the bodies down the wharf on stretchers. Others brought bodies up from the ice-filled hold.

Then came the second and third class passengers, whose remains were sewn up in canvas bags. The bodies of the first class passengers, all embalmed and identified, were in the coffins on the stern, and were the last to be brought ashore. It took almost three and a half hours for the unloading to be completed.

By 10 am, as soon as they began coming ashore, the coffins were loaded on to the waiting teams — thirty of them — and began their 3,000-foot-long journey to the Mayflower Curling Rink. Apparently, the clergy's request to avoid the area had been heeded: small groups of people, clustered at street corners or along the pavements, witnessed the passage of coffins from the dockyard. They uncovered their heads as the horse-drawn hearses clopped past. The city itself was in deep mourning: everywhere there was black bunting. Draped photographs of the lost liner formed the centrepiece of displays in downtown businesses' windows. The tolling of the church bells continued.

At the Mayflower rink, friends and relatives had already gathered in the viewing room, which was well-filled by the time the first hearse arrived through a ring of police. The bereaved's faces clearly

showed the difficult ordeal that lay ahead for them. As the first rough coffin was carried into the rink and placed on one of the white benches, a hush fell upon them.

The second coffin followed, then a third, as hearse after hearse arrived. The coffins were borne into the darkened rink gently, reverently, and placed in the main rink (if embalmed at sea) or in the embalming area.

At first, relatives were permitted in the main rink to watch the coffins being unloaded, but soon orders came that everyone be excluded until all bodies were ready for identification. The expectancy of finally determining a loved one's fate was replaced by anguish at the delay. Most waited in the observation room, some pacing impatiently, others occasionally stepping outside into the sun for air. A makeshift hospital, set up in one of the large dressing rooms, stood ready to help those finding the identification process too stressful. A full set of restoratives and smelling salts was kept at the ready under the watchful eye of a trained nurse, Miss Nellie Remby.

The coroner's staff had set up a temporary office on the second floor. In contrast to the solemn, hushed environment of the rink below, this area bustled with staff members doing the necessary documentation for each victim. Never had the Halifax coroner's office had such a large number of cases to process at one time. To the office were brought the canvas bags containing the deceased's valuables. A log was kept of each bag and its contents, which were ordered held until they could be given to authorized claimants.

As the procession of hearses continued, the crowd outside began to grow, drawn mainly by curiosity. Vantage points were hard to find, and every window seemed occupied by three or four heads, except where photographers had ensconced themselves to take pictures of the scene.

As the undertakers worked, one of them, too, received a painful surprise. Frank Newell, from Yarmouth, Nova Scotia, unexpectedly encountered the body of his uncle, first class passenger Arthur W. Newell, and collapsed from the shock.

Once all bodies had been prepared, the dreaded moment arrived, and loved ones were admitted to identify the deceased. Each claimant was asked for identification, so that no possible error could occur. In the case of those representing the families of the deceased, notarized letters of authorization or formal powers of attorney were required. Once the claimants' identity had been established, viewing of the bodies was permitted. It was a harrowing ordeal

for all but the strongest.

Those victims whose identities were established beyond doubt were released. Those who had not been claimed remained in the shadowy interior of the curling rink.

As *Minia* continued her search in the North Atlantic, preparations went forward for the first of the burials to take place in three Halifax cemeteries. In cases where decomposition had begun, where identification had proved to be impossible, or where family or friends had indicated such a wish, interment would take place at once. By late on the evening of Thursday, 2 May, the authorities had prepared for the burial of 59 bodies, most unidentified, in the non-sectarian Fairview Cemetery. Late in the evening, however, Rabbi Jacob Walter visited the curling rink and determined that nine of the victims were of the Jewish faith. At his request, they were separated from the others, to be interred in the Baron de Hirsch Cemetery. The rabbi was not, however, granted sufficient time to inspect the remaining coffins.

As Friday, May 3 began so, too, did the funeral arrangements at Fairview Cemetery. A large group of spectators had gathered, the Royal Canadian Regiment Band was in place, and the clergy were on hand to officiate in the commitment. The plan was to inter the bodies in long trenches, each body eventually to have its number engraved on the tombstone when installed, so that remains could be exhumed, if necessary, in the future.

When the service had begun, it was discovered that ten coffins were missing. Consternation was put aside for the moment, and the burial services proceeded. Later inquiries revealed that Rabbi Walter, during the memorial service in town, had gone to Fairview Cemetery, where the caskets were arriving from the Mayflower Rink for interment, opened the caskets, satisfied himself that ten contained victims of the Jewish faith, and directed the undertaker's team and several leading citizens of Halifax's Jewish community to take them to the adjacent Baron de Hirsch cemetery.

Nineteen bodies now there, the Jewish community put on extra men digging graves on Friday afternoon, intending to inter all before sundown, which marked the beginning of the Sabbath, when such activities would not be permitted.

Once the authorities found out, they stopped the plan. The original nine were interred, as planned.* The disputed ten were placed in the Jewish cemetery's receiving vault, pending a determination in the matter, since their burial permits stated that their interments were to be at Fairview.

---

*Ironically, among them was Michel Navratil, in actuality a Catholic. Because he had travelled under the assumed name of 'Hoffman', it was believed he was of the Jewish faith. Only one other victim in Baron de Hirsch Cemetery was ever identified: F. Wormald, a saloon steward.

Meanwhile Rabbi Walter was granted an opportunity to inspect all remaining bodies at the morgue, and reported that of the 190 bodies brought in, 44 were those of Jewish victims. As the Halifax *Evening News* reported, 'It will probably be found that the whole difficulty is one of misunderstanding. The Jewish cemetery has room for only about 75 bodies altogether'.

That it had been a misunderstanding was soon apparent. One body was soon identified as that of a man bearing an Irish surname from Galway. Others were victims for whom the White Star Line had received instructions from family members. At a conference between White Star and Rabbi Walter, it was further discovered that four bodies were those of Roman Catholics, and they were designated for interment in Halifax's Mount Olivet Cemetery.

The ten 'missing' caskets eventually were returned to the Mayflower rink on the authority of White Star and provincial authorities. The *Evening News* added, 'The coffins were somewhat damaged in the frequent changes to which they were subjected and it is said that someone will have to pay for new ones'.

Even when victims' identities were firmly established, problems sometimes occurred. The remains of Stanley H. Fox, a travelling salesman of Rochester, New York, were quickly identified. Within 24 hours, his body had been claimed by Lydia Fox, the victim's sister-in-law, who said she had come on behalf of his widow, Cora Fox, who was 'prostrated in Rochester' by the news of her husband's death.

Officials, convinced of Lydia Fox's identity and her authority to act, at her request directed Fox's body to be shipped via train on the evening of 1 May. One hour before the train left, the authorities received a telegram from Cora Fox, directing that the body not be forwarded in Lydia's care, and that personal effects be retained by the authorities. Baffled, the offials decided not to detain the body, but did retain the personal effects, consisting chiefly of $70 and two watches.

When the train was about an hour out of Halifax, White Star agents received information suggesting that some sort of fraud, perhaps involving insurance, was being perpetrated. Immediately they telegraphed to Truro, ordering the body to be taken off the train. As the *Evening News* put it, 'Mrs Lydia Fox, if that be the sister-in-law's name, and if indeed she be a sister-in-law, did not know anything about [the off-loading of the body]. She believes it

still on board, speeding with her to Rochester'.

Eventually, no less than the Mayor of Rochester wired Halifax, and directed that the body be sent to the widow. The authorities complied, and sent the effects along as well.

As the first interment day, Friday 3 May, arrived, the city paid its respects in a series of services. The first, at 9.30 am, was conducted at St Mary's Cathedral by Dr Foley, its rector, with the province's Catholic archbishop and six other priests participating. The cathedral was filled to overflowing. The four bodies, all unidentified females,* were placed on a catafalque in the sanctuary. Messrs Mitchell, Jones and a large group from White Star's Halifax agency attended the services, following which the bodies were removed to Mount Olivet Cemetery, where interment was conducted at 4 pm.

Soon, another service was held at the Brunswick Street Methodist Church, under the auspices of the Halifax Evangelical Alliance.

The building's interior was draped with purple and black. Large clusters of pink and white carnations, a gift of Mrs Hugh R. Rood, wife of a first class passenger lost in the disaster, were banked near the pulpit. The Lieutenant Governor of Nova Scotia, officers of the cruiser *Niobe*, officers of the garrison at the Citadel and a Masonic delegation were in attendance. The Very Reverend Dean Crawford used Psalm 90 as the text for his Scripture reading, while the Rev Dr McKinnon of the Presbyterian College at Pine Hill delivered the sermon.

A band from the Royal Canadian Regiment provided accompaniment for the hymns, which included 'Forever with the Lord', the 'Hymn for the Survivors of the Titanic' by Hall Caine (sung to the tune of 'O God Our Help in Ages Past'), and finally, 'Nearer, My God, To Thee'. After the benediction, the regimental band played the Dead March from 'Saul' as a postlude.

At 3 pm the Fairview interments began, some fifty victims being laid to rest on the gentle, grass-covered hillside overlooking the lower reaches of Bedford Basin, known as Fairview Cove. Present were the Royal Canadian Regiment band and a band of pipers in Highland costume. At the service's conclusion, the bands and those present joined in singing 'Nearer, My God, To Thee'.

On Saturday, 4 May, there was but a single burial at Fairview. The little boy, among the first victims found by the *Mackay-Bennett*, remained at the Mayflower rink, unclaimed and unidentified†,

---

*Subsequently only one, third class passenger, Margaret Rice, was identified.

†The child, fair haired, has been tentatively identified as two-year-old Gosta Leonard Paulsson, who boarded at Southampton with his mother, two sisters and brother (the oldest of whom was eight years old).

All were lost. Gosta's grave, unbeknown to anyone at the time, was placed within feet of his mother's final resting place. His sisters and brother were not found.

despite all efforts of White Star and provincial personnel. Many individuals and institutions had offered to sponsor the funeral for the little one but, at Captain Lardner's request, the men who had found him were given permission to extend this final expression of care and remembrance.

The memorial service was held at St George's Anglican Church, located at Brunswick and Cornwallis Streets, not far from the dockyard where the cable ship lay. Canon Kenneth O. Hind, who had been present when the little boy was found, now presided. In attendance were 75 officers and crew from the *Mackay-Bennett*. The church was filled with flowers; all of Halifax had been deeply touched by the child's tragic plight. At the service's conclusion, the little white casket, heaped high with flowers, was borne by six sailors from the *Mackay-Bennett* to the hearse, where it was conveyed to its final resting place.

Later, the cable ship's crew again saw to it that the child would not be forgotten: together they commissioned his headstone, larger than many of the others in Fairview. On it, the poignant inscription, 'Erected to the Memory of an Unknown Child Whose Remains Were Recovered after the Disaster to the Titanic, April 15th, 1912'.

Meanwhile, the *Minia* had not had an easy time of it at the disaster site. The bad weather had continued without respite. After a week of searching, she had recovered just seventeen bodies. Two, those of unidentified firemen, were buried at sea. The fifteen brought to Halifax included Charles M. Hays, president of the Grand Trunk Railway; Joseph Fynney, a second class passenger; three third class passengers, and ten crew members. On 3 May Captain DeCarteret gave up the quest and returned home. *Minia* arrived at quarantine outside Halifax Harbour at 2 am on Monday, 6 May, but did not proceed to the dockyard for five hours. She, too, berthed at coaling wharf number 4.

Hays' body was taken directly to Snow's private mortuary on Argyle Street, where it was prepared, placed in a casket and taken to the North Street railway station. There it was put aboard the private rail car *Canada* for transport to Montreal. The other bodies were taken to the Mayflower rink.

Within a day or so, the letter *Minia*'s temporary wireless assistant Francis Dyke had been writing during the week was posted to his mother, with the added comment, 'I honestly hope I shall never have to come on another expedition like this as it is far from pleasant. The Dr and I are sleeping in the middle of 14 coffins (for the time being) they are all stacked round our quarters aft. The *Titanic* must have blown up when she sank, as we have picked up pieces of the grand staircase + most of the wreckage is from *below* deck, it must have been an awful explosion, too, as some of the main deck

planking 4 ft [*sic*] thick was all split and broken off short.'

Yet one more attempt was made to find *Titanic*'s victims. The Canadian Ministry of Marine and Fisheries ship *Montmagny* was despatched on 3 May from Sorel, Quebec, as *Minia* headed home. After picking up supplies and personnel from Halifax on 6 May, *Montmagny* cruised around the Gulf of St Lawrence. Aboard were the undertakers J. R. Snow and Cecil Zink, the Rev Mr Prince and Rev Father McQuillan, and Captain Peter Johnson, who was replacing the ship's regular captain, F. X. Pouliot, who was also aboard.

Weather again made progress difficult upon arrival in the disaster area. The Rev Mr Prince said:

'On Friday [10 May] there was a dense fog and at the best we could not see clearly more than a couple hundred yards from the vessel. The morning was not far advanced before we began to see a succession of drifting wreckage. Once the ship was stopped, an oak newel post [was] picked up. A bedstead was seen, also hats, polished and white painted woods, and a great square of probably forty feet dimensions, which may have been part of the ill-fated steamer's deck'.

Despite the weather, the body of Harold Reynolds, a steerage passenger, was recovered on Friday morning. He was found clinging to a life preserver. One report said the body had apparently slipped through the life ring. 'It is supposed that the unfortunate man's hand caught in the line [around the ring] and thus he perished,' said the report.

At 2.30 pm two more bodies were found: those of a fifteen-year-old Syrian girl, and C. Smith, a bedroom steward. On Saturday, at 3 pm one more body — the last of the voyage — was recovered. It was a crew member, with no marks to identify him. He was buried at sea with 'suitable services', according to a despatch received from Captain Johnson.

Montmagny arrived at Louisburg, Nova Scotia, on Monday, 13 May. The three bodies were put ashore and shipped to Halifax via the Sidney & Louisburg and the Canadian National Railways.

After rebunkering, *Montmagny* left port at 11 pm on the 14th, returning to search, unsuccessfully, for more bodies. On the second trip, the only objects sighted were small pieces of wood, very scattered, to the east of the disaster site. She cruised back and forth as far as the Gulf Stream before departing from the area on Sunday, 19 May. At the conclusion of her search, the unused caskets, supplies and equipment were unloaded and she resumed her normal duty.

As *Montmagny* headed to port for the second time, White Star chartered yet one more vessel to search. *Algerine*, owned by Bowring Bros of St John's, Newfoundland, left St John's on 15 May with fifty coffins and a quantity of embalming fluid.

Only a single body was recovered, that of James McGrady, a saloon steward. It was assigned number 330.* *Algerine* returned to St John's on 8 June, when McGrady's body was trans-shipped to Halifax via Bowring's *Florizel,* arriving 11 June.

The searches by *Minia, Montmagny* and *Algerine* had not delayed interments in Fairview and Mount Olivet cemeteries. On 10 May, 33 bodies were interred at the former, and the body of Mr William Carbines was shipped by Snow & Co to New York, where it was to be trans-shipped back to England in the company of Mr Carbines' two brothers.

Also on the 10th, two chests of unclaimed effects removed from the bodies of *Titanic* victims were taken by M. R. Lownds, an employee of White Star's Halifax agents, from the Mayflower rink to the provincial treasurer's office. The property's value was estimated at between $50,000 and $75,000.

Of the 209 bodies brought to Halifax by *Mackay-Bennett* and *Minia,* there now remained but four in the Mayflower rink. The hushed tones, the distraught loved ones largely had gone now. Medical examiner W. D. Finn and White Star's representatives collected their papers and closed their temporary offices, departing for the last time from the rink.

On Saturday, third class passenger Sigurd Moen's body was forwarded to New York for shipment to Bergen, Norway, for interment. Steward Arthur Lewis' body was buried at Fairview in the morning, second class passenger Arthur McCrae following in the afternoon. The last body from the rink, that of third class passenger Karl Wiklund, was moved to Snow's funeral home where, with the incoming bodies on *Montmagny* and *Algerine,* it would await relatives' instructions. It was subsequently interred at Fairview on 14 May.

The scenes of anguish that had filled the rink were over, now. The dead and living had arrived and departed. As Saturday's evening shadows crept over Agricola Street, the Mayflower Curling Rink, its place in the chronicles of Halifax and of the world assured, finally, for the first time in two weeks, fell silent.

The last burials, involving those found by *Montmagny* and *Algerine,* took place in late May and early June. First class passenger Serrando Ovies y Rodrigues, interred at Fairview on 3 May, was exhumed and reburied at Mount Olivet on 15 May. On 12 June, the last of all, steward James McGrady, was laid to rest in Fairview, amongst his shipmates and the passengers he may have served.

Soon a carpet of grass erased the scars where the trenches and graves had been dug. Nature, the great healer, was at work. Mankind, who had designed *Titanic* to withstand Nature's forces, tried yet again for permanence. Within a year, dark grey granite headstones were installed over each grave. Virtually identical in design, the vast majority recorded the vital statistics with uniform brevity. A name, the words 'Died April 15, 1912', and a body number. No mention of *Titanic,* unless the family had asked — or perhaps paid for — a supplementary inscription.[†]

Mindful of its responsibility, the White Star Line deposited $7,500 with the Royal Trust Company of Canada for perpetual care of the graves of *Titanic*'s dead.[‡]

Though the city of Halifax turned to other matters it, too, did not forget. The 150 persons, strangers whom history had brought to its hallowed and storied ground, were at peace beneath the silent, sentinel gravestones. As the sun descended each afternoon in the City by the Sea, the markers' lengthening shadows pointed toward the harbour, whence they had come.

---

*The four ships recovered 328 bodies in all; pages 324 and 325 in the record book apparently were not used, for reasons unknown.

[†]In the case of the unidentified (about (about half of the 150 buried in Halifax), the stones' topmost line was left blank, in the forlorn hope that identification eventually would be made. Despite the authorities' meticulous recording of descriptions and even the taking of photographs, none of those unidentified when buried later had the stones' upper line filled in.

[‡]The trust fund was supplemented with an additional deposit in 1930. While details are lacking, it is known that the Cunard Line contributes to some extent to the graves' upkeep, having assumed the duty at the time of its 1934 merger with White Star. The cemetery association apparently pays for spring and autumn plantings of flowers.

Left The clock tower on Citadel Hill overlooks the busy harbour that is to receive the victims of the *Titanic* disaster. (Halifax Regional Library.)

Second left In this area of the city's waterfront, the cable ship *Mackay-Bennett* usually docks. (Halifax Regional Library.)

Third left Chartered by the White Star Line, the *Mackay-Bennett* is the first of four vessels to search the wide Atlantic for *Titanic*'s victims. Her crew is to be paid double wages for the difficult work that lies ahead. (Authors' collection.)

Below Captain W. H Lardner has a break as crewmen take aboard one of 100 coffins the *Mackay-Bennett* is to carry. (*New York Evening Journal.*)

Bottom left One by one, the coffins are stowed in the vessel's holds. (*Philadelphia Inquirer.*)

Bottom As departure time approaches, several tons of ice are brought aboard. (*Halifax Morning Chronicle.*)

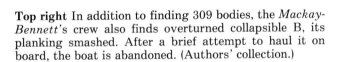

Top Shortly after noon on Wednesday, 17 April, the *Mackay-Bennett* steams out of Halifax Harbour and heads for the disaster site. (Bob Forrest collection.)

Top right In addition to finding 309 bodies, the *Mackay-Bennett*'s crew also finds overturned collapsible B, its planking smashed. After a brief attempt to haul it on board, the boat is abandoned. (Authors' collection.)

Above Stacks of coffins visible on her stern, her flags flying at half-mast, the cable ship *Mackay-Bennett* enters Halifax Harbour on the morning of 30 April. (Russ Lownds collection.)

Second right Slowly she proceeds through a harbour empty of its usual commerce, on towards the naval dockyard. (*Harper*'s.)

Third right Once the *Mackay-Bennett* is moored at the dockyard, her grim deck cargo is readily apparent. (*Harper*'s.)

Right On the naval dockyard's coaling wharf number four, tents for officials and undertakers have been set up, awaiting the *Mackay-Bennett*'s arrival. (*Harper*'s.)

Left From their establishment on Argyle Street, John Snow and Sons direct the handling of *Titanic*'s victims. Mr Snow asks for, and receives, the help of virtually every undertaker in Canada's Maritime Provinces in preparing the bodies. (Public Archives of Nova Scotia.)

Inset Mr Snow (left) and his business manager emerge from a planning meeting with White Star, Canadian and provincial government officials. (*The Casket*.)

Bottom left As the *Mackay-Bennett* is warped to her dock, hearses and extra coffins lie ready. (Public Archives of Nova Scotia.)

Top right A guard of honour of twenty sailors from the Canadian Navy's cruiser *Niobe* forms at the dockside. (Authors' collection.)

Right Slowly, the coffins are removed from the *Mackay-Bennett*. A hearse bears the body of John Jacob Astor out of the dockyard as a crowd of reporters and the curious watches. (*Harper's*.)

Right The procession of hearses enters the grounds of the Mayflower Curling Rink on Agricola Street. As the first coffins arrive, there is virtually no crowd watching. . . (*The Casket*.)

Below. . .but as the seemingly unending line continues, onlookers — always quiet, always respectful — begin to gather. (Arnold Watson collection.)

Below right Inside the rink, canvas cubicles, each capable of enclosing three coffins, have filled the main room. Only when all victims have been prepared and brought out into the room are friends and relatives permitted to enter. (*The Casket*.)

THEO. N. VAIL, PRESIDENT

RECEIVED AT

113.B.Kn.36 NL

Besten Mass April 26th.12.

Frank A Smith

Halifax NS Halifax Hotel

Richard's body reported found better return with it at once,will meet you in Portland,see white star officials for everything necessary look sharp for my brother's body wire me fully as soon as you can,

Z L White 1111pm

Above The Halifax Hotel establishes an information bureau where the latest news regarding identifications and recovery ships' movements may be obtained. Yet, sometime, the impetus to act comes from outside Halifax, as in this case. (Public Archives of Nova Scotia.)

Right The employees of White Star Line's Halifax agents, A. G. Jones and Company Ltd, are besieged with requests for assistance in locating and identifying the remains of loved ones. (Russ Lownds collection.)

UNITED SUPPLY COMPANY

DAVID NETTER & CO., PROPRIETORS

DEALERS IN

LABELS, CORKS, BOTTLES, ESSENTIAL OILS, FLAVORING EXTRACTS AND COLD LUNCH SUPPLIES

441 AND 443 MARKET STREET

PHILADELPHIA, PA.,   May 8,   1912.

Mr. R. Lonnds.

Halifax, N. S.

My Dear Sir:-

Confirming telegram sent you last night, charges pre paid, which read as follows:-

Has the Minia recovered body with initials of H. K. Herman Klaber his height was six feet, sandy complexion, high forehead, straight nose, brown hair, weight one hundred and ninety pounds, am sending photograph care White Star Dominon Line, Halifax. Kindly compare with bodies. If found or not found wire me at my expense.

Mr. Klaber's family has been reconciled to the fact that he has given up his life on the Titanic. Naturally they desire me to use my best efforts as to any information concerning the remains that may be brought to shore, possibly his body is one of them. Unfortunately Mr. Klaber's family lives in California and I am oblig- ed to act in there stead. I have had the photograph of Mr. Klaber sent to you by Mrs. Netter, and kindly request you to compare same with bodies recovered by the Minia. If you find any resemblance wire me at my expense and I will come to Halifax.

Thanking you for favors shown and when ever you are in Philadelphia I will be pleased to have you call. Trusting these few lines find you well are the wishes of,

Yours respectfully,

DN/EP.

P. S.⁺ Show phtograph of Mr. Klaber to Dr. W. D. Finn, Coroner, and oblige,

Below left Other letters bring poignant requests for the personal effects of those lost. The letter, with original spelling and punctuation preserved, reads, 'Dear Sir, I have been inform by Mr F. Blake Superintendent Engineer of the White Star Line, Trafalgar Chambers on the 10th that the body of my Beloved Son Herbert Jupe which was Electrical Engineer No. 3 on the Ill Fatted Titanic has been recovered and Burried at Sea by the Cable Steamer "Mackay-Bennett" and that his Silver Watch and Handkerchief marked H.J. is in your possession. He bought him half of the same when he was at Belfast with the R.M.S. Olympic to have a new Blade put to one of Her Perpellors. We are extreemly oblidged for all your kindness to my Precious Boy. He was not Married and was the Love of our Hearts and he Loved his Home. But God gave and God has taken him. Blessed be the Name of the Lord. He has left an aceing [aching] Void in our Home which cannot be filled. Please send along the Watche and Handkerchief marked H.J. Yours Truly, C. Jupe. His mother is 72 last April 4th. His Father is 68 Last Feb. 9th.' (Public Archives of Nova Scotia.)

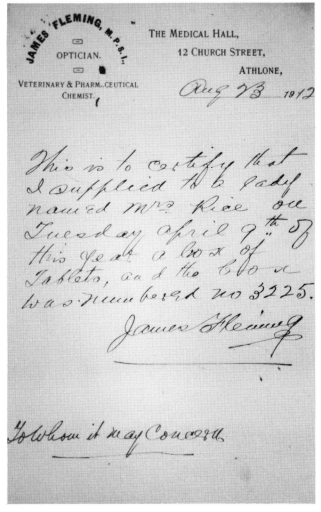

Top Vincent Astor (right) arrives on his private rail car, *Oceanic,* to make arrangements for the shipment of his father's remains back to the United States. *(Harper's).*

Above right Meanwhile, the difficult task of identifying the victims continues at the Mayflower Rink. A chemist supplies details about a pill box that third class passenger Margaret Rice had upon her person, permitting her identification. (Public Archives of Nova Scotia.)

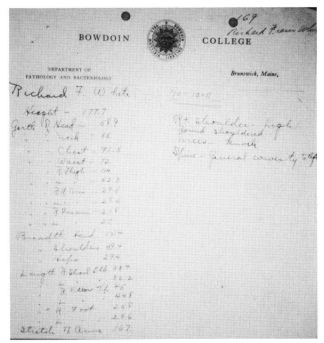

Right Bowdoin College forwards the measurements it took of Richard F. White during his last routine physical examination on campus. (Public Archives of Nova Scotia.)

241

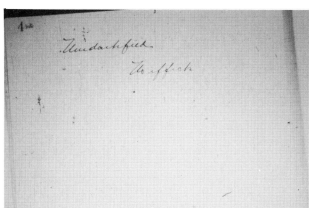

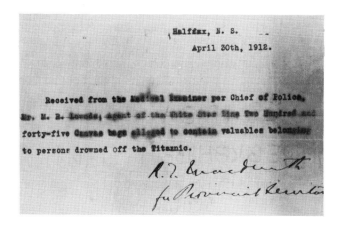

NO. 123   MALE.   ESTIMATED AGE, 24.   HAIR DARK.

CLOTHING—Brown jacket, uniform vest; black pants.

EFFECTS—One razor; discharge book A.

STEWARD.   NAME IN BOOK—FRED. TAMLYN,
20 Southampton St., Southampton.

NO. 124   MALE.   ESTIMATED AGE, 50.   LIGHT HAIR AND MOUSTACHE.

CLOTHING—Blue serge suit; blue handkerchief with "A. V."; belt with gold
buckle; brown boots with red rubber soles; brown flannel shirt; "J. J. A."
on back of collar.

EFFECTS—Gold watch; cuff links, gold with diamond; diamond ring with
three stones; £225 in English notes; $2440 in notes; £5 in gold; 7s. in
silver; 5 ten franc pieces; gold pencil; pocketbook.

FIRST CLASS.   NAME—J. J. ASTOR.

Above left Pictures found on the bodies also provide valuable clues. In this case, a victim's likeness (marked 'x' by the person doing the inventory) is found on a photograph in his possession. Lift attendant William Carney is thus identified. (Public Archives of Nova Scotia.)

Initially, the details of a victim's physical description, content of pockets, clothing, etc, is recorded by hand in a ledger, whose page numbers correspond to the body number. **Top** John Jacob Astor's record, and the subsequent disposition of his remains and personal effects are noted. (Public Archives of Nova Scotia.)

Above Later, the White Star Line sends printed lists of the recovered bodies to its major agencies, in a continuing effort to achieve identification. Identities, if known, were also included. (Public Archives of Nova Scotia.)

For some, there is nothing to be recorded. **Middle left** This is the record sheet for body number 4, who became known as the 'unknown child'. Recent research indicates this may well have been two-year-old Gosta Leonard Paulson. (Public Archives of Nova Scotia.)

Left As activities at the Mayflower Curling Rink come to a close, Matthew Russell Lownds, an employee of A. G. Jones, White Star's Halifax agent, is detailed to bring unclaimed personal effects to the provincial secretary's office. (Russ Lownds collection.)

Above The first of several memorial services is held at St Mary's Cathedral on Friday, 3 May. (Halifax Regional Library.)

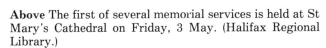

Top right The cable ship *Minia* is chartered by White Star to take over search operations when the *Mackay-Bennett* returns to Halifax. (Maritime Museum of the Atlantic.)

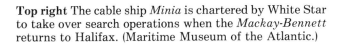

Second right Her departure from Halifax is delayed by a shortage of coffins, but the James Dempster Company works into the night to supply the ship's needs. (*Daily Mirror*.)

Third right The *Minia* recovers two pieces of woodwork from the lost liner. The pattern in this piece suggests the first class lounge as its source. (Arnold Watson collection — Public Archives of Nova Scotia.)

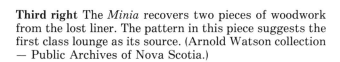

Right The beautiful craft of expert wood carvers is evident in this detail of the other piece found by *Minia*. (Arnold Watson collection — Public Archives of Nova Scotia.)

Above A boat from *Minia* recovers another *Titanic* victim from the cold waters of the North Atlantic on the morning of 26 April. A *Mackay-Bennett* crewman snaps the photograph before his ship returns to port. (Public Archives of Nova Scotia.)

Middle left The Canadian government vessel *Montmagny* is the third to take up the search, commencing on 6 May. Four victims are recovered during her first voyage, none during her second, which began on 14 May. (Canadian Ministry of Transport.)

Left Rabbi Jacob Walter (centre) and two workers pause following the installation of grave stones in the *Titanic* section at Baron de Hirsch Cemetery in Halifax. A mix-up in who was to be interred in the Jewish cemetery has delayed proceedings briefly. (Russ Lownds collection.)

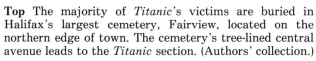

Top The majority of *Titanic*'s victims are buried in Halifax's largest cemetery, Fairview, located on the northern edge of town. The cemetery's tree-lined central avenue leads to the *Titanic* section. (Authors' collection.)

Top right In three gently curving rows, the marker stones over *Titanic*'s dead bear silent witness to the human cost of the night of 14-15 April. (Authors' collection.)

Among those interred in Fairview is John Law ('Jock') Hume, the violinist of *Titanic*'s orchestra. (Authors' collection.)

The faithful service of Ernest E. S. Freeman, secretary to J. Bruce Ismay, is remembered in this marker stone, paid for by Freeman's anguished employer. Ismay also sees to it that Freeman's family is well provided for. (Russ Lownds collection.)

Words from a verse of the hymn 'Nearer, My God to Thee' appear on the grave stone of Herbert Cave, a saloon steward. (Russ Lownds collection.)

The tragic story of the Paulson family — mother and children — is told in a few words. (Authors' collection.)

The *Mackay-Bennett*'s crew provide the marker for the 'unknown child'. (Authors' collection.)

Right Nineteen of *Titanic*'s people are at peace in Halifax's Catholic cemetery, Mount Olivet. (Authors' collection.)

Chapter Seventeen

HOMECOMING

From the moment the ocean closed in over *Titanic*'s stern at 2.20 am on 15 April, the surviving crew were unemployed. Their wages stopped, their families' financial status jeopardized, they hoped for a quick return home. Perhaps for less personal reasons, their employer, the White Star Line, likewise hoped for an immediate return voyage. Each day the crew spent in New York made it more likely that misinformation or adverse publicity might be disseminated to the public through conversations with newspaper reporters eager for a 'scoop'.

Even as *Carpathia* returned to New York, Bruce Ismay, mindful of this potential, had despatched a series of telegrams to the company's offices. It was imperative, he felt, to return *Titanic*'s surviving crew to England as quickly as possible. The first of the telegrams sent over Ismay's special 'personal signature' was explicit enough. It was received in New York at 5.35 p.m. on 17 April:

'Most desirable *Titanic* crew aboard *Carpathia* should be returned home earliest moment possible. Suggest you hold *Cedric*, sailing her daylight Friday unless you see any reason contrary. Propose returning in her myself. Please send outfit of clothes, including shoes, for me to *Cedric*. Have nothing of my own. Please reply.

YAMSI'

He sent another message on the morning of the rescue ship's arrival:

'Steamship "Carpathia" via Siasconsett, Mass, April 18, 1912
'Islefrank, New York:
'Very important you should hold *Cedric* daylight Friday for *Titanic* crew. Reply.

YAMSI'

Several hours later Ismay received a negative response from P. A. S. Franklin, IMM's American vice president:

'Ismay, *Carpathia*:
'Have arranged forward crew *Lapland*, sailing Saturday, calling at Plymouth. We all consider most unwise delay *Cedric*, considering all circumstances'.

Ismay, unaware of the situation developing in New York, persisted:

'Steamship "Carpathia", via Siasconsett, Mass, 'Islefrank, New York:
'Think it most unwise keep *Titanic* crew until Saturday. Strongly urge detain *Cedric* sailing her midnight if desirable.

YAMSI'

Yet another telegram, apparently from Ismay, arrived without signature soon thereafter:

'Steamship "Carpathia", via Siasconsett, Mass, 'Islefrank, New York:
'Unless you have good and substantial reason for not holding *Cedric*, please arrange to do so. Most undesirable have crew New York so long'.

Franklin, aware of Senator Smith's imminent investigation and the growing public clamour for full disclosure of the facts, brought the wirelessed discussion to a close:

'Ismay, *Carpathia*:
'Regret after fullest consideration decided *Cedric* must sail as scheduled. Expect join *Carpathia* at quarantine, but can not remove boats as everything arranged for steamer proceed dock immediately'.

Thus it was that *Cedric* sailed on Friday, 19 April, without *Titanic*'s crew on board. Placed on the Red Star liner *Lapland*, they had little to do but await Saturday's sailing — or one of Senator Smith's subpoenas. Press contact was, at least temporarily, not possible.

A crowd gathered at Pier 61 to watch *Lapland* depart on 20 April with 172 *Titanic* crew on board, 38 others having been detained at Senator Smith's request. Her flag still fluttered at half-mast as she backed away from the pier.

Five additional crew were removed from the ship once she was underway. They, too, would testify at the Senate inquiry, and would not be going home yet.

For the 167 more fortunate ones, *Lapland*'s

eastbound crossing was uneventful. The crew, including nineteen stewardesses, spent the time resting, recovering from the ordeal they had experienced. There was time to think of colleagues and friends lost, and anticipation of reunions with loved ones.

It was shortly after 7 am on Monday, 29 April when *Lapland* was sighted in Plymouth Harbour, and 45 minutes later she dropped anchor far from the docks, in Cowsand Bay. The day was sunny and mild. Immediately, three tenders were despatched to the ship. One conveyed the liner's first and second class passengers to Millbay Docks, and they immediately departed via train for London. The second tender brought in the mail and specie which *Lapland* had carried.

The third tender, *Sir Richard Grenville*, had left the dock at 6.30 am. On board were two White Star Line directors, Harold Sanderson and E. C. Grenfell; Mr Wolverstan, a Board of Trade representative, accompanied by four assistants; Mr Furniss, a solicitor for the White Star Line; Mr W. Woolven, the local Receiver of Wrecks and Collector of Customs; Mr J. Bartholomew, White Star's Southampton victualling superintendent; and Mr Frank Phillips, the company's Plymouth agent.

The crew's enthusiasm at returning home soon faded when it became clear they were not to be disembarked. The Board of Trade intended to begin taking depositions immediately. But two visitors stopped the plan before it started. Mr Thomas Lewis, president, and Mr Cannon, secretary of the British Seafarers' Union, had requested permission to board *Lapland* with the White Star and Board of Trade representatives, to advise the men about the legal proceedings now under way. They were refused.

Lewis and Cannon would not take 'no' for an answer. Quickly they arranged for a small boat to take them out to *Lapland,* and through a megaphone they advised *Titanic*'s crew not to make any statement until they, as union representatives, were taken aboard.

As the tender left *Lapland,* it followed a slow and circuitous route, manoeuvring around the harbour for several hours, apparently trying to 'shake off' further interference from the union officials. But the crew had followed the advice, and refused to say a single word to Board of Trade officials, who were forced to allow Messrs Lewis and Cannon aboard *Sir Richard Grenville.* Mr Lewis invited the crew to ask for him upon their leaving the dock. To expedite departure, the nineteen *Titanic* stewardesses were the first to give statements on board the tender. It was not until almost noon that the survivors landed, some with a varied collection of kitbags and simple luggage.

At first, many believed they would be released upon arrival ashore. Instead, amid considerable, but ineffective, protest they were herded into the dock's third class waiting room, which was sealed off from the inquiring press, the public and loved ones by the dock yard's high iron fence. A contingent of dock police, assisted by the local police force, vigorously enforced the exclusion of unauthorized persons.

The taking of depositions resumed. Some were served with formal subpoenas requiring their appearance at the Board of Trade's inquiry, to be held in London. Regardless of their potential value to the inquiry, however, all surviving crew also had to appear before the Receiver of Wrecks before they could be released.

Accordingly, provision had been made for them to stay overnight in the waiting room, if necessary, until all statements had been taken and appearances completed. Bedding was installed, and long tables set up to feed the crew. Through the room's windows, piles of loaves of bread inside the waiting room could be seen from the dockyard gate.

From time to time, some were able to exchange greetings through the front windows with friends in the crowd. During their detention, the crew were given no information about arrangements for their departure. Each member was asked to pledge his word of honour that he would make no statements for publication — a promise that quickly evaporated.

At about 1 pm some survivors left the waiting room, and through the bars of the dock gates complained bitterly of their confinement. Others related their experiences to friends and the press with varying degrees of accuracy. At about 1.30, the gates swung open, and a crowd of seamen were allowed to leave. A mêlée erupted as waiting press representatives vied for 'exclusives' from *Titanic*'s crew.

Some 85 seamen and firemen left Plymouth via a special train for Southampton that departed at 6 pm. Remaining behind were stewards and stewardesses (whose travel plans inexplicably had been cancelled), cooks and victualling assistants.

At Southampton, even as the men were being released, an open-air service celebrating the crew's return to England was held at the Marlands, and was attended by Territorials, Army and Navy Reserve men, and a crowd of 50,000 civilians.

As the afternoon turned to dusk, and dusk to night, hundreds began to gather at Southampton's West Station. The gates were guarded by police, who admitted only relatives of the survivors and several dignitaries to the platform area. Southampton's Mayor, Councillor H. Bowyer, RNR, and Mr P. E. Curry, White Star's local manager, were on hand. The dominant mood of the expectant though hushed crowd was one of thankful joy.

The train's journey had been expedited and, fully

45 minutes ahead of schedule, it steamed slowly into the station. Station porters found it almost impossible to control the crowd as the train jolted to a stop. Men and women struggled to reach the moving carriages, and fiercely tugged at the handles of the compartment doors. There were many happy cries as face after face was recognized at the carriage windows. The surviving crewmen were pulled from the cars by the welcoming crowd. Tears flowed from men and women alike.

Slowly, the giant crowd dissolved into a series of tiny groups, each the focal point for an emotional reunion. The station platform was frequently illuminated by press photographers' flashguns.

For some, the waiting would continue. Halting, hesitating questions about the fate of loved ones not on board the train were sometimes answered with the happy confirmation of survival; in other cases, there were just shrugs of the shoulders, a whispered word or two, a shake of the head, or averted eyes.

Outside, the crowd continued to burgeon, and as the crewmen and their families made their way from the station, a narrow lane opened through the midst of the crowd, who greeted the survivors with cheers and applause. The Mayor, himself an old sailor, nodded and smiled at the men as they recognized him.

With their kit bags on one shoulder — and, frequently, a child on the other — the 85 seamen made their way out into the city they called home.

A railroad guard's shrill whistle signalled the train's departure, but the journey was a short one to the Docks Station. As the train made its way through the city, crowds lining the route cheered the men on. The scenes at the train's terminus, a blending of joy and grief, echoed those at West Station.

The second contingent of *Titanic* survivors, 86 stewards and the stewardesses, was allowed to leave around midday on Tuesday, 30 April, and boarded another special train departing in the late afternoon. It was believed that the train would arrive shortly before eight o'clock, and by that hour hundreds of people had massed on the platform, within the station, and in the adjacent streets, many anxiously seeking news of loved ones.

At 9 o'clock, word was received that the train had arrived at Redbridge, two miles away, and several minutes later the engine's white lights could be seen in the distance. Immediately, people mounted baggage carts, seats, anything that provided a viewpoint. As the train drew to a stop, prolonged cheers filled the air. Soon, the survivors and their families were reunited.

Another large crowd awaited the train's arrival at Docks Station but here the atmosphere was quite different upon the train's arrival: cheers were replaced by silence, broken only by an occasional sob as husband met wife and mother greeted son. One woman, disconsolately leaving the station without having seen her son, was stopped by a hand on her shoulder. Turning, she beheld him, and fainted from the shock. Mr Storry, the secretary of the stewards' union, placed mother and son in a taxi and sent them home.

Said the *Southern Daily Echo:*

'The scenes at the Dock Station were pathetic in the extreme. Not a man who witnessed them was able to look on unmoved. Most of them, indeed, had to turn away to check a tear and to clear their throats. Another touching incident was the quest of an elderly lady for a lad named Finch. [H. Finch, a steward.] He was an adopted son, and she had heard that the previous night a returning fireman had asked, "Is there anyone here for Finch?" That brought her to the station full of hope, but, alas, her search was in vain'.

With *Lapland*'s arrival, many of *Titanic*'s surviving crew were reunited with their families. But for the 43 crew detained by Senator Smith, the waiting was to continue. Eventually, as their testimony was completed, they, too, were allowed to sail for home.

One week after the first group of men arrived in Southampton, the joyous scenes of welcome were re-enacted, although on a smaller scale, when *Celtic* brought some of the crew to Liverpool on 6 May. Among them were lookouts Reginald Lee and Frederick Fleet, and quartermaster Robert Hichens.

On 9 May, Florence Ismay, her maid, Bruce's brother Bower and Henry Concannon, a White Star manager, sailed to Queenstown on *Oceanic*. They awaited the arrival of *Adriatic*, with Bruce Ismay and *Titanic*'s surviving officers aboard.

Tired, deeply distressed and strained by the past three weeks' events, Ismay at last was reunited with his family. There were a few brief hours of consolation and thanksgiving.

Adriatic proceeded to Liverpool, arriving at the Princes Landing Stage at 7.30 am on 11 May. The Ismays waited until nearly all first class passengers had departed before they left the ship. As they descended the gang-plank, they were quite surprised and deeply touched when the assembled crowds broke into applause and expressions of concern and support. It seemed a marked contrast to his treatment in America, and White Star's chairman managed a tight smile. His wife, behind him, beamed broadly.

Henry Concannon had preceded the Ismays, and had distributed a written statement to the press:

'Mr Ismay asks the gentlemen of the Press to extend their courtesy to him by not pressing for any statement from him. First he is still suffering from the very great strain of the *Titanic* disaster and subsequent events.
'Again because he gave the American Commission a plain and unvarnished statement of fact, which has been

fully reported; and also because his evidence before the British Court of Inquiry should not be anticipated in any way. He would, however, like to take this opportunity of acknowledging with full heart, the large number of telegraphic messages and letters from public concerns, and businesses and private friends to him and confidence in him, which he very much appreciates in this, the greatest trial of his life'.

The press courteously withheld its questions and, enveloped in the cheers of the crowd, the Ismays entered their car and drove to 'Sandheys', their Georgian-style home near Liverpool, for some much-needed rest.

Titanic's surviving officers were greeted by relatives at the pier, but were tight-lipped when it came to answering reporters' questions.

In contrast, the arrival of *Arabic* in Liverpool the next day passed virtually unnoticed. She, too, had brought home someone inextricably linked to the *Titanic* disaster. The body of Wallace H. Hartley, the ship's bandmaster, was placed on a hearse for the sixty-mile journey to Colne, his home town.

On 18 May, another *Titanic* hero, junior wireless operator Harold Bride, arrived on board the *Baltic*.

He was greeted by his father. Bride subsequently was to serve aboard the liner *Medina* in 1913 and the Royal Navy's net layer HMS *Mona's Isle* in 1918 and 1919. He then faded utterly from view, into the solitude of his memories.

The crew was home, now, in the care of families and loved ones. For each of them, life would never be the same. It would have a special meaning, a unique significance. For some, there would be a new life's work, the sea having lost its allure. For those who continued sailing, there were frequent flashbacks to the night of 14-15 April 1912. For all, there were recurring thoughts of the 697 crew not so fortunate, those who would never again know a family's love.

Yet another test lay ahead, one for which the vestiges of *Titanic*'s crew, all men and women of the sea, had scant experience. The subpoenas issued at Plymouth were carefully placed on mantlepieces or tucked under desk blotters or in the pockets of the crew's best outfits, where they were objects of occasional, worried glances. The opening day of the Board of Trade's inquiry into the loss of the *Titanic* was drawing near. . .

Above Flags still flying at half-mast, the Red Star Line's *Lapland* departs from New York City on 20 April with 172 of *Titanic*'s crew on board. (*Boston Post*.)

Above right The ship is stopped before she can leave New York Harbour, so that five additional crew can be served with subpoenas to testify before Senator Smith's committee. (Authors' collection.)

Right Meanwhile, at Plymouth, preparations are under way to receive — and detain — *Titanic*'s crew. Bedding and tables are installed in a third class waiting room at the dockside to house and feed the crew until questioning, the taking of depositions and the subpoenaing of witnesses for the forthcoming Board of Trade inquiry can be completed. (*Daily Mirror*.)

Homecoming

Left The *Lapland* arrives at Cawsand Bay, off Plymouth, on 28 April, carrying most of the surviving crew of *Titanic*. (*Daily Sketch*).

Second left The liner anchors in the middle of the bay. *Titanic*'s men line the rails of the tender *Sir Richard Grenville* which will take them ashore. (*Daily Sketch*.)

Third left The crewmen watch intently as landing preparations proceed. (*Daily Mirror*.)

Bottom left As *Lapland*'s passengers watch from above, *Titanic*'s crewmen field a few questions from reporters in circling harbour craft. (*Daily Mirror*.)

Top right At first prevented from going on board the *Sir Richard Grenville* to counsel the crew about their legal status before their questioning by Board of Trade representatives can begin, officials of the Seafarers' Union address the survivors from a boat alongside the tender. Later, the union's president and secretary are allowed on board. (*Daily Mirror*.)

Second right *Sir Richard Grenville* docks. Her pier is virtually deserted as officials close off all public and press access to the men. (*Illustrated London News*.)

Third right The interrogation and subpoenaing of the men begins. They unhappily await their turns to go before Board of Trade officials. (Private collection.)

Fourth right Time passes, and the men are given a meal during their enforced detention at Plymouth. (*Illustrated London News*.)

Below The men are at last allowed to go outside for a breath of fresh air. A group of stewards and cooks watches the press. (*Daily Mirror*.)

The strain of the ordeal and the anger over their detention shows on the men's faces. (*Illustrated London News*.)

The stewardesses fare little better, and gather near some pier machinery. (*Illustrated London News*.)

Virtually trapped behind the tall gates of the dockyard, *Titanic*'s crew are besieged by reporters' questions shouted through the steel bars. (Lloyd's *Deathless Story*.)

The crowd grows as relatives strain to see the crew. Police guard the side entrance, and visitors' credentials are carefully checked. Those crew near the fence have already given depositions, but are, nevertheless, still detained. (*Daily Sketch*.)

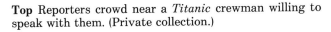

Top Reporters crowd near a *Titanic* crewman willing to speak with them. (Private collection.)

Above right Four detained crew members make the best of their unfortunate situation. (*Illustrated London News*.)

Above left Trimmer A. Hunt lights his brother's cigarette through the dock gates. One of his first questions to his brother was an inquiry about the latest football results. (*Daily Sketch*.)

Above middle Fireman John Thompson (left) awaits his release. (Private collection.)

Middle right Their detention at Plymouth over, *Titanic*'s crew arrives at the Southampton train station for the longed-for reunions with their families. (Private collection.)

Right Quartermaster James Humphreys carries his kit from Southampton station. (*Daily Sketch*.)

Far right A happy mother escorts her son, able seaman C. H. Pascoe, who is joined by his young brothers for the trip home. (*Daily Sketch*.)

Left For these three Southampton families, the long wait is over. Trimmers A. Hunt and A. Hebb, and Greaser G. Pregnall re-join their loved ones. (*Daily Sketch.*)

Middle left For the less fortunate, there are distributions of relief payments at the union headquarters in Southampton. (Private collection.)

Below The formalities must be observed. Each surviving crewman must 'sign off' on the ship's articles. Note that the date of discharge is shown as 15 April 1912, and the place of discharge is noted as 'Lat 41.16N, Long 50.14W'. The crew's pay had stopped when *Titanic* sank. (Public Record Office.)

254

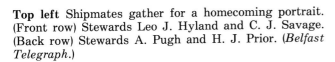

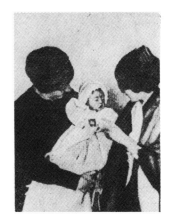

Top left Shipmates gather for a homecoming portrait. (Front row) Stewards Leo J. Hyland and C. J. Savage. (Back row) Stewards A. Pugh and H. J. Prior. (*Belfast Telegraph.*)

Top middle Steward Alfred Pugh receives a summons to appear at the forthcoming Board of Trade Inquiry. It later transpires that his testimony is not required, after all. (THS).

Top right The surviving crew of *Titanic* march to a memorial service in Southampton. (Lloyd's *Deathless Story.*)

Above On 6 May the *Celtic* brings look-out Reginald R. Lee (right) and quartermaster Robert Hichens (left) to Liverpool. (*Daily Mirror.*)

Second right Look-out Frederick Fleet (right of centre) is escorted from the *Celtic* on 6 May. (*Daily Sketch.*)

When the *Adriatic* docks in Liverpool on 11 May, seven-week-old survivor Vera Dean and her brother Bertram steal the show. According to one newspaper, she 'was the pet of the liner during the voyage, and so keen was the rivalry among the women to nurse this lovable mite of humanity that one of the officers decreed that first and second class passengers might hold her in turn for not more than ten minutes'. Photographers get ready to 'snap' the happy children, who could not know their father had been lost in the disaster. (*Daily Mirror.*)

Left His prolonged detention by Senator Smith now over, White Star managing director Bruce Ismay descends the gang-plank of the *Adriatic* at Liverpool on 11 May. Mrs Ismay beams as she follows her husband. Behind her is Harold Sanderson; he and Mrs Ismay went to Queenstown to meet *Adriatic* and the weary Bruce Ismay. (*Daily Graphic*.)

Middle left The Ismays walk to their waiting automobile. . . (*Daily Mirror*.)

Below. . .and get in, surrounded by well-wishers, reporters and the curious. (*Daily Mirror*.)

Bottom left The crowd cheers, and one man leans forward to express best wishes to the Ismays. (*Daily Sketch*.)

Bottom middle Also on board the *Adriatic* is Harold Godfrey Lowe, *Titanic*'s fifth officer. . . (*Daily Graphic*.)

Bottom. . .who is soon reunited with his sister Josie and his father. (*Daily Sketch*.)

Right Third officer Herbert John Pitman is met by relatives at the *Adriatic*'s pier in Liverpool. (*Daily Sketch*).

Right Third officer Pitman (left) and second officer Charles H. Lightoller exchange a few words upon arrival in Liverpool. (*Daily Graphic.*)

Below The 'signing off' process continues, with those crew detained for the American inquiry completing the necessary paperwork. (Public Record Office.)

Left Off the *Baltic* comes *Titanic*'s surviving radio operator, Harold Bride (centre), who is met by his father (left) in Liverpool. (*Daily Sketch*.)

Second left The White Star liner *Arabic* brings the body of bandmaster Wallace H. Hartley back to England, arriving 12 May. (*Authors' collection*.)

Third left The heroism of Hartley is commemorated in this postcard, published in his home town of Colne, in Lancashire, at the time of his burial. (Robert DiSogra collection.)

Middle left As a throng watches, the casket of Wallace Hartley is carried from the Bethel Independent Methodist Chapel in Colne. When younger, he had served as a chorister there. (*Daily Graphic*.)

Bottom The solemn, half-mile-long procession through his hometown brings Wallace Hartley to his final resting place in the cemetery outside Colne. (*Daily Graphic*.)

Left As he is laid to rest, the strains of 'Nearer, My God, to Thee' swell through the valley. The service concludes with the sounding of 'The Last Post' by a dozen boy scouts. (Arnold Watson collection.)

Chapter Eighteen

THE BRITISH INVESTIGATION

The Board of Trade Inquiry... The British Investigation... The Mersey Commission... Synonymous, at one time or another, with the body convened by the British Board of Trade to sit under the benign but watchful eye of the Wreck Commissioner to find the answers to some — if not all — of the questions surrounding the *Titanic*'s loss.

Horatio Bottomley, MP, knew how to communicate. His oratorical posturings in the House of Commons had become legendary in the six years since his first election. Bottomley was a populist and a spellbinder. He used his own publication, *John Bull*, to further his political ambitions by posing in its pages questions which frequently proved embarrassing to the establishment.

On 22 November 1910, Horatio Bottomley asked the House of Commons if the Board of Trade's president was aware that the new steamship being built *(Olympic)* was provided with only fourteen lifeboats. The Honorable Member received from the Board of Trade the response that the aggregate capacity of the boats — whatever their number — exceeded the statutory requirements.

Through articles in *John Bull*, Bottomley pursued the lifeboat question. In the December 1910 issue appeared a letter in which an anonymous naval architect described how he had worked with the designer of *Olympic* and *Titanic* (then Alexander Carlisle, who had left Harland and Wolff on 30 June 1910; in August, he joined the firm of Axel Welin, designer of the davits being built for the two new liners). The 'anonymous naval architect' was actually Axel Welin himself, and in his letter he stated that the davits he had designed for *Olympic* and *Titanic* could carry three or even four lifeboats each, although he had no idea of how many the builders or owners were likely to install.

In February 1911 Bottomley questioned the Board of Trade's president: 'Would the President state the date of the last regulations made by the Board in reference to the number of lifeboats necessary to be attached to passenger vessels; and whether having regard to the increased tonnage of modern ships he will consider the desireableness of revising such regulations?'

The Board of Trade answered, 'These regulations were last revised in 1894. The question of their future revision is engaging the serious attention of the Board of Trade and I have decided to refer the matter to the Mercantile Shipping and Advisory Committee for consideration and advice...'

Indeed, the question already had been brought to the Board's attention. On 9 March 1910, Axel Welin had sent to the Board of Trade a blueprint in which sixteen of his new double-acting davits were incorporated into one of *Titanic*'s plans. Using the davits to their designed capacity would permit a total of 64 boats to be carried.

Carlisle personally believed *Olympic* and *Titanic* should have at least 48 boats installed, though he felt it was not his place to ask for any particular number, this question being left to the owners and the Board of Trade to decide. But a week after receiving Welin's proposal the Board of Trade responded in a letter that '*Titanic* and *Olympic* are each to be fitted with 32 boats which are to be carried under 16 sets of double-acting davits, eight on each side'. And in July 1910, after Carlisle's departure, the builders submitted to the Board of Trade a print showing the number and arrangements of boats to be carried: eight lifeboats on each side, sixteen in all...

The advisory committee met during the early part of 1911. Carlisle, now with the Welin Davit and Engineering Co Ltd, attended two meetings. He took with him two plans: one showed *Titanic*'s original lifeboat distribution; the other was based on the Welin davit, which could carry up to four lifeboats on each set. Carlisle appeared in May 1911, actually during the committee's last two meetings, and as he later said, 'They had already come to certain conclusions on certain points'.

The committee rejected Carlisle's proposal and, though disappointed, he viewed the committee's

consideration of additional boats as encouraging. Thus, even though rebuffed, he signed the committee's report.

During the days following the disaster, the public focused its attention on the tragedy itself and on *Carpathia*'s dramatic rescue of survivors. Initial suggestions that lifeboat capacity may have been inadequate were met with the response that the capacity was sufficient — indeed, more than required — to meet the statutory requirements of both England and America.

The first public comment to the contrary appeared in the London *Daily Mail*'s 18 April issue. In an interview, Alexander Carlisle called the Board of Trade's lifeboat regulations archaic, noting that while *Titanic*'s number of boats had proved to be inadequate, it exceeded the Board's requirements. Carlisle further mentioned that his original plan had provided for more than forty boats.

At the British Inquiry, both Bruce Ismay and Harold Sanderson denied ever having seen Carlisle's plans. The Board of Trade tried to discredit his testimony by not even referring to it in their final report. But by that time, an issue had arisen whose notoriety appeared far more significant to the public than the boat question. . .

On Tuesday 16 April, Horatio Bottomley, MP, gave notice that on 18 April he would ask Sydney Buxton, Board of Trade president, '. . . Whether he can state the exact lifeboat accommodation which was provided on the *Titanic*, and what proportion it bore to the authorised number of passengers and crew'.

The Board of Trade was anxious to investigate, lest jurisdiction be awarded to some other body or court. Having written the rules, the board desired to hold an inquiry into these same rules, on its own home ground, with yet another set of its own rules to guide the hearing. Under this circumstance it is remarkable that the inquiry was conducted, in the main, and for the period, quite fairly — although the results were not totally impartial.

Lord Mersey — John Charles Bigham, Baron Mersey of Toxteth (Lancashire) — had served the Bench long and faithfully. As Mr Justice Bigham he was president of the Probate, Divorce and Admiralty Division of the High Court. He received authority to serve as Wreck Commissioner for the United Kingdom in a warrant dated 23 April 1912, signed by the Right Honourable Robert Threshire Earl Loreburn, Lord High Chancellor of Great Britain.

Names of the assessors to assist Lord Mersey were submitted to the Home Secretary, who approved them on 23 April. They were honourable men, highly skilled in their professions (all dealing directly with the sea and maritime affairs), fully capable of using their knowledge and expertise to evaluate the complex evidence laid before them.

Captain Arthur Wellesley Clarke was an Elder Brother of Trinity House, and had served many years as Trinity Master in Admiralty Court; Professor J. Harvard Biles, occupant of the Chair of Naval Architecture at Glasgow, was a leading authority on ship construction. Navy presence was represented by Rear Admiral, the Hon Somerset Arthur Gough-Calthorpe, while Commander Fitzhugh C. A. Lyon, formerly in the Navy, had already acted as assessor in many marine inquiries. Mr Edward C. Chaston of Newcastle-on-Tyne was senior engineer assessor on the Admiralty list for appointment to Board of Trade inquiries.

The 'Order for Formal Investigation', which granted authority to the inquiry under Section 466 of the Merchant Shipping Act of 1894, was initiated by the Board of Trade and signed on 30 April.

Site for the hearings was the Drill Hall of the London Scottish Regiment, in Buckingham Gate, just down the road from Buckingham Palace. Selected because of its size, in anticipation of large public attendance, the capacious, glass-roofed hall with its series of galleries had abominable acoustics. Sounds were dispersed and subdued, rather like a series of muffled echoes, and the search for a more suitable hearing room began at once. (It was not until the hearings' penultimate day — on Monday, 1 July, when the Scottish Drill Hall proved unavailable for the day — that the hearings moved to Caxton Hall, though by then all witnesses had been heard, and the inquiry's only activity involved intramural deliberation.)

Rows of seats faced the dais on which Lord Mersey sat, flanked on either side by his assessors. Behind them were hung dark maroon curtains, while in front was mounted a sounding board, in an attempt to improve the acoustics. The witness stand, to the left of the dais, was also covered by a sounding board. Behind it was a twenty-foot-long half-model of *Titanic* supplied by Harland and Wolff, and next to it extended an immense North Atlantic map showing lanes and ice locations. Counsel and press filled the front rows, facing the dais. The remaining space was for spectators, who also filled the galleries.

Appearing as the Board of Trade's counsel were Sir Rufus Isaacs, KC, the Attorney General; Sir John Simon, KC, the Solicitor-General; Mr Butler Aspinall, KC, Mr S. T. Rowlatt and Mr Raymond Asquith.

A formidable battery of counsel represented the White Star Line. Headed by the Right Honourable Sir Robert Finlay, KC, MP, the group included Mr F. Laing, KC; Mr Maurice Hill, KC; and Mr Norman Raeburn, and was instructed by Messrs Hill, Dickinson and Co.

Mr Thomas Scanlan, MP (instructed by Mr

Smith, solicitor) appeared for the National Sailors' and Firemen's Union; Mr Clement Edwards for the Dockers' Union; Mr C. Robertson Dunlop was allowed only to watch the proceedings in an advisory capacity on behalf of *Californian*'s owners, master and officers. Third class passengers were represented by Mr W. D. Harbinson, instructed by Mr Farrell, solicitor, while Mr Henry Duke, KC, appeared for Sir Cosmo and Lady Duff-Gordon.

On the hearing's first day, 2 May, the Attorney General presented a list of 26 questions whose consideration would constitute the scope of the inquiry.

After reading the 'Order for Formal Investigation', Sir Rufus Isaacs orally summarized the questions for Lord Mersey:

'The Questions 1 to 8 inclusive relate to what happened before the casualty and before there is any question or suggestion of a warning that *Titanic* was approaching ice. Questions 9 to 14 relate to the suggestion of warning given to the *Titanic* and ask what was done with regard to lookout or other precautions before the casualty; that is to say, it is suggested by those questions that those responsible for the navigation of the *Titanic* were warned that they were approaching ice; and then the Questions are put in order to ascertain what was done and the Court may answer what it finds as a fact was done by those responsible for the *Titanic* after they received such warning, if they did receive it. Then, my Lord, Question 15 is a question relating to the casualty itself. Questions 16 to 24 relate to the events after the casualty, as to what steps were taken either to save the vessel or to save life. Then there is a general question, 25, which relates to the construction and equipment of the *Titanic* as a passenger steamer and emigrant ship for the Atlantic service; and Question 26, which relates to the rules and regulations under the Merchant Shipping Acts and the administration of those Acts and the rules and regulations, invites such recommendations or suggestions as the Court may think fit to make with a view to promoting the safety of vessels and persons at sea.'

The questions were acceptable to White Star's counsel. (At a later date an addition to Question 24 became the crux of the entire investigation; it was not even implied in the question's original form.*) The day's proceedings closed with the court's consideration of Mr Thomas Lewis' application to represent the British Seafarers' Union at the hearings.

Friday, 3 May (the second day, but the first

during which witnesses were heard) began with the interrogation of look-out Archie Jewell regarding his department's routines. Jewell's responses to a lengthy series of questions earned a rare word of thanks from Mersey. The only other witness that day was Joseph Scarrott who, in his answers, provided a graphic description of the sinking and its immediate sequel.

Early in the day, Attorney General Isaacs requested an extra day to prepare questions for *Titanic*'s crew who were to appear as witnesses. Mersey granted Monday, 6 May, and himself suggested that he and the commission's members would benefit from an examination of *Titanic*'s sister ship, *Olympic*, at Southampton. He proposed to use the free day to accomplish such an end.

Accordingly, on Monday morning, Lord Mersey, accompanied by the Honourable Clive Bigham (his son, and the commission's secretary) and four of the five assessors boarded the 10.15 Bournemouth/Weymouth express at London's Waterloo Station. Arriving at Southampton a few minutes after noon they were joined by assessor J. Harvard Biles, who had motored down. The entire commission was met at Southampton's West Station by White Star's Harold Sanderson, and driven to the White Star Dock where *Olympic* was moored. They were received at the dock by Mr P. E. Curry, the company's manager at Southampton, and were immediately conducted aboard.

After touring portions of *Olympic* relating to their investigation — including, among other things, a demonstration of a watertight door's operation — Mersey and the assessors appeared on deck, and the press, who had been rigidly excluded, could photograph — at a considerable distance across the water, from the dock's opposite side — the lowering of one *Olympic* lifeboat, as the assessors watched closely.

Following lunch on board, Mersey, his son and Professor Biles returned to London on a special train. The commission's other members remained aboard *Olympic* overnight, continuing their inspection.

In contrast to the dignified court and the worldly press, *Titanic*'s crew members who testified in London during the next four days seemed almost naïve as they appeared for their brief moments in notoriety's spotlight. Dressed in their Sunday best

---

*Question 24, as first presented, read as follows: 'What was the cause of the loss of the *Titanic* and of the loss of life which thereby ensued or occurred? Was the construction of the vessel and its arrangements such as to make it difficult for any class of passengers or any portion of the crew to take full advantage of any of the

existing provisions for safety?'

On 24 June the Attorney General, Sir Rufus Isaacs, proposed a new sentence for insertion between sentences one and three of the original. It read, 'What vessels had the opportunity of rendering assistance to the *Titanic*, and, if any, how was it that assistance did not

reach the *Titanic* before the steamship *Carpathia* arrived?'

The supplemental sentence was introduced in the absence of Mr C. Robertson Dunlop, adviser to the *Californian*'s owners and officers, but with his knowledge of its proposed inclusion.

they took the stand, one after another, to answer questions put to them by the Attorney General and other counsellors — questions they already had been asked during preliminary examinations.

One after another they told where they had been, what they had been doing at the time of the collision. They added details of their working areas aboard *Titanic* and their participation in loading and lowering the lifeboats.

Fireman George Beauchamp; quartermaster Robert Hichens, at the wheel when the collision occurred; able-bodied seaman William Lucas; leading stoker Frederick Barrett, who related the moving story of engineers Shepherd and Harvey; look-out Reginald Lee; able-bodied seaman John Poigndestre; steward James Johnson, who told of following Thomas Andrews as the latter made his post-collision inspection of the ship.

Plain, simple men — wise in the ways of their trades: greaser Thomas Ranger, trimmer George Cavell, fireman Alfred Shires, leading stoker Charles Hendrickson; trimmer Thomas Dillon, whose testimony about engine movements immediately after the collision interested the court. ('Following the collision the engines stopped for 1½ minutes, then went slow astern for two minutes, stopped for about half a minute and then went ahead for two minutes before finally stopping. . .')

At the close of testimony on the fifth day, 9 May, the Attorney General proposed to limit further examination of the crew to one man from each lifeboat, to which the court agreed without comment. The crew members' testimony provided a general backdrop, an overall picture of the disaster and how events progressed on that dreadful night. It formed a preliminary basis on which more ranging questions of a technical nature, and concerning administrative procedures, might be formulated.

But before the owners' testimony and the builders' evidence were heard, before *Titanic's* surviving officers were questioned, the master, officers and crew of the Leyland Line steamer *Californian* were interrogated.

A full consideration of their testimony and its implications can be found in Peter Padfield's book, *The Titanic and the Californian**, whose contents appear to clear *Californian's* Captain Stanley Lord of the allegations later cast by the court: that his vessel was close to the sinking *Titanic*, and that, in spite of knowledge of the stricken liner's distress signals, he took no steps to alert his own crew or to attempt a rescue.

Captain Lord, while represented by counsel provided by his employer, was not formally a party to the investigation, and thus was given no

opportunity to suggest to that counsel what navigational and technical facts might have verified the truth of his evidence.

One witness followed another. More of *Titanic's* crew testified; then Sir Cosmo and Lady Duff-Gordon during the tenth day on 17 May. (Sir Cosmo and his lady were able to convince the court that the nature of their departure from the sinking *Titanic*, with twelve persons in a boat intended for forty, was within the acceptable bounds of civilized behaviour.) Second officer Charles Herbert Lightoller gave calm and considered responses to more than 1,600 questions put to him, doing much to stave off criticism of the manner in which *Titanic's* navigation had been conducted; the other surviving officers — Pitman, Boxhall and Lowe — testified regarding navigation and the ship's evacuation.

On 20 May, and in agreement with counsel, Mersey decided to grant a recess when everyone involved — himself, the assessors and counsel — could review testimony to date, and prepare for the remainder of the hearings. The recess began after the fifteenth day (24 May), but only after Mersey expressed moderate irritation regarding the inquiry's length. The court reconvened on 4 June for the sixteenth day.

During that session, *Californian's* crewman Ernest Gill had simply recapitulated his American inquiry testimony, and an effort was made to vindicate his previously questionable statements using evidence given to the court by *Californian's* officers and crew.

Joseph Bruce Ismay appeared on the stand immediately following Ernest Gill. During the answers to the 849 questions put to him during days sixteen and seventeen, Ismay convinced the court that he was not responsible for *Titanic's* navigation and that he boarded a descending lifeboat only when there were no other passengers — male or female — in the vicinity.

Harold Sanderson testified during days seventeen and eighteen, largely about the relationships between the Board of Trade and shipowners, and about how owners must conform to Board-imposed regulations. Towards the end of his testimony he made it evident that White Star Line vessels equalled and often exceeded Board rules in their construction and lifeboat capacity.

The testimony of Edward Wilding, Harland and Wolff naval architect, regarding *Titanic's* construction and technical features, was followed by that of Leonard Peskett, Cunard's naval architect, who had assisted in designing *Lusitania* and *Mauretania*. Mr Peskett's principal testimony related to watertight doors and bulkheads, and compartmentalization.

The Right Honourable Sir Alexander M. Carlisle appeared on 10 June. His testimony, though brief,

---

*Hodder & Stoughton, London, 1965.

was vital: it put on public record the 18 April interview he had given to a London *Daily Mail* reporter, in which he had stated that the number of lifeboats on both *Olympic* and *Titanic* had been far fewer than that which he, as one of the designers, had initially proposed. Attorney General Isaacs attempted to discredit Carlisle by reminding him that, as a member of the Board of Trade's Advisory Committee on Life-Saving Appliances, he had signed the committee's 1911 report whose recommendations — if adopted — would have resulted in not more, but fewer lifeboats than were then required. Carlisle stated regret at having signed a report with which he did not concur. ('I must have been soft. . . I was not going to be a dog in a manger. . .')

But Carlisle succeeded in what he had set out to do: to have his original intent regarding *Titanic*'s lifeboats made a part of public record.

Sir Walter J. Howell, as chief of the Marine Department and an assistant secretary of the Board of Trade, underwent a gruelling examination. Sir Walter's testimony gave official credence to the fact already known: that, under existing Board of Trade regulations, *Titanic* was certified to carry a number of passengers (3,547) considerably in excess of her lifeboat capacity.

Examinations of the Board of Trade's various ship surveyors followed, including a series of questions to William David Archer, principal ship surveyor. Mr Archer stated that he had expressed in a February 1911 report to the Board of Trade's Marine Department that *Titanic*'s boat accommodation should be for 2,493 persons — a far higher capacity than that eventually provided (1,178). Mr Archer could not answer why his report was not acted upon, except to say that it was referred to the Advisory Committee, whose action had already been described by Alexander Carlisle.

Mr Archer further testified that the engine room and stokehold bulkheads of *Titanic* as originally designed did not reach as far as intended (to D, or the saloon, deck). He accepted this condition after being shown a builder's calculation that even if the first and second compartments and the firemen's passage were simultaneously flooded, the vessel would sink only two feet six inches by the head.

After seeing the calculation, Archer himself ascertained that with the vessel down 2½ feet by the head, the top of the bulkhead between the fourth and fifth watertight compartments would then be 15½ feet above the waterline. He added that he then felt he had insufficient grounds for insisting that the bulkhead's height be raised, or for withholding the declaration of seaworthiness.

On 18 June, the next-to-last-day witnesses appeared. The commission heard testimony from Sir Norman Hill, chairman of the Merchant Shipping Advisory Committee. The twenty-member group was appointed by the Board of Trade's president from names submitted by shipping associations. Its function was to advise the Board during its formulation of policies and regulations.

In April 1911 a seven-man sub-committee was formed to advise the Board on extending the existing lifeboat scale so it might deal with vessels of more than 10,000 tons. The sub-committee had invited Alexander Carlisle to the two sessions it had held.

The sub-committee's report was submitted in July 1911 and the full committee was still considering it at the time of *Titanic*'s loss. For vessels for 45,000 tons and upwards, the report called for a minimum of sixteen boats under davits, with at least eight boats readily available for attachment to the davits. The arrangement would provide for a total minimum capacity of the boats to be 8,300 cubic feet.

Several minutes later, Sir Norman stated that the committee was considering substantial additions to lifeboat accommodation, perhaps for every person on board. He added that, since the disaster, the committee had met 21 or 22 times, a sharp contrast to the two short meetings it had held in order to reach its initial recommendation. Sir Norman concluded his testimony by cautiously recommending motor lifeboats and several other safety features receiving committee consideration.

Also on 18 June appeared Guglielmo Marconi, inventor of a wireless telegraphy system extensively used aboard ships. Signor Marconi testified briefly concerning marine telegraphy's functions and his company's rules relating to emergencies at sea.

Among the last witnesses heard during 18 and 19 June, the final days of open hearings, were masters and retired masters of North Atlantic liners: Joseph Ranson of the *Baltic;* John Pritchard, formerly of *Mauretania;* Hugh Young, retired, formerly of the Anchor Line; and John Fairful and Andrew Braes, both retired Allan Line masters. One after another, the men testified that they did keep or had always kept up the speed of their vessels in clear weather, regardless of ice warnings.

The public hearings drew to a close. While many British newspapers still reported the proceedings in detail, general interest had waned. Since the Duff-Gordons' testimony, attendance at the hearings had declined. Even Bruce Ismay's appearance caused little more than a brief flurry. Much of the remaining testimony was technical in nature, dull and uninteresting. And then there were the terrible acoustics. . .

On 19 June Sir Ernest Shackleton, master mariner and Antarctic explorer, gave technical testimony regarding ice and icebergs, including the

distance ('about five miles') from which ice might be seen on a clear night.

Edward Wilding, recalled, described the results of several turning tests made since the disaster using *Olympic:* running at about 74 revolutions, about 21½ knots, from the time the order was given to put the helm hard over until the vessel turned two points took 37 seconds, during which time *Olympic* had travelled between 1,200 and 1,300 feet. Wilding concluded his testimony with data concerning the strength of bulkheads and their rivets.

After a two-day adjournment the commission met on Friday 21 June, its 28th day, for the final session of public hearings. Arthur Henry Rostron, *Carpathia*'s captain, described rescue details for the commission. He also verified for the record the contents of an affidavit he had executed on 4 June in New York, saying that on the morning of the rescue, as it became light at the disaster site, he observed two ships to the northwards, about seven or eight miles distant. Neither ship was the *Californian.* 'One of them', he said, 'was a four-masted steamer with one funnel, and the other was a two-masted steamer with one funnel. I never saw the *Mount Temple* to identify her. The first time I saw *Californian* was at about 8 o'clock on the morning of 15th April. She was then about five or six miles distant, bearing west-southwest true and steaming towards *Carpathia...*'

Captain Rostron also stated emphatically that 705 survivors were landed at New York. But Attorney General Isaacs insisted *Carpathia*'s purser had prepared a supplementary list, adding six names — purportedly of first class passengers — to Rostron's total. The commissioner accepted Isaacs' figures, and '711' became the inquiry's officially recognized number of survivors.

On Friday 21 June, Arthur Ernest Tride, master of the steamship *Manitou*, was asked by Mr Aspinall, the Board of Trade's counsel, 'Is your practice as to reducing speed [ie, not reducing speed] the same as the practice of the various other masters in that [ie, the Red Star Line] fleet?'

The witness responded, 'Yes,' and was dismissed. The answer was to question number 25,622, the hearings' last.

The analogy of prosecution, defence and judge is not the best one to describe the structure of the Mersey Commission, which did not constitute a court of law, *per se,* but only an investigative body. However, the terms do help to define the position of Sir Rufus Isaacs (defending the Board of Trade's policies), and Sir Robert Finlay (defending the White Star Line's procedures and employees). It helps to place in their proper spots such

'prosecutors' as Mr Thomas Lewis of the British Seafarers' Union; Mr L. S. Holmes of the Imperial Merchant Service Guild; Mr Cotter, appearing on behalf of the National Union of Stewards; Mr Roche, of the Marine Engineers' Association; Mr W. D. Harbinson, appearing on behalf of the third class passengers; Mr F. Laing, for Harland and Wolff; and Mr C. Robertson Dunlop, for the owners and officers of *Californian.* It places Lord Mersey and his assessors in the position of hearing evidence and arguments by counsel, and drawing conclusions enabling them to answer questions placed before the commission.

To determine guilt or innocence was not the commission's province. Their function was to establish right or wrong; to accept — even praise — right; to correct wrong.

Following the questioning of witnesses, counsels for the several interested parties were allowed to present argument on their clients' behalf, interpreting witnesses' testimony in a light best suited to their clients' interests.

Much of Day 28 was taken by these deliberations, which continued for eight more full days — Monday to Saturday, 24 to 30 June; Monday 1 July and Wednesday 3 July. The last two days of argument were heard at Caxton Hall, the Scottish Drill Hall having been booked prior to the hearings for an examination.

It was a detailed evaluation of testimony and evidence: of testimony by *Titanic*'s officers and crew, by Mr Ismay, by other vessels' masters; by naval architects, Board of Trade surveyors and wireless operators... Of evidence in the form of reports by William David Archer; by the Merchant Shipping Advisory Committee considering an amendment to life-saving appliance rules; 'Instructions to Commanders' of various shipping companies; ships' logs and scrap logs; copies of plans for *Titanic* and *Olympic...*

Reiteration and interpretation, examination and definition — all so that Lord Mersey and his assessors had the broadest spectrum of information on which to base their findings.

Strangely missing — because they had not been heard in testimony — were examinations of passengers' accounts, although their rights as human beings were well represented by Mr Harbinson.

During a three-hour questioning by Lord Mersey, counsel for *Californian*'s owner and Captain Lord, Mr Dunlop demonstrated his interpretation of the vessel's position, and offered names of several vessels known or thought to have been in the disaster site's vicinity.* In closing, Mr Dunlop

---

*Those mentioned by Mr Dunlop were the following: *Trautenfels,* *Paula, Memphian, Campanello* and *President Lincoln.*

Among other vessels not named by Mr Dunlop, but which are known to

made the point that it was not until 14 June, a full month after Captain Lord's appearance at the inquiry, that the Board of Trade added a question to the commission's list relating to *Californian* and the part her navigation may have played in the disaster. Dunlop added that should Captain Lord be prosecuted in the future, he ought to have had notice of the question *before* he entered the witness box, and to have been allowed to hear other witnesses' evidence before he gave his own testimony.

Presenting, in essence, a defence of the Board of Trade's rules, Attorney General Sir Rufus Isaacs took three days in his summation. One of his principal points was the submission by the life-saving appliances sub-committee to the main Merchant Shipping Advisory Committee in April 1911, in which an increase in lifeboat capacity aboard large liners was recommended. Further, that on 29 June 1911, the Advisory Committee had forwarded a copy of the sub-committee's report to the Board of Trade, recommending that their consideration be given to the report's findings.

On 3 July, the inquiry's 36th and final day, and in support of the Board of Trade's ship construction rules, Sir Rufus reiterated figures given earlier in Sir Robert Finlay's address to the commission: that during the preceding ten years, British ships, while carrying more than 3½ million passengers, had suffered losses of just 73 persons.

Under Lord Mersey's questioning, Sir Rufus described the questions Mr Horatio Bottomley put in the House of Commons in November 1910 and February 1911 to the Board of Trade, and the answer given in February, that 'the question of the revision of the [lifeboat] rules was engaging the serious attention of the Board. . .' But Sir Rufus and the Board lost ground when the commissioner observed, '. . . Under the regulations of the subcommittee, which were adopted by the Advisory Committee, if the *Titanic* had been provided with lifeboat accommodation according to their recommendations, she would not have had as much lifeboat accommodation as she in fact had'.

To which the Attorney General could only respond, 'That is so'.

In remarks filling more than 5½ pages of fine print, Sir Rufus made his statement regarding the *Californian* and her master, Captain Stanley Lord, in making no attempt to investigate signals of distress, distress signals [sic] from *Titanic*. The Attorney General's final point was, 'If you compare the *Titanic* evidence with the *Californian* it is abundantly plain that the distance between them

must have been comparatively small, certainly within five to seven miles, and could not have been nineteen to twenty miles as the captain of the *Californian* suggests'.

Nowhere in his thousand-word closing statement did Sir Rufus Isaacs refer to equipment, construction or life-saving appliances as contributing to the disaster. Rather, he emphasized navigation and speed in proximity to ice.

Lord Mersey, in promising to submit his commission's conclusions within a reasonable time, brought the inquiry to a close.

As a jury retires to consider its verdict, so did the commissioner and his assessors retire from public view to study the minutes of testimony, the exhibits and the arguments of council. On 30 July the Mersey Commission presented its findings. Summarized in the briefest form, they were:

That the collision of the *Titanic* with the iceberg was due to the excessive speed at which the ship was navigated, that a proper watch was not kept, that the ship's boats were properly lowered, but that arrangements for manning them were insufficient; that the Leyland liner *Californian* might have reached the *Titanic* if she had attempted to do so; that the track followed was reasonably safe with proper vigilance; and that there was no discrimination against third class passengers in the saving of life.

The court exonerated J. Bruce Ismay, chairman and managing director of the White Star Line, and Sir Cosmo Duff-Gordon, one of the passengers, from allegations of improper conduct.

The judgment recommended more watertight compartments in ocean-going ships, the provision of lifeboats for all on board, as well as a better look-out.

Among Lord Mersey's other findings:

He praised the general conduct of the passengers and crew, but regretted that none of the boats, especially number 1, had attempted to save the drowning.

He commended Captain Rostron of the *Carpathia* very highly.

He was convinced that those on board the *Californian* had seen the *Titanic*'s signals at a distance of eight or ten miles and could have reached her without risk and thus saved the lives of many or all.

In conclusion, Lord Mersey severely blamed the Board of Trade for its failure to revise the shipping rules of 1894.

Recommendations included installation and 24-hour manning of wireless equipment aboard foreign-going passenger and emigrant ships; frequent lifeboat drill by crewmen; and the convening of an international conference to consider mutual adoption of regulations regarding safety at sea.

The minutes of the commission's testimony are a

---

have been in the vicinity, were the *Etonian, Mount Temple, Parisian, Birma, Saturnia, Almerian, Pisa, Dora, Bruce* and the schooner *Dorothy Baird.*

In addition, the possible presence of the Norwegian sealing vessel *Samson* and the Gloucester (Massachusetts) schooner *Premier* was not known until later.

matter of public record, as are most of the reports and evidence Lord Mersey and his assessors used to reach their conclusions. It would surely seem that the British inquiry — unencumbered by subjective judgment, having at its command the best technical advisors' testimony, and conducted hard by the land of *Titanic*'s birth — would be as unprejudiced as it was possible for an investigative body to be.

Perhaps, based on testimony and evidence, this is so. It is likely, given the historical period in which the investigation was conducted, that there can be little fault found with the inquiry's decisions.

But decisions which remain untempered by time's passing become rigid. They lose the plasticity of history. Different generations have different standards of judgment. Considering Mersey's conclusions objectively is close to impossible when regarding them in the light of present-day knowledge.

While *Titanic* was superbly constructed, there was a fatal flaw in her design. And the design was within acceptable standards of the time. While *Titanic* was operated well within safety standards, there was a flaw in her navigation. And the navigation was certainly within accepted rules of the day. The capacity of *Titanic*'s lifeboats exceeded that required by existing regulations: she was certified to carry 3,547 passengers and crew while offering lifeboat space to but 1,178. Yet, according to rules then in effect, she might legally have provided space for only a few more than 700.

And while *Californian* was one of the vessels in proximity to the sinking *Titanic*, evidence strongly suggests there were at least three and possibly as many as five others which may have been closer, and whose lights could well have been viewed at various times from both *Californian* and *Titanic*.

Just as the perspective of time has caused re-examination of design, navigation and lifeboat capacity, so should it effect a re-evaluation of *Californian*'s role in the disaster and a reconsideration of the culpability of her master, Captain Stanley Lord.

But the Mersey Commission's jurisdiction and legal bearing are well summed up by the London *Daily Telegraph* following the release of the findings:

'It must be borne in mind that Lord Mersey's court was not in the ordinary sense a court of justice, and the results of its deliberations must not be regarded as a judgment. It follows that the report is not final and conclusive in regard to the various debatable matters with which it deals, and were it necessary to discuss any of them hereafter in a court of justice, they could be reargued as if there had never been any investigation into the why and wherefore of the *Titanic* disaster.

'At the same time it is quite clear that a court of justice or a jury would hesitate long before expressing dissent from the conclusions at which these eminent experts arrived.

'Technically speaking, the report is not the last word, but in practice it would probably be treated as if it were. It is difficult to suppose, for instance, that any court which had to inquire into the responsibility of the owners of the ship would disregard the expression of opinion of Lord Mersey and those who sat with him, and this particular point is one of vital importance. For if "fault or privity" can be brought home to the owners of the *Titanic*, the limitation of liability laid down by the Merchant Shipping Act — £15 per ton for loss of life, £8 per ton for loss or damage to goods — is wiped out and the damages of sufferers are left at large. . .'

Top right The execution of the 'Order for Formal Investigation' constitutes the legal authority under which the British Board of Trade's inquiry into the loss of *Titanic* is held in London. (Public Record Office.)

Right Steward Alfred Pugh receives a formal summons, signed by Lord Mersey, to appear before the British Inquiry. Later, it is determined that his testimony is not necessary. (THS.)

Far right The Scottish Drill Hall, in Buckingham Gate, London, is chosen as the site for the British Inquiry's hearings. (Authors' collection.)

M. ~~7985~~ 19~~12~~   D21022b/12

THE MERCHANT SHIPPING ACT, 1894.

Order for Formal Investigation.

WHEREAS, on or about the 14th day of April 1912, the British steam ship "Titanic" ~~of Liverpool~~ of Liverpool Official Number 131428 struck ice in or near Latitude 41° 46' N Longitude 50° 14' W North Atlantic Ocean and on the following day foundered and loss of life thereby ensued or occurred

and whereas a shipping casualty has occurred, and the Board of Trade have ~~and a preliminary inquiry~~ requested a Wreck Commissioner appointed under this Act to hold a ~~has been held respecting the same~~ Formal Investigation into the said shipping casualty and he has consented to do so.

Now, the Board of Trade in pursuance of the powers vested in them by Section 466 of the Merchant Shipping Act, 1894, do hereby direct that the Formal Investigation shall be held into the said shipping casualty ~~by a Court~~ in the ~~of Summary Jurisdiction in the~~ Scottish Hall Buckingham Gate London S.W

Annexed hereto is a statement of the Case upon which the said Formal Investigation has been ordered.

Dated this ⅄ day of April 1912

An Assistant Secretary to the
Board of Trade

(x) (64137) WL 22C3/87 500 4.09 W B & L

The British S team Ship Titanic
of the Port of Liverpool . Official Number 131 428 .

STATEMENT OF CASE.

The following is a statement of the Case on which a Formal Investigation is ordered :—

The above-named Ship left Queenstown for New York on ~~the~~ or about the 11th day of April 1912, with a crew of about 892 hands all told and about 1316 passengers, ~~and about~~
————— tons of ————— ~~cargo~~
On the night of Sunday the 14th day of April 1912 ~~at~~ ————— M., the weather being ————— the wind blowing ————— from ————— with the sea ————— and the ~~current being~~ ————— the vessel was under ~~making about~~ ————— knots ————— the vessel struck ice in or near Latitude 41° 46' N Longitude 50° 14' W North Atlantic Ocean and at about 2 a.m on the following day foundered in about the same locality and loss of life thereby ensued or occurred.

Dated this ————— day of April 1912 .

Initials of
Professional Officer.

An Assistant Secretary to the
Board of Trade

Copy

IN THE COURT OF THE WRECK COMMISSIONER
FOR THE UNITED KINGDOM.

WHEREAS the Board of Trade has requested me, the undersigned, a Wreck Commissioner for the United Kingdom, to hold a Formal Investigation into the circumstances attending the loss of the British steam ship "Titanic", of Belfast, in the North Atlantic Ocean, on or about the 15th day of April 1912, and the loss of life which thereby ensued or occurred:

AND WHEREAS it appears to me that you are likely to give material evidence therein you are hereby summoned to appear before my Court sitting in the Scottish Hall Buckingham Gate Westminster London S.W on Friday the 3rd day of May 1912 at 10.30 o'clock in the forenoon to testify what you know in such matter.

Given under my hand this 29th day of April 1912.

Signed   Mersey

Wreck Commissioner for the
United Kingdom.

1 Inst
72 Orchard Lane
Southampton

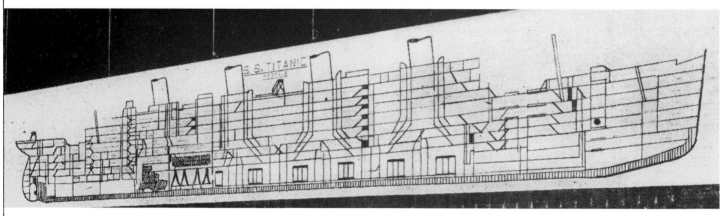

S.A.T. Rowlatt

Raymond Asquith

Rufus Isaacs

Butler Aspinall KC

Top To assist Lord Mersey, his assessors and witnesses, a large track chart of the North Atlantic and a 20-foot half-model of *Titanic* supplied by her builders are installed in the hearing room. (*Daily Sketch*.)

Above A large-scale longitudinal plan almost 40 feet long allows the court to understand the complexities of *Titanic*'s structure. (*Daily Sketch*.)

Left Representing the Board of Trade at the inquiry as counsel are Raymond Asquith, S. A. T. Rowlatt, Butler Aspinall, KC and the Right Hon Rufus Isaacs, KC, MP, Attorney General. (*Daily Sketch*.)

The British Investigation

Right Sir John Charles Bigham, Baron Mersey of Toxteth, is appointed a Wreck Commissioner of the United Kingdom to preside over the inquiry. Lady Mersey is an occasional visitor to the proceedings. (*Daily Sketch*.)

Below right Sir Robert Finlay, KC, MP, arrives at the Scottish Drill Hall to lead the White Star Line's representation. (*Daily Sketch*.)

Below far right *Olympic*'s Captain Herbert J. Haddock (left) and White Star managing director Harold Sanderson arrive at the inquiry. (*Daily Sketch*.)

Below The inquiry's nautical assessors are chosen because of their many years of experience with ships and the sea. They include Captain Arthur Wellesley Clarke, an Elder Brother of Trinity House; Mr Edward C. Chaston, RNR, senior engineer assessor to the Admiralty; Commander Fitzhugh C. Lyon, RNR; J. Harvard Biles, professor of Naval Architecture at Glasgow; and Rear Admiral the Hon Somerset Gough-Calthorpe. (*Daily Sketch/Daily Mirror/Illustrated London News*.)

Bottom right In the cavernous, echoing Scottish Drill Hall, the 'Formal Investigation into the Loss of the SS *Titanic*' begins with opening statements on 2 May 1912. (*Daily Sketch*.)

Sir John Charles Bigham, Lord Mersey

Lady Mersey

Sir Robert Finlay

Herbert J. Haddock and Harold Sanderson

Captain A.W. Clarke

Edward C. Chaston

Commander F.C. Lyon

Professor J. Harvard Biles

Rear Admiral S.A. Gough-Calthorpe

Thomas Scanlan, MP Archie Jewell, lookout

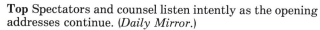

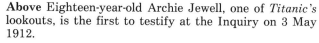

Top Spectators and counsel listen intently as the opening addresses continue. (*Daily Mirror*.)

Above left Labour organizations representing various constituencies among *Titanic's* crew also attend the Inquiry. Mr Lewis, president of the National Seafarer's Union, arrives with several union members, all *Titanic* crew summoned to testify. **Above middle** Mr Thomas Scanlan, MP represents the National Sailors' and Firemen's Union of Great Britain and Ireland at the proceedings. (*Daily Sketch*.)

Above Eighteen-year-old Archie Jewell, one of *Titanic's* lookouts, is the first to testify at the Inquiry on 3 May 1912.

Left above The first question of the inquiry, 'Is your name Archie Jewell?' is to be followed by 25,621 others in 28 days of testimony from 96 different witnesses. Archie Jewell describes being awakened in his forecastle bunk by the collision. (*Daily Mirror*.)

Left After enduring more than 330 questions, and describing his leaving the ship in lifeboat 7 and subsequent rescue, Archie Jewell is excused. Lord Mersey says to him, 'Thank you, Jewell; and if you will allow me to say so, I think you have given your evidence very well indeed'. The modest lookout simply responds, 'Thank you, Sir'. (He is one of the few witnesses to be thanked by the Court.) (*Daily Sketch*.)

Right On 25 April, one week before the inquiry begins, the Board of Trade orders a test-lowering of one of *Olympic's* lifeboats while the liner is at Southampton ... (*Daily Sketch*.)

Right middle ... and on 6 May the inquiry visits Southampton, where lifeboat number 9 repeats the demonstration for Lord Mersey and his assessors, peering over the rail to the right of the outswung davits. (*Daily Graphic*.)

Below Among the first to testify back in London are (left to right) leading fireman Charles Hendrickson; fireman Samuel Collins; greaser Thomas Ranger; fireman George W. Beauchamp; and look-out Reginald R. Lee, who was on duty at the time of the collision. (*Daily Sketch*.)

Testimony from the crew of the *Californian* spans two days of the inquiry. **Bottom right** Captain Stanley Lord arrives at the Inquiry. He is summoned solely as a witness; weeks after he leaves the stand, it is suggested that he was negligent in not going to the *Titanic's* assistance.

Bottom far right Wireless operator Cyril Evans and apprentice James Gibson await their turn to testify.

Charles Hendrickson and Samuel Collins

Thomas Ranger, greaser

George W. Beauchamp, fireman

Reginald R. Lee, lookout

Captain Stanley Lord

Cyril Evans and James Gibson

Far left *Californian* personnel take a break during the proceedings: (left to right) apprentice James Gibson; wireless operator Cyril Evans; chief officer George F. Stewart; second officer Herbert Stone; and third officer Charles V. Groves.

Left Captain Lord and chief officer Stewart leave the inquiry on 14 May.

Far left Assembled at the Scottish Drill Hall are (left to right) *Californian* fireman G. Glenn; greaser W. Thomas; wireless operator Cyril Evans; apprentice J. Gibson; second officer H. Stone; able seaman W. Ross; third officer C. Groves; and chief officer G. Stewart.

Left Third officer Charles Victor Groves leaves the Inquiry. (*Daily Sketch /Daily Graphic*.)

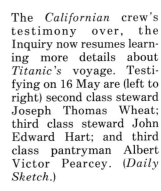

Joseph Thomas Wheat,
second class steward

John Edward Hart,
third class steward

Albert Victor Pearcey,
third class pantryman

The *Californian* crew's testimony over, the Inquiry now resumes learning more details about *Titanic*'s voyage. Testifying on 16 May are (left to right) second class steward Joseph Thomas Wheat; third class steward John Edward Hart; and third class pantryman Albert Victor Pearcey. (*Daily Sketch*.)

Harold Lowe and Mr
and Mrs Lightoller

Sir Cosmo Duff-Gordon

Lady Duff-Gordon

Far left A long ordeal awaits two of *Titanic*'s surviving officers, fifth officer Harold Godfrey Lowe (left) and second officer Charles Herbert Lightoller, who arrive with Mrs Lightoller at the Board of Trade hearings in London. Over a four-day period, Lowe answers more than 300 questions, while Lightoller, as *Titanic*'s senior surviving officer, calmly responds to more than 1,600. (*Daily Mirror*.)

Bottom previous page The only *Titanic* passengers summoned to testify before the Inquiry are Sir Cosmo and Lady Duff-Gordon, who arrive on 17 May. (*Daily Mirror.*)

Look-out George Symons describes the £5 cheque he received from Sir Cosmo Duff-Gordon following their rescue from boat 1, a boat built for forty that contained only twelve people. Sir Cosmo (left) listens intently. (*Daily Sketch*).

Sir Cosmo takes the stand to deny any impropriety in his gift to the crewmen of boat number 1. (*Daily Sketch.*)

Lady Duff-Gordon recalls her entry into boat 1: '...Somebody hitched me up from the deck and pitched me into the boat and then I think Miss Franks [Miss Laura Francatelli, her secretary] was pitched in. It was not a case of getting in at all. We could not have got in, it was quite high'. (*Daily Sketch.*)

The source of much controversy, Sir Cosmo's £5 cheque is examined by one of the recipients, able seaman Albert Edward James Horswell. (*Daily Mirror.*)

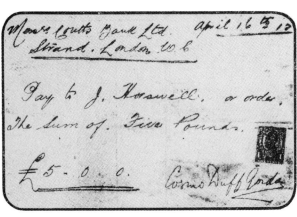

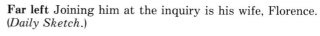

Above far left Following their testimony, Sir Cosmo (behind the door), secretary Miss Francatelli and Lady Duff-Gordon leave via a rear entrance to the Scottish Drill Hall, hoping to escape reporters and photographers. Unsuccessful in the attempt, Sir Cosmo gets into his automobile. (*Daily Mirror/Daily Sketch*.)

Another object of intense public and journalistic interest is White Star's managing director J. Bruce Ismay, who testifies on 4 and 5 June 1912. In answers to the 849 questions put to him, he describes the company's financial structure, the decision-making process behind *Titanic*'s design, his non-involvement in decisions involving the ship's navigation, his activities during the evacuation, and his profound sorrow at the loss of the ship and her people.

Far left Joining him at the inquiry is his wife, Florence. (*Daily Sketch*.)

Above left On 5 June, standing before the large model of his company's most tragic vessel, Ismay responds to an interrogator's question. (*Sphere*.)

Above Ismay lights a cigarette as he leaves after the first day of testimony. (*Daily Sketch*.)

Left Following his partner Bruce Ismay to the stand, Harold Sanderson testifies on 5, 6 and 7 June. He, too, denies having ever seen plans for an increased number of boats on *Titanic*.

Captain Maurice Harvey Clarke **far left** the Board of Trade's assistant emigration officer at Southampton, describes his inspection of the *Titanic*'s lifesaving equipment prior to her 10 April departure.

The Right Hon Alexander Montgomery Carlisle **left**, former chairman of the directors of Harland and Wolff, describes how he attempted unsuccessfully to increase *Titanic*'s lifeboat capacity. (*Daily Sketch*.)

Top right The inquiry moves to London's Caxton Hall on 3 July for its final session, the Scottish Drill Hall having been booked for an examination on that date. As Lord Mersey and his assessors begin drafting the Inquiry Report, the total cost is tabulated. It comes to £20,549 5s 10d ($99,664), of which £1,000 ($4,850) is Lord Mersey's stipend as Wreck Commissioner. (Authors' collection.)

Below Naval architect Edward Wilding, who is to succeed the late Thomas Andrews as Harland and Wolff's managing director, gives instructions for removal of the great *Titanic* model — its usefulness now over — from the Scottish Drill Hall. He concludes his letter by expressing pleasure that the shipbuilder's reputation remains an excellent one, a fact due in large measure to Wilding's forthright and knowledgeable testimony, and the firm's full co-operation at the inquiry. (Harland and Wolff Ltd.)

Overleaf Lord Mersey's Report is issued on 30 July 1912. In it, he writes, '. . .The ship seen by the *Californian* was the *Titanic*, and if so. . .the two vessels were about 5 miles apart at the time of the disaster. . .When she first saw the rockets, the *Californian* could have pushed through the ice to open water without any serious risk and so have come to the assistance of the *Titanic*. Had she done so she might have saved many if not all of the lives that were lost'.

Never having been named as a defendant, never having been legally represented at the hearings, Captain Lord is anguished at the Court's finding. He writes to Walter J. Howell, assistant secretary to the Board of Trade, putting forth a strong case on his own behalf.

His request for Howell's assistance in bringing the truth before the public is repeatedly declined; because he is not a named defendant, the Board of Trade reasons, he is not entitled to a hearing of his case. And thus, the 75-year-old controversy known as the '*Californian* incident' begins. (Public Record Office.)

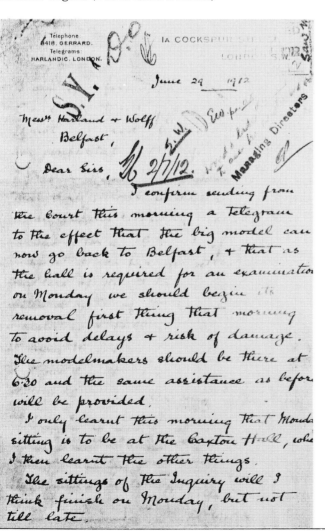

10 Ormonde St
Liscard
Cheshire
Aug 10/12

The Assistant Secretary
Marine Dept
Dear Sir

With reference to Lord Mersey's report on the "Titanic" disaster, he states the "Californian" was 8 to 10 miles from the scene of the disaster, I respectfully request your attention, as master of the "Californian" to give you a few facts which prove she was the distance away, that:- I gave my 17 to 19 miles; (Apl 14th 6.30pm I sent my position to the "Antillian" & "Titanic", this gives me 17 miles away, and you will see it was sent some hours before the disaster.

Apl 15th about 0.30am gave my position to S.S. "Virginian" before I heard where the "Titanic" sunk, that also gave me 17' away. I understand the original Marconigram were in Court.

The evidence of Mr Goshall of the "Titanic" who was watching the steamer they had in view, states she approached them between one and two am, the "Californian" was stopped from 10.30pm to 5.15am next day

The steamer seen from the "Californian" was plainly in view from 11.30pm, the one seen by the "Titanic" was not, according to her lookout men seen until 0.30am.

Capt Rostron of the "Carpathia" states when at the scene of the disaster, it was daylight at 4.30am I could see all around the horizon, about 8 miles north of me (this was the direction the "Californian" was) there were two steamers, neither of these was the "Californian"

---

cont.

Had the "Californian" been within 10 miles from the "Titanic" she would have been in sight at this time from the "Carpathia", as she was in the same position as when stopped at 10.30pm the previous evening.

With regard to my own conduct on the night in question, I should like to add a little more. I had taken every precaution for the safety of my own ship, and left her in charge of a responsible officer at 0.30am, with instructions to call me if he wanted anything, and I lay down fully dressed.

At 1.15am (25 minutes after he had seen the first signal) the officer on watch reported the steamer we had in sight was altering her bearing, in other words was steaming away, and had fired a rocket. I did not anticipate any disaster to a vessel that had been stopped nearby for an hour, and had ignored my three signals, and was then steaming away, I asked him was it a Co's signal, and to signal her and let me know the result. It is a matter of great regret to me that I did not go on deck myself at this time, but I didn't think it possible for any seaman to mistake a Co's signal for a distress signal, so I relied on the officer on watch.

Altho' further signals were seen between 1.15am & 2.0am I was not notified until 2.0am, and then I had fallen into a sound sleep, and whatever message was sent to me then, I was not sufficiently awake to understand, and it was sufficient indication to anyone that I had not realised the message, by the fact that I still remained below, curiosity to see a vessel pushing through the ice would have taken me on deck. The message sent to me at 2.0am was I heard later, to the effect that the

---

cont.

steamer we had in sight at 11.30pm, had altered her bearing from SSE to SW½W (to do this she must have steamed at least 8 miles, the "Titanic" did not move after midnight and had fired 8 rockets, and was then out of sight.

The question of drink has been raised as the reason I could not be raised. I don't drink, and never have done.

Further signals were seen after 2.0am but the officer was so little concerned about them, that he did not think it necessary to notify me. I was called by the Chief Officer at 4.30am, and in conversation he referred to the rockets seen by the second officer, I immediately had the wireless operator called, heard of the disaster, and proceeded at once, pushing through field ice to the scene, and I would have done the same earlier had I understood, as I had everything to gain and nothing to lose.

There is the conversation between the second officer and the apprentice whilst watching the vessel, that they thought she was a tramp steamer, this is their opinion at the time, which is most likely the correct one.

My employers, the Leyland Line, altho' their nautical advisers are convinced we did not see the "Titanic", or the "Titanic" see the "Californian", say they have the utmost confidence in me, and do not blame me in anyway, but owing to Lord Mersey's decision and public opinion caused by this report, they are reluctantly compelled to ask for my resignation, after 14½ years service without a blot of any description, and if I could clear myself of this charge, would willingly reconsider this decision.

If you consider there was any lands

---

aboard the "Californian" the night in question, I respectfully draw your attention to the information given here, which was given in evidence, which also proves was not on my part.

I am told that at the inquiry I was a very poor witness, this I don't dispute, but I fail to see why I should have to put up with all this public odium, through no fault or neglect on my part; and I respectfully request you will be able to do something to put my conduct on the night in question, in a more favourable light to my employers and the general public

I am Sir
Your Obedient Servant
Stanley Lord

Chapter Nineteen

LIMITATION OF LIABILITY

On 7 May 1915 the Cunard liner *Lusitania*, near the end of her 202nd transAtlantic crossing, was torpedoed and sunk by a German submarine ten miles south of the Old Head of Kinsale, off Ireland's south-eastern coast. Among the mail she carried were many letters to British claimants against the White Star Line summoning them to appear at New York on 17 May. At that time their claims for losses suffered in the *Titanic* disaster would be heard. The letters' loss caused Judge Julius M. Mayer of the United States District Court to postpone the proceedings for limitation of liability in the *Titanic* case until the British claimants might properly respond.

Lusitania had departed from New York on her final voyage on Saturday 1 May. On the preceding day, her captain, William Thomas Turner, appeared at 11 am before Notary Public John Crandall at 165 Broadway, New York City, to give testimony pertaining to the loss, three years earlier, of *Titanic*. Captain Turner, as master of one of the largest vessels then afloat, responded to questions concerning icebergs, watertight integrity of ships, the speed of liners through ice-fields, and the posting of ships' look-outs under various weather conditions. When answering the final question put to him, which concerned flotation, the captain responded, 'My dear sir, it all depends on the size of the compartments, the amount of buoyancy; if she has buoyancy she will float; if she has not, she will do down'.

Exactly one week, two hours and several minutes later, Captain Turner's expertise was to suffer a test which, on 30 April, he could not have conceivably imagined.

The British inquiry under Lord Mersey found neither J. Bruce Ismay nor Captain Smith guilty of negligence. Claimants who had awaited the inquiry's results, believing their claims might better be filed in England, now turned to United States courts. They hoped, in filing their claims in America, to rest upon the Senate investigation's findings to sustain their charges of negligence.

The United States District Court had jurisdiction over the case. And, because *Titanic* had been sailing towards the Port of New York, and because White Star's main American office was in that city, it fell to the Southern District Court of New York State to hear and adjudicate the petition.

Dockets for the United States District Court, Southern District, New York are maintained in large, wheat-coloured buckram-bound volumes. In volume 55, on page 279 appear the first entries for the case whose ultimate settlement would not take place for more than six years: 'In re: Petition of the Oceanic Steam Navigation Company Limited for Limitation of its Liability as Owner of the Steam Ship *Titanic*'. The docket for 'The *Titanic* Case' was henceforth identified as '55/279'.

The case was assigned to District Court Judge Charles M. Hough, who proceeded with the initial aspects of the case, while at the same time considering its acceptability under United States law. The court appointed Mr Henry W. Goodrich as commissioner. He was to report the value of the *Titanic* as to all items, excepting moneys received from the British government under mail contracts.

After due investigation, which included an appraisal of the lifeboats — the only tangible salvage from the lost liner — Commissioner Goodrich stated the value of *Titanic* and her pending freight on 15 April 1912 was as follows:

Value of 13 lifeboats and one collapsible boat		$4,972.00
Value of equipment of lifeboats		474.31
Prepaid freight		2,025.25
Gross passenger	money	$94,581.90

Less railway fares paid by the petitioner	$3,637.68	
Less board of third class passengers	643.76	
	$4,281.44	4,281.44
	$90,300.46	90,300.46
TOTAL		$97,772.02 (£20,159)

It was this amount, $97,772.02 (£20,159) against which claims totalling $16,804,112 (£3,464,765) were filed. It became the court's responsibility not only to receive and verify claims against the Oceanic Steam Navigation Company but also to determine if such claims had any legal validity. If so, the court was to apportion payment of each claim on the basis of available funds.

In response to advertisements placed in the *New York Times* on various dates between 6 October 1912 and 13 January 1913 by William Henkel, United States Marshall for the Southern District of New York, claimants for damages were ordered to present their claims prior to the morning of 14 January 1913. This filing date was extended to allow additional claimants to file.

On 22 February 1913, the United States District Court handed down a decision enabling claimants to file suit in that court, a move which had been opposed by attorneys for the steamship company.

When the preliminary legal skirmishing was completed, actual determination of the *Titanic*'s owners' liability was undertaken in a series of hearings and trials which did not commence until June 1915.

The White Star Line had retained the prestigious New York law firm of Burlingham, Montgomery and Beecher to represent its interests. Appearing at most of the hearings was Mr Charles Burlingham himself, usually accompanied by another of the firm's partners.

Most claimants were represented by the law firm of Hunt, Hill and Betts; other claimants were represented by attorneys from four other firms; finally, there were several claimants who were represented by individual attorneys.

Between initiation of the action and the time when hearings actually began (from September 1912 to June 1915), Judge Hough had withdrawn from the case due to ill health. The judge in whose court the case actually was heard was Judge Julius M. Mayer.

The claims against *Titanic*'s owners were filed under four 'schedules'. The types and average claim amount for each were as follows:

Schedule A	Loss of Life	$35,376 (£7,294)
Schedule B	Loss of Property	6,743 (£1,390)
Schedule C	Loss of Life and Property	40,601 (£8,371)
Schedule D	Injury and Loss of Property	10,834 (£2,234)

Claims by individuals ranged from $41.04 (£8 10s 5d) (by the United States of America, for value of registered mail which had been lost) to $177,352.75 (£36,567) by Mrs Charlotte D. M. Cardeza, wife of a Philadelphia, Pennsylvania, millionaire. The largest claim of all for lost property was filed by Laura Moore, an agent for several shippers whose goods had been lost; her claim totalled more than $222,690 (£45,915).

The largest claim for loss of life — $1,000,000 (£206,185) — was filed by René Harris, widow of theatre magnate Henry B. Harris. Among the more unusual property claims filed were the following:

Eugene Daly	Set of bagpipes	$50
Emilio Portaluppi	'1 picture of Garibaldi, signed by him and presented to my grandfather'	$3000
Annie May Stengel	Copy of *Science and Health*	$5
William Carter	1 Renault 25 hp automobile	$5000
	2 dogs, $100 and $200 each	$300
Charlotte Cardeza	14 trunks, 4 bags, a jewel case and a packing case	$177,352
Hokan Björnström-Steffanson	Oil painting by Blondel, 4 by 8 feet 'La Circassienne Au Bain'	$100,000
Margaret Brown	3 crates of ancient models for the Denver Museum	$500
Helen Wilson	1 Arab costume	$5
Stuart Collette	Handwritten college lecture notes, 2 year course	$50
Edwina Troutt	Marmalade machine	8s 6d
Thomas F. Myles	[as baggage] 50 lb butter, 10 lb tea	$15
Robert W. Daniel	Champion French bulldog, Gamin de Pycombe	$750
Harry Anderson	Chow dog	$50

The claimants wished to prove negligence, the petitioner wished to limit its liability by proving that negligence had no part in the disaster. In the British courts, in the case of *Ryan v Oceanic Steam Navigation Co Ltd*, the jury found for the claimants. The company appealed, but on 9 February 1914, Lord Justice Vaughan Williams dismissed the case, and thus upheld negligence in *Titanic*'s navigation. Many claimants withdrew their actions in the United States District Court following this decision, and refiled them in British courts.

The United States actions continued. Between mid-April and the end of July many hearings were held. Edward Wilding appeared to describe in detail *Titanic*'s construction and safety features. In London, Alexander Carlisle gave a sworn deposition in which he reiterated his British inquiry testimony about the inadequacy of *Titanic*'s lifeboat capacity. A far greater number of passengers appeared and testified than had at either the Senate or Board of Trade investigations, including Mr John B. Thayer, Karl Behr, W. J. Mellor, Mrs Jacques Futrelle. . .

Under American law the owners' liability would have been limited to the salvage value, about $97,000 (£20,159). Early in the hearings, and in a separate decision, Judge Holt of the District Court ruled that British law applied to the total limit of claims. This amount, $16,804,112 (£3,464,765) had

to be divided *pro rata* among the claimants. By December of 1915 a tentative settlement was agreed upon by lawyers on both sides.

On 28 July 1916, Judge Mayer signed the decree ending all *Titanic* suits. The amount distributed among all claimants was $663,000 (£136,701).

In a speech to the Senate of the United States on 28 May, Senator Isidor Raynor of Maryland points out the inherent unfairness of existing American liability and Admiralty law concerning the rights of maritime disaster victims to recover damages. 'Look at it for a moment,' he says. 'The owners of the *Titanic* can come into court and surrender their freight money, the pending freight, and there is no recovery against them in any State or Federal court. No matter how many suits are brought in the State [or]. . .Federal courts, the owners of that ship, no matter how able they may be financially to answer in damages, can go into the Federal courts, sue out an injunction, have a trustee appointed, bring the ship, if it exists. . ., bring pending freight into the court, and escape all liability whatever for injury to passengers, for injury to goods, or for any cause whatever.'

But before the Congress can act to change the law, the White Star Line initiates proceedings in the United States District Court for the Southern District of New York to limit its liability. The case, begun in August 1912, is assigned Admiralty docket number 55-279. (Library of Congress.)

Centre Hearings begin in the Post Office building (left foreground) in New York City, then move to another courtroom in the new Woolworth Building, the world's tallest. (Authors' collection.)

Judge Charles Hough is selected to hear the case. Justice Hough is a likely candidate for a United States Supreme Court nomination when illness forces him to leave partway through the case. . . (Authors' collection.)

. . .and it is Judge Julius M. Mayer who sees the case through to its conclusion in 1916. (*National Cyclopedia of American Biography*.)

Representing the White Star Line at the hearings is Charles C. Burlingham, a veteran of Senator Smith's Washington investigation. (Burlingham, Underwood and Lord.)

Senator Isidor Raynor

Judge Julius M. Mayer

Judge Charles Hough

Mr Charles C. Burlingham

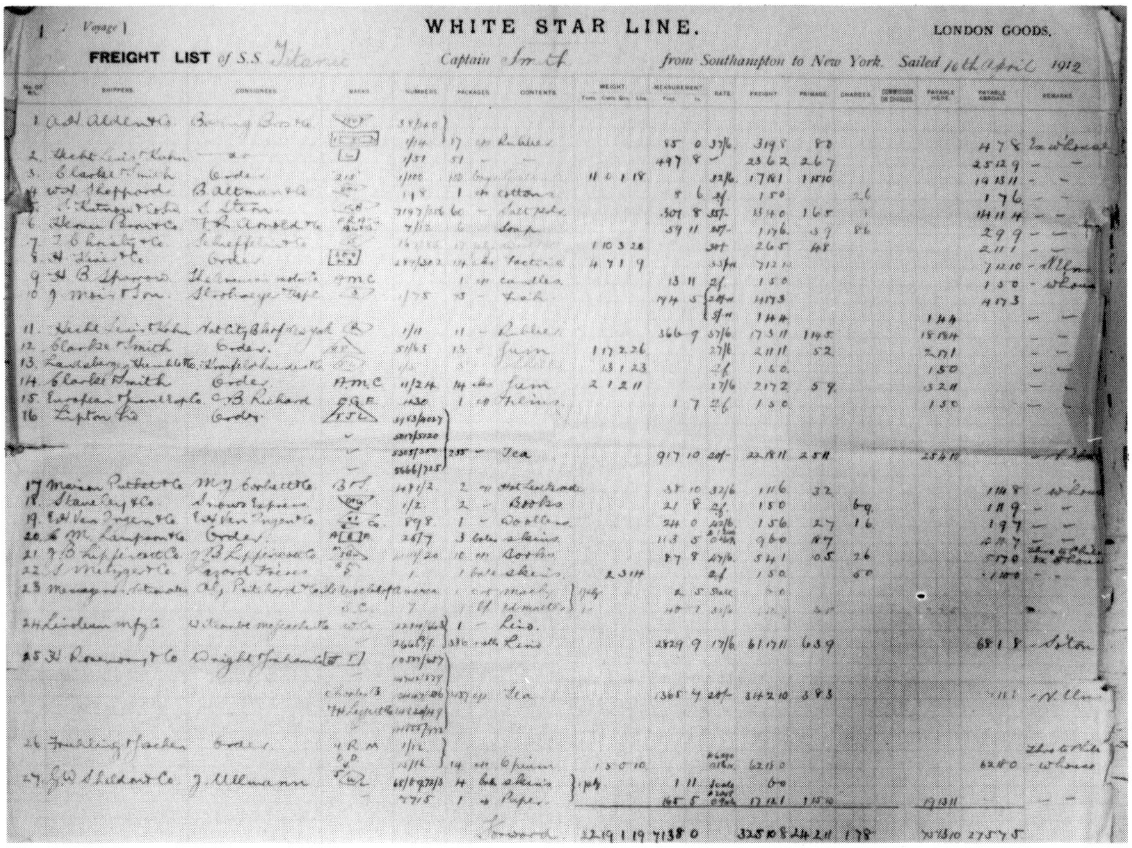

1 Voyage 1

WHITE STAR LINE. LONDON GOODS.

FREIGHT LIST of S.S. Titanic Captain Smith from Southampton to New York. Sailed 10th April 1912

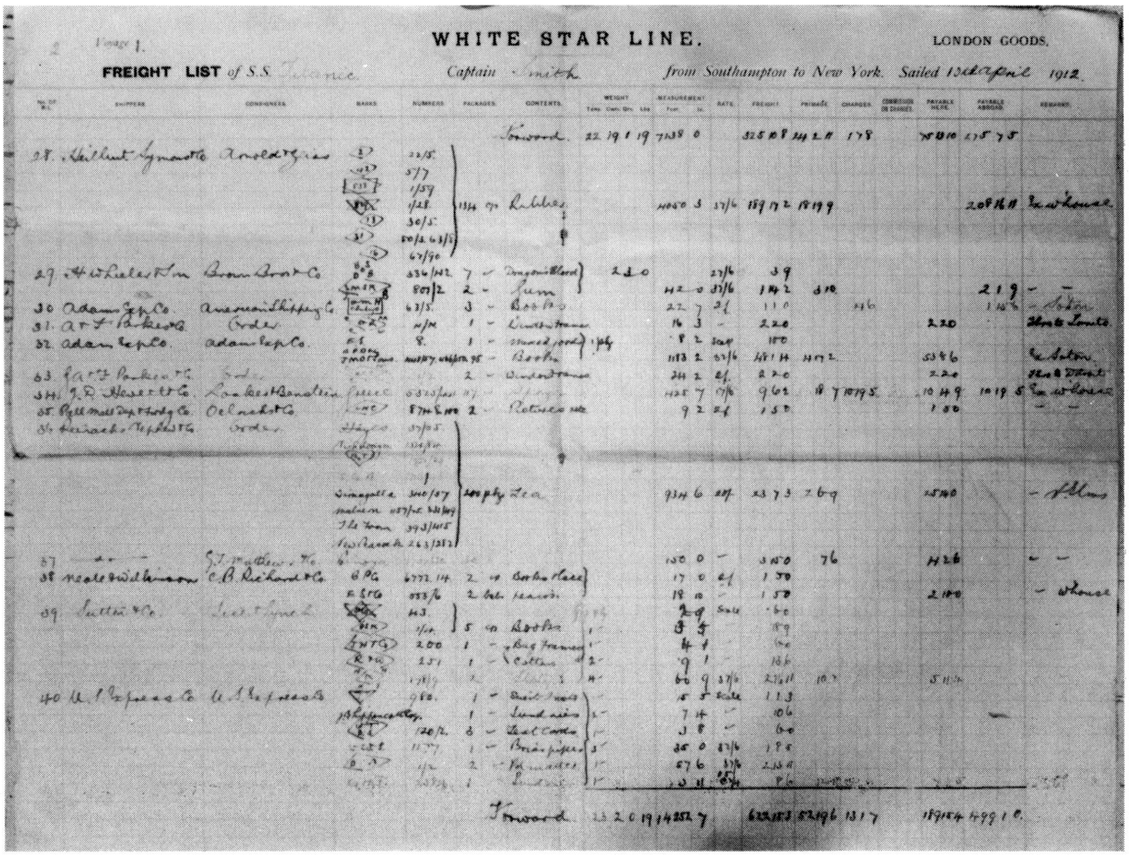

2 Voyage 1.

WHITE STAR LINE. LONDON GOODS.

FREIGHT LIST of S.S. Titanic Captain Smith from Southampton to New York. Sailed 10th April 1912.

Left One of the court's first tasks is to assess the freight monies that the White Star Line had received for the carriage of cargo aboard the *Titanic*. To do so, the company is ordered to produce the office carbon copies of the ship's cargo manifest. (The original was lost with the ship; the carbon was brought to the United States on the *Mauretania* several days after the disaster.) The sheets bear proof that the cargo was strictly a low-grade commercial one. (National Archives.)

Right The *Titanic*'s thirteen lifeboats — the only salvage recovered from the ship — are carefully examined to determine their current value. (Private collection.)

Below and overleaf Inspectors from the C. M. Lane Lifeboat Company in Brooklyn, New York, list the contents of the boats, now in storage at White Star's Pier 59. The impact of the souvenir hunters who visited the boats on the evening of their arrival on board *Carpathia* is clearly noted in the lists of 'missing' equipment and markers. The boats are later joined by collapsible A, returned to New York following its discovery on 13 May by the *Oceanic*. (National Archives.)

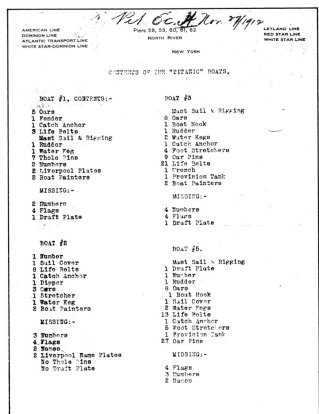

AMERICAN LINE
DOMINION LINE
ATLANTIC TRANSPORT LINE
WHITE STAR-DOMINION LINE

Piers 58, 59, 60, 61, 62
NORTH RIVER

NEW YORK

LEYLAND LINE
RED STAR LINE
WHITE STAR LINE

CONTENTS OF THE "TITANIC" BOATS.

BOAT #1, CONTENTS:-

5 Oars
1 Fender
1 Catch Anchor
3 Life Belts
Mast Sail & Rigging
1 Rudder
1 Water Keg
7 Thole Pins
2 Numbers
2 Liverpool Plates
2 Boat Painters

MISSING:-

2 Numbers
4 Flags
1 Draft Plate

BOAT #2

1 Number
1 Sail Cover
8 Life Belts
1 Catch Anchor
1 Dipper
3 Oars
1 Stretcher
1 Water Keg
2 Boat Painters

MISSING:-

3 Numbers
4 Flags
2 Names
2 Liverpool Name Plates
No Thole Pins
No Draft Plate

BOAT #3

Mast Sail & Rigging
8 Oars
1 Boat Hook
1 Rudder
2 Water Kegs
1 Catch Anchor
4 Foot Stretchers
9 Oar Pins
21 Life Belts
1 Wrench
1 Provision Tank
2 Boat Painters

MISSING:-

4 Numbers
4 Flags
1 Draft Plate

BOAT #5.

Mast Sail & Rigging
1 Draft Plate
1 Number
1 Rudder
8 Oars
1 Boat Hook
1 Sail Cover
2 Water Kegs
13 Life Belts
1 Catch Anchor
5 Foot Stretchers
1 Provision Tank
27 Oar Pins

MISSING:-

4 Flags
3 Numbers
2 Names

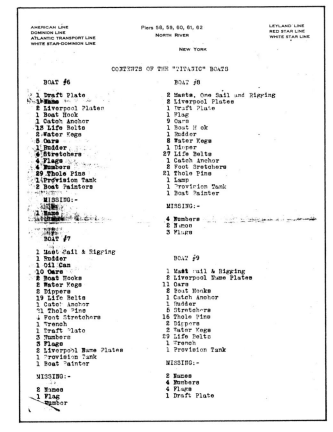

AMERICAN LINE
DOMINION LINE
ATLANTIC TRANSPORT LINE
WHITE STAR-DOMINION LINE

Piers 58, 59, 60, 61, 62
NORTH RIVER

NEW YORK

LEYLAND LINE
RED STAR LINE
WHITE STAR LINE

CONTENTS OF THE "TITANIC" BOATS

BOAT #6

1 Draft Plate
1 Name
2 Liverpool Plates
1 Boat Hook
1 Catch Anchor
13 Life Belts
2 Water Kegs
5 Oars
1 Rudder
5 Stretchers
4 Flags
4 Numbers
29 Thole Pins
1 Provision Tank
2 Boat Painters

MISSING:-

1 Name

BOAT #7

1 Mast Sail & Rigging
1 Rudder
1 Oil Can
10 Oars
2 Boat Hooks
2 Water Kegs
2 Dippers
19 Life Belts
1 Catch Anchor
21 Thole Pins
4 Foot Stretchers
1 Wrench
1 Draft Plate
3 Numbers
3 Flags
2 Liverpool Name Plates
1 Provision Tank
1 Boat Painter

MISSING:-

2 Names
1 Flag
1 Number

BOAT #8

2 Masts, One Sail and Rigging
2 Liverpool Plates
1 Draft Plate
1 Flag
9 Oars
1 Boat Hook
1 Rudder
8 Water Kegs
1 Dipper
27 Life Belts
1 Catch Anchor
2 Foot Stretchers
21 Thole Pins
1 Lamp
1 Provision Tank
1 Boat Painter

MISSING:-

4 Numbers
2 Names
3 Flags

BOAT #9

1 Mast Sail & Rigging
2 Liverpool Name Plates
11 Oars
2 Boat Hooks
1 Catch Anchor
1 Rudder
5 Stretchers
16 Thole Pins
2 Dippers
2 Water Kegs
29 Life Belts
1 Wrench
1 Provision Tank

MISSING:-

2 Names
4 Numbers
4 Flags
1 Draft Plate

AMERICAN LINE
DOMINION LINE
ATLANTIC TRANSPORT LINE
WHITE STAR-DOMINION LINE

Piers 58, 59, 60, 61, 62
NORTH RIVER

NEW YORK

LEYLAND LINE
RED STAR LINE
WHITE STAR LINE

CONTENTS OF THE "TITANIC" BOATS

BOAT #10
1 Mail Sail & Rigging
Numbers
1 Flag
1 Liverpool Plate
1 Draft Plate
25 Thole Pins
2 Catch Anchors
2 Water Kegs
10 Oars
2 Boat Hooks
1 Rudder
39 Life Belts
6 Foot Stretchers
1 Di-per
1 Provision Tank

MISSING:-
3 Flags
1 Liverpool Plate
2 Names

BOAT #11
1 Mast Sail & Rigging
2 Liverpool Plates
4 Numbers
4 Oars
1 Wrench
2 Water Kegs
32 Life Belts
1 Oil Can
1 Catch Anchor
4 Stretchers
28 Thole Pins
1 Draft Plate
2 Flags
1 Provision Tank
2 Boat Painters

MISSING:-
2 Names
2 Flags

BOAT #12.
1 Mast Sail & Rigging
4 Numbers
4 Flags
2 Liverpool Name Plates
1 Draft Plate
23 Thole Pins
1 Catch Anchor
2 Water Kegs
2 Boat Hooks
7 Oars
1 Rudder
1 Dipper
1 Wrench
4 Stretchers
35 Life Belts
1 Provision Tank

MISSING:-
2 Names

BOAT #13.
1 Mast Sail & Rigging
4 Numbers
1 Oil Can
1 Rudder
2 Boat Hooks
10 Oars
2 Water Kegs
5 Foot Stretchers
12 Life Belts
1 Catch Anchor
1 Dipper
21 Thole Pins
1 Provision Tank
1 Boat Painter

MISSING:-
2 Names
2 Liverpool Plates
4 Flags
1 Draft Plate.

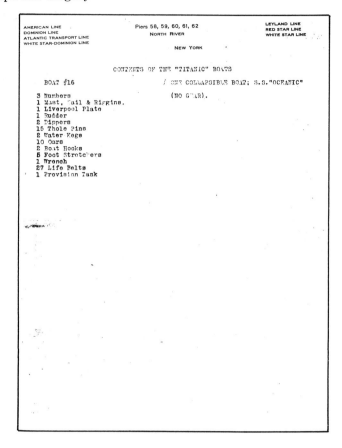

Below To the inventory is appended a valuation of the now used, sometimes damaged equipment found in the boats. (It appears that none of the boats is ever re-used, and that all rotted away in a small boat-builder's yard in Brooklyn.) (National Archives.)

Below The court also examines the revenue received by White Star from the sale of passenger tickets. A now-torn page from the company's handwritten ticketing list shows the net passage money to be £17,677 12s ($85,733). (National Archives.)

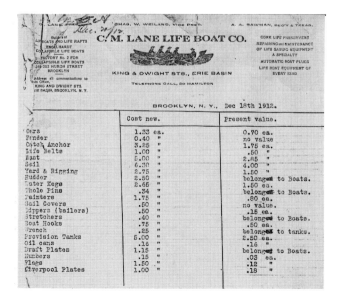

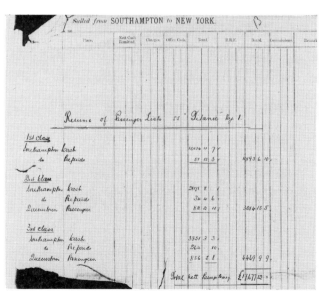

Limitation of Liability

During the limitation of liability hearings, hundreds of claims are filed against the White Star Line for loss of life, loss of property, cargo losses, injuries, etc. The largest claim by a passenger is that of Philadelphia's Mrs Charlotte Cardeza **right**. It totals $177,352.75 (£36,567) and fills eighteen single-spaced typewritten pages **below and overleaf**. (*Philadelphia Inquirer*.)

Mrs Cardeza's list offers insight into the lifestyle enjoyed by those occupying one of *Titanic*'s two 'Millionaires' Suites'.

While Mrs Cardeza notes that her jewels had been entrusted to the purser's safe, she does not know that they — and all other jewels left behind as evacuation proceeded — were later taken from the safes by the purser's staff. (National Archives.)

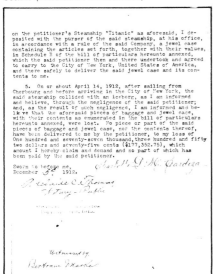

Brought Forward,	21,342.10
Hair pins, safety pins, gold, and toilet articles,	100.
2 lace scarfs.	90.
1 piece albatross.	15.
1 piece pink brocade.	8.50
No. 4 Drawer of Mendel.	
Music box, little bird.	350.
Leather picture frame.	25.
Mother-of-pearl and lace fan.	250.
Large beaded bag.	126.
Small beaded purse.	72.
Opera glasses.	125.
2 mosaic frames	20.
2 silver frames.	50.
2 silver and gilt frames.	64.
Vuitton dress trunk.	80.
12 handerchiefs, Hutchinson, N. Y. (6 with Mechlin lace edge, 6 with Val. lace edge)	36.
12 fine real lace handerchiefs with monogram.	48.
11 fine handkerchiefs with coat-of-arms. Wixler, Zuirich	67.
6 fine double hemstitched handerchiefs with "Cardeza".	35.
1 fine glove handerchief, Mechlin lace, embroidered monogram.	8.
1 fine glove handkerchief, Pont de Paris lace.	10.
2 Florence lace sachet sacks or bags.	15.
1 Glove fine linen handkerchief, embroidered "Cardeza"	5.
Pink dressing sack. Vienna.	8.80
1 Singlet swan, light weight. Altman & Co.	1.18
1 Singlet swan, light weight. Saks & Co.	1.25
2 Singlets swan, light weight, tag 118	2.36
5 " " " " Wanamakers.	6.50
2 Singlet Star, " "	3.00
2 " swan " " low neck	2.00
2 pair medium weight wool tights,	13.
2 " white silk knickers. London.	15.
1 " pink silk " "	8.
2 " " " tights. Bon Marche, Paris.	14.
2 " " " underwaists, Bon Marche, Paris.	8.
1 " " " Singlet with crochet.	6.
1 " " " drawers. New York.	4.58
1 " white " "	4.58
Carried Forward,	23,039.85

[illegible] flannel nightgowns. [illegible]	20.
White and blue knit jacket.	12.
White Shetland wool auto scarf. Vienna.	8.
3 camel 's hair knit jackets, heavy. Paris.	12.
17 pairs black silk stockings, embroidered and lace	150.
4 pairs black wool stockings	16.
4 " fancy colors silk stockings,	20.
4 " white " "	20.
2 " " cotton "	5.
4 " pink wool "	16.
2 pink silk chemises	35.
3 pairs silk drawers.	47.
2 pairs chimaloons,	1[illegible].
[illegible] wrap	27.
4 pairs drawers, lace and embroidery,	85.
1 embroidered chemise	9.
Night gown, English style, wreath and bees. Rouff, Paris.	[illegible]
Combination, Empire, style, wreath and bees. Rouff, Paris.	28.
1 pair drawers. wreath and bees, Rouff, Paris.	19.
1 pair drawers. butterflies and wreaths, antique lace. Rouff, Paris.	24.
1 corset cover butterflies and wreaths, antique lace, Rouff, Paris.	21.
2 combinations and drawers to match. English embroidery. Rouff, Paris.	50.
2 corset covers and drawers to match. English embroidery. Rouff, Paris.	1[illegible].
2 white china silk underwaists. Rouff, Paris.	1[illegible].80
1 Pink china silk underwaist. Rouff, Paris.	8.40
1 White satin waist, covered with chiffon. Redfern, Paris.	30.
2 White satin waists. Low neck.	50.
2 Pink underwaists. Lord & Taylor.	4[illegible].
1 White satin gamp. Lord & Taylor.	18.
1 Pink satin gamp. Lord & Taylor.	18.
1 White satin, short sleeves underwaist, covered with chiffon.	2[illegible].
1 White satin low neck underwaist. Ungar, Vienna.	20.
2 Pink china silk underwaists. Ungar, Vienna.	42.
Fel Toir curtain. Wixler, Zurich.	600.
3 heavy Lourve silk nightgowns.	75.
2 Pink silk nightgowns. Rouff, Paris.	40.
3 " " " New York.	75.
3 " thin silk nightgowns. "	66.
1 Brusse " "	30.
2 lace bureau scarfs, Rouff, Paris.-$190.-$230.	420.
7 Carried Forward,	25,311.06

Brought Forward,	25,311.05
Long near seal coat trimmed with ermine. Dresden.	800.
Long ermine coat. New York.	1,400.
Chinchilla coat, Irish lace. New York.	6,000.
Chinchilla stole. Ungar, Carlsbad.	1,400.
Silver Fox stole. New York.	2, 350.
Ermine stole and Muff. Dresden.	180.
Fur lined gloves for auto.	3.
Steel comb for furs.	
Long white moth bag for ermine coat.	1.50
1 Pink Paradise.	75.
1 Elephant's breath Paradise.	80.
2 Pink "	125.
1 Black aigrette.	100.
1 light blue aigrette	80.
Small breast of Paradise.	20.
White ostrich feather, 20" long.	35.
Bunch of 13 white feathers.	42.
Long gray and white ostrich feather.	50.
5 white ostrich feathers.	120.
2 purple ostrich feathers.	35.
2 natural ostrich feathers.	50.
7 black ostrich feathers.	130.
1 black ostrich feather, extra long.	35.
7 Omdurman ostrich feathers.	35.
2 large white ostrich feathers.	70.
1 large white aigrette.	200.
1 blue ostrich feather	25.
Louis Vuitton Hat Trunk.	60.
7 black veils.	11.
1 black lace veil.	8.
3 black and white veils.	4.
1 blue lace veil	8.
1 blue lace veil.	3.50
3 colored veils.	6.
6 colored scarfs.	72.
5 auto. veils.	50.
5 scarfs.	55.
2 silk and lace theatre caps. Lord & Taylor.	25.75
White and coral hair band. Lord & Taylor.	23.50.
Pink band, gold tassel. Lord & Taylor.	17.90
2 pink roses.	5.
Blue hat, feather band and paradise. Valette, Paris.	54.
Bordeaux velvet hat, very long ostrich feather. Valette, Paris.	85.
Black velvet hat, chinchilla band and Paradise. Valette, Paris.	150.
Carried Forward,	39,393.20

Brought Forward,	39,393.20
Velvet hat with ermine. New York.	85.
Seal hat with ermine. Dresden.	40.
Light blue velvet hat with pink roses. Valette, Paris.	50.
22 hat pins.	[illegible]
6 gold hat pins: (Moonstone and amethyst, dull gold, enamel butterfly and pearls, Baroch pearl, Carlsbad amethyst, 2 small amethyst.)	270.
9 assorted hat pins: ([illegible] brilliants, amethysts and brilliant, murray scarab and lotus, Turkish, Ural mountings, amber, yellowstone, blue stone.)	139.
9 Bar pins: (Carlsbad garnets, sapphires, turquoise, re-constructed ruby and brilliants, miniature with brilliants, enamel and blue stone, enamel and lotus flower.)	500.
Louis Vuitton Hat Trunk.	60.
Large black straw hat, yellow Paradise. Valette, Paris.	76.
Light green velvet hat, black and green ostrich feathers, Valette, Paris.	80.
Large black velvet hat, black ostrich plume. Lord & Taylor.	55.
Mauve hat, ostrich feathers. Valette, Paris.	70.00
Champagne straw hat, pink ostrich feathers. Valette, Paris.	75.
White linen parasol, Swiss embroidery. Lucerne.	18.
White taffeta silk parasol, hand painted, porcelain handle. Lord & Taylor.	60.
Red taffeta silk parasol. Vienna.	35.
White applique lace parasol. Redfern, Paris.	300.
2 Yeager wool caps for hunting.	3.
1 pair wool stockings for hunting.	2.
1 pair corsets. Redfern, Paris.	35.
2 Girdles. Paris.	24.
2 pair garter suspenders } 2 white silk laces. } in silk ribbon bag.	8.
Tissue paper.	
Carried Forward,	41,464.20

Brought Forward,	41,464.20
Louis Vuitton Shoe Trunk.	100.
1 pair satin slippers, gilt rhinestone buckles.	16.
1 " kid "	7.
1 " blue kid slippers, stockings to match.	10.
1 " light blue satin slippers, stockings to match. Paris.	18.
1 pair blue satin slippers.	1[illegible].
1 " rose satin slippers, Paris.	16.
1 " white kid slippers, silk and wool stockings.	12.
1 " covert cloth gaiters.	8.
1 " white canvas "	5.
1 " black velvet "	12.
1 " long gaiters.	14.
Package shoe laces, ribbons, etc. for shoes and slippers.	4.
1 pair new white kid slippers, large gilt buckles.	9.
1 " " " " " enamel "	9.
1 " " " " "	6.
1 " black satin slippers, rhinestone buckles and silk stockings.	21.
1 " black satin slippers, pink roses.	1[illegible].
1 " purple satin slippers and stockings to match green slippers,	18.
2 " red felt bedroom slippers, fur tops.	6.
1 " pink satin slippers quilted. Paris.	9.
1 " " " bedroom slippers, white fur.	1[illegible].
11 pairs of shoes and 1 pair patent leather laced, heavy soles.	1[illegible].
Innovation Steamer Trunk.	[illegible]
White jersey petticoat. Redfern, Paris.	[illegible]
4 lace and embroidered pillow cases, Rouff, Paris.	1[illegible]0.
Pink satin pillow slip. Rouff, Paris.	[illegible]
White silk knitted scarf, heavy fringe. London.	[illegible]
2 silk nightgowns. Rouff, Paris.	[illegible]0.
Embroidered chemise and drawers.	30.
2 pairs silk stockings, white feet.	8.
1 pair black wool stockings,	[illegible]
2 pink satin underwaists. Ungar and Redfern, Paris.	[illegible]
Pink satin gamp. Lord & Taylor.	1[illegible].
2 china silk underwaists.	1[illegible].40
1 Pink silk ribbed underwaist.	[illegible]
Carried Forward,	42,409.

Brought Forward,	42,409.
3 singlets.	3.75
1 flannel skirt and cambric hair jacket.	19.
5 auto veils.	25.
6 pairs white silk gloves.	15.
1 pair gray suede gloves.	2.
Blue serge waist. Lord & Taylor.	90.
Light blue dress trimmed with silver. Ungar, Vienna.	340.
White satin dress, applique lace. Lord & Taylor.	350.
Blue taffeta dress, Samases yoke. Lord & Taylor.	200.
White camel's hair coat. Redfern, Paris.	210.
Blue serge suit trimmed with old rose. Lord & Taylor.	200.
Gray suit trimmed with Irish lace. Lord & Taylor.	210.
Blue flowered wrapper. Vienna.	50.
Gray squirrel fur coat.	200.
Carry all--Innovation Flexible bag.	28.
2 steamer rugs.	40.
Auto rain coat. London.	50.
White sweater.	15.
2 summer blankets in pink case.	51.
Iron attachments, wisk, shoe and hat brush.	5.00
Medicine chest and contents about	50.
Dress suit case,	500.
Pink silk nightgown and dressing sacque.	36.
Brushes, combs and toilet articles, about	50.
Carried Forward,	45,153.75

Brought Forward,	45,153.75
Goyard Tray Trunk.	58.
White embroidered dress, Paris.	70.
Blue polka dot dress, Paris.	125.
Blue lace evening dress. Paris.	250.
Embroidered bird dress. Paris.	225
Veils Paris.	100.
Gloves Paris.	200.
Underwear "	400.
Hat pins "	100.
Blue silk dress. Berlin	240.
Lace waist "	80.
Lace gown "	300.
Tailor suit. "	200.
Hat "	75.
White Baby lamb coat. Russia.	1,500.
Mink stole and muff. "	600.
Mole skin muff and coat. Paris.	400.
Tailor suit. "	225.
Blue and silver dress. "	375.
Tailor suit, trimmed ermine "	300.
Blue silk coat and skirt. Irish lace, Paris.	250.
Evening dress, "	275.
Evening coat " "	200.
Tailor suit "	225.
Bonbonniere "	1,000.
Hat Trunk	60.
Hats, Paris.	742.
Hair goods and hair ornaments.	246.
Souvenir spoons, etc.	350.
19 enameled boxes	300.
Automobile trunk,	40.
" " contents.	575.
2 leather bags,	45
Contents of 3 packing cases.	
Pipes.	100
Gold Turkish coffee cup,	200.
Carlsbad embroidery	300.
Amethyst and garnets unmounted,	100.
Carlsbad lace,	100.
" glass.	500.
Dresden pictures.	75.
" china	300.
Pink and satin brocade	300.
Red and gold "	400.
Brown and gold "	250.
12 Carried Forward,	58,109.75

Brought Forward,	58,109.75
Silver and gold brocade.	90.
Russian lace	150
Lacquered hand painted boxes	225.
Russian silver enamel tea set	500.
12 China plates Royal Vienna	1,200.
10 Gold and embossed salt shakers and spoons	200.
Pictures from Rome,	400.
Plates " "	80.
Tortoise shell, monogram in gold.	340.
Paintings	90.
Water colors (Serento)	400.
Fancy woodwork	100.
Brocade from Florence.	350.
Embroidery " "	175
Lace from Florence	90.
Steins	100.
Crystal rock bowl.	1,000.
Table and bed linen --Nurnberg,	7,500.
Cash	5,600.
Carried Froward,	72,599.75

SCHEDULE B.

Contents of jewel case, deposited with Purser.

Jewel case,	$65.
2 Bracelets, 15 diamonds in each,	2,000.
Necklace, 63 imitation pearls, clasp of 10 diamonds and 1 ruby,	500.
Bracelet, 1 diamond, 2 emeralds, 1 amethyst, 1 ruby, 1 sapphire, and 1 topaz.	800.
Chain and medal, gold. Immaculate Conception,	18.
Sunburst, 84 diamonds.	1 500.
Pendant and platinum chain, pink pearl surrounded by diamonds,	1,800.
Pendant, aqua marine surrounded by 38 diamonds, 4 diamonds in clasp,	1,350.
LaValliere, with platinum chain, canary marquise, white marquise, 22 small diamonds,	2,200.
Pin, three feathers in diamonds, Bailey, Banks & Biddle,	800.
Pin, four-leaf clover, in green enamel and diamonds. Dent, London.	200.
Pin, diamond spray and opal flowers, Doneth, Vienna.	1,500.
Pin, 8 diamonds and 8 opals,	1,250.
Pin, 5 sapphires, 5 rubies, 5 emeralds and 15 diamonds, Tiffany, London.	795.
Chain, blue enamel and pearls.	140
Chain, platinum, Tiffany.	20.
Brooch, miniature, surrounded by diamonds and turquoise. Wescott & Bailey.	450.
Bar pin, 3 re-constructed rubies, 12 diamonds and white enamel.	68.
Locket, Turquoise, surrounded by 2 rows of diamonds and diamond clasp.	487.
Pendant, Monganite surrounded by diamonds, platinum chain with 16 diamonds.	2,017.
Bar pin, 14 diamonds. Tiffany, London.	425.
2 small Bar pins, 6 diamonds in each, Tiffany, New York.	350.
Talisman, white jade and 10 rubies.	100.
Necklace, turquoise matrix and gold. Tiffany, Paris.	382.
Ring, Vegitable diamond solitaire.	800.
Ring, Diamond solitaire.	500.
Ring, 3 diamonds, set deep.	325.
1 Carried Forward,	20,902.

Brought Forward,	20,902.
Ring, Burmah ruby and 2 diamonds. Tiffany, New York,	14,000.
Marquise ring, ruby and 32 diamonds, Caldwell & Co.	1,000.
Ring, ruby, opal and 14 diamonds,Westcott & Bailey.	1,500.
Ring, water opal and 2 diamonds.Bailey,Banks & Biddle.	1,000.
Ring, Hungarian opal and 12 diamonds.	530.
Ring, Montana opal and 12 diamonds.	350.
Ring, Mexican opal, 20 diamonds and 18 cleaines. Westcott & Bailey.	550.
Ring, 3 diamonds and 2 emralds.	600.
Ring, emerald and 65 diamonds.	2,400.
Ring, emerald and 10 diamonds.	2,650.
Marquise ring, Ceylon Sapphire and 32 diamonds.	800.
Ring, Star sapphire and 19 diamonds.	500.
Ring, blue enamel , 9 diamonds.	60.
Egyptian scarab.	125.
Ring, turquoise and 16 diamonds.	800.
2 clasps for Pendants, one gold mounted with diamonds ,one platinum with diamonds.	65.
2 Yacht club pins, enamel.	30.
Pin, reconstructed ruby and 2 diamonds.	100.
Pin, opal.	45.
Glove buttoner, gold.	8.
Bracelet, Egyptian enamel.	80.
Anklet, gold.	65.
Garter buckles, gold with 3 diamonds.	100.
Pendant,blue marquise diamond, 419/64 carats. Tiffany, New York.	9,000.
White oblong diamond, 3 7/82 carats Old Indian stone.	3,000.
Pink diamond, 6 7/16 carats. Tiffany, New York.	20,000.
Pendant and chain, platinum and diamonds.	300.
Pendant, 1 large diamond,19 29/32 carats. Tiffany, London.	13,000.
Small leather auto bag,gold fittings. London.	150.
Pin, opals and diamonds. Gompers,Paris.	65.
Bracelet,opals,ruby and diamonds.	100.
Plaque . Gest,Monte Carlo.	1,000.
Chain, platinum and diamonds. Gest, Monte Carlo.	400.
Plaque,diamonds and sapphires. Gest,Monte Carlo.	800.
Carried Forward,	101,135.

Brought forward,	101,135.
Set of cuff buttons, shirt studs and waistcoat buttons, white enamel,sapphires and diamonds. Hartog, Paris.	468.
1 pair cuff buttons, 3 shirt studs, Moonstones,surrounded by rubies. Hartog, Paris.	110.
Jewelry, Stickers, Monte Carlo.	200.
1 Pearl ribbon chain with diamond slides and clasps, Gompers, Paris.	960. —
1 necklace,diamonds set in platinum.Gompers,Paris.	400.
1 collarette and jabot of diamonds, jewelled clasp. Hartog, Paris.	1,120.
1 Chinese ring, diamonds and sapphires. Hartog. Paris.	560.
	$104,753.

------------o----------

Schedule A.,	$ 72,599.75
Schedule B.,	104,753.00
	$ 177,352.75

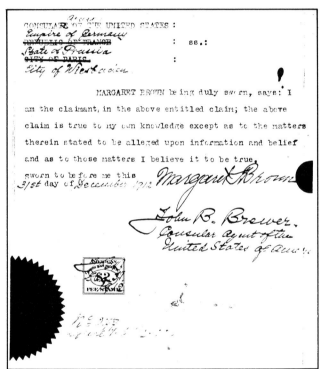

Denver socialiate 'Molly' Brown **top right** files a much more modest claim against the company... (Bain Collection, Library of Congress.)

Executed in Wiesbaden, Germany, before an American consular agent, Mrs Brown's claim fills but a single page **above and right**. Always eager to try to improve her social standing in her community, she was bringing home, among other things, 'ancient models for Denver Museum'. (National Archives.)

SCHEDULE A.

Street furs	$ 300.00
Ermine Collarette	75.00
Ermine Opera Cape	500.00
Brussels Lace Gown	375.00
Persian Over dress	175.00
6 Dinner Gowns ($75) each	450.00
Green Lace Gown	175.00
1 Sealskin Jacket	700.00
4 Gowns ($200 each)	800.00
1 necklace	20000.00
Odd laces	200.00
1 Pearl Brooch	150.00
14 hats	225.00
6 lace shirtwaists,	75.00
6 Embroidered waists, lace	140.00
Silk hosiery	75.00
Lingerie	300.00
Souveniers (Egypt)	500.00
3 crates ancient models for Denver Museum	500.00
2 Japanese Kimonas	50.00
1 Black Satin Gown	150.00
1 blue and white serge gown	75.00
3 satin evening gowns	450.00
1 Irish lace gown	150.00
3 dozen gloves	50.00
1 hat	35.00
6 shoes (10 Each)	60.00
4 tailored gowns and 2 coats	500.00
3 shoes	36.00
1 evening wrap	150.00
4 Evening slippers	16.00
Brown velvet gown	200.00
Brown velvet coat	100.00
2 black gowns	150.00
	$27087.00

IN THE DISTRICT COURT OF THE UNITED STATES

SOUTHERN DISTRICT OF NEW YORK.

In the Matter of the Petition of the)
Oceanic Steam Navigation Company, Lim-) CLAIM OF
ited, as Owner of the Steamship Titanic,) MRS. ALLEN O. BECKER.
etc., for Limitation of Liability.)

STATE OF MICHIGAN)
) ss.
COUNTY OF BERRIEN)

MRS. ALLEN O. BECKER, being duly sworn, says:

I am a resident of Benton Harbor, Michigan. On April 15th, 1912, I was one of the passengers on the late Steamship Titanic, at the time of her collision with an iceberg, as set forth in the libel and petition herein. By reason of the said collision, and as I am informed and believe and charge, through the fault of said petitioner, the Oceanic Steam Navigation Company, limited, or of its agents and servants in charge of the Steamship Titanic, and without fault on my part, the said Steamship Titanic was sunk and became a total loss.

By the sinking and destruction of said steamship, I lost my personal effects and property, which went down with said vessel, to the value of upwards of *Two Thousand One Hundred + Eighty four $84/100 Dollars*

That a true list and inventory of the articles and effects so lost is annexed hereto, marked "Exhibit A," to be taken as part of this claim; that all and every the articles set forth were owned by me and were in my possession on said steamship, and were all totally lost with said steamship, and as I am informed and verily believe, no part of said articles has been raised or salved from the wreck thereof; that the values therein stated are the true and correct market values of the property at the time of said collision, to the best of my knowledge, information and belief.

WHEREFORE, I present a claim for damages against said petitioner in these proceedings, to the amount of *$2184 84/100* no part of which has been paid.

Mrs Allen O. Becker

SWORN TO before me, this *16th* day of December, 1912.

Edward E. English
Notary Public.

1	Large rug,	$ 28.00
1	Oriental rug (India),	50.00
1	" " "	50.00
1	" " "	50.00
1	" " "	50.00
1	" " "	35.00
1	" " "	35.00
1	" " "	25.00
1	Large camel's hair rug (India),	15.00
1	Small " " "	10.00
1	" " " "	10.00
1	" " " "	10.00
1	" " " "	10.00
1	" " " "	10.00
1	Pair Oriental bead portierres,	20.00
1	Irish linen hand embroidered bed spread,	15.00
1	Oil painting,	100.00
6	Water colour paintings,	6.00
2	Oil paintings,	10.00
40	Books,	50.00
1	Carved walnut table (India),	25.00
1	" " "	25.00
1	" tabourette "	5.00
4	" " "	16.00
1	Bamboo table	2.00
1	Hammered brass jardinier (India),	5.00
1	Turquoise picture frame "	3.00
1	" " "	2.00
1	" " "	1.00
6	Oriental brass finger bowls "	6.00
1	Large brass tray "	4.00
1	" " "	3.00
1	Small " "	2.00
1	" " "	1.00
1	Brass brush and comb tray "	1.00
2	" powder boxes "	2.00
1	Silver jewel case,	3.00
1	Carved wood jewel case	4.00
1	Olive wood ivory top jewel case (India)	5.00
1	Bible, large,	6.00
1	" "	2.00
1	" small,	2.00
1	Silk embroidered table cover (India),	5.00
1	Pair silk " portierres "	20.00
3	" portierres "	6.00
3	" embroidered window curtains (India)	15.00
1	Large linen table cloth,	10.00
1	" " "	8.00
1	" " "	5.00
1	" " "	3.00
1	" " "	3.00
1	" " "	3.00
3	Dozen linen napkins,	15.00
1	Gold picture frame,	4.00
4	Silk Como rugs (India),	20.00
1	Linen hand embroidered center piece,	2.00
2	Lace center pieces,	3.00
6	Yards real lace,	25.00
	FORWARDED,	**$821.00**

Left and below Second class passenger Mrs Allen O. Becker reports the loss of her own possessions, and those of her three children. The family was returning to the United States due to young Richard's illness, but fortunately Mr Becker had remained in India, where he was a missionary. (National Archives.)

Right Mrs Lulu T. Drew, also a second class passenger, seeks recompense for the loss of her husband James V. Drew, as well as for their possessions, and asks for the return of their passage money. There is no mention of the belongings of eight-year-old Marshall Drew who, like his aunt, was saved. (National Archives.)

	BROUGHT FORWARD,	$ 821.00
1	Real lace collar,	10.00
1	Pair solid gold spectacles,	25.00
1	" gold glasses,	7.00
1	Maltese lace collar,	5.00
1	Silver tea set,	25.00
1	" nut dish,	10.00
1	Solid silver tea set (India),	24.00
1	Silver tea canister,	25.00
1	Solid silver mustard pot (India),	5.00
1	" " bon bon dish "	5.00
1	" " " "	2.00
1	Hand painted chocolate pitcher,	5.00
1	China dresser set,	5.00
4	Hand made quilts,	16.00
6	" " comforts,	12.00
8	pillows,	16.00
1	Dozen linen sheets,	24.00
3	" hemstitched linen pillow slips,	15.00
1	Finger ring, 5 rubies,	25.00
1	" " 5 sapphires,	25.00
1	" " 4 opals,	10.00
1	" " 5 rubies,	15.00
1	Pin, pearls and diamond,	5.00
1	Solid gold pin,	6.00
1	" " "	3.00
1	Gold coin necklace,	5.00
1	Silver necklace with coral (India),	6.00
1	Coral necklace, (Egypt),	3.00
1	" " "	10.00
1	Necklace, silver and turquoise (India),	5.00
1	Solid gold necklace, moonstone cross pendant (India),	12.00
1	Diamond pin,	25.00
1	Ruby pin (India),	4.00
8	Silver bar pins, (India),	4.00
1	Hand embroidered dress (India),	75.00
1	" " shirt waist (India),	15.00
1	" " "	13.00
40	Yards silk (India),	40.00
1	Piece gray cloth, gold bordered (India),	14.00
1	" pink " " "	14.00
1	" tan " " "	14.00
1	Hat pin, gold inlaid "	2.00
1	" " " "	2.00
4	Silver hat pins "	4.00
1	Hat,	4.00
1	" linen,	2.00
1	Tan silk suit,	30.00
1	Silk dress,	18.00
1	" "	12.00
1	Mohair dress,	10.00
1	Serge suit,	25.00
1	Gray cloth skirt,	5.00
1	Black " "	5.00
7	White shirt waists,	21.00
	FORWARDED,	**$1545.00**

	BROUGHT FORWARD,	$1545.00
1	White mohair skirt,	7.00
1	Black silk shirt waist,	3.00
1	Blue messaline silk waist,	5.00
1	White " " "	7.00
1	" lace waist,	6.00
1	Sweater,	3.50
	Ruth's sweater,	2.75
	Marion's sweater,	2.25
	Richard's sweater,	2.00
1	Silk petticoat,	5.00
1	Hot water bottle,	1.50
1	Saratoga trunk,	18.00
1	Steamer trunk,	8.00
1	" "	7.00
1	Suit case,	5.00
1	Leather hat box,	5.00
1	Hand satchel,	7.50
1	Kodak,	8.00
6	Cambric night gowns with hand made lace,	28.00
6	" petticoats " " "	20.00
4	Knit combinations,	4.00
6	Cambric " "	22.00
6	Pairs stockings,	1.50
1	Pair shoes,	4.00
1	" "	3.50
5	" gloves,	10.00
3	Silver belt buckles,	9.00
4	" " buckets for Dr. Baer,	5.75
1	Dozen coffee spoons for Dr. Wolf,	5.75
1	Wool petticoat,	1.50
1	Crocheted hand bag,	5.00

Ruth's Clothes.

1	Hat,	3.25
6	Cambric night gowns, trimmed hand made lace,	18.00
1	Silk dress,	5.00
1	Mohair dress,	6.00
1	Linen dress,	3.00
4	Gingham dresses,	12.00
2	White dresses,	10.00
1	Cloth jacket,	5.00
6	White aprons,	3.00
2	Yards ribbon,	4.80
1	Pair shoes,	2.50
1	" "	2.00
6	stockings,	1.50

Marion's clothes.

2	Dozen cotton dresses,	24.00
2	Mohair "	6.00
6	Cambric undersuits,	3.00
6	" petticoats trimmed hand made lace,	10.00
	FORWARDED,	**$1887.55**

	BROUGHT FORWARD,	$1887.55
6	Night gowns,	3.00
6	Pairs stockings,	1.50
1	Pair shoes,	2.00
4	Yards ribbon,	2.40
1	White serge coat,	2.50
3	Blue cloth "	2.50
1	Tan silk "	4.50
1	Pique jacket,	2.00
1	Hat,	2.00

Richard's clothes.

2	Dozen cotton dresses,	24.00
1	Mohair dress,	2.00
1	Silk "	3.00
6	Pairs stockings,	1.50
1	Pair shoes,	2.00
1	" "	2.00
6	Cambric petticoats,	4.00
4	Flannel "	5.00
12	Pairs drawers,	6.00
4	Combination undersuits,	4.00
2	Caps,	2.00
6	Ferris waists,	1.50
6	Night gowns,	4.50
10	Ebony elephants,	10.00
1	Fountain pen,	4.00
1	" "	3.50
1	Pair scissors,	1.00
1	" "	.50
1	" "	.25
26	Brass gods (India),	5.50
1	Silk embroidered piano cover (India),	15.00
1	Clock,	3.00
1	" "	1.00
1	Set carpenter's tools,	5.00
1	Fancy pillow,	2.00
5	Solid silver napkin rings (India),	15.00
1	Large drawn thread table cloth (India),	25.00
1	Small " " tea " "	5.00
1	Solid silver dresser set,	10.00
1	Hammered brass jardinier (India),	3.00
1	Pair ornamental vases "	6.00
3	" " brass candlesticks (India),	6.00
1	Cloisenne card tray (India),	3.00
1	" bowl "	3.00
1	" vase "	5.00
1	" " "	5.00
2	Dozen large Turkish bath towels,	24.00
5	" hand towels,	15.00
2	Steamer rugs,	10.00
2	" chairs,	7.00
1	Leather traveling writing case,	6.00
1	White Kashmir shawl,	15.00
	TOTAL,	**$2184.20**

Below Second class passenger Miss Lucy Ridsdale had arrived at London's Waterloo Station on the morning of 10 April with luggage weighing about 100 pounds more than the allotment. (*Railway Magazine.*)

With legal proceedings now under way, she files with her claim the sage green excess luggage receipt to help prove the extent of her loss **centre right**.

And as additional proof, submits the grey coupon given her by *Titanic*'s baggage master when she checked in her luggage on board **bottom**. (National Archives.)

UNITED STATES DISTRICT COURT
FOR THE SOUTHERN DISTRICT OF NEW YORK

IN THE MATTER of claim of Lulu T. Drew as administratrix of the goods, chattels and credits of JAMES V. DREW and personally against the Steamship Titanic and the OCEANIC STEAM NAVIGATION COMPANY LIMITED, owner of Steamship TITANIC,

AFFIDAVIT

STATE OF NEW YORK)
) ss
COUNTY OF NEW YORK)

LULU T. DREW being duly sworn deposes and says: That she resides in the Village of Greenport, County of Suffolk in the State of New York. That she was duly appointed as administratrix of the personal property of JAMES V. DREW deceased by the HONORABLE SURROGATE'S COURT in and for the County of Suffolk on the 8th day of February, 1913, certificate of said Letters of Administration are hereto annexed; that the said JAMES V. DREW, deceased, departed this life on the 15th day of April in the year one thousand nine hundred and twelve having lost his life on the Steamer "TITANIC" owned and operated by the OCEANIC STEAM NAVIGATION COMPANY. That this claim is made by your deponent as administratrix as aforesaid for loss of personal property and loss of passage money amounting to the sum of FIVE HUNDRED DOLLARS ($565.00), schedule of which is hereto annexed and made a part of this affidavit, and the deponent individually further makes claim as the widow of the said deceased for the loss of his companionship, maintenance and support to her damage in the sum of FIFTY THOUSAND DOLLARS ($50,000.00).

Sworn to before me this
10th day of February, 1913.

Lulu T. Drew

NOTARY PUBLIC. Westchester County
Certificate filed in New York County
New York County No. 49
New York Register No. 4206

SCHEDULE

4 Overcoats
7 hats (2 ladies and 5 mens'
5 Suits of Clothes
About 15 pairs of gloves
12 suits of men's underwear
12 shirtwaists
5 dresses
Kimona
2 bath robes
3 pairs of Artics
6 pairs of shoes
12 pair of hose
2 Doz. and half handkerchiefs
24 pairs of ladies underwear
18 Collars
12 Neckties
6 pairs cuffs
2 Thermos bottles
Hot Water Bag
6 Under Skirts
2 Dress Shirts
Gold Watch and Chain
3 pairs of cuff links
Stick Pin
2 Three Tie Clasps
1 suit case
Toilet Articles, shaving outfit
Steamer Rug
2 Umbrellas
Lot of antique China
1 Satchel and 2 Trunks   Valued at $500.00

Passage Money Secon Cabin   65.00
                                         _____
                                         $565.00

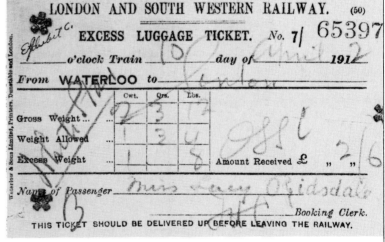

LONDON AND SOUTH WESTERN RAILWAY. (50)

EXCESS LUGGAGE TICKET. No. 7| 65397

o'clock Train 10 day of April 1912

From WATERLOO to London

	Cwt.	Qrs.	Lbs.
Gross Weight	2	3	14
Weight Allowed	1	2	4
Excess Weight	1		8

Amount Received £ " 2 " 6

Name of Passenger   Miss Lucy Ridsdale

Booking Clerk.

THIS TICKET SHOULD BE DELIVERED UP BEFORE LEAVING THE RAILWAY.

Exhibit D.

COUPON.

AN DEN PASSAGIER: Man reisse diesen Zettel ab und behalte ihn. Nachdem alles Gepäck am Landungsplatz abgeladen ist, zeige man diesen Zettel dem Oberzollbeamten daselbst. Letzterer wird dann einen Inspector beauftragen, die Untersuchung vorzunehmen. Die Beglaubigung ihrer Unterschrift muss persönlich gemacht werden, ehe die Besichtigung des Gepäckes beginnen kann. Alles Gepäck muss für Untersuchung geöffnet werden.

AU VOYAGEUR: Detachez et gardez ce coupon. Apres que tout votre bagage a ete debarque sur le quai presentez le coupon au chef de douane qui designera un inspecteur pour en faire la verification. Votre declaration devra etre faite en personne avant qu'on puisse proceder a l'inspection de votre bagage. Chaque colis doit etre ouvert pour la verification.

AL PASSEGGIERE: Staccate e ritenete questa cedola. Quando tutto il vostro bagaglio sara sbarcato, presentate questa cedola all' ufficiale doganale dello sbarcatoio, il quale mandera un ispettore per fare la visita. La vostra dichiarazione dovra essere fatta personalmente prima che si possa procedere all' ispezione del vostro bagaglio. Tutto il vostro bagaglio dovra essere aperto per l'ispezione.

Detach and retain this coupon until ALL your baggage is delivered by the steamship company upon the wharf. Then present it to the Customs officer there in charge, who will detail an Inspector to make the examination. Before this can proceed, you must acknowledge, IN PERSON, your signature upon the declaration. All baggage must be opened for inspection.

2—5937

31438D

1

United States District Court

SOUTHERN DISTRICT OF NEW YORK.

In the Matter

of

2 The Petition of the OCEANIC STEAM NAVIGATION COMPANY, LIMITED, for Limitation of its Liability as Owner of the Steamship "TITANIC."

THE CLAIM OF *Chung Foo* ALLEGES AS FOLLOWS:

I.

That *he* is a citizen of the ~~United States and a citizen and resident~~ *Hongkong, China*
3 of the State of

II.

That the above-named petitioner is and at all times herein mentioned was a corporation organized and existing under the Laws of the United Kingdom of Great Britain and Ireland, and an English registered company and a common carrier, and the owner of the steamship "Titanic." At the times hereinafter mentioned the said steamship "Titanic" was
4 a British sea-going ship, and upon information and belief had been duly registered pursuant to the Laws of the United Kingdom of Great Britain and Ireland, and hailed from the port of Liverpool in said Kingdom and was one of a line of cargo and passenger steamships operated by petitioner between Southampton and New York.

III.

That on or about April 10, 1912, this claimant took passage at Southampton, England, on the said steamship "Titanic" under a contract previously made between this claimant and the petitioner herein,
5 for a valuable consideration paid to petitioner, by the terms of which contract petitioner agreed safely to transport this claimant as a passenger, together with *his* luggage and personal effects from Southampton to New York.

IV.

That while on said voyage and on the high seas in or near latitude 41 d. 46 m. N., longitude 50 d. 14 m. W., said steamship "Titanic" collided
6 with a large iceberg on or about April 14th, 1912, and shortly afterward sank, causing the death of a large number of persons and the loss of the cargo, baggage and personal property contained in said vessel. That such loss of the steamship "Titanic" and the lives and property of persons on board thereof was caused by the wrongful acts, fault and negligence of petitioner, Oceanic Steam Navigation Company, Limited, and of petitioner's agents and servants in the navigation of said vessel and in failing to make the said vessel seaworthy and properly

1

7 manned, equipped and supplied, and otherwise, and such loss and destruction of lives and property was with the privity, fault and knowledge of the petitioner, and occurred without fault on the part of this claimant.

V.

That included in the property so lost and destroyed as aforesaid were certain luggage and personal effects, the property of this claimant,
8 which petitioner had contracted safely to transport from Southampton to New York. The said property was never salved or recovered and an itemized list thereof, with the market values of each item at the date of such loss, is annexed hereto and made a part hereof marked Schedule "A." No credits have been given thereon and no payments have been made on account thereof.

VI.

That by reason of the premises claimant has been damaged in the
9 sum of $ *96.16*

WHEREFORE claimant hereby makes and files this claim against the above-named petitioner, Oceanic Steam Navigation Company, for the sum of $ *96.16* and prays that the Commissioner appointed to receive claims herein will report to the Court that the said sum is due to this claimant and should be allowed to ~~him~~ out of any funds deposited in the Registry of the Court in this proceeding and that
10 this Court decree that this claimant recover from the petitioner herein damages as aforesaid with interest and costs and for such other and further relief as may be just.

HUNT, HILL & BETTS,
Proctors for Claimant,
Office and Post Office Address,
165 Broadway,
Borough of Manhattan,
New York City, N. Y.

11

12

2

6

Left To save both money and time, many third class passengers' claims are mass-produced, with spaces to be filled in on their behalf. Chung Foo, one of six Chinese sailors travelling on *Titanic*, submits his claim for $96.16 (£19.83). (National Archives.)

Re Titanic Disaster

42, GEORGE STREET,
DUMFRIES.
Scotland

U.S. Commissioner District

Dear Sir

I note from a copy of the Evening World of Aug 16th sent to us by Mr R Paul 215 East 122nd N.Y. that claims for loss should be presented to you.

Herewith I beg to present a claim for $2500 on account of the loss of my son and two fine violins that he had with him on approval one by J B Guadagnini £200 and one by Thomas Dodd £120. He was but 21 years of age and had these items on the voyage with him for

(2)

the purpose of choosing one of them as a life Instrument, neither of them was insured unfortunately and though the Music Contractors have been sued in the Liverpool Courts for compensation no redress has been obtained. The Mansion House fund have paid £92 declining at the same time any liability, while a personal note to Bruce Ismay of the White Star line has also failed to obtain any satisfaction.

My son John Law Hume would at this time have been permanently resident here with us and would have been worth at least £100

(3)

per annum to us, with this object in view this property was bought 4 years ago jointly by us for £500 on a £400 Bond at 4/p £300 of which I am now quite hopelessly faced with alone and as I am now 50 years of age it is most unlikely that I can hope to clear it off without some assistance, the £92 paid being but a small portion. I'll be obliged if you will kindly file this claim and put it forward with the others against the White Star line.

Faithfully Yours

A Hume

(Father)

Left The death of *Titanic*'s violinist John Law 'Jock' Hume was a double ordeal for his family. There was anguish over his loss... (*Illustrated London News*.)

Below left ...and despair about a very special loan the young musician had signed for before the voyage, as this letter **below left** from Hume's father, written on mourning paper, explains. (National Archives.)

Above and right Meanwhile, in England, the father of third class passenger Patrick Ryan enlists the aid of Thomas Scanlan, MP (who had appeared at the Mersey inquiry) to bring suit against the Oceanic Steam Navigation Company, seeking damages for his loss. The allegations against White Star are quite similar to those found in American claims. The plaintiff filed additional details of his claim against White Star, who responded with a statement of defence. (Public Record Office.)

Far right The High Court of Justice serves a writ upon the White Star Line, summoning them to the trial. (Public Record Office.)

Writ issued the 3rd day of July 1912.

BETWEEN   THOMAS Ryan   Plaintiff
                       and
THE OCEANIC STEAM NAVIGATION
COMPANY LIMITED   .   Defendants.

S T A T E M E N T of C L A I M.

The Plaintiff brings this action for the benefit of himself the father of Patrick Ryan deceased he having suffered damage from the Defendants' negligence in carrying the said Patrick Ryan on their Steamship "Titanic" on a voyage from Queenstown to New York whereby the said Patrick Ryan was drowned in consequence of the said ship colliding with an Iceberg and foundering in the North Atlantic Ocean on the 15th April 1912.

Particulars of negligence.

The negligence of the Defendants servants consisted in this that they navigated the said Ship at an excessive speed and at an improper speed in view of the conditions then prevailing namely the exceptional darkness of the night the hazy condition of the atmosphere the absence of wind and movement of the sea at and immediately preceding the time of the collision and of the presence of icebergs and fields of ice in the course of the said vessel: that while knowing of the presence of the said ice they failed to alter their course or to diminish their speed so as to avoid the same and failed to provide a sufficient and proper look-out therefor and to supply look-out men with Binoculars: that no adequate lifeboat accommodation was provided on the said Ship having regard to the number of passengers and crew she

was then carrying: and that the Defendants failed to have the said crew sufficiently drilled and organized for the work of manning filling and launching such lifeboats as were provided.

Particulars pursuant to Statute are as follows :-

Thomas Ryan the father of the deceased.

The nature of the Claim in respect of which damages are sought

The said Patrick Ryan was a Cattle Dealer and had been earning about £2 per week and was the sole support of the Plaintiff, who by his said death has lost all means of support and living.

The Plaintiff claims damages.

THOMAS SCANLAN.

DELIVERED this 12th day of October 1912 by HERBERT Z. DEANE of 265 Strand London,W.C. Solicitor for the Plaintiff.

1.

In the High Court of Justice.

King's Bench DIVISION.   1912 . R , No. 1111

BETWEEN   Thomas Ryan   Plaintiff.
                       and
The Oceanic Steam Navigation
Company Limited   Defendants

GEORGE THE FIFTH, by the Grace of God, of the United Kingdom of Great Britain and Ireland, and of the British Dominions beyond the Seas, King, Defender of the Faith, TO The Oceanic Steam Navigation Company Limited whose registered office is situate at 30 James Street Liverpool

of
in the of

We command you, that within eight days after the service of this writ on you, inclusive of the day of such service, you do cause an appearance to be entered for you in an action at the suit of Thomas Ryan

And take notice that in default of your so doing, the plaintiff may proceed therein and judgment may be given in your absence.

WITNESS, RICHARD BURDON, VISCOUNT HALDANE OF CLOAN, Lord High Chancellor of Great Britain, the 3rd day of July in the year of Our Lord One thousand nine hundred and twelve

N.B.—This writ is to be served within twelve calendar months from the date thereof, or, if renewed, within six calendar months from the date of the last renewal, including the day of such date, and not afterwards.
The defendant may appear hereto by entering appearance either personally or by Solicitor, at the Central Office, Royal Courts of Justice, London.

5000/2/12—[3481] 5000 7/21• O.& S. 1151 [380]

The Plaintiff's claim is for damages for the loss sustained owing to the death of his son Patrick Ryan whilst a passenger on the "Titanic" the property of the Defendants owing to the negligence of the Defendants

THIS WRIT was issued by Herbert Z Deane
of   and
whose address for service is   265 Strand
                                        WC
agent for

solicitor for the said plaintiff who resides at Askeaton Limerick Ireland

THIS WRIT was served by me

on the defendant
on   the   day of   19

Indorsed the   day of   19 .

(Signed)

(Address)

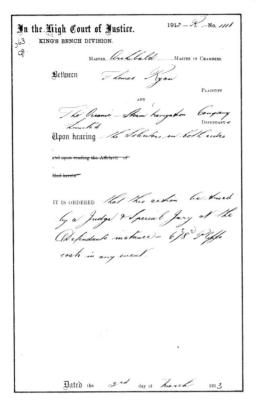

Far left At the company's request, it is ordered that the action be heard before a judge and special jury. (Public Record Office.)

Left Before the Honourable Mr Justice Bailhache, the jury hears five days of evidence before rendering its verdict in June 1913. It finds the *Titanic*'s navigation negligent in terms of speed, and awards a judgment against the White Star Line for £100 ($485) to Mr Ryan, and to the family of James Moran, whose case was one of several consolidated with the Ryan action.

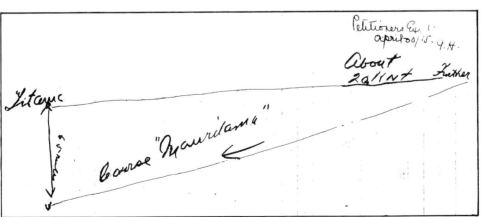

Far left Back in New York, Cunard's Captain William T. Turner is one of the witnesses at the limitation of liability hearings. Appearing on the stand on 30 April 1915, the Captain is asked what he would have done differently if he had the same information as Captain Edward J. Smith. (Private collection.)

Left In pencil, Turner sketches on a yellow pad a southward course deviation he would have ordered for safety's sake, knowing he was sailing into danger. Having completed his testimony, Captain Turner returns to his command, which leaves New York on the following day, 1 May. Six days later, he is swept from the bridge as *Lusitania* is torpedoed by a German submarine within sight of the Irish coast. (Retraced from the original; National Archives.)

Chapter Twenty

REMEMBRANCE

The first memorials to *Titanic*'s victims were the church services in commemoration of the dead and thanksgiving for the living. At London's St Paul's Cathedral; at Southampton's St Mary's Church; in Belfast, New York, Paris — the world wept and worshipped while the grief was still strong.

As the days passed the enormity of the loss of life became evident, and relief programmes were established. To fund them, memorial concerts, theatrical performances and benefits were presented in theatres, concert halls and even athletic stadiums throughout the United Kingdom, the United States and the colonies.

The first specific group to be memorialized were the musicians. Plaques were dedicated in Liverpool, Boston and New York to mark the valour of these gallant men. Another monument, of a 'broken column' style, was dedicated in 1915 in the New South Wales mining community of Broken Hill. A concert in London's Royal Albert Hall and another at New York's Broadway Theatre raised funds specifically for the relief of the musicians' families.

Two memorials appeared at Southampton, one for the engineers, another for the stewards and other crew. At New York, the Seamen's Church Institute building, then nearing completion, incorporated a replica of a lighthouse in its design. (When the building was demolished in 1968, the lighthouse was carefully moved to the South Street Seaport Museum, where it now stands.) Another splendid memorial to *Titanic*'s engineers overlooks the Liverpool Landing Stage.

Plaques, monuments, statues proliferated rapidly. Never has a single event resulted in the creation and dedication of so many memorials to so many groups and individuals.

One of the finest memorials is the Widener Library at Harvard University, dedicated by the Widener family to Harry Elkins Widener*, while surely one of the most beautiful is the cloister at Godalming, Surrey, to the memory of chief wireless operator John Phillips.

With the passing years, the event becomes dim in the minds of men. But the monuments stand, an assurance that — as long as tides ebb and flow, as long as people sail the seas — the memory of *Titanic*'s courageous and gallant men and women will never fade.

---

*As a condition of the grant for the library's construction, Mrs Widener stipulated that all future Harvard graduates must pass a swimming course.

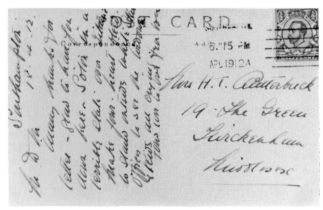

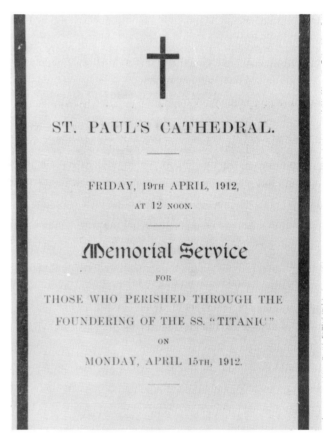

ST. PAUL'S CATHEDRAL.

FRIDAY, 19TH APRIL, 1912,
AT 12 NOON.

Memorial Service

FOR

THOSE WHO PERISHED THROUGH THE
FOUNDERING OF THE SS. "TITANIC"

ON

MONDAY, APRIL 15TH, 1912.

Alexander M. Carlisle

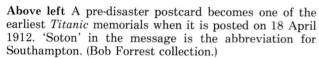

Above left A pre-disaster postcard becomes one of the earliest *Titanic* memorials when it is posted on 18 April 1912. 'Soton' in the message is the abbreviation for Southampton. (Bob Forrest collection.)

Far left One day later, on 19 April, a throng gathers on the steps of St Paul's Cathedral in London. Inside, the first of many memorial services in Great Britain is conducted. (Lloyd's *Deathless Story*.)

Below far left The Cathedral's cavernous interior is quickly filled with more than 2,000 people, and attendants post signs turning many mourners away. (*Daily Mirror*.)

Left The cover of the St Paul's memorial programme is simple, yet powerful. (Bob Forrest collection.)

During the service, Alexander M. Carlisle, former Harland and Wolff managing director and designer of the lost ship, is overwhelmed with emotion, and faints. (*Daily Mirror*.)

Bottom left Though less formal in its environment, one of the first American attempts to aid the bereaved families occurs on 20 April, at the Polo Grounds in New York City. Composer and showman George M. Cohan distributes a special issue of the *New York American* to baseball fans. Sales proceeds and gate receipts are donated to the newspaper's funds for the victims' families. (*New York American*.)

Above In the ship's home port of Southampton, White Star sailors march to a memorial service in honour of their fallen colleagues. (*Daily Mirror*.)

Top right United in mourning, the crewmen near the site of the 20 April service. . . (*Daily Mirror*.)

. . .which fills St Mary's Church **middle right**. (Southern Newspapers plc.)

Right On 22 April, the Catholic community fills Westminster Cathedral in London for a *Titanic* memorial service. (Lloyd's *Deathless Story*.)

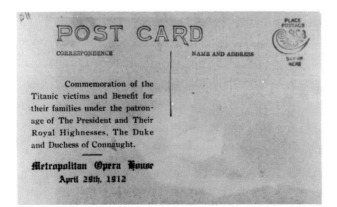

Far left In London's Cambridge Theatre, a benefit concert is held two weeks after the disaster. (Bob Forrest collection.)

Middle left The needs of the many suffering families are acute, and the Palace Theatre offers a cinematic benefit on 29 April. (Authors' collection.)

Left Across the Atlantic, New Yorkers attend a benefit performance at the Metropolitan Opera House. (Authors' collection.)

Left The first half of the Metropolitan Opera programme concludes with the hymns 'Autumn' and 'Nearer, My God, to Thee'. (Authors' collection.)

Far left and bottom far left To raise additional funds, a special memorial postcard is sold in the Opera House lobby. (Authors' collection.)

Bottom left London's Hippodrome sponsors a benefit matinée performance on 30 April. (Bob Forrest collection.)

Top right Their Majesties King George V and Queen Mary attend yet another *Titanic* benefit performance... (*Daily Graphic*.) ...at the Royal Opera House in Covent Garden. The programme cover depicts a stylized angel rising from the sea. The inside cover bears the names of the benefit's organizers. (Authors' collection.)

Right Nearly 500 performers from seven orchestras and the Orchestral Association fill London's Royal Albert Hall with music, under the batons of seven noted conductors. The 24 May gathering of musicians was billed as 'the greatest professional orchestra ever assembled', and commemorated the heroism of *Titanic*'s bandsmen. (Private collection.)

Remembrance

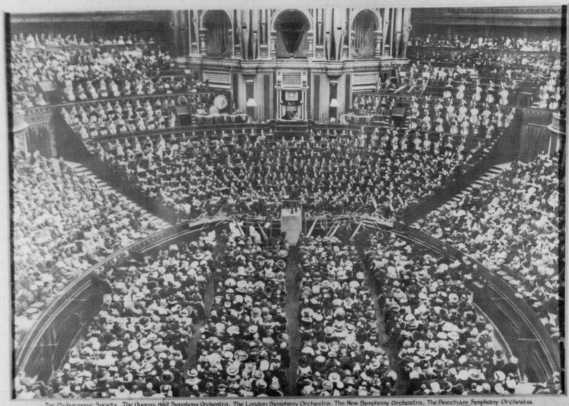

THE GREATEST PROFESSIONAL ORCHESTRA EVER ASSEMBLED.

Far left In the Lancashire town of Colne, following the 14 May burial of Wallace Hartley, a beautiful monument to the bandmaster is placed in a city park. (Arnold Watson collection.)

Left The cover of the Century Theatre's programme dramatically depicts an early, proposed design for the Women's Titanic Memorial. . . (Authors' collection.)

Below left . . .and the benefit performance in New York on 6 December launches efforts to raise funds for the memorial. (Authors' collection.)

Below Even with the passage of time, memorials to *Titanic* and her people continue to be dedicated. On 3 November, the Musicians' Mutual Protective Union unveils a plaque at its hiring hall in the Yorkville (New York) casino. The current (1986) whereabouts of this graceful plaque are not known. (Authors' collection.)

Above right In late 1912, a memorial panel is unveiled in New York's Grace Church, commemorating the heroic sacrifice of Edith Evans, who gave up a seat in a lifeboat to a woman who had children waiting at home. (Authors' collection.)

Top middle Another American memorial has special meaning to President William Howard Taft. The fountain commemorates the heroism of Archibald Butt, the President's military aide, and Francis Millet, the sculptor. Behind the Washington, DC fountain may be seen the fence of the White House, where Butt spent so many hours in his country's service. (Authors' collection.)

Above On 15 April 1913 the dedication service is held at the Seamen's Church Institute of New York for a unique *Titanic* remembrance... (Mr and Mrs Arthur Dodge.)

...the Titanic Memorial Lighthouse, mounted on the Institute's roof **top right**. Topped by a black time ball that dropped each afternoon at 1 pm, the lighthouse is fitted with a green light ('the colour of hope') that can be seen from New York Harbour, *Titanic*'s destination. In the late 1960s, the Institute's building is razed, and the Titanic Memorial Lighthouse becomes a prominent feature of the South Street Seaport Museum, where it is incorporated into an information booth's design. (Authors' collection.)

Middle right Two years and two weeks after the liner's loss, her home port again remembers her native sons. A large crowd watches on 29 April 1914 as the Union Jack... (Mariners Museum, Newport News, Va.)

...is gently lowered to reveal the memorial to *Titanic*'s engineers, located in Southampton's East Park. (Southern Newspapers plc.)

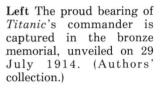

Far left Helen Melville Smith stands silently after unveiling a life-sized statue of her father, Captain Edward John Smith, RD, RNR, in Lichfield, England. (Authors' collection.)

Left The proud bearing of *Titanic*'s commander is captured in the bronze memorial, unveiled on 29 July 1914. (Authors' collection.)

Far left Even as Great Britain mourns the loss of another of its liners, *Lusitania*, to the horrors of war, the sacrifices of *Titanic*'s stewards are not forgotten. On 27 July 1915 the stewards' memorial fountain is unveiled in Southampton. (THS.)

Left By 1972, the memorial is endangered by vandals and a deteriorating environment. On 15 April, the 60th anniversary of *Titanic*'s loss, it is unveiled in its new location, within the ruins of Southampton's Holy Rood Church. Destroyed by bombing raids on the port during World War II, the Church serves as a memorial to Great Britain's merchant seamen, and as a quiet sanctuary from the bustle of the city. (Authors' collection.)

Right The grieving employees of Macy's Department Store join other New Yorkers in subscribing funds for this memorial, commemorating the undying love of Isidor and Ida Straus. The fountain, located at Broadway and West 106th Street, is one of three Straus memorials in New York; another is a plaque in the lobby of the store the couple founded. (Authors' collection.)

Right The people of Liverpool, the White Star Line's 'home town', also commemorate the loss of *Titanic*'s engineers with a monument near the Royal Liver Building and the Princes Landing Stage. While fund-raising continues, the monument's design is modified to include the engineers lost during World War I. (Authors' collection.)

Far right In the city of the liner's birth, Belfast, a beautiful statue depicting two mermaids claiming a victim from the sea is dedicated in 1920. Fifty years later, it being deemed a traffic hazard, the statue is moved from the front to the eastern side of Belfast's City Hall plaza. (Harland and Wolff Ltd.)

Right In Comber, County Down, Thomas Andrews' many friends remember him through construction of Thomas Andrews Memorial Hall, now used as a primary school. (Authors' collection.)

Left An unceasing memorial to *Titanic* begins in March 1913 when the British Board of Trade charters the *Scotia* for duty as an ice patrol ship. White Star fits the ship out for its new duty, on behalf of the Atlantic steamship companies. *Scotia* departs Dundee, Scotland, on 9 March 1913 for a two-month tour off the Grand Banks of Newfoundland. She succeeds the American cruisers *Birmingham* and *Chester*, which were sent to report on ice conditions in the spring of 1912, following *Titanic*'s loss. (Authors' collection.)

Second left As *Scotia* completes her voyage, a more permanent arrangement for tracking icebergs is set in motion. In April 1913 the International Ice Patrol is created. Under the aegis of the United States Coast Guard, though funded by all the nations engaged in North Atlantic shipping, the Ice Patrol establishes a yearly vigil, interrupted only by war, using vessels such as the *Modoc*. (National Archives.)

Third left An extract from the log of the United States Coast Guard Cutter *Modoc*, dated 15 April 1923: 'At daybreak arrived at lat. 41.46', long. 50.14' where *Titanic* sank after colliding with an iceberg, on April 15, 1912. The engines were stopped and at sunrise colors were half-masted. At 10 a.m., 75th meridian time, by request all stations within range observed radio silence for five minutes and the patrol carried out memorial exercises for those who had perished on this spot 11 years ago, including a general muster, a memorial address by Lieutenant Smith, prayer by Surgeon Laye, three volleys, and taps. The following message was received from the Agent of Marine, Halifax: "Halifax desires to be associated with you in your memorial service over *Titanic* grave today." Upon conclusion of these exercises, the vessel proceeded to occupy oceanographic stations 263 and 264. . .' The 1923 service is the first in a series of on-site memorials that continue to the present day. (United States Coast Guard *Report* for 1923.)

Below far left Lord William James Pirrie **far left** whose vision it had been to construct the *Titanic* and her two sister ships, is buried in Belfast in June 1924. His bust above the monument looks towards the still-active Harland and Wolff shipyards. (Harland and Wolff Ltd.)

Left After several years of preparation, the Women's Titanic Memorial is unveiled in a Washington, DC ceremony in the presence of Mrs William Howard Taft on 26 May 1931. Sculptress Gertrude Vanderbilt Whitney used a photograph of her brother, Alfred Gwynne Vanderbilt, as the model for the statue's face. Ironically, Vanderbilt was lost in the *Lusitania*'s sinking. In 1972 the memorial is dismantled carefully at its original Potomac River site, to make way for the Kennedy Center for the Performing Arts; it is replaced in a new waterfront park in Washington's southwestern corner. (Authors' collection.)

EPILOGUE

During the summer of 1985 an expedition headed jointly by Dr Robert D Ballard of the Woods Hole Oceanographic Institution and Jean-Louis Michel of the *Institut Français de Recherche pour l'Exploitation des Mers* discovered *Titanic*'s wreckage. The engineers and oceanographers aboard the American research vessel *Knorr* were assisted in their quest by scientists from the United States Navy and the National Geographic Society.

(A full description of the technical aspects of their success appeared in the Woods Hole Oceanographic Institution's quarterly journal, *Oceanus*, Winter 1985/86.)

Near *Titanic*'s bow a bollard, used to secure docking lines, casts its shadow behind a deck railing. A broken upright stanchion from the railing extends outwards from the ship. (Woods Hole Oceanographic Institution.)

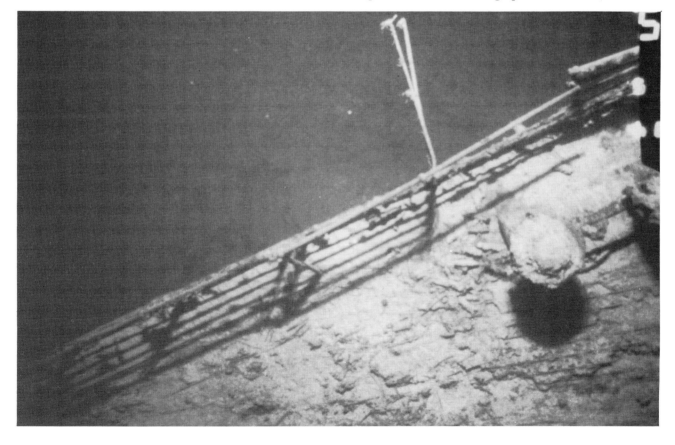

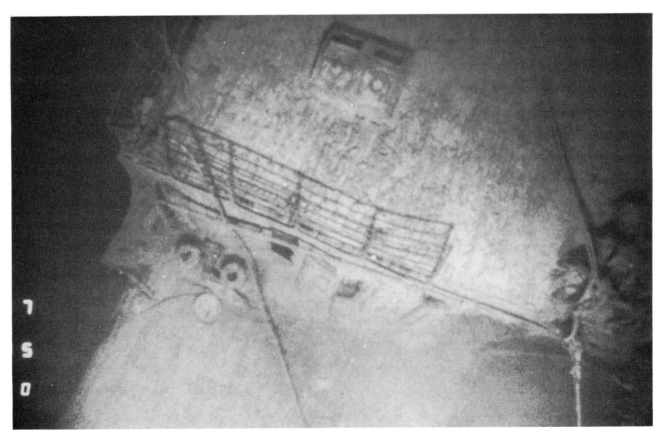

Left The powerful windlasses and massive chains of *Titanic*'s bow anchors lie fixed and frozen for eternity. Capstans (lower left) and the access hatch to the forward chain locker complete the picture. (Woods Hole Oceanographic Institution.)

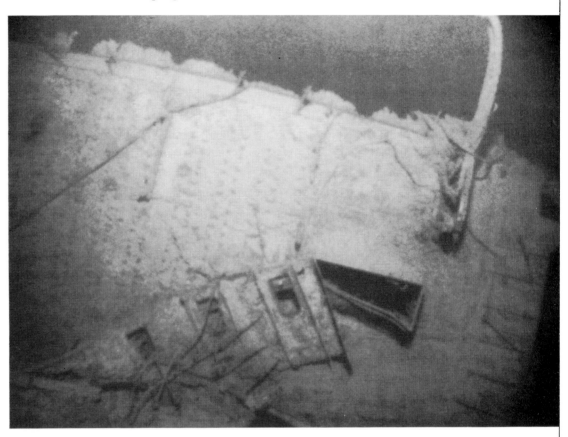

Below left The port side of the shelter deck's forward well, facing towards the bow. At the far left, the forward port side gangway stands open (or is missing). The door to the lamp room is to the right of the two bollards, while still further to the right is the third class port side entrance, its door missing. (Woods Hole Oceanographic Institution.)

Above right The boat deck's port side: bow to the left, stern towards the right. The davit remains turned outwards after having launched collapsible D; the windows are those in the outer bulkhead of the officers' quarters; for *Titanic* they would be those of chief officer Wilde's and first officer Murdoch's cabins. The dark oblong appears to be the upper cowling from the ventilator on the port side roof of the officers' quarters. (Woods Hole Oceanographic Institution.)

Right As *Titanic* sank, the forward funnel collapsed, leaving a gaping hole in the liner's superstructure. (Woods Hole Oceanographic Institution.)

This dramatic photograph shows the collapsed roof over the grand staircase at the first class entrance's starboard side. The dark area at the bottom is the central part of the staircase, over which the magnificent glass dome extended. Towards the bow, on the left, can be seen a portion of the roof over the forward cabins and officers' quarters; the specific area represents passenger cabin 'W'. An electric deck winch, intended for lowering and hoisting lifeboats, perches on top of the roof of cabin A35. At the extreme right is the enclosed vestibule opening upon the first class entrance. (Woods Hole Oceanographic Institution.)

The story of *Titanic* began in 1867. The final chapter is yet to be written.

On September 1, 1985, not far from the traditional location of the vessel's sinking, the American-French expedition discovered *Titanic*'s hull, resting in two sections on the floor of the North Atlantic.

When the final chapter for *Titanic* is composed, it will consist of photographs of the ship's interior, of broken walls, smashed windows and rotted staircases. Yet even the ravages of time and erosion, and the ultimate ravages of great pressure and impact shock, can never dispel or totally destroy the corridors where Astors and Wideners once strolled. Nor can they remove from our memories the reception halls and dining rooms and private suites with their coloured silk hangings and crystal lamps and multi-hued carpeting.

Perhaps, in viewing these ghostly photographs, we shall catch a faint glimpse of the elegance and beauty that was, hear faintly the sounds of the string orchestra as it plays once again for Hays and Millet and Butt and Molly Brown. Perhaps we shall hear the strains of Eugene Daly's bagpipes or the distant murmur in steerage, even now never fully silent.

As we see boilers, pistons, and cylinder beds strewn across the ocean floor, to our ears might come the far-off hiss and rumble of the great engines. Perhaps we might sense the vibrations that drove the vessel onward. Then, in a sudden burst of reality, we might hear distantly, once again, three rings of the crows' nest bell: 'Iceberg right ahead, sir. . .'

In the photographs to come we shall surely see the actual places where the bravest of the brave hewed out their mighty deeds of heroism and self-sacrifice which shall never fade.

Then we shall truly be able to envision the pride and splendour, the glorious drama, the terrible tragedy, the form, the legend which has become — and ever shall be —

TITANIC

APPENDICES
I: *Titanic* Collectibles

Within 72 hours of the *Titanic*'s loss, entrepreneurs on both sides of the Atlantic were already 'cashing in' on the tremendous public interest in the ship and her people. Among the first available *Titanic* souvenirs — and among the more readily obtainable today — were memorial postcards. More frequently than not they featured photographs of *Olympic*, rather than *Titanic*. In other cases, *Mauretania* was used as a stand-in for *Titanic,* and even for the rescue ship *Carpathia.* Some were issued with blatant spelling or factual errors; others went through several different printings as the number of people lost in the disaster was revised.

Titanic postcards are prized by collectors. Bargains may still be found in some shops, and at some postcard shows, but, typically, the price of *Titanic* postcards has risen dramatically in recent years, with few discernible links between the commonness of the cards and the prices realized.

Left White Star's *Olympic,* taken during her maiden voyage, fills in for her sister ship in this memorial card issued soon after the disaster. (Authors' collection.)

Below left Another early, post disaster memorial card employs an actual photo of the liner, taken as she departed from Southampton. (Robert DiSogra collection.)

Below 'Nearer My God to Thee' and its role in *Titanic*'s story are captured on a French postcard that offers the hymn's verses in two languages. (Authors' collection.)

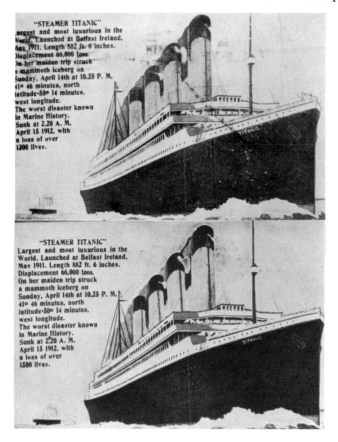

Above left Initially, this postcard is issued with its last line of text noting that 'over 1300 lives' had been lost. As the full magnitude of the disaster becomes known, a revised version is published. (Robert DiSogra collection.)

Above A view of *Titanic* (actually *Olympic* taken while she was in Harland and Wolff's fitting out basin) is transformed, through the magic of the artist's work, into a view of the lost liner at sea, and at the moment of collision with the iceberg. (Robert DiSogra Collection.)

Middle left Five heroes of the disaster are remembered in this rare postcard. (Robert DiSogra collection.)

Left An unusual full-colour postcard depicts Captain Smith rescuing a child and bringing him to the overturned collapsible. The card's reverse side bears the notation that it was published in New York by 'The White Star Publishing Company', though certainly the White Star Line had nothing to do with its issuing. (Authors' collection.)

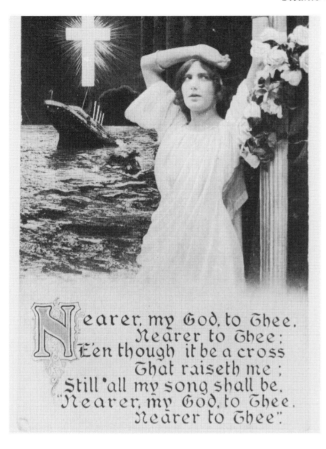

Steamer Titanic Sinking, April 15, 2:20 A. M.

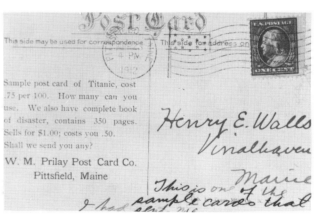

'THE TITANIC' S. S.: 882 ft. long; the largest boat in the world

Above Among the more famous *Titanic* memorial postcard series is that published by Bamforth & Company Ltd in England. The six-card set illustrates verses of 'Nearer, My God, to Thee', with *Titanic* sinking in the background and a mourning woman in the foreground. The cards were published in black and white and sepia versions. (Authors' collection.)

Top right In absolute contrast to the actual conditions that night, huge waves whip the North Atlantic to a frenzied froth as lifeboats leave *Titanic*. (Robert DiSogra collection.)

Middle right To encourage dealers to stock its new *Titanic* memorial cards, the Prilay Post Card Company sends out samples of its wares and the rates for bulk lots. The sample card has been mailed within eight days of *Titanic*'s loss. Once again, *Olympic* has her bow disfigured with the painting-in of *Titanic*'s name. (Bob Forrest collection.)

Right Factual errors abound on this memorial card, which calls *Titanic* an 'American Liner', and notes the number lost as 1,635. (Bob Forrest collection.)

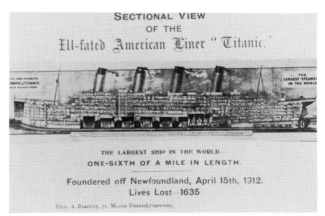

Also popular among collectors are the many pieces of music written in reaction to the disaster. More than 300 songs commemorate the loss of *Titanic*. One song, 'It Was Sad When the Great Ship Went Down', is virtually a standard sung by scouts and other children around camp fires in the United States. Many of the works attempted to tell the liner's story musically, much as a tone poem would. Rumbling keys in the piano's bass range often portrayed the impending collision. *Carpathia*'s dash to the *Titanic*'s aid is rendered in stirring march music.

Titanic sheet music often can be found at 'flea markets' and antique shows.

Right A view of the ship in Belfast complements the front cover of 'The Titanic Wreck', published, ironically, by the Majestic Music Publishing Company. (Authors' collection.)

Below Lifeboats leave the stricken ship on the cover of 'Just as the Ship Went Down'. (Authors' collection.)

Below right A mountain of ice blocks the path of *Titanic* on the cover of 'My Sweetheart Went Down with the Ship'. One of the composers is prominently featured, too. (Authors' collection.)

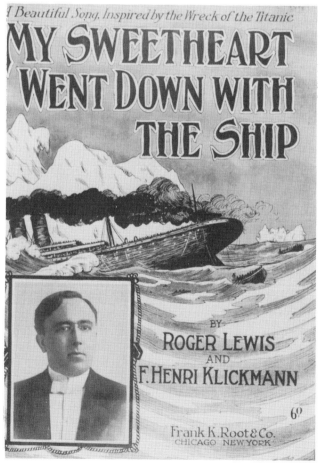

There are virtually no objects from the *Titanic* for collectors to seek. And those that do survive command premium prices. In 1986, a 3¼ inch by ½ inch cardboard ticket, apparently a weigh ticket from a scale on board, sold in the United States for $5,000 (£3,570).

Titanic's name did not appear on her dinnerware, her tableware, her linens, or any other shipboard items. Authentication of articles alleged to be from the ship is extremely difficult and fraught with the potential for fraud. Entrepreneurs in the 1970s, without any fraudulent intent, issued brass key tags bearing the words 'Captain's Office, SS Titanic'. Still available for perhaps $5 (£3.50) in novelty stores, one was purchased from an unscrupulous person by a Florida gentleman, believing it to be genuine, for $150 (£105).

In March 1986, a battered lifeboat from the 1953 Twentieth Century Fox movie *Titanic* was offered for sale in Atlantic City, New Jersey, advertised in antique trade journals and reported in *The New York Times* as 'the only surviving lifeboat from the *Titanic*'. The $40,000 (£28,000) asking price apparently deterred all those wishing to purchase 'Lifeboat Number 6, Molly Brown's boat'. Particularly in the case of such objects, the policy *caveat emptor* should prevail.

Happily, many quite genuine memorial pieces, though not off the ship, may be found in antique shows and 'flea markets', offering the *Titanic* collector tangible remembrances of the liner. . .

Above left The self-sacrifice of Isidor and Ida Straus is remembered in this Yiddish piece, 'The Titanic's Disaster', published in New York. (Authors' collection.)

Left A tin candy box bears a full-colour painting of *Olympic* or *Titanic*. (Bob Forrest collection.)

Below A memorial whisky jigger, made of porcelain, commemorates *Titanic*'s loss. (Bob Forrest collection.)

Above A commemorative plate features a hand-painted rendering of *Titanic*'s last night afloat. (Bob Forrest collection.)

Below A reverse painting on glass is a fine example of early 20th Century folk art. (Bob Forrest collection.)

II: The Safety of Life at Sea

Perhaps nowhere is the legacy of *Titanic* more apparent than in the significant changes and improvements in the field of maritime safety. At the initiation of the British government — in response to one of the recommendations from Lord Mersey's inquiry — the first International Conference on the Safety of Life at Sea (SOLAS) conference was held in London in 1913 and 1914. Thirteen nations reached agreement on watertight and fire-resisting bulkheads, life saving appliances, fire prevention and fire-fighting appliances on passenger ships, and there was general acceptance of the principle of 'boats for everyone' on board ocean-going passenger ships.

World War I prevented much of the Conference's work from coming into force on an international scale, but two important areas that did were the establishment of the International Ice Patrol and the regulation of wireless and its use in sending distress signals.

Further SOLAS conventions were held in 1929, 1948 and 1960. Their combined impact has made ocean transport an exceptionally safe mode of travel. The *Titanic*'s safety legacy clearly could be seen in the successful rescue of more than 700 passengers and crew from the burning Dutch liner *Prinsendam* off the Alaskan coast in 1980, and in the evacuation of the Russian cruise ship *Mikhail Lermontov* following grounding off New Zealand in early 1986.

Right Today there are lifeboats for everyone on board an ocean-going vessel, and both passengers and crew are required to attend lifeboat drill at least once per week. Boat crews are fully trained and certified; boat capacities are prominently marked. The lifesaving equipment of *Queen Elizabeth 2* is another of the lessons learned through *Titanic*'s loss. (Authors' collection.)

Below Industry-wide implementation of improved watertight sub-division and provision of 'inner skins' was one of the many lessons learned from the *Titanic* disaster. The lost liner's sister ship was among the first to incorporate the new features, as described in this contemporary advertising broadside. (Authors' collection.)

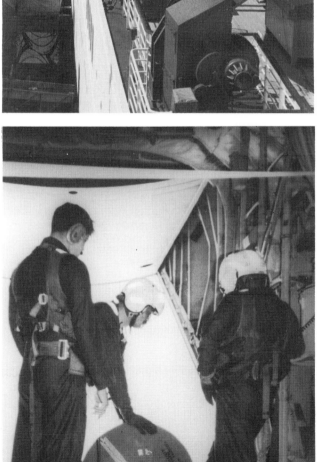

Top Round-the-clock radio service is now mandatory; for those ships unable to carry the requisite number of operators, automatic radio alarms are required. These sound an alarm immediately upon receipt of an incoming distress message. Radio operators are required to 'listen out' (cease transmissions) for three minutes each half hour, standing by for distress calls. A special frequency is set aside for distress messages, which have priority over all other radio traffic. New, more powerful radio equipment ensures contact with shore stations and other ships. (Marconi Company Ltd.)

Above Established in 1913, the International Ice Patrol guards the sea lanes of the North Atlantic, helping to ensure that *Titanic*'s tragedy will not be repeated. A C-130 transport plane, based at Elizabeth City, North Carolina, is prepared for an Atlantic mission, to spot icebergs that are a potential danger to shipping. (United States Coast Guard, International Ice Patrol.)

Left Three Coast Guardsmen prepare to drop a TIROS Oceanographic Drifter Buoy from the C-130. The device parachutes into the ocean, and monitors currents and water temperatures which, when combined with iceberg sightings, is used to predict iceberg movements. Data from the buoy is relayed to an orbiting satellite, which transmits the information to Toulon, France, Washington, DC and Groton, Connecticut, headquarters of the International Ice Patrol. Each day, a detailed map showing ice locations is sent via radio to ships in the North Atlantic. (United States Coast Guard, International Ice Patrol.)

III: Yesterday, Today and *Titanic*

There are many tangible reminders of *Titanic* and her dramatic story to be found in the places associated with her. With just one exception, none is designated a landmark or memorial. But their mere presence reminds one of the great liner and the role that each of these sites played in her tragically short history.

Above The former White Star Line offices still stand at 30 James Street, Liverpool the only *Titanic*-related site acutally a designated landmark (though for its architectural and business associations, rather than because of the ship.) Bruce Ismay was said to have had his office in the lowest level of the right 'turret' of the building, which is constructed of pink and white brick. White Star moved into the building in December 1897. From this building, negotiations were handled with the builders over *Titanic*'s design. (Authors' collection.)

Top left The shipyards of Harland and Wolff continue to produce the world's finest ships, although the place where *Olympic* and *Titanic* were built has radically changed. Berths two and three are now a car park and bulk storage area, the huge Arrol Gantry having been torn down in the late 1960s. The slipways were located in the space now seen between the two buildings with 'corrugated' roofs; *Titanic*'s stern entered the River Lagan in the space at the picture's right edge. Today, ships are no longer constructed in the traditional manner, but in huge sections. No longer do ships 'go down the ways'; instead, they are floated out of the building dock. (Authors' collection.)

Middle left Oceanic House, White Star's London office in Cockspur Street near Trafalgar Square, is now a bank. Only minor decorative touches — the topping of a lamp post with a miniature replica of a Viking ship, and the building's name — indicate its former role. (Authors' collection.)

Bottom far left Berth 44 in Southampton still plays host to ships, such as this naval vessel from an Arab country, but most liners now dock at the new Queen Elizabeth II terminal. Ocean Terminal which served for many years as the home of Cunard's Queens, was torn down in the early 1980s, having been declared superfluous. In the distance on the right can be seen the Cunard offices, which in 1912 were the South Western Hotel, at which many of *Titanic*'s passengers stayed the night prior to the ship's departure. (Authors' collection.)

Top right Scott's Quay — White Star's pier — lies dilapidated and deserted in Cobh, formerly Queenstown, Ireland. In the distance, the yacht club building looms on the other side of Kennedy Park. Although Cobh was *Titanic*'s last port of call, virtually no mention of her can be found in the town's library; a small display at the town museum recalls the ship. Of more interest to the citizens is *Lusitania*; more than 300 victims of the Cunarder's torpedoing are buried in the churchyard cemetery about two miles from town. (Authors' collection.)

Middle right The site of joyous reunions between *Titanic*'s people and their relatives and friends, Cunard's Pier 54 in New York City was extensively damaged by fire in the 1930s, and rebuilt to a design essentially similar to the original. Abandoned, rotting, its lower level used only as a car park, the pier was scheduled for demolition to allow construction of a supehighway ('Westway') on Manhattan's western side. The highway plan was abandoned in 1985, and future plans for Pier 54's site are uncertain. In the faded, chipped paint over the boarded-up gates a visitor can still see the words 'Cunard Line' and, underlying those, 'Cunard-White Star'. (Diane R. Prignoli.)

Right The former Snow's Funeral Home (left) and the adjacent, former Royal College of Art (right) still stand in Argyle Street in Halifax, Nova Scotia, though Snow's establishment has since moved to a new location. The city's common fronts the property. (Authors' collection.)

IV: *Titanic* Deck Plans

One of many exhibits produced before the limitation of liability proceedings in New York was a set of deck plans bearing the official Harland and Wolff seal, and the date 29 April 1912. The original plans were drawn to the scale of 1/32″ = 1 foot.

The authors have modified the plan* to correct numerous minor imperfections (rooms shown with no doors, missing features, unclear numbering or labels, etc), and the result is the most accurate and detailed set of *Titanic* plans available. They appear

on the front and rear endpapers of this book. For the first time, *all* passenger staterooms are numbered. Crew areas are fully identified.

On the plans may be located the ship's dog kennels (long thought to be on an upper deck, but actually near the third class galley on F deck — a logical place, since ships' butchers were responsible for feeding pets then); the fifty-line telephone switchboard and the maids' and valets' dining saloon, both on deck C; and the two last-minute staterooms of A deck (A36 occupied by Thomas Andrews, and A37).

The plan is presented through the courtesy of the National Archives.

V: *Titanic's* Cargo Manifest

Yet another document produced at the New York limitation of liability hearing was the office 'carbon copy' of the *Titanic*'s cargo manifest. While the original document was lost on board the ship, the carbon was sent, as was prevailing practice, to the port of destination aboard another ship, in this case Cunard's *Mauretania*.

Far from confirming the persistent legend that *Titanic* was a 'treasure ship', the document reaffirms the mundane, ordinary nature of the cargo, worth just $420,000 (£84,000) in 1912.

The manifest was published in at least two New York newspapers on 20 April 1912, where would-be treasure-seekers might certainly examine it. The carbon copy, preserved in the National Archives, is now faded and torn. In many places it is very difficult to read and impossible to reproduce; hence it has been necessary here to present the manifest in newly typeset form.

With the cargo stowage diagram — published for the first time elsewhere in this volume — the document makes an eloquent statement about the possible motives of those wishing to disturb *Titanic*'s wreck, which they may well destroy in their searches for non-existent riches.

Cargo Manifest
RMS *Titanic*

Wakem & McLaughlin	1 case wine
Thorer & Praetorius	1 bale skins
Carter, W.E.	1 case auto
Fuchs & Lang Mfg Co	4 cases printer's blankets
Spaulding A.G. & Bros	34 cases athletic goods
Park & Tilford	1 case toothpaste,
	5 cases drug sundries
	1 case brushware
Maltus & Ware	8 cases orchids
Spencerian Pen Co	4 cases pens
Sherman Sons & Co	7 cases cottons
Claflin, H.B. & Co	12 cases cotton laces
Muser Bros	3 cases tissues
Isler & Guve	4 bales straw
Rydeman & Lassner	1 case tulle [netting for
	scarves or veils]
Petry, P.H. & Co	1 case tulle
Metzger, A.S.	2 cases tulle
Mills & Gibb	20 cases cottons,
	1 case gloves
Field, Marshall & Co	1 case gloves
NY Motion Picture Co	1 case films
Thorburn, J.M. & Co	3 cases bulbs
Rawstick & H.Trading Co	28 bags sticks
Dujardin & Ladnick	10 boxes melons
American Express Co	25 cases merchandise
Tiffany & Co	1 cask china,
	1 case silver goods
Lustig Bros	4 cases straw hats
Kuyper, P.C. & Co	1 case elastic cords
	1 case leather
Cohen, M. Bros	5 packages skins
Gross, Engle Co	1 case skins
Wilson, P.K. & Son	61 cases tulle
Gallia Textile Co	1 case lace goods
Calhoun, Robbins & Co	1 case cotton laces,
	½ case brushware
Victor & Achiles	1 case brushware
Baumgarten, Wm & Co	3 cases furniture
Spielman Co	3 cases silk crepe
Nottingham Lace Works	2 cases cotton
Naday & Fleischer	1 case laces
Rosenthal, Leo J. Co	4 cases cotton

Wakem & McLaughlin	25 cases biscuits,
	42 cases wines
Leeming, T. & Co	7 cases biscuits
Crown Perfume Co	3 cases soap perfume
Meadows, T. & Co	5 cases books,
	3 boxes samples,
	1 case parchment
Thomas & Pierson	2 cases hardware,
	2 cases books,
	2 cases furniture
American Express Co	1 case elastics,
	1 case gramophone,
	4 cases hosiery,
	5 cases books,
	1 case canvas,
	1 case rubber goods,
	3 cases prints,
	6 cases films,
	1 case tweed,
	1 case sero fittings
	[syringes?],
	a quantity of old oak
	beams,
	1 case plants,
	1 case speedometer,
	1 package effects,
	2 cases samples,
	8 cases paste,
	3 cases camera and stand,
	4 cases books
Sheldon, G.W. & Co	1 case machinery
Maltus & Ware	15 cases alarm apparatus,
	11 cases orchids
Hempstead & Sons	30 cases plants
Brasch & Rothenstein	2 cases lace collars,
	2 cases books
Isler & Guve	53 packages straw
Baring Bros & Co	68 cases rubber,
	100 bags gutta [percha]
Altman, B. & Co	1 case cottons
Stern, S.	60 cases salt powder
Arnold, F.R. Co	6 cases soap
Shieffelin & Co	17 packages wool fat
American Motor Co	1 package candles
Strohmeyer & Arpe	75 bales fish

Titanic's Cargo Manifest

National City Bank of New York	11 bales rubber		1 case eggs,
Kronfeld, Saunders & Co	5 cases shells		1 case whiskey
Richard, C.B.	1 case films	International News Co	10 packages periodicals
Corbett, M.J. & Co	2 cases hat leather, etc	Van Ingen, E.H. & Co	1 parcel
Snow's Express Co	3 cases books	Sterns, R.H. & Co	1 case cretonne [silk]
Van Ingen, E.H. & Co	1 case woollens	Downing, R.F. & Co	1 case iron jacks,
Lippincott, J.B. & Co	10 cases books		1 case bulbs
Lazard Freres	1 bale skins		1 case hosiery
Aero Club of America	1 crate machinery,	Jacobson, James	
	1 case printed matter	Carbon Machinery Equipment Co	1 case clothing
Witcombe, McGrachlin & Co	856 rolls linoleum	Sanger, R. & Co	3 cases hair nets
Wright & Graham Co	437 casks tea	Flietmann & Co	1 case silk goods
Gillman, J.	4 bales skins	Rush & Co	1 case hair nets
Arnold & Zeiss	134 cases rubber	Blum, J.A.	3 cases silk goods
Brown Bros & Co	76 cases dragon's blood,	Tiedeman, T. & Sons	3 cases silk goods
	3 cases gum	Costa, F.	1 case silk goods
American Shipping Co	5 cases books	Tolson, A.M. & Co	1 case gloves
Adams Express	35 cases books	Mathews, G.T. & Co	2 cases books and lace
Lasker & Bernstein	117 cases sponges	Tice & Lynch	5 cases books,
Oelrichs & Co	2 cases pictures, etc		1 bag frames,
Stechert, G.E. & Co	12 packages periodicals		1 case cotton,
Milbank, Leaman & Co	3 cases woollens		2 cases stationery
Vandegrift, F.B. & Co	63 cases champagne	US Export Co	1 case scientific instruments,
Downing, R.F. & Co	1 case felt,		1 case sundries,
	1 case meal,		3 cases test cords,
	3 cases tennis balls,		1 case briar pipes,
	1 case engine packing		1 case sundries,
Dublin, Morris & Kornbluth	2 packages skins		2 cases printed matter
International Trading Co	1 case surgical instruments,	Pape, Chas & Co	1,196 bags potatoes
	1 case ironware	Sauer, J.P. & Co	318 bags potatoes
Pitt & Scott	4 cases printed matter,	Rusch & Co	1 case velvets
	1 case cloth	Mallouk, H.	1 case laces
Davies, Turner & Co	4 cases printed matter,	Bardwill Bros	8 cases laces
	1 case machinery,	Heyliger, A.V.	1 case velvet
	1 case pictures,	Peabody, H.W. & Co	13 bales straw goods
	1 case books,	Simon, A.I. & Co	1 case raw feathers
	1 case merchandise,	Wilson, P.K. & Sons	2 cases linens
	1 case notions,	Manhattan Shirt Co	3 cases tissues
	1 case photos	Broadway Trust Co	3 cases coney skins [rabbit]
Sheldon, G.W. & Co	1 case elastics,	Prost, G.	1 case auto parts
	2 cases books,	Young Bros	1 case feathers
	1 box golf balls,	Wimpfheimer, A. & Co	3 cases leather
	5 cases instruments	Brown Bros & Co	15 cases rabbit hair
American Express Co	2 parcels merchandise	Goldster, Morris	11 cases feather
Vandegrift, F.B. & Co	1 case merchandise	Cobb, G.H.	1 case lace tissue
Budd, S.	1 parcel merchandise	Anderson Refrig Machinery Co	11 cases refrigeration apparatus
Lemke & Buechner	1 parcel merchandise	Suter, Alfred	18 cases machinery
Nicholas, G.S. & Co	1 case merchandise	American Express Co	1 case packed packages,
Walker, G.A.	1 case merchandise		3 cases tissues,
Adams Express Co	4 rolls linoleum,		2 barrels mercury,
	3 bales leather,		1 barrel earth,
	1 case hats,		2 barrels glassware,
	6 cases confectionery,		3 cases printed matter,
	5 cases books,		1 case straw braids,
	1 case tin tubes,		3 cases straw hats,
	2 cases soap,		1 case cheese
	2 cases boots	Meadows, Thomas & Co	3 cases hosiery
Wells, Fargo & Co	3 cases books,	Uchs & Hegnoer	3 cases silk goods
	2 cases furniture,	Cauvigny Brush Co	1 case brushware
	1 case pamphlets,	Johnson, J.G. Co	2 cases ribbons
	1 case plants,	Judkins & McCormick	2 cases flowers

Spielman Co	1 case gloves	
American Express Co	18 cases merchandise	
Wakem & McLaughlin	6 bales cork	
Acker, Merrall & Condit	75 cases anchovies,	
	225 cases mussels,	
	1 case liquor	
Engs, P.W. & Sons	190 cases liquor,	
	25 cases syrups	Austin, Nichols
Schall & Co	25 cases preserves	
NY & Cuba SS Co	12 cases butter	Order
	18 cases oil,	
	2 hogsheads vinegar,	
	19 cases vinegar,	
	6 cases preserves,	
	8 cases dried fruit,	
	10 bundles of 2 cases wine	
DuBois, Geo C.	16 hogsheads wine	
Hollander, H.	185 cases wine,	
	110 cases brandy	
Van Renssaller, C.A.	10 hogsheads wine,	
	15 cases cognac	
Brown Bros & Co	100 cases shelled walnuts	
Bernard, Judas & Co	70 bundles cheese	
American Express Co	30 bundles cheese,	
	2 cases cognac	
Moquin Wine Co	1 case liquor,	
	38 cases oil	
Knauth, Nachod & Kuhne	107 cases mushrooms,	
	1 case pamphlets	
Lazard Freres	25 cases sardines,	
	3 cases preserves	
Acker, Merrall & Condit	50 cases wine	
Dubois, Geo F.	6 cases vermouth,	
	4 cases wine	
Heidelbach, Ickelheimer & Co	11 cases shelled walnuts	
Brown Bros & Co	100 bales shelled walnuts	
First National Bank of Chicago	300 cases shelled walnuts	
Blechoff, H. & Co	35 bags rough wood	
Baumert, F. X. & Co	50 bundles cheese	
Rathenberger & Co	190 bundles cheese	Holders of original bills of lading
Haupt & Burgi	50 bundles cheese	
Sheldon & Co	40 bundles cheese	
Percival, C.	50 bundles cheese	
Stone, C.D. & Co	50 bundles cheese	
Phoenix Cheese Co	30 bundles cheese	
Petry, P.H. & Co	10 bundles cheese	
Reynolds & Dronig	15 bundles cheese	
Fouger, E.	41 cases filter paper	
Munro, J. & Co	22 cases mushrooms,	
	15 cases peas,	

3 cases beans,
10 cases mixed vegetables,
13 cases peas,
25 cases olives,
12 bundles capers,
10 bundles fish,
20 bundles merchandise
25 cases olive oil,
14 cases mushrooms
14 cases factice,
13 cases gum,
14 casks gum,
285 casks tea,
8 bales skins,
4 cases opium,
3 cases window frames,
8 bales skins,
8 packages skins,
1 case skins,
2 cases horsehair,
2 cases silk,
8 bales raw silk,
4 packages hair nets,
200 packages tea,
246 cases sardines,
30 rolls jute bagging,
1,962 bags potatoes,
7 cases raw feathers,
10 cases hatters' fur,
3 cases tissue,
1 case rabbit hair,
31 packages crude rubber,
7 cases vegetables,
5 cases fish,
10 cases syrups,
2 cases liquors,
150 cases shelled walnuts,
15 bundles cheese,
8 bales buchu,
2 cases grandfather clocks,
2 cases leather
79 goat skins,
16 cases calabashes,
5 bales buchu,
4 cases embroidery,
3 barrels wine,
12 cases ostrich feathers,
4 cases feathers,
3 bales skins,
33 bags argols,
3 bales sheep skins

INDEX